# THE CHAMPAGNE MUMM
## ADMIRAL'S CUP

CHAMPAGNE MUMM
ADMIRALS CUP

# THE
# CHAMPAGNE
# MUMM
## ADMIRAL'S CUP
### THE OFFICIAL HISTORY

## TIMOTHY JEFFERY

BLOOMSBURY

First published in Great Britain 1994
Bloomsbury Publishing Plc, 2 Soho Square, London WlV 5DE

Copyright 1994 by Timothy Jeffery

The moral right of the author has been asserted

A CIP catalogue record of this book is available from the British Library

ISBN 0 7475 19838

Designed by AB3
Produced by Brown Packaging Ltd, 255–257 Liverpool Road, London N1 1LX
Printed in Italy

To Jenny and Kate

## ACKNOWLEDGEMENTS

The sheer breadth of 40 years' racing for the Champagne Mumm Admiral's Cup has meant that I have not been able to tackle this book without considerable assistance.

Sir Peter Green, Sir Edward Heath, Mary Pera and Robin Aisher were especially generous with their time and hospitality. The Commodore of the Royal Ocean Racing Club was kind enough to let this be the Official History of the RORC's most famous event, while Alan Green and Janet Grosvenor and their full-time staff at 20 St James's Place were an unstinting source of support and assistance. It was a researcher's dream to be permitted to roam freely among old files buried deep in the bowels of the clubhouse. Janet Grosvenor, in particular, was especially helpful and did not seem to mind my annoying habit of coming through with 'just one last query' at the moment she was at her busiest.

John Crookshank was most encouraging in the very early days of this project, as were Keith and Kenneth Beken, whose photographic archive is a national treasure and a wonderful place to lose oneself. It is an honour to have their work, along with that of Franco Pace, Daniel Forster, Kos Evans, Jonathan Eastland, Alastair Black, Rick Tomlinson, Gilles Martin-Raget, Malcolm White, Kaoru Soehata and Philippe Plisson, gracing the pages of this book. Peter Whyte created the endpapers – a pictorial history in themselves – while the book's exceptional design is the work of designer Hugh Adams of Carrickfergus and AB3 Design.

Many others have contributed in no small measure: Sir Peter Johnson, Gérard de Ayala, Nigel Croney, Anthony Churchill, David Welch, Piet Vroon, Syd Fischer, the Commissioners of Irish Lights, RNAS Culdrose, After srl,Christine Forest and John McLaughlin.

More than anything, this is a book about the yachts which have carved furrows in the Solent, out into the Channel and round the Fastnet Rock and back. Special acknowledgement is due to Olin Stephens, Ron Holland, Doug Peterson, German Frers Jr, Bruce Farr, William de vries Lentsch, Jim McCurdy, Jean-Marie Finot, Friedrich Judel and Rolf Vrolijk for permission to reproduce some of their most outstanding yachts. Fittingly, Simon Rogers, whose father Jeremy made the yachts *Moonshine* and *Eclipse* stars of British teams in 1977 and 1979, re-drew the designs for reproduction.

ADMIRAL'S CUP

# CONTENTS

# INTRODUCTION

BY SIR PETER GREEN,
DONOR AND TRUSTEE

IN THE WINTER of 1952–3, after Myles Wyatt had returned from the USA, having taken part in the Bermuda Race with his famous yawl Bloodhound, he talked about how we could persuade American owners to participate in Royal Ocean Racing Club and other races in the United Kingdom and Europe.

At that time, the New York Yacht Club was actively setting about reviving the America's Cup which had not been contested since 1937 and we thought it was an appropriate time to launch a perpetual challenge cup for offshore racing. I was travelling frequently to the USA in those days and many senior members and owners in the Cruising Club of America were friends, so I was able to talk to them about such a challenge. While they showed some interest in the idea, they pointed out that their transatlantic commitments for races or cruises to Ireland, Spain and Scandinavia had already been made several years in advance. We realised that to ensure US participation we would have to plan the opening races to take place some years ahead.

In some ways this was probably a benefit because we were able to cast out some of our more elaborate ideas. As our night-time talks grew longer and the level of the Plymouth Gin bottle fell ever lower, the more expansive our thinking became: a series based on the Fastnet, Bermuda and Sydney-Hobart races; even a round Britain race whose sailing instructions would read 'Start from anchor on the Royal Yacht Squadron line and proceed via Solent or Spithead, leaving the British Isles and all outlying islands (including Rockall) on either hand.'

Such wild notions were quickly dispelled and with the able assistance of Buster de Guingand, the Trust Deed for the new series was drawn up, laying down the flexible format of a mixture of inshore and offshore races. The only compulsory race is the Fastnet, arguably one of the best and most challenging courses for an offshore race. Selwyn Slater found the prize – originally a horse-racing prize for a challenge in the reign of William IV and it was first contested in 1957.

The management of those early series was, by today's standards, very amateurish. As the numbers of teams showed a welcome and exciting increase over the years, a new approach was needed and sponsorship by Champagne Mumm provided financial support for this. As a result, the type of yachts became more grand-prix, the pattern of inshore races changed and scoring system modified to reduce weighting in favour of the offshore race. Within reason, this is welcome and will, I sincerely hope, ensure that the Admiral's Cup continues as one of the pre-eminent yacht racing challenges.

The Trust Deed, now nearly forty years old, with the Trustees and the Management Committee, who actually plan and manage each series, has stood up well. It is my hope that the Cup will not, like the Whitbread, become a series for professionals. The IYRU, the RYA and the RORC rules should ensure this does not occur. It would also be totally contrary to the wishes of the five donors if the stipulation of the Fastnet being a compulsory component was ever changed. In my opinion it would destroy the whole concept of the Admiral's Cup.

The Trust Deed even thought to provide for ultimate disposal of the Cup if it is not put up for challenge for seven years! But four decades of success has demonstrated that the Admiral's Cup has proved resilient, adaptable and, above all, hugely popular.

HAVING COMPETED IN THREE Admiral's Cups and captained the British team twice, I can vouch that the series is second in international yacht racing only to the America's Cup. It has built up this position in less than 40 years whereas the battle for the America's Cup has continued for nearly a century and a half.

Tim Jeffery has produced an excellent account of the Admiral's Cup, describing the way in which it was brought into existence by far-sighted members of the Royal Ocean Racing Club, and the changes which have taken place both in the nature of the races and their organisation. He includes a detailed description and analysis of each challenge, together with rather more light-hearted and usually favourable comments on some of those who have taken part in them.

The 1979 Fastnet Race justifiably receives a separate chapter to itself and, having competed in six Fastnets, I can vouch for the accuracy of the compelling account which he provides of these great contests.

We are indeed grateful to Champagne Mumm for supporting this work in addition to the long-standing and forward-looking sponsorship which has been given by them to the races for the Admiral's Cup itself.

Long may the Cup remain foremost in British and international yacht racing.

(Jonathan Eastland)

'As a keen and experienced yachtsman, I believe the sport of yachting is an ideal way for a company dealing in luxury goods to promote its name and fine products throughout the world.

When I first became Chairman of Champagne Mumm, I asked for research to be undertaken to find an international event of commensurate style and status. At that time I had no idea that this connection would last for almost three decades, as Mumm will sponsor the Champagne Mumm Admiral's Cup into the twenty-first century. Such a long sponsorship makes yachting history.

We are pleased to continue our commitment and look forward to continuing friendships with the Commodores of the Royal Ocean Racing Club and the many owners and skippers of yachts around the world who make the Champagne Mumm Admiral's Cup such a success.

The Champagne Mumm Admiral's Cup is one of the greatest offshore racing events and I am happy to have contributed to its renown and international interest for the many yachtsmen who dream of competing in the world championship of yacht racing.'

Baron Alain de Gunzburg
Chairman G H MUMM & CIE

'At CORUM our main passion is, of course, to create very particular watches. When we created our model bearing nautical flags on the dial we wanted, naturally enough, to give it a name from the world of sailing. As I am passionately fond of sailing, I have always thought that the Champagne Mumm Admiral's Cup is one of the greatest and certainly the most beautiful nautical events in the world.

So, the name of our famous watch simply became Admiral's Cup by CORUM! And when we won it, we of course celebrated the victory with Mumm champagne.'

Jean-René Bannwart
President of CORUM

**ADMIRAL'S CUP**

**CORUM**

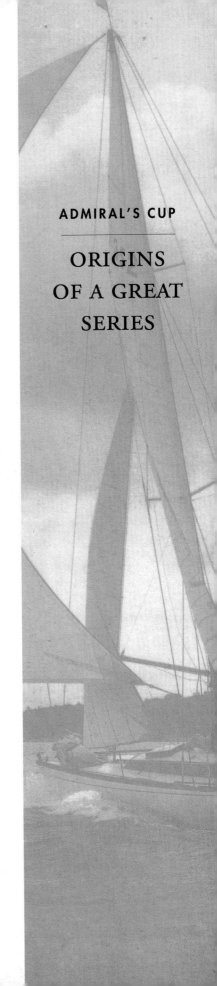

THE ADMIRAL'S CUP may be synonymous with Mumm champagne, but it started with Plymouth Gin. Like many a tale, this one begins over a drink – or several – for it was Sir Myles Wyatt and his great friend Peter Green who nurtured the idea of an international off-shore yacht race series. They knocked the idea about ashore and while racing. Some of the notions were out-landish, others less so; and the series we know now was the distillation of them all. Five-boat teams, a race around the islands of Britain and even a series linking the Bermuda, Sydney-Hobart and Fastnet Races all sprang from imaginations in which perhaps there was initially more gin talking than reasonable thought.

Still, just as Weston Martyr had before them, when he dreamed up the idea of the Fastnet Race in the Royal Western Yacht Club's bar in Plymouth back in 1924, so Myles Wyatt and Peter Green let their fertile minds wander over the idea of giving the still-fledgling sport of ocean racing a boost. Their plans crystallised in time for the 1957 season.

At the time there was talk of reviving the Ameri-ca's Cup, dormant since 1937 because of the crippling costs of the magnificent J-Class yachts, the war and the austerity which followed. But as ocean racing had already claimed their hearts, Sir Myles Wyatt and Peter Green's thoughts focused on an offshore series, not dayboats and day races. 'Our first ideas were extremely extravagant,' remembers Peter Green, then an insur-ance underwriter, later chairman of Lloyd's of London and knighted for his efforts. 'The series was to have been for teams of boats which competed in the Fastnet race, the Bermuda Race and the Sydney-Hobart. But in the cool light of dawn, after too much Plymouth Gin, we realised that wouldn't really be possible.'

Over one particularly spectacular dinner, a pro-posal to include a race around all the islands of Britain

seemed a crackerjack scheme. Between the claret and the port, the rules were whittled down to the bare essentials: competing yachts would have to start at anchor off the Royal Yacht Squadron's line at Cowes; from there, they could sail out of the Solent to either the east or the west – depending on their expectation of the forecast – and pass to seaward of all islands, including the solitary outpost of Rockall, on the way back to Cowes.

They thought it would have been a very interesting course, but when cold reflection triumphed over spir-ited debate, they accepted such a race would take just too long. Even so, almost forty years later, the notion of crews racing each other in contrary directions still appeals to Sir Peter Green as a one-off challenge.

'Myles was a tremendous deep-water sailor,' recalls Green, who like his friend and another of the original donors, Geoffrey Pattinson, came from Essex's rural lands near Colchester. 'He cruised *Tyger* all the way to Spitzbergen, and we did once think of taking her down to do circumnavigation of Tierra del Feugo.'

Gradually the Grand Plan drew in its horizons, with the Dinard Race considered a suitable curtain raiser, because of its pleasant course and the run ashore in the twin ports standing astride the River Rance–Dinard and St Malo. To this would be added the Channel Race, two races in the Solent during Cowes Week and the Fastnet Race. 'In fact, when we began to talk to other countries about it, they said that if we brought in the Dinard Race it would make the whole thing too long,' said Peter Green.

Dinard was dropped from the proposed programme and in 1956 a letter was sent to the Commodore of the Cruising Club of America, enquiring as to the possi-bility of them being able to raise a team to compete against the British. The letter was private, though the

Myth of Malham, *Britain's most famous racing yacht of the 1950s and 1960s. Her owners, Captain John Illingworth and Peter Green, were two of the Cup's five donors (Beken of Cowes)*

new series could not be entirely divorced from the Royal Ocean Racing Club as Sir Myles Wyatt held the office of Admiral of the Club while Peter Green was the incumbent Commodore.

The gauntlet thrown down to the Americans was this:

A PRIVATE CHALLENGE FROM A GROUP OF ENGLISH
YACHT OWNERS TO THE AMERICANS:-

*"It is the intention of certain British Owners to offer a Challenge Cup to be competed for between not less than three and not more than five privately owned yachts drawn from each side.*

*So far as possible, the English yachts will be of the same approximate rating as those the Americans wish to send.*

*The races in which this would be decided are the Channel Race starting August 2nd (220 miles), the Britannia Cup (day race) on August 6th, the New York Yacht Club Cup (day race) on August 8th and the Fastnet Race (605 miles) starting on August 10th.*

*All these races to be sailed on 1957 RORC rating and according to RYA (Royal Yachting Association) rules and for the offshore races RORC Special Regulations.*

*The method of scoring would be the winning boat on RORC handicap in each race would score 6 points with 3 entries per side, 8 points 4 entries a side, or 10 points with 5 entries a side; the second boat 5, 7, 9 and so on in finishing order. For the Channel Race, the points so given to be multiplied by 2 and for the Fastnet Race to be multiplied by 3, the winning team to be that with the most points."*

Following its delivery in late 1956, the challenge was dealt with by G W Blunt White, chairman of the New York Yacht Club's Transatlantic Race Committee. In a letter to Peter Green dated 4 January 1957, Blunt White wrote: 'The other day I had lunch with Geoffrey Julian and Alf Loomis in New York. This gave us an opportunity to discuss a private challenge from certain English yachtsmen, which has already received some publicity in this country.'

Blunt White admitted that the NYYC were behind in arrangements for their Transatlantic race and that

*Selwyn Slater was also a donor. His* Uomie *was in the first British team (Beken of Cowes)*

invitations had just been sent out to potential partici-pants. Since any yachts likely to rise to the British challenge would come from those who had raced across 'The Pond', Blunt White requested: 'I would like to ask if you could postpone your closing date until some time later in the spring than March, when we will def-initely know how many yachts from the USA propose to sail in the Transatlantic Race. Presumably, all such would seriously consider sailing on to England after the finish, and this would make for a fine summer of sailing and racing.'

The closing date was put back to noon on 30 April. Blunt White was optimistic that the Philadelphia judge, Curtis Bok, would enter and was certain that Carl Koch would join the team in his 40ft masthead yawl, *Jen*. As it was, both dropped out, leaving Blunt White's own 46ft *White Mist*, William Snaith's 47ft *Figaro* and Richard Nye's 53ft *Carina* as the American contenders. Ironically, as principal instigator, Myles Wyatt was denied the opportunity to race in the inaugural series because the Americans were unable to send more than three yachts. So his *Bloodhound*, a 63ft yawl built by Camper & Nicholsons, winner of the Fastnet in her first season in 1939 and later owned by the Queen and the Duke of Edinburgh, stood down.

With *Bloodhound* excluded, three smaller yachts were left: Peter Green's own and famous *Myth of Malham*, which he shared with the redoubtable Captain John Illingworth; Selwyn Slater's *Uomie*; and *Jocasta*, owned by Essex fruit farmer Geoffrey Pattinson.

When the four owners of three yachts decided they ought to join Sir Myles Wyatt and put up a trophy for their challenge, it was Selwyn Slater who tracked down a horse racing cup through a silverware dealer friend. Selwyn Slater had all manner of contacts in all sorts of fields, and was a man who could come up with almost anything if asked. The Cup, initially called The Gold Cup, dated from the early 1830s, when William IV was still on the throne, and cost a reasonable £250, with a further £50 to have an old inscription removed and a new one engraved. The silver gilt piece was re-gilded too. This trophy is a finely figured, nicely proportioned lidded bowl, though arguably it is spoilt somewhat by

the wooden base now bearing the names of its subse-quent winners. Many would say it is a far finer piece than the more gaudy America's Cup.

It was the America's Cup, however, which made the Americans the natural sailors to challenge, ever since they had relieved the Squadron of that particular Cup in 1851. Because of its station as a fashionable town favoured by royal patronage, regattas in the Solent made Cowes the pre-eminent sailing venue in the country and the only logical place to anchor the new series.

While there were many day races, and several notable long-distance ocean races, big yachts did not really start racing offshore until after World War II. Before then, there were few long-distance races besides the blue water classics, and the notion of spending a weekend passage racing overnight was not well sub-scribed. The yachts being cruisers first and foremost, offshore races in the Channel were often looked upon as no more than a means to deliver the yacht to a cruis-ing ground.

A zealous advocate of offshore racing for its own sake was Captain John Illingworth. Still in the Royal Navy, Illingworth made his mark before the war with the Laurent Giles-designed and innovative *Maid of Malham*, forcing the pace of yacht design. Fractional rigs, in which the forestay height is less than the height of the mast, are pretty much the norm on racing yachts now, as they were before the war. Yet so radical was Illingworth's insistence that *Maid* should have a full height foretriangle that Chris Ratsey was unwilling to make jibs for her.

When the Royal Ocean Racing Club resumed its programme after World War II with the Dinard Race, in 1945, Illingworth shook the sport up, not only by building a yacht expressly for racing, but also by giving Jack Giles a precise brief on what she should be like. *Myth of Malham* became the hottest racing yacht for over a decade.

The Illingworth influence worked in many ways, for as well as gingering up the sport, he was a co-donor of the Cup with Peter Green. That friendship was launched when Peter Green's future wife, Pam, sailed with Illing-worth on *Myth* in the 1949 Fastnet, as did Mary Pera (née Blewitt), who later became RORC secretary. After that Fastnet, Illingworth took one of his other yachts, *Minx of Malham*, to La Rochelle, where Peter Green had also raced with Michael Mason aboard *Latifa*, and struck up friendships with both Illingworth and Pam.

By 1953, Green had finished with the Lloyd's YC *Lutine* and, looking around for a new yacht, built the tiny Class III boat *Mouse of Malham* with Illingworth. 'She might have been called *Midden of Malham*, such was her state after a race,' commented Peter Green. He persuaded Illingworth to get *Myth* out again, and they raced her together, including in the very first Admiral's Cup. Later Green bought his partner out and Illingworth concentrated on his own design and building business, Aero Marine, at Emsworth in Chichester Harbour.

At the close of the initial series, a committee of management was formed with Myles Wyatt and Peter Green, the Royal Ocean Racing Club's secretary, Alan Paul, and a representative of the Royal Yacht Squadron. The Royal Yacht Squadron's line had been used for the Cowes Week races and they had welcomed the additional entries to their prestigious Britannia Cup and New York Yacht Club Challenge Cup races. They had, however, required assurances that there would be no team racing amongst the Admiral's Cuppers which would wreck either event for other yachtsmen. 'We were able to say that as the boats were so varied in size, it would be very difficult to indulge in the sort of team racing tactics seen in dinghies or one-design yachts, and besides, our object really was to bring people who enjoyed racing to England to take part in our races. The Admiral's Cup was little more than a soupçon on top,' recalled Peter Green.

When the five men presented the Cup to the Royal Ocean Racing Club, a Deed of Gift was drawn by E. P. 'Buster' de Guingand, then both a committee member and solicitor to the Club and whose brother, Major-General Sir Francis de Guingand, had played such a prominent role in the Normandy landings at the close of World War II. Among the clauses of the Deed was a provision for the Cup reverting to the RORC if it was not contested for seven years.

Its central plank was that the Fastnet Race had to be part of the series. It was the only race to be specified and, some would say, it remains the most important provision. Having the Fastnet as the climax to the series has shaped the character and atmosphere of each Admiral's Cup, for the race brings an inescapable sense of occasion. With the points being loaded up for the race and its reputation for being physically tough and tactically taxing, it served the useful sporting purpose of ensuring that the Cup has never been won until the Fastnet has run its course.

While Sir Myles Wyatt did not compete in the child of his creation, he imbued it with its offshore character and, through his office of Club Admiral, gave the Cup its name.

*T*N THE WORDS of the late Sir Owen Aisher, patriarch of Britain's most famous sailing family, the Royal Ocean Racing Club 'is quite simply the most marvellous club in the world.' He was its treasurer for many years, held the office of Admiral for a while, donated *Griffin* to the RORC as its second club yacht, and made the name *Yeoman* the best known in British offshore racing. The success of the Club is due to those who run it. They are great enthusiasts for the sport and, as a man who raced in his nineties, it is a quality Sir Owen appreciated to the full.

The Club's participation in the sport follows a continuous thread back to 1925, when the then Ocean Racing Club was formed by a small band of people headed by Lieutenant-Commander E. G. Martin, whose express aim was 'to provide annually one ocean race of not less than 600 miles in length to be sailed under the Yacht Racing Association rules and such special regulations as are considered by the committee to be necessary'.

This was the Fastnet and the race made the Club what it is today. It was organised by another small group, again led by George Martin but propelled along with great enthusiasm by a yachting writer, Weston Martyr. Like others, he had taken note of the formation of the Cruising Club of America, similar to Britain's Royal Cruising Club, some of whose members held a race from New London, in Long Island Sound, to Bermuda in 1922.

That race became a classic. Martyr, who sailed in the 1923 race and again in 1924, found sufficient British owners of cruisers to start the first Fastnet from Ryde, Isle of Wight, on 15 August 1925. In advocating the new race, Martyr had written in *Yachting Monthly*: 'It is without question the very finest sport a man can engage in; for to play the game at all it is necessary to

process, in the very highest degree, those hallmarks of a true sportsman: skill, courage and endurance.'

Among those stimulated by Martyr's proposal was Claud Worth, a member of the Royal Cruising Club and famous for voyaging aboard *Tern IV*. 'Are our latitudes suitable for public ocean races?' he challenged in *The Field*. It was his use of ocean, coupled with Martyr's deep water experiences to Bermuda, that brought the word ocean into currency. Without it sailing around UK waters would have been more properly described as offshore and the RORC would have been a club with the same initials but a different name.

Following Weston Martyr's victory with *Jolie Brise* in the inaugural 1925 Fastnet, a meeting of like minds was held at the Royal Western Yacht Club in Plymouth. They formed the Ocean Racing Club, whose 34 founder members paid a £1 subscription and fulfilled an entry requirement in sailing the Fastnet Race. Sir Philip Hunloke, the King's sailing master aboard *Britannia*, was president, George Martin the Commodore, and Malden Heckstall-Smith theSsecretary and Measurer. Martyr wrote some time later: 'We decided to make our own rating rules and I well remember saying to Martin it would not be long before many yachts would be built to them.'

By 1928 a second race, the Channel Race, had been created, and although an application made a year later for Royal status was declined, the Club eventually became the Royal Ocean Racing Club in November 1931.

The Club gently fostered the appeal of racing offshore, such sport previously being the reserve of rich owners and their professional crews who, more often than not, raced during the summer and were fishermen in winter. The sailing instructions for the first Fastnet contained the telling requirement that: 'No

*Sir Myles Wyatt, Admiral of the Royal Ocean Racing Club in 1957 when he and Peter Green, Captain John Illingworth, Selwyn Slater and Geoffrey Pattinson donated the Admiral's Cup*

restriction will be placed on the number of amateurs carried but no more paid hands will be permitted than can be normally accommodated in the forecastle.' By the mid-1920s, there was a growing body of educated and adventurous Englishmen wanting to go to sea in the small yachts.

But it was not spiralling growth. In 1933, the Fastnet entry had dwindled to just six, and a despairing Martyr wrote in *Yachting World*: 'What is the matter

*The bar, heart of the RORC's clubhouse at 20 St James's Place*

with us? We've got the ships, we've got the men, and if we haven't got the money then neither have the Americans just now.'

Martyr's contributions were immense. The Fastnet remains one of the world's great races, while the fostering of design rules and the nurturing of newcomers to the sport remain close to the Club's heart. The Club's first Commodore, E. G. Martin, gave the RORC its signature: the seahorse with its reversed tail – Hippo campus Rorcus. Martyr even carved the original

pattern, above which a crown was placed when royal status was granted.

Initially, the Club had no fixed abode, using assorted premises in London for its meetings. By 1935 it was using rooms at 3 Burlington Street and the following February, with membership having reached 600, a clubhouse was opened at 2 Pall Mall, right in the heart of London's clubs. It sounded grand, but consisted of no more than half a dozen rooms above a shop. Britain's great designers of the day, Charles E. Nicholson, William Fife and Alfred Mylne were among those who attended the housewarming party.

In the black days of war, when drink was virtually unobtainable, a direct hit from a bomb in November 1940 destroyed the premises, tragically killing the steward. Several members searched the ruins and emerged bearing a blanket-covered stretcher, whereupon a small crowd removed their hats as the stretcher passed, unaware that the 'body' was two cases of precious gin. Many of the Club's records were saved and transferred to 20 St James's Place, a building tucked away in a backwater between Pall Mall and Piccadilly, on which a lease had been obtained. King Haakon of Norway opened the new clubhouse in July 1942, and there the Club remains today, in a location now deemed of immense value. Among its wartime activities the RORC ran a design competition, open to allied prisoners of war, for a 32-35ft LWL cruiser-racer. The instructions and drawing materials were put out by the Red Cross, and first prize went to Flight-Lieutenant Walsh of the RAF.

Straight after the war, the Club was in a precarious state, with few members, less money and the building's owner trying to eject the RORC from its dilapidated premises. The end of the war did not see the last of the Club's structural problems, either. Years later, when the new Jubilee Underground line was constructed, the building was badly disturbed and required urgent remedial work, which was still in progress when the Queen and Prince Philip visited the clubhouse for the RORC's fiftieth birthday in 1975.

Racing resumed after the war with an event from Cowes to Dinard, but even that was not without problems. The eight boats were escorted by a destroyer and had to round a buoy in Torbay to avoid the minefields still in the Channel.

In 1952, the freehold to 20 St James's Place was purchased. Since the RORC did not have the means to raise the £17,500 asking price, the Club took the novel step of borrowing £10,000 from the vendor, a loan paid off within a year through members' loans and debentures. When the freehold on 19 St James's Place came up for purchase in 1959, that was also bought and a huge amount of work was undertaken on the combined premises.

While Peter Peterson guided the RORC through the war years, when the clubhouse was a great meeting place for members on leave and honorary members from the Services, the busy post-war years led to the appointment of a Club Secretary in 1947. The first was the jovial and well-liked Alan Paul, nicknamed Postle, who had aided the RORC during the war, when not engaged with the Admiralty Ferry Service or the London Fire Service.

A yacht designer manqué, he had been well schooled by Malden Heckstall-Smith and went on to handle technical matters with aplomb. Postle had won many design competitions and his keen eye was cast expertly over many a line drawing. Ever since its inception, the RORC had run its own design rule and Paul guided its development by assisting the amateur committees. His wise counsel to the RORC's committees over the years was priceless, for after the war the rule came under intense pressure. John Illingworth's *Myth of Malham* was described as 'the heartiest slap in the face of conventional yacht architecture ever experienced', a foretaste of the pressure to which the IOR design rule was subjected in later years.

Alan Paul's influence and hard work were immense, yet he still found time to make another significant contribution to the sport when London solicitor Bernard Morgan sought Paul's guidance regarding Morgan's cherished dream of large sailing ships bringing youngsters together from different countries, an organisation which became the Sail Training Association

When Alan Paul took over in 1947, the membership

numbered 700 and boasted the 'precarious tenancy of a dilapidated clubhouse'. By the time Alan Paul left the club in 1972, the membership had risen to nearly 3000, and some concessions to the changing times had been made, alternatives to the Fastnet and shorter RORC races now considered as part of the qualifying process.

For much of that time all of the Club's functions – membership, house, rating and racing – were handled

*Alan Paul, RORC Secretary from 1947–1972, steered the Admiral's Cup through its formative years*

by the Apostle, ably assisted for many years by Hope Kirkpatrick, who was a formidable asset to the Club. A concert pianist and broadcaster in Ireland before the war interrupted her degree studies at Trinity College, Dublin, she served in London as an officer, driving every form of Army transport from staff cars to tracked vehicles. In the 1950s, 1960s and early 1970s, results were generated by tables rather than computer, and the sight of Postle and Hope working elapsed times into corrected times in the corner of a cross-Channel club was a familiar one.

Alan Paul was succeeded by Mary Blewitt, better known as Mary Pera following her marriage to an Italian naval captain. He had sailed with Illingworth aboard *Mouse of Malham*, affectionately known as the *Baby Belsen*, and did for Italy what Illingworth had done for the UK in promoting offshore racing.

A skilled navigator, Mary Pera had guided *Myth of Malham* to a Fastnet victory and *Bloodhound* across the Atlantic, and was also renowned for the navigation books she wrote under her maiden name and which have run to ten editions since 1950. She demystified the art of celestial navigation for many sailors, using methods developed by the RAF in the war. 'There were a lot of Navy people who were particularly tiresome,' she reflected. 'They gave themselves airs, as if they were the only ones who could navigate, but it was wasn't that difficult.' Only the advent of the Global Positioning System at the end of the 1980s spelt the virtual demise of celestial skills.

Living in Rome in the 1960s, Mary Pera regularly travelled to London to attend meetings of the RORC main committee. She also brought the 1969 Italian Admiral's Cup team to England, overcoming enormous difficulties. Her husband had died just weeks before their *La Meloria* was due to be trucked across Europe with her two team mates, itself a hugely difficult exercise, and Mary Pera had developed rheumatoid arthritis and was unable to sail, but undaunted, she saw Italy's first challenge through.

It was two years later that British owner Ron Amey said to her at the 1971 Admiral's Cup prizegiving in Plymouth Guildhall: 'You know Mary, the sort of person we want to succeed The Apostle is someone like you.' It crystallised her thoughts about coming back to the UK and, accepting the job, she became the Club's Secretary in May 1972.

The 1973 Cup was Mary Pera's first and led to an organisational shake-up. A query over the Australian twins *Ginkgo* and *Apollo* highlighted the fact that the Admiral's Cup was, and remains, a club-run event. The Offshore Racing Council's chief measurer, Robin Glover, had made checks on the boats and noted that, according to his computer, they should have rated higher. It was the eve of the series and he asked Mary Pera what to do. Should the boats be fully remeasured? If they were, the Australians would be indignant. If they were not, but went on to do well, other countries might be aggrieved. None of the flag officers was available to advise and decide. 'It wasn't a decision for the executive branch at all, but in the end I decided to do nothing. Fortunately, the Australians didn't win, but I jolly well made sure the responsibility for important decisions like that was not left without being covered by a flag officer again', she recalled.

Alan Green arrived the year before Mary Pera as Assistant Secretary, coming to the Club from Malta. Few appreciate the improvements to the safety standards of offshore racers that this meticulous and considered man has carefully built up through the Club's special regulations over twenty years. Besides the obvious improvements in such things as harnesses and liferafts, Alan Green has carefully nurtured the culture of skippers and crews looking at their own vessels, assessing their equipment and of considering their responsibility in putting to sea. He is also regarded by many as an exceptional race officer. Anyone listening to the radio traffic from committee vessels at others events around the world will realise the economy and precision of the words he uses to get the job done.

His own evenly paced delivery, where words are weighed before they are spoken, makes it easy to conclude he is cautious and conservative. In fact, Alan Green has quite radical ideas, but as an executive conducting the policy created by committees and the Club's elected officers, he rarely reveals his own views. He is ably backed up by Janet Grosvenor, who works with an undemonstrative efficiency. She is the sort of person whom all the world loves and, by knowing the wives and children of members and visitors, she has the unobtrusive influence that women can achieve within a male-dominated hierarchical organisation.

Alan Green became Secretary in 1978, and in 1991 both his title and that of Janet Grosvenor changed to Director and Deputy Director of Racing and Special

Events to reflect the growing complexity of running both a domestic racing programme and a world-class event such as the Champagne Mumm Admiral's Cup. David Minords joined the Club as general manager to look after the very considerable membership, financial and house matters.

With the growth of the Admiral's Cup, RORC has found itself having to fulfil a number of functions at once: a members' club; its role as trustee under the trophy's Deed of Gift; host and race manager; organiser of the British team; and its self-appointed role of 'world leader in offshore racing'.

For Alan Green, the diverse roles are compatible in the 1990s and he has a carefully considered explanation of them. 'The RORC is more than a members' club. It's an organisation of essentially like-minded supporters of the sport of offshore racing worldwide and its principal objective is the promotion of offshore racing. In that unambiguous aim it is probably different from many, if not most, clubs and its promotion is expressed, in particular, through race organisation. Therefore by pursuing top class, international standard race organisation we also express our aspirations to lead the world. In fact, you will find that the Champagne Mumm Admiral's Cup alone has led the world. There have been many copies of it, and the level rating world championships came after the Admiral's Cup and were modelled, I believe, on the Admiral's Cup. And in the detail of running the event there have been numerous other examples of leads – the narrowing of the rating bands was one. In this evolution of the event there is always a balance to be struck between responding and striking new ground which people don't expect. A great deal of development is evolutionary.

'I've never understood why there should be any problem with us running the team as well as running the event. Perhaps that's because I run the event and I know we do it objectively and there's never any shadow of suspicion. We've always set up the British team management as distinctly different people. Although they are all Club people, they are absolutely separate and I, personally, never have anything to do with the British team and have always made a point of distancing myself. Any facilities we have requested, such as weather forecasts, have been for the event and made available to all. Indeed I've never had communication with the British team group. So it's easy for me to be content about it because I know that's the position, though on at least one occasion it was thought and believed there was some kind of stitch-up going on.'

Little imagination is required to work out that one of these instances was the rating scandal over Peter de Savary's *Victory of Burnham* in 1983, when many people, including the designer Ed Dubois, alerted the Club that certain measurements were not as expected and that the rating seemed too favourable, but these signals were not acted on fully by the RORC's Rating Office in Lymington. The alleged favourable treatment of Graham Walker's one-tonner *Indulgence*, which made the 1989 British team despite missing a compulsory trial, also brought indignant outcries that the RORC's chinese walls, which are meant to separate its various functions wherever a conflict of interest could be construed, had failed to work. This was one of several run-ins between the Club and Walker, who was uncomfortable with the Club running both the team and the event, and the way the yacht's owners felt their contribution diminished as soon they became part of the RORC's 'own' team. The 1989 fuss was worthy of the MCC debate in 1992-93, in which England's cricket selectors were put under the spotlight by indignant members of MCC, who could not understand why David Gower, as England's highest scorer of Test runs, had been omitted from a tour of India.

'We are alert to the problem of conflicting interests,' says Alan Green, 'but there never has been the suggestion of anything improper in the way of selecting the British team.'

The growing commercialisation of sport led the RORC into trademark registration in the late seventies. The first was Hippo campus Rorcus, the RORC's own seahorse insignia which is so recognisable because of its reversed tail. Progressively more and more marks have been registered in different classes in a growing number of countries around the world now handled by an outside agency as opposed to the Club's own staff.

THE PARADOX OF COWES is one of a small country town whose name is synonymous with a blue chip sport. Furthermore, a narrow band of water separates it from the mainland, yet Cowes in appearance is more like a dormitory of Southampton on the mainland than the small villages and resorts dotted around other parts of the Isle of Wight.

It could be Devizes or Lancaster, or any one of a number of small English towns which are largely unprepossessing. Yet history has made Cowes the world capital of yachting – a watering hole for kings and kaisers, a playground for captains of industry and princes of commerce – although this patronage has largely failed to realise the town's modest aspirations. There are none of the elegant Edwardian terraces and crescents of spa towns such as Bath or Harrogate, nor lingering reminders of a golden past such as in Brighton, for Cowes was essentially a warship-building town up until the 1960s.

That did not prevent a writer in the *Southampton Herald* from gushing, in 1824: 'Every scheme which human ingenuity can devise and labour can accomplish is being carried out to render this highly favoured spot of the most alluring and attractive description. Cowes people fairly challenge any watering place in England to compete with or produce a collection of such brilliant stars of fashion as at present illuminate our hemisphere.'

Essentially the town's modest station was due to the fact that the season in Cowes was, and is, short. Only for a week a year, or three weeks in an Admiral's Cup year, is the town centre-stage. The great and good come, and in their wake follow the press photographers, the diarists from the social pages and the whole supporting cast of party planners, accommodation agents, paid crews, PR people and the plain curious.

The rest of the time, the town's population worry about the decline of light industry, the tough trading conditions for shops and small business, planning shopping trips to Southampton, the children's school results and the countless humdrum details of daily life familiar in any town, in any country.

The standard image of Cowes is that of an event shoe-horned in between Glorious Goodwood and the start of the grouse-shooting season. That may have been so in the luxuriant era of Edwardian yachting when Edward VII was on the throne, but the numbers who visit Cowes for social reasons alone are modest. It is the sailing which keeps drawing them back. The Castle, clubhouse of the Royal Yacht Squadron, effectively became 'centre-soul, the seat of all moral intellectual life and the spring of all its hopes, fears, plans, tales and jealousies', according to one writer in Edward VII's time.

The early growth of Cowes was due simply to the fact that it was an admirable seaport. Located at the northern tip of the diamond-shaped island, its harbour was protected and the River Medina gave access inland to Newport, the capital.

For sailors the world over, Cowes is known as the home of the Royal Yacht Squadron. 'The world's most exclusive yacht club' is inevitably tagged "the Squadron", and while many senior British yacht clubs enjoy a royal patron, only the Squadron can number HM The Queen as its patron and HRH The Duke of Edinburgh as its admiral. It's true that the Squadron has a respectable number of blue-bloods among its membership, but it is far from exclusive in the Palm Springs or Monaco sense of the word. There is something endearingly British about it, with families counting several generations of members, while an egalitarian streak is apparent in the number of RN members.

*Edwardian splendour at Cowes Week in the 1930s, with the J-class yacht* Candida *manoeuvring for the start*

*West Cowes Castle today, home of the Royal Yacht Squadron since 1858, and the abiding image of yachting at Cowes (Franco Pace)*

Point to the west, Yarmouth castle, Calshot castle and West Cowes. It is 'The Castle' at west Cowes that became the home to the Royal Yacht Squadron, after it was founded as a loose association under Lord Grantham at an inaugural meeting at the Thatched House Tavern in St James's Street, London.

On George IV's acession to the throne, what was simply the Yacht Club in 1820 became the Royal Yacht Club, with a regular regatta programme in place. Already in 1815 there had been much interest in the match between the yachts of two of the forty-two founding members: Joseph Weld's 60-ton cutter *Charlotte* and Thomas Assheton-Smith's 65-ton cutter *Elizabeth*. With a 2000-guinea wager at stake – a considerable sum then – the *Hampshire Telegraph* remarked that the three race match would 'afford as much sport as any race that was ever contested by the highest mettled courses at Newmarket'.

In 1826 the purchase of a house on the site of what became the Gloster Hotel, and the putting up of a gold cup for an annual regatta off Cowes, finally gave yachting in the town some permanence. Its cachet was enshrined in a letter dated 4 July 1833 from William IV to the club secretary: 'I have it commanded from His Majesty to acquaint you for the information of the Commodore and the Officers of the Royal Yacht Club, that as a mark of His Majesty's gracious approval of an institution of such national utility, it is his gracious wish and pleasure that it shall henceforth be known and styled as The Royal Yacht Squadron, of which His Majesty is graciously pleased to consider himself the head.'

Progressively through the 1800s, the town became the object of gentrification. John Nash built East Cowes castle for himself; the artist Turner was a guest, painting scenes of the great races; one of Nash's associates created Northwood Park above the town in East Cowes, which is now owned by the Medina Borough Council and used as function rooms. Nash himself, who is buried in one of his churches, St James in East Cowes, designed the tower of St Mary's Church, whose congregation is swelled each year by yachtsmen for the Cowes Week service.

Cowes was a port long before the first seeds of yachting were sown in Pepys' time, when Charles II and his brother, the Duke of York, sailed on the Thames in 1661. As a shipbuilding centre, it constructed ships of the line for Henry VIII, while his fortifications of the Solent to guard the Cowes, Southampton and Portsmouth harbours remain familiar landmarks: Hurst

There was little gentlemanly behaviour evident afloat in those days, especially when large wagers were at stake. Sailors today lament that the fun has gone out of racing, and that it has become too serious, with the desire to win overriding the simple thrill of competition.

Well, affairs were no better in the last century. In his superb book *Sacred Cowes*, Anthony Heckstall-Smith retells the story of a race to the death between Lord Belfast's *Louisa*, Mr Assheton-Smith's *Menai* and Mr Weld's *Lulworth*. *Menai* ran aground, leaving *Lulworth* and *Louisa* to slug it out. 'They sailed back into the Solent neck-and-neck, and were only separated by a few seconds as they rounded the last marker boat off Yarmouth. As they neared Cowes, the two yachts came into collision. *Lulworth* on the port tack, was about to cross the finishing line when she ran into *Louisa*, which was on the starboard tack. *Louisa's* crew drew their cutlasses and knives and cut away the earring of *Louisa's* boom as well as her reef pendant leaving her disabled. As the race had been sailed in the lightest of winds, the collision took place late at night, just as the Roads were ablaze with light from fireworks let off in honour of the King's birthday. In the midst of this display and while the yachts anchored in the Roads were firing their cannon, the crews of *Louisa* and *Lulworth* were fighting each other like wild cats and slashing at each other's rigging with their cutlasses that flashed and glinted in the light of the fireworks.'

Queen Victoria and Prince Albert made their summer home on the island from 1846 onwards, building Osborne House to the east of Cowes with the aid of architect and developer Thomas Cubbitt, who produced a quirky combination of Italian renaissance and Belgravia in style.

By 1851, Cowes was sufficiently considered to be the home of British yachting for the schooner *America* to come and challenge the pride of the British fleet. It was the year of the Great Exhibition, and whether or not *America* sailed the course correctly, the pretender from the colonies won the race around the Isle of Wight. The Queen's enquiry as to which yacht was the runner-up was answered with the famous phrase, 'Ma'am, there is no second.' The America's Cup legend had been born.

New Year's Day 1858 saw a light lit in the Squadron's new home, West Cowes Castle. It had become, according to a report in *The Observer*, 'no mean fortress, that rendezvous of the princely and squire'. The Castle remains the Squadron's home today.

The Prince of Wales made Cowes' reputation. No matter that he was small and rotund, had a hacking cough and spoke with a guttural German accent. The lawns of the Squadron became the most exclusive in the world and, though far from crowded, they were impossible to gain entry to. 'Cowes is no longer a half civilised resort of rough sailormen; it is Court,' wrote a contemporary observing the town's rise in status in the late 1800s.

It's curious to reflect that it was largely because of his amorous associations and financial scandals that the future Edward VII was so popular, whereas a hundred years later the fabric of the British monarchy seemed less secure in the light of such revelations. The public revelled in his colourful life, which was, after all, an antidote to the apparently joyless Queen Victoria.

*Royal Yacht Squadron gate detail (Gilles Martin-Raget)*

*The former Ratsey & Lapthorn sail loft in which* Britannia's *mainsail was made, was restored after World War II by Sir Max Aitken. The Prospect was donated to the Royal Ocean Racing Club as a museum and function room*

*The Prospect, a familiar sight on the River Medina (Gilles Martin-Raget)*

The Queen's grandson, the German emperor William II, joined the Squadron in 1889, bought the Scottish America's Cup challenger *Thistle*, renamed her *Meteor* and raced her at Cowes in 1892. In 1896 the Kaiser turned up with a new *Meteor*, the second largest cutter ever built. Tellingly, she was one foot longer on the waterline, at 89ft, than the Prince of Wales' famous and beloved *Britannia*, which he raced when he became King Edward VII, with the yacht passing in turn to his son, George V. *Meteor* had been built with the express aim of beating *Britannia*.

The rivalry with *Meteor* was not to the Prince of Wales' liking. Neither had 'Willie's' arrogance been to Queen Victoria's, especially when he visited her in the magnificent 4000-ton steam yacht *Hohenzollern*, which overshadowed the 2000-ton paddle steamer *Victoria and Albert*. Tsar Nicholas II, another relation, was a more welcome visitor with his milder manner, despite the magnificence of his royal yacht, *Standart*, while another visitor was the King of Spain's *Hispania*. For the International Regatta of 1911, the zenith of big-boat racing, the Spanish king put up a trophy – huge, ornate and solid gold with upswept handles in the form of mermaids – and there were other cups from the royal houses of the UK, Norway, Denmark, Sweden and, of course, Germany.

The German Emperor's attitude troubled the Prince of Wales further. 'The regatta,' he is said to have commented while still Prince of Wales, 'used to be a pleasant relaxation for me; since the Kaiser takes command it is a vexation.' It was an annoyance ended by World War I. The Kaiser's brother was staying with the Prince of Wales but three days before war was declared, with the Cowes regatta abandoned only at the last minute, *Meteor II*, on her way to the Solent, returned to Germany but *Germania*, owned by the Krupp steel-making and armaments family, was captured and escorted to Southampton.

Years later, in 1947, Sir Max Aitken, son of the British newspaper baron Lord Beaverbrook, purchased the former Ratsey & Lapthorn sail loft when it was a rat-infested and bomb-damaged ruin following World War II. Sir Max patiently restored the building in which *Bri-*

*tannia*'s mainsail had been made, and among the treasures he collected in his private museum were the tillers from both *Britannia* and *Meteor*, momentoes of an era brought up all standing by the Great War. This building, now known as the Prospect, was donated to the RORC by Sir Max Aitken. Also on display is the Squadron's Cowes regatta programme for 4-7 August 1914, featuring the flags of *Germania*, *Meteor* and *Hispania*: 4 August was the day war broke out.

After World War I, Cowes was deathly quiet. In 1919, many of the Kaiser's cups were returned to him in the Netherlands, where he lived in exile. That winter, prominent members of the Squadron sought an audience with King George V, asking him to consider commissioning *Britannia* for the next season. It was felt he alone could breathe life back into the sport. Mindful of how his actions might be construed in the austere aftermath of war, the King agreed only after careful deliberation, and immediately Sir Thomas Lipton made plans to race his *Shamrock* again, joined by the likes of *White Heather*, *Nyria*, *Westward* and *Terpsichore*.

While the Squadron had been one of the last bastions of the aristocracy and gentry, it was evident that the war had dealt a blow to the *ancien régime*. As Anthony Heckstall-Smith noted: 'Soaring taxation and death duties had impoverished the old aristocracy so that they could no longer afford to own large yachts...The men who built the yachts to race against the King were all tradesmen of one kind or another. Tommy Lipton, the grocer, Sir Charles Allom, the antique dealer and house decorator, Sir Howard Frank, the estate agent, Lord Waring, the shopkeeper, W. I. Stephenson, the chairman of Woolworths, Sir William Berry, the newspaper proprietor, Hugh Paul, the malt-ster, T. O. M. Sopwith, the aeroplane maker, T. B. Davis, the ex-stevedore, Mortimer Singer, the sewing machine manufacturer – all great names in the world of commerce and finance, but none of them, when they first became owners of large yachts, members of the RYS.' The conclusion seemed to be that it was easier to become a member of the House of Lords than it was the Royal Yacht Squadron.

While the Big Class continued its racing, sailing in

*Royal yachts have graced Cowes Roads since the 1800s, but budget cuts mean that 1997 may prove Britannia's farewell appearance (Franco Pace)*

the Solent prospered. Many of the smaller classes created then remain active today: the Redwings, Victories, XODs, Sunbeams and so forth, though the days are long gone when 6-metres and 12-metres flourished.

Two other people helped keep Cowes centre stage, though they could not have been more different. Between the wars, the Squadron was vexed by the question of ladies. They could scarcely enter the Castle though they were permitted to take tea on the lawn and listen to Mr Clifford Essex's band. In 1924 a committee meeting ruled that even the grounds were barred to women if they wore trousers. That the Squadron could be scandalised by trouser-wearing women, given

the proclivities of some its members, is merely a sign of those times. One acute problem which had to be faced was that if women were not allowed into the Castle, how should the Squadron provide la toilette for female guests of a member?

The solution seemed to be the purchase of Castle Rock, later the Royal Corinthian YC's premises. Negotiations went on for years until it was bought from right under the Squadron's nose by Rosa Lewis, who owned London's Cavendish Hotel in Jermyn Street, and was a friend to the good and the great. The Cavendish was said to be a gift of Edward VII.

Rosa Lewis opened the ballroom as the ladies'

annexe, while by night younger members of the royal family, ageing peers, alluring actresses and Americans young and old could be found enjoying Rosa's plentiful food and drink. Warm natured, of great beauty, and no respector of either her own pronunciation or another's station, she added greatly to the aura of Cowes by her colourful presence . She eventually sold her 'little place' in Cowes to the Squadron. At a profit.

After World War II, it was Uffa Fox who helped place Cowes in the minds of people who had no interest in sailing at all. He was an extraordinary man capable of quite outstanding feats, the most daring of which was to cross the Channel in a two-man sliding-seat dinghy and cruise the Brittany coast.

His first design office was one of the old floating bridges which he kept upstream on the Medina. One ramp formed the gangway to the shore while the other was used to launch his boats, which he built on the deck in between. He designed all manner of boats, built many of them in his own works, wrote fantastically detailed books on design and exhibited exceptional prowess as a racing sailor and seaman.

In the 1950s and early 1960s his name came to wider prominence through his sailing with the Duke of Edinburgh and the young Prince Charles aboard the Dragon *Bluebottle* and Flying Fifteen *Coweslip*. Uffa Fox was also the source of considerable evening merriment, with ripe yarns and ribald sea shanties. Photographs of Uffa sailing with the royal family kept Fleet Street's interest in Cowes alive, their presence a continuing thread which maintained the town's name as the home of yachting.

By 1965 the yachting correspondent of *The Times* was committing to print the thought that: 'It is tempting perhaps to think of the Week as one of those timeless, unchanging features of British life which we are supposed to cherish. But this would be false. Not only have the boats changed in size and shape and the accents and attitudes of their owners altered, but there are some notable changes ashore as well. The social life goes on as usual but administratively Cowes loses a little of its garden party atmosphere each year and becomes more like the important national fixture that

it is.' Already the tensions between those who saw Cowes Week as a regatta and those who sought something more from it were emerging.

When the Australian Admiral's Cup yacht *Camille* performed the extraordinary feat of sailing the Britannia Cup course twice in succession in 1965, an achievement made possible by there being no time limit in the sailing instructions, her crew were rather put out to find that the Squadron knew little of their efforts. 'Presumably, the committee decided that after a certain hour social commitments take precedence over sailing,' said *The Times*' writer. 'This in a way typifies an underlying conflict of interests: a prominent Australian has been quoted as saying that they come over here to race, not to go to parties.'

Cowes was still far from being a sporting event, the reporter concluded, despite signs of change, such as a link from the island to London to facilitate the computing of results. 'The old snobbery, ignorance and philistinism still persist, revictualled each year by the swarms of gossip writers and photographers.' One reason, perhaps, why accredited yachting correspondents are still not given the freedom of the yacht clubs?

From 1957, the offshore fleet took more of an interest in the town because of the Admiral's Cup. Since then the RORC has conducted considerable soul searching about whether the venue should be changed, the Isle of Wight press usually picking up the fact that several in-depth appraisals have been made.

This was despite steady improvements. Swinging moorings gave way to trots; the Groves & Guttridge marina was built and used from the 1971 Admiral's Cup onwards. This marked the end of Gosport being used as the starting base for the series with the fleet heading to Cowes only after the Channel Race. With tents and caravans, the marina took on the look of an ocean-racing dinghy park and proper event centre.

By the 1970s, though, the image of Cowes was becoming tarnished. The toilet and shower block in Groves & Guttridge was a disgrace; trying to get petrol or diesel was far easier in other Solent yachting centres; the standards of accommodation were falling. To many it seemed that Cowes was simply resting on its laurels.

Although the Royal Ocean Racing Club's requirements to run the Champagne Mumm Admiral's Cup have not changed much, finding them all in one place is not easy. They need a good, centrally positioned marina; good depth of water; good access at all states of the tide; reasonable proximity to the inshore racing areas; good transportation; a range of nearby accommodation; the presence of clubs and restaurants and facilities for crews. Clearly Cowes does not fit the bill entirely, but then few places do. 'We've looked from time to time at places as far apart as Brighton and Torquay,' says the RORC's Alan Green, 'including Poole, Lymington, Southampton, Portsmouth. But

there is a sentimental attachment to Cowes and the fact that many overseas visitors like sailing from Cowes is a practical consideration, even though we try to make the decision an objective one. The fact that the Royal Yacht Squadron is there, and that it is regarded as a great place from which to sail by many people from overseas, cannot be ignored.'

Accommodation in Cowes has long troubled the RORC, for the small number of hotels, the high cost of rented accommodation and its varying standards have caused visitors considerable anguish over the years. 'We have always encouraged the local authorities, and the Cowes' clubs to keep working to improve the

*Cowes' shipbuilding and sea-faring past is reflected among its older houses (Gilles Martin-Raget)*

accommodation,' admits Alan Green. 'I must say, I've always been disappointed that Cowes has never yet really seemed to come up with tourist board accommodations' management of a style equal to that of Torquay, say, or many other resorts.' As a consequence, visitors who have found top digs or a good accommodation agent treasure their finds jealously, for a good house can transform a stay in Cowes.

In 1987, Crispin Lowe bought the Groves & Guttridge marina, which was the home of the Admiral's Cup and also bore the brunt of the 800 yachts and 5000 crews which came to Cowes Week. A young and able businessman, he had worked in the London property and pop business. Once he'd kept an S & S 34 called *Ancasta* in Groves & Guttridge and had used that name when he entered the yachting business in the early 1980s, building up a big new boat-sales and brokerage concern before purchasing the marina.

Lowe had attracted financial backing from Lazard Brothers bank and James Gulliver, former head of the Argyll food retailing giant. His stated aim to upgrade facilities and attract more events to a world-class yachting venue was widely welcomed. But when the the first of many development schemes was unveiled, Lowe ran into a barrage of strong local resistance. A large study development plan was prepared by Donaldson, the Jermyn Street chartered surveyors who are best known for developing many huge retailing schemes, including the UK's first regional shopping centre at Brent Cross. When terms such as 'speciality and other retailing' were used, along with 'residential accommodation, business space and tourist-related activities', alarm bells started to ring in certain quarters.

The debate polarised between two groups. Some saw the marina as a business opportunity – but not one that could possibly survive entirely on the basis of just eighty berths, which could never generate enough income to pay the costs of marina operation. The other view was that this was a get-rich-quick scheme. It flew in the face of the clubs who created and ran the racing, turned a blind eye to the fact that big events needed full repair, maintenance, storage and lifting facilities on site (and not upstream in other yards

as the developers suggested) and that a retail, residential and heritage centre was an attempt to make up for past failings to develop tourist and visitor facilities.

'I am dismayed by the proposals to run down Ancasta Marina for the benefit of the developers,' said the late Major Peter Snowden in 1988, who as the then Secretary of the Cowes Combined Clubs and Solent Cruising & Racing Association was at the fulcrum of the town's yachting interests.

Stalemate ensued. Marina charges went up as Ancasta sought to defray the cost of their investment. New plans were drawn. And still there was no real improvement in the toilets and showers. By 1991, Ancasta Marina went into receivership. There was no work for the yard's skilled labour force and the very fabric of it began to crumble, with the concrete apron starting to subside and become unsafe.

Those who had resisted the plans for an on-site hotel, apartments and shops, formed their own lobby – Cowes Yachting – whose aim was to promote the yachting business in the town and actively encourage clubs and classes to come to Cowes. In concert with the Cowes Waterfront Trust, which was closely associated with the Harbour Commissioners, they bought the marina from the receivers in January 1993 for £11 million.

The Trust is working in partnership with local government, tourist and rural development agencies, with the aim of bringing the site into some form of public ownership. Their immediate task was to carry out engineering work to the sea wall, apron and the pontoons, plus some dredging. A new harbour office, marine trade shops, light industrial units, toilets and showers were also part of the refurbishment. Crews will be able to work on their boats on the site, which is both convenient and provides the pit-lane atmosphere the public like so much, while major repair work will have to be done elsewhere. The old Groves & Guttridge name will be borne by a full-service yard further upstream.

And with Cowes Yachting speaking of plans to work with tourist boards to grade accommodation standards and set targets for pricing, 1993 might prove to have been the watershed in Cowes' renaissance.

FROM THE VERY FIRST, the Admiral's Cup was a joint venture with the Royal Yacht Squadron, the RORC running its accustomed Channel Race and Fastnet Race to open and close the series, with the RYS's Britannia Cup and New York Yacht Club Challenge Cup interleaving the offshore races on the Tuesday and Thursday of Cowes Week. In 1957, this cooperation was very informal, the results of the Admiral's Cup yachts extracted from the RYS's lists to score the private Britain v. America contest.

The scoring was simplicity itself. For the six yachts representing the gentleman's challenge by the British to their three American counterparts, the winner accrued six points, the second-placed yacht five and so on. The combined points of the New York Yacht Club and Britannia Cup inshore races plus the Channel and Fastnet Race determined the result. Though the Admiral's Cuppers comprised a handful of yachts within much larger fleets, it was their scores in relation to each other which counted.

The Channel Race of 1957 hinged on the tide at Beachy Head, the results shaped by the overnight beat east along the south coast of England from the Owers to Beachy Head. *Lutine*, though not an Admiral's Cup boat, was alone among Class I in making the tide and Myles Wyatt and Peter Green's *Myth of Malham*, of Class II, just about did, but between there and the Royal Sovereign Light Vessel the tide was running progressively stronger. Dick Nye's *Carina* from the USA and Selwyn Slater's *Uomie*, behind the smaller *Myth*, lost progressively more time, and as the race progressed without freak or fortune there was no way the bigger boats could have made up the time on the little British boat.

*Myth* winning the Channel Challenge Cup for the best corrected time and *Uomie* in second place, gave Britain a magnificent start. *Uomie* went one better by winning the Britannia Cup on the Tuesday of Cowes Week, having wriggled clear from a muddled start. *Myth of Malham* experienced an uncharacteristic foul up with a riding turn on her yankee sheet winch just before the gun. She tacked, all but became hove-to and had to wear right round and partly lower the sail before it could be cleared.

Having thwarted American plans for a good showing in the Admiral's Cup by failing to make the Channel Race start, *Figaro* came good in Thursday's New York Yacht Club Challenge Cup, winning the 29 mile race by more than a minute and a half, superbly backed up by a fourth from *Carina* and a fifth from *White Mist*. Ideal conditions in the Channel contrasted with the tough 1955 race, for an easterly breeze, consistent in direction and strength, made for a straightforward race.

The 1957 Fastnet provided a dramatic final act for the new event, being one of those heavy-weather affairs that has made the race a classic. The start was especially difficult for the race committee as it was in a rising gale, though the shelter the Isle of Wight shore gave from the south-westerly did offer some respite. Any postponement would probably have resulted in cancellation, for within a few hours of the gun the forty-three-boat fleet was plugging into a robust Force 9, and after two days more than half the fleet had retired, battered and bruised, as conditions worsened. Twelve yachts managed to finish, including all three Americans. One contemporary described the conditions as the dirtiest he had seen as the fleet soldiered on under storm jibs and deep reefs, or even trysails, out to the Rock.

Buster de Guingand, the RORC's vice-commodore, was racing on Dick Nye's *Carina II* and wrote in *Yachting World*: 'The foredeck crew were frequently invisible from the cockpit when they were covered by the sea

*Bill Snaith's* Figaro *from the USA leading the Admiral's Cup fleet off the Royal Yacht Squadron start line (Beken of Cowes)*

and spray driving over *Carina*'s weather bow. The ex-12-metre *Vanity* was a little ahead at this point and we saw her leap out of the sea and without exaggeration we saw her keel several feet aft of the mast.' Given a Twelve's deep draught and heavy displacement, *Vanity*'s acrobatics say much about the sea state. In the van of the fleet, the wind moderated and freed on the way to the Rock, only to veer and increase so that they had to beat a fair way back to Plymouth.

Through it all, Nye drove his beamy shallow draught Rhodes-designed yawl with verve and skill, and that despite the yacht cracking three ribs forward, lifting the deck in places and having to be pumped virtually the entire way around the course. The two-year German built hull was made to work hard for her glory, with her helmsmen in watches of four rotated every hour to keep them sharp.

De Guingand described the ride back from the Rock when the wind was still free as 'the finest sailing of the race. Until we reached the Scillies we were making 8-8.5 knots and surfing at times to 9.5 knots.' *Carina* averaged an astonishing 8.3 knots for the course, no doubt helped by Nye's exhortations to his crew. 'Is every man a tiger?' he bellowed. 'Grr! Grr!' was their theatrical reply. Little wonder Nye uttered the famous words as *Carina* steamed past the Plymouth breakwater: 'OK boys, we're over now; let the damn boat sink.'

Despite having the lowest rating but one among the sixteen Class I entries, *Carina* was first to the Rock and held her lead back home to collect an array of silverware. Her elapsed time of four days 10½ hours was only a couple of hours longer than *Carina*'s time two years before in a less arduous race.

As in the transatlantic to Santander earlier in the year, the American pair of *Figaro* and *White Mist* again finished within a minute of each other, though the redoubtable John Illingworth was two hours ahead in *Myth of Malham* to take Class II and secure Britain's narrow victory by 70 points to 68.

De Guingand's account is a cameo on ocean racing as it was then. Generations since, brought up on dry-suits, caffeine tablets, sleep snatched while lashed to the lifelines on the weather rail and token food should

*Dick Nye's Carina won the Transatlantic Race en route to the Admiral's Cup and completed her 1957 season in Europe as winner of the Fastnet Race (Beken of Cowes)*

consider this: 'During the first night, the anthracite stove in the cabin was lit and kept alight throughout the race. This proved to be a real life saver. There was no denying it was wet and cold on deck and to be able to come off watch to a warm, comparatively dry cabin and strip and rub down and at the end of one's spell below to climb back into clothes, which though perhaps not dry, had at least been warmed by the stove, was a great boost to morale.

'On the subject of morale, one must mention Sandy Sanderson, our whole-time cook. Up at six in the morning, he unfailingly produced a hot breakfast (starting with porridge) for both watches and then cleared up. Bouillon was at call at any time. He then would provide a good lunch with either hot soup and cold pudding or a good fried steak and mash potatoes. In the evening he invariably produced a first-class hot meal and plenty of it. Before he turned in, everything was cleared up and ready for the night watches to brew up their grog, soup or coffee as they might feel disposed.'

It was not unrelieved hedonism. Far from it. Foul-weather clothing was little more than oil-impregnated cloth with water coursing through neck, arms and leg apertures almost unchecked. And those who lost nails handling heavy cotton, or the early Terylene and Dacron sails in filthy weather will swear that the equally awkward Kevlar is actually more pleasant to wrestle with.

At the close, the impact of the fledgling series seemed limited, and there was no obvious sign that the seeds of something quite special had put down roots. *Rudder*, the long-established American journal, did not even mention it when praising Dick Nye and *Carina* for repeating their 1955 Transatlantic Race and the Fastnet triumphs 'for a unique place in yachting history'.

## SHORT TACKS

• Selwyn Slater named his yacht *Uomie* as in You Owe Me. He built her with a modest fit-out below, intending to add more comfort later.

**ABOVE:** Carina's haul of trophies, including best corrected time in the 1957 Fastnet Race (Beken of Cowes)
**BELOW:** Blunt White's White Mist *was the second highest scorer in the USA team. Safety regulations required a dinghy to be carried on deck (Beken of Cowes)*

Proof of just how fledgling a series the Admiral's Cup still was can be found in the Royal Ocean Racing Club's main committee minutes. The series did not warrant its own agenda item, but was buried as a footnote to the Fastnet Race report under the general Season's Racing sub-heading.

The Americans seemed to be of the same mind: the Admiral's Cup was not sufficiently alluring in itself to make it worth crossing the Atlantic for a second time, although Dick Nye did bring his beautiful 53ft *Carina* back across 'the Pond' to race the Channel Race, Cowes Week and to try to win a third Fastnet. She nearly did too, taking the Class I laurels and placing third overall, missing out on a memorable triple by 51 minutes on corrected time. Fortunately, interest was strong elsewhere and the Netherlands and France ventured to Cowes, where the Dutch came within an ace of victory.

The Dutch visitors were familiar faces. A. W. Goudriaan's *Olivier van Noort* and plywood manufacturer Cornelius Bruynzeel's *Zeevalk* had been to Cowes before, though W. N. H. van der Vorm's *Zwerver* was all new. By contrast, the French team was pretty much unknown, comprising F Hervé's *Eloise II*, Jean-Claude Menu's *Marie Christine III* and G. Caripeau's *St François*.

The international spirit, epitomised by the Admiral's Cup, was growing. Three British yachts sailed the 1958 Bermuda Race, the prime fixture in the Cruising Club of America's season which reciprocated America's attendance in Cowes the summer before, while Geoffrey Pattinson took Selwyn Slater's *Uomie* down to the Sydney-Hobart Race, the first time a British boat had taken part since 1945.

The defending British team had a familiar look to it. John Illingworth and Peter Green were back with *Myth of Malham*, as was Selwyn Slater – though this time with *Ramrod*, a replacement for *Uomie* and built by Port Hamble to Arthur Robb's designs. They were joined by the Royal Ocean Racing Club's own yacht, *Griffin*, which had previously been Owen Aisher's own *Yeoman III* and winner of the 1951 Fastnet. Curiously, though the Aisher name is synonymous with the British offshore scene and one of his sons, Robin, went on to captain three British Admiral's Cup teams, the patriarch of the Aisher clan never sailed in the Cup himself. It was *Yeoman III*'s subsequent owners – Sir Giles Guthrie, banker and sometime chairman of British Overseas Airways Corporation, a forerunner of the present day BA, and Charles Gardener, a landowner who later bought the Groves & Guttridge marina site in Cowes – who, in 1987, presented the Club with its own yacht, which sailed with a crew of trainees in the 1959 Cup

Perfect conditions for the Channel Race were matched by a very good result for the British team. A steady Force 3 put a premium on the key decision – when to tack on the return leg from the Le Havre light vessel to the Solent. Selwyn Slater got it so right that *Ramrod* came to the line with the much larger *Carina* to win the Channel Challenge Cup by fourteen minutes, as well as the open class for big boats, while *Griffin* justified her selection with Major Gerald Potter and his trained crew winning Class II, in which *Myth of Malham* came third.

Light winds and spring tides made concentration the requirement of the Cowes Week races, sailed under blissful summer skies. The word on the waterfront was 'Have you seen *Anitra*?' *Yachting World* explained about the Swedish yawl, which went on to win the Fastnet and sailed in the 1961 Admiral's Cup for her country: 'The perfection of her varnished topsides and the beauty and delicacy of her fittings was such that, as with a really beautiful woman, everyone stared at her.'

The spring tides were taken advantage of to send

*Selwyn Slater's cutter* Ramrod, *winner of the 1959 Channel Race (Beken of Cowes)*

the Britannia Cup fleet round the Isle of Wight, though what seemed like a good idea turned out to be a long and frustrating affair. The Squadron's start line was extended northwards to South Bramble buoy. *Ramrod* attempted an audacious start: kedged by the stern, she had full sail set, ready to up anchor the moment before gun fired. But the blanketing effect of the surrounding thirty-four-boat fleet meant that she was slow off the mark, though she did avoid being swept over prematurely and having to make up against the tide again.

Several hours after the gun, the leaders had barely made the Forts off Spithead, and only the first few got round the back of the Island to St Catherine's Point before the tide turned and the flood started to run. *Myth* was among several which bounced off the rocks at St Catherine's, trying to cheat the tide. With such a gate there, it was not surprising the bigger boats tri-

umphed, with the Dutch *Zwerver* winning both fleet and Admiral's Cup honours, while others struggled through the night to complete the loop back to Cowes.

A pleasant morning breeze promised a more satisfactory race for the New York Yacht Club Challenge Cup, but the wind failed as the day's heat grew, leaving the Solent glassily calm by the early afternoon. Many of the dayboat classes retired and *St François* from France was the best of the nine Admiral's Cuppers. Britain went into the Fastnet, scoring triple points, with a three-point lead over the Netherlands.

Whereas 1957 had been rumbustious, the 1959 race was slow and murky. As Alfred Loomis so rightly put it: 'Superlatives are usually employed in describing the 605 miles race around the Fastnet, but this race was not the fastest, or the slowest, or the hardest or softest. It was the most exasperating.'

The leaders had scarcely enough wind to get round Portland Bill before the foul tide started running. The smaller boats did not make it though, forced to kedge or drift backwards. The contrariness of offshore racing was found by those anchoring off Portland. In twenty fathoms, they found that genoa sheets, mooring lines and anchor warps had to be added to the chain rode before sufficient scope was out and their anchors held. And so it was at the next tidal gates, Start Point and the Lizard, as the fleet was sorted into a natural pecking order.

Proof that minutes do count in a race which takes four days or more was provided by *Myth of Malham* which, like *Carina*, was attempting a third Fastnet victory. She ran aground when tide-dodging in the Solent and the twenty minutes lost while the dinghy was launched, kedge laid and the yacht pulled off, was pretty much the margin *Myth* missed collecting a fair tide around Portland Bill and Start Point. Twice she had to anchor, waiting for the flood to slacken or the breeze to gather some backbone. One on top of the other, the setbacks meant that *Myth* was nine hours behind race winner *Anitra* at the Rock, and fourteen hours at the finish. Falling at such hurdles was not the method Illingworth expounded in his classic book, *Offshore*.

*France joined Holland in challenging in Britain in 1959. St. Francoise was the second lowest scorer among the nine yachts, not starting the Britannia Cup and retiring from the Fastnet (Beken of Cowes)*

Dick Nye's *Carina* (*left*) leads
*Ramrod* (*centre*) and Cornelius
Bruynzeel's *Zeevalk* (*right*)
at the start of the 1959 Fastnet Race
(*Beken of Cowes*)

Compounding the lack of breeze was fog, which dogged the fleet until a sharp change in the weather brought a gale from the south-west, which sent the fleet scurrying home. With all three French yachts pulling out, the fate of the Admiral's Cup depended on how the Dutch and British fared. In Class I, *Olivier van Noort* and *Zwerver* finished second and fourth, sandwiching third-placed *Ramrod*, while a second for *Griffin II* and a valuable fourth for *Myth* in Class II gave victory to Britain by 135 points to 123.

The benefit of having visiting yachts was not unnoticed in the UK. Group Captain E. F. Haylock wrote this editorial in *Yachting World*. 'However keen home competition may be, it is always sharpened when an international flavour is introduced. Without it, there is always the danger of getting into a rut. A stranger may well spring surprises and keep us on our toes.' Focusing on Sven Hansen's *Anitra* from Sweden, Teddy Haylock added: 'Among the foreign competitors in the Fastnet race, there was one yacht with which none could compare in finish, design, construction, gear, and in general efficiency.'

## SHORT TACKS

• Selwyn Slater continued injecting humour into his boat naming. *Ramrod*'s concealed message was 'I'm going to ram Rod Stephens'.

• A member wrote disapprovingly to the RORC committee about having lady members sleeping at the Club. But as alterations to the bathrooms had been completed 'lady sleepers' could book up to two rooms.

• Inflatable liferafts were not permitted. Instead dinghies carried on deck had to be 'fitted with adequate and permanent buoyancy compartments and must have oars and rowlocks permanently lashed thereto.'

• Prince Philip, the Duke of Edinburgh, 'consents' to become an honorary life member of the RORC.

• One half of the Club's premises, 19 St James's Place, was bought for £18,500.

THE WORLD WAS WAKING UP to what was happening in the UK. In the USA, *Rudder* magazine noted that 'the Fastnet lived up to its reputation for bitter weather'. And then, almost as a footnote to the Dutch success with *Zwerver*, added dryly: 'The Fastnet was the last race of a team event among cruising yachts and our side became the winner with 220 points. The prize was the Admiral's Cup.'

There was more to it than that, even before a gale ravaged the 95-boat Fastnet fleet.

The Channel Race saw Britain open their third defence with some of the cast beginning to look like old friends: *Myth* was back for a third appearance in Britain's line-up, despite being fourteen years old, and there was a second show for *Griffin II*. They were joined by Ren Clarke's *Quiver II*, a new Charles Nicholson design which teased the RORC rating rule pretty hard by having the bow girth station pushed well aft, and was significantly one of several new boats which had been built not only expressly for racing but with a view to making the Admiral's Cup team.

*Yachting World* commented: 'There are plenty of precedents for this particular type of "rule cheating" and students of yacht design can see exactly the same treatment in *Hestia*, a Sparkman & Stephens design.... It is the designer's job to get the best out of any particular rule, just as it is the rule-maker's job to devise a formula which gives a fair result.'

*Quiver III* won her first two offshore races and, once selected, became the cornerstone of the British team, and the second-highest scorer in the series after the van der Vorms' *Zwerver*. With the USA returning, the 1961 series was a five-cornered event: Britain, the USA, the Netherlands, Sweden and France. The Americans celebrated their return by taking first blood in the

Channel Race to gain a huge lead, scoring 76 of a possible 84 points and moving well clear of Britain – in second place with 46 points – with a first, fourth and fifth place.

The Channel Challenge Cup was won by Jakob Isbrandtsen's *Windrose*, a US team yacht four years before and notable for the clipper bow. Back in vogue with the 1993-94 generation of the Whitbread Round the World maxis, it serves the same purpose now as then: a built-in bowsprit.

The traditional Channel Race course was a triangle from Southsea, east towards the Royal Sovereign Light Vessel by way of the Owers, south to Le Havre and back to the Solent via the Nab Tower. The outcome was clinched on the French side of the Channel with the leading pack hardening up on to port tack on their way back across to England and tacking when the tide started flooding up Channel. Yet it was those who sagged to the east who benefited when they found a younger easterly breeze and the American yawls were among them. They were the lucky ones, for the smaller boats which were slow out of the Solent were becalmed half a day off the Owers, not making it back to Cowes until Monday, a full day adrift of the big boats.

Yet the Americans squandered their 30-point advantage inshore in what must have been a classic Cowes Week. The royal presence was strong in numbers while Erik Maxwell in *Sceptre*, Tony Boyden in *Flica II* and Lord Craigmyle in *Norsaga* ensured the Week was graced by racing 12-metres, savouring their America's Cup-inspired revival.

*Quiver III* scored a great double among the AC boats in the two Solent races, dominating despite the especially difficult conditions of a near windless Britannia Cup. *Anitra*, Sven Hansen's winner of the 1959 Fastnet,

*The Royal Ocean Racing Club's own boat Griffin III was top boat in 1959, but was only the sixth best yacht in 1961 (Beken of Cowes)*

*Ren Clarke's* Quiver III *was the top British performer, second to* Zwerver *from the Netherlands (Beken of Cowes)*

dragged her anchor while kedged before the start gun and spent nearly an hour trying to restart correctly, eventually retiring.

*Quiver III*'s win was a double in a second sense, for in the Britannia Cup she was second to her Nicholson-designed near-sister-ship, *Fedalah*. 'Both boats were designed by C. A. Nicholson,' noted *Yachting World*, 'and both sailed by men who know the Solent backwards.' And backwards was the operative word, for all the yachts were kedged at the start and *Anitra* was not alone in falling astern over the line prematurely. The Nicholson twins, *Fedalah* and *Quiver III*, repeated their first-second finish two days later in the New York Yacht Club Challenge Cup.

Things were not good for the USA boats. *Cyane*, Henry B. du Pont's sloop, overstood a mark in the Britannia Cup race and placed eleventh. In the New York YC trophy race, Jakob Isbrandtsen's *Windrose* retired, leaving the USA just a 13-point cushion on the eve of the nineteenth Fastnet race. A record-sized fleet lay restless at anchor in Cowes Roads or on the trots in the Medina, perhaps sensing something in the air. Though two offshore races are rarely the same, the Dinard race only a month before and supposedly a 'ladies race' had been pretty grim. Of the eighty starters, only ten had finished.

The 1961 Fastnet started tamely enough, with a brisk Force 4-5 for the best down the Solent, dropping by the Needles. Abeam of Start Point the breeze stayed light, interspersed with heavy showers, but on the second night at sea the air became uncommonly clear. Crews reported seeing the looms of the lights on Start

Point, the Eddystone and Lizard simultaneously and by Monday morning most of the fleet was becalmed.

Some resorted to sailor's lore. Alf Loomis, an American navigating Lloyd's Yacht Club's *Lutine* wrote: 'I received permission from the skipper to look southeast and whistle very quietly. I have never been one who dared to stick a knife in the mast or toss a coin over the side for a farthing's worth of wind.'

The wind arrived with a vengeance, and by the time the big boats had cleared the Runnelstone buoy off Land's End, the radio was forecasting a deep depression off south-western England. The Fastnet fleet were already in it. The wind increased in tandem with the onset of fog as Force 4 increased to 7 in under two hours out of the south-east, before it backed sharply to the north-east. Running sails came down, more or less in order, and with a further back to the north, the fleet plugged into a headwind under working sail. Eventually the wind backed all the way round to north-west as the system passed over the fleet.

Among those damaged was *Windrose*, winner of the Channel Race two weeks before, who broke her boom, and *Cyane*, who snapped her tiller while running square under spinnaker. Neither breakage was disastrous but harmed America's chances of a successful defence, for *Cyane* eventually placed ninth in Class I, while *Windrose* recovered well to be second in Class II and third in fleet. The greatest damage was among non-AC boats. Adlard Coles in *Cohoe III* gained plenty of material for his seminal work *Heavy Weather Sailing*, describing the gale as one of the briefest but most violent he had experienced in home waters.

The big boats did not round until Tuesday, with *Quiver III* the leader on corrected time at the Rock, before a fading breeze at the Lizard snuffed out her chances, while Otto van der Vorm and his young crew, aboard his father's *Zwerver*, sailed superbly and made the best of their fortune to win Class I and fleet honours.

Alf Loomis, after a rumbustious race navigating *Lutine*, concluded that the Admiral's Cup was 'a series of races which might one day supersede the matches for the America's Cup in prestige and sentimental value'.

He might have underestimated the value of the America's Cup growth, but he read the Admiral's Cup's potential pretty well. Most important of all, the USA's victory by dint of a well-prepared and well-financed team demonstrated that Britain could be beaten on their home turf – a vital message to get across for an international competition.

## SHORT TACKS

• HRH Prince Phillip, the Duke Edinburgh, sailed virtually every day of the ten-day Cowes Week, not only in the Royal Dragon *Bluebottle* and the Flying Fifteen *Coweslip* with the legendary Uffa Fox but, on the final Saturday, aboard *Sceptre*, Britain's 1958 America's Cup challenger.

*Olle Wettergren's Dione formed part of Sweden's first team (Beken of Cowes)*

THE AMERICANS' WIN in 1961 goaded the British to adopt formal trials for the team. Three offshore races and a compulsory pair of inshore races were nominated, and owners began building yachts expressly with the aim of representing Britain in the series.

Announcement of the British team was delayed until the last possible moment and it was notable that selectors were also required for the first time: Myles Wyatt, RORC Vice-Commodore Michael Vernon and the RORC Secretary Alan Paul. Given that five other countries were dispatching teams, it was evident that the task of winning the Cup was not becoming any easier.

A particularly cold British winter did not seem to hold up the new launchings and most were racing by May. Cowes had been especially busy. Clare Lallow built the 30ft LWL (43ft LOA) sloop *Clarion of Wight* for Derek Boyer and Dennis Miller, a partnership established with a previous yacht, *Pym*. *Clarion* was planked up from mahogany, though her bottom four strakes were teak. She was an Olin Stephens design and boasted performance instruments, uncommon if not unknown on racing yachts then. That was because Miller owed his prowess in small-boat racing and meteorology to his flying days in the Fleet Air Arm. The pair split up after *Pym*, but following unsuccessful seasons campaigning on their own, they joined forces again. *Clarion*, it would turn out, proved to be Sparkman & Stephens' first really successful design to the British RORC rule.

Upstream, the Souter yard completed *Outlaw* for Lord Beaverbrook's son, the Hon. Max Aitken. He had turned to John Illingworth, who had started his own successful design business with his partner Angus Primrose and, not surprisingly, there was a lot of *Myth of Malham* in the new 48-footer. Built from eight skins of mahogany, she was very light for her length and copied *Myth*'s reverse sheer and short bow overhang, as well as sporting Illingworth's favoured masthead cutter rig carried on a spindly mast.

Joining them as team-mates was Ron Amey, a Gosport man who was in the gravel and aggregates business, who had hung up his motorcycle racing goggles and asked Camper & Nicholsons to develop *Quiver III*'s design into his new *Noryema III*. She carried a mast a foot taller than that on *Quiver* to boost her sail area. Though Charles E. Nicholson, as creator of the sublime 1934 J-Class sloop *Endeavour*, is thought of as the last of the truly great British designers, his son Peter was very much involved in the concept, detailing and steering of these yachts.

Interestingly, while many commentators believe the production yachts of the 1970s – such as the Swan range of which a later *Noryema* was one – to be the last of the genuine cruiser-racers to be built for international top level racing, Peter Nich would argue that the true dual-purpose boats ended with *Noryema III*.

This was an era when Britain was trying throw off the last of cruising mentality, though cockpits were still snug, saloons had tables and crews had their cook. British yachts also had Lloyd's Register of Shipping, a classification society whose 100 A1 certification was deeply ingrained in the British psyche as being an absolute prerequisite for a yacht to be considered a yacht.

Rod Stephens, whose ideas on decks, rigs and layout so complemented the designs created by his brother Olin, said rather uncharitably of early 1960s British ocean racers: 'We used to reckon they were all right in a blow, just slogging through that short chop you get in the Channel, when finesse didn't matter too much. You only had to look at their fittings. They were heavy, inefficient.'

*Derek Boyer's and Dennis Miller's* Clarion of Wight *on her day at Clare Lallow's yard in Cowes. As top yacht, she led Britain's successful recapture of the Cup from the USA (Beken of Cowes)*

The USA, Sweden, the Netherlands and France all came back and were joined by newcomers Germany. As defenders, the Americans were a highly fancied team. But it was the Swedes who opened the series strongly in the Channel Race with *Vagabonde* (Gunnar Lindberg) and *Staika III* (Sven Roden) winning Classes I and II and taking first and second overall. The start 'should have provided the most glorious spectacle ever seen from the beach at Southsea, but, as it happened, the 119 yachts were drifting around in sepulchral gloom,' noted *Yachting World*.

It was not a good race for Britain or America. *Noryema III*, on port tack, forced the USA's *Windrose* about soon after the start and was penalised 50 per cent after protest. *Bolero*, owned by Mrs S. A. Langmuir, and Hans-Otto Schumann's *Rubin* from Germany were working along the Bracklesham Bay shore towards the entrance to Chichester Harbour and thence the Owers, when *Bolero* hit a submerged section of the Mulberry Harbour which had been used in the Normandy beach landings. She stayed put for five hours and suffered considerable hull damage.

With more sail than most contemporary yachts, *Vagabonde* moved nicely in the light first half of the race to take the Channel Challenge Cup. The results vindicated the desire to bring overseas yachts to the UK, for among the first three yachts in each class there were some six nations represented.

Sweden had a lead of 34 points over France, in second place, and stayed ahead when the small turtle-decked double ender, *Staika III*, won the Britannia Cup, though Britain staged a recovery, with *Clarion* and *Noryema* finishing fourth and fifth and *Outlaw* victorious in the protest room to deny points to her protagonist. Essentially it was a small boat race with light winds, strong tides, frequent kedging and much bunching of the fleet. Still, at this stage Britain was only fourth: Sweden stood on 119; USA 93, the Netherlands 81, Britain 79, France 76 and Germany 65.

However, familiarity with the Solent counted in Britain's favour in the New York YC Cup, sailed in fresher conditions, when *Clarion*, *Outlaw* and *Noryema* filled the top three places, elevating Britain to second

*Hans-Otto Schumann's* Rubin *demonstrated her owner's long-held fascination with the science of sailing with her ventilated spinnaker (Beken of Cowes)*

place on 130 points, one ahead of the USA and four behind Sweden, with the triple-points Fastnet and the promise of more lively weather to come.

It proved a great race for Britain, for not only was the Admiral's Cup reclaimed from the Americans, but *Clarion*'s overall fleet win to gather up the Fastnet Cup made her the first British yacht to win the race's principal prize. The win could have cost *Clarion* and Britain dear, for the British yacht was involved in a start-line collision but survived the ensuing protest.

Dreary overcast skies and a south-westerly Force 6 greeted the starters. *Outlaw* hit bad luck straight away when her gooseneck broke as her crew were rolling down a reef. She made her way up the Solent under jib

only while the gooseneck was repaired and, with lace holes in the mainsail, she was able to use an alternative reefing method. Bill Snaith's *Figaro* lost half an hour when her inflatable dinghy blew overboard and inflated automatically, and just as her crew finished hauling it back onboard and deflating it, her mainsail split from luff to leech as squalls thumped off the island shore.

After a beat to Land's End, the wind perversely veered so making the leg out to the Rock another beat, though the breeze moderated before dying completely off the famous light. Trouble continued to plague the fleet. The Dutch Admiral's Cupper *Corabia*, owned by Mrs J. Kaars and sailed by Hans Zuiderbaan, lost her rig near the Longships light.

Thanks to *Clarion*'s victory, *Outlaw* placing well and *Noryema* edging in ahead of the USA's *Windrose*, Britain won back the Cup by 250 points to the Americans' 237. Their win was accounted for in part by the Americans and Swedes, who had done well inshore, appearing slower to cram on the sail when the wind dropped during the Fastnet.

## SHORT TACKS

• *Noryema* was so named because it spelt her owner's name, Ron Amey, backwards.

• Alan Paul, the RORC's Secretary, was known as The Apostle, or Postle, because of his name, sparse beard and prominent brow.

*Outlaw, owned by Sir Max Aitken and Bobby Lowein, was built by Soutar's yard in Cowes (Beken of Cowes)*

*Hans Otto-Schumann first sailed for Germany in 1963. Four decades later, the longest Admiral's Cup competitor was part of Germany's 1993 winning team (Jonathan Eastland)*

# 1965

N 1965 TWO DÉBUTANTES, Australia and Ireland, swelled the number of competing countries to eight. It's odd to think that the Admiral's Cup was still being compared with the America's Cup, and favourably so.

The money spent building 12-metres in 1964 was small change when put against the sums devoted to building ocean racers for eight teams. What's more, as contemporary observers were at pains to point out, the Admiral's Cuppers had twenty-five years of useful life in them, racing and cruising. Evidence for that was the evergreen *Myth of Malham*, back this time in the Irish team in the hands of her new owners, David and Brigit Livingston.

But it was the Australians who were making the most noise. Hugh Somerville, yachting correspondent of *The Sunday Times*, liked what he saw in the Australian challenge by racing aboard Gordon Ingate's *Caprice of Huon* in the Queen Victoria Cup race a month before the Admiral's Cup, the Australian boats having sailed over from Dunkirk, after shipping from Sydney. Noting the shame of the British team not racing ('to keep their powder dry'), while the visitors had come halfway round the world to race, Somerville wrote: 'This delightful Australian yacht is 32ft on the waterline and was designed by Robert Clark in 1949. Her plans were sent out to Australia and she was built by a Tasmanian septuagenarian singlehanded. He took three years to build a superb boat. I was most impressed by the cheerful dedication of her crew and the way in which she was equipped and sailed. Her owner has a nice touch with a boat and we may well find that she and her Australian team-mates produce a serious challenge for the major silverware during Cowes Week.' They did.

The Australians were remarkably confident and no one took too seriously the protestations of Cruising Yacht Club of Australia commodore, Bill Psaltis. 'We have come over here to race, to learn and to see what our standard is.' Others remembered Australia's previous foray into the international big yacht scene in 1962, when their 12-metre *Gretel* came closer to winning the America's Cup than any other challenge save Sir T. O. M. Sopwith's *Endeavour* back in 1934. In a joint venture between Qantas and the British Tourist Authority, the Admiral's Cup had already been flown out to Sydney and put on display at the Royal Sydney Yacht Squadron to help promote the Australian team and the event. Another aim of the promotion was to try to persuade Australians to forsake their winter for the British summer!

The Aussies even went to Southampton University to study the Solent tides but, unlike Somerville's assessment, other commentators were not so optimistic of their chances. David Palmer of *The Financial Times* concluded: 'None of the Australian helmsmen has ever raced in the Fastnet. Two of their boats are two years old, and the other is fifteen; the average age of the twenty-seven crew members is forty-one. If such a challenge came from anywhere but Australia, it would be treated as a pleasant piece of sporting eccentricity.'

Perhaps the most fancied yacht of the Australian line-up was *Freya*, a 32-footer designed, built, owned and sailed by Trygve and Magnus Halvorsen of Sydney. Not only had their yard built *Gretel*, but they had campaigned *Freya* to become top points scorer in the CYCA's series. That the brothers had by then already sailed in seventeen Sydney-Hobarts and won four of them said much about their calibre.

The Americans continued to race with one hand tied behind their back, for their yachts were designed to the CCA rule used in the USA and tended to be penalised under the RORC's own rating rule. As yet,

*Caprice of Huon was built in an orchard in Tasmania for Gordon Ingate. She was top Admiral's Cupper in the Channel Race (Beken of Cowes)*

there was no international rule for offshore handicapping, unlike inshore classes and though S & S had developed their line of RORC-rule boats, no American owner had taken the plunge to build a boat solely for Admiral's Cup racing. Nonetheless their line-up was very impressive. Bill Snaith had a new *Figaro* and in addition to his sons, McLeod and Jock, he counted Nassau's Bobby Symonette and Newport's Norris Hoyt in his crew. Jakob Isbrandtsen and *Windrose* had been top scorers and second-highest scorers in previous US teams, while Irving Pratt numbered America's Cup skipper Bus Mosbacher in the crew of *Caper*, his eight-year-old Phil Rhodes-designed 56ft sloop.

It was far from plain sailing for the Australians, however, despite heroic efforts from *Caprice of Huon*, which won the Channel, Britannia Cup and New York Yacht Club races. Several non-Admiral's Cup yachts such as *Fedalah* and *Roquette* had done the double in winning the big prizes in Cowes Week, but no Admiral's Cup yacht, before or since, had won three races on the trot.

*Dennis Miller steering Firebrand in 1965 (Beken of Cowes)*

## DENNIS MILLER

*Firebrand's owner was said to symbolised the single-minded dedication of money and energy that makes a winner. 'Money? We never talk about money,' said Miller in mid-series. 'It's rather like telling all and sundry what your house cost. Energy? We try, and we try hard. Well, most people like winning and if you are going to win you have to put a lot of work in. You pay attention to detail.'*

*Miller was one of the first of a new breed of modern owners: rich, assertive and bringing the sort of flourish to his sport that stood as a complete contrast to his industrial business, Harmo Industries, which was a major component supplier to the British car industry. 'Everything is a race,' he said of the drive he brought to his sport and business alike.*

*Firebrand was £13,000 of timber beautifully put together, and he spent another £7,000 getting her ready for the Admiral's Cup. With a flat in Cowes and a power boat, he took his racing very seriously. After the 225-mile Channel Race, he chose not to rest on the Sunday but to compete in the Morson Challenge Cup, one of the minor prizes at Cowes Week. He won.*

*Miller may have started something of a trend, with a special crew uniform featuring Firebrand branded on the shoulder patches.*

Britain led after the Channel Race, their team including a new Lallow-built S & S-designed 43ft *Firebrand* for Dennis Miller and a pair of new Camper & Nicholsons-designed and built yachts which were

improvements on Peter Nicholson's own *Roquette*, star of the 1964 season. They were Ren Clarke's *Quiver IV* and Ron Amey's *Noryema IV*. Not even making the start of the race were the three Germans, held up in Calais by poor weather.

In the 33-mile Britannia Cup, two British navigators in the Australian team made the same mistake by heading off in the wrong direction after the first lap of the course. *Caprice of Huon* sailed a faultless race to win again, but *Freya* and *Camille of Seaforth* were originally shown in the results as disqualified for missing out a mark. Yet what had actually happened was that *Freya* realised her mistake and turned back to round the mark correctly, losing some twenty minutes in the process and then, on finishing, told *Camille*, who went back out and resailed the entire course. A feisty Gordon Ingate, 'Wingnut' to his friends, let fly at the navigational error. 'We represent Australia and if we can't beat the British and everyone else without taking bad advice from their yachtsmen, we should never have sent a team.'

The Squadron were unaware of all of this – hence the DSQs in the results – as the race officers had gone ashore to the Royal London YC ball, one of the highlights of Cowes Week. The Australians had to wait until the morning to hand in their declaration, whereupon their team picked up another six points.

*Camille*'s re-run of the course was possible only because there was no time limit for the race in the sailing instructions, which prompted the Swedish crew of *Vagabonde* to ask if they could resail the Britannia Cup course the following day, a chance she was denied 'because she had been on her mooring all night'.

Britain's turn for trouble came in the New York Yacht Club race, when *Firebrand* struck a buoy and was disqualified. The same happened to *Windrose* after she knocked off her golden figurehead in a collision with the Italian non-AC boat *Al Na'ir*, steered by Rod Stephens. But a third and sixth for *Quiver IV* and *Noryema IV* – the latter having recovered from a poor start after being baulked by *Bloodhound* with Prince Philip, Prince Charles and Princess Anne aboard – against a ninth and tenth for *Freya* and *Camille*, meant

*Highest points scorer in the 1965 series was Ren Clarke's* Quiver IV.
*The crew's method of sitting-out was soon banned (Beken of Cowes)*

that the Australians went into the Fastnet with just a fourteen-point advantage.

Australia found the twenty-first race frustratingly light. The quietest Fastnet for a couple of decades was not what they had ordered. Soft breezes and smooth water were about as welcome as warm beer.

Of special interest was the performance of a little Class III American boat. *Rabbit* was not a team yacht, but was the first stab at yacht design by a Boston busi-

nessman and showed great if erratic speed. With a saucer-like hull, short fin keel, trim tab, separate rudder and low-windage clean decks, she threw out the old notion that a yacht's forte should be upwind pointing. The little boat went like a rabbit when her sheets were eased and she won the Fastnet Cup, only the second Class III yacht to do so. Her owner and designer was Dick Carter, of whom much more was to be heard.

Class wins for *Quiver* and *Noryema* were enough

*The enduring partnership of Dutch ship owner Piet Vroon and boat-builder Frans Maas first raced in the Admiral's Cup with* Tonnerre de Breskens *(Beken of Cowes)*

to hoist Britain's score ahead of Australia to regain the Cup 420 points to 376. The USA, the previous winners, could do no better than fourth.

Royal patronage of the event was vigorous, with the Duke of Edinburgh hosting a cocktail party aboard the Royal Yacht *Britannia* in Portsmouth Dockyard on 29 July, at which team organisers, owners, wives and, yes, crews were invited. That year, even the fireworks, the traditional and spectacular climax to Cowes Week, featured portraits of the Queen and the Duke of Edinburgh, made from thousands of individual fireworks.

The official dinner was held at *HMS Vernon*, also in Portsmouth Dockyard. The correspondence between RORC secretary Alan Paul and Commander Michael Fawcett is a nice vignette of the period. 'On considered reflection I am very sorry to tell you that I can not offer berths in *HMS Vernon* for any yachts. When we were discussing this and I offered the facility, I stupidly forget the security restrictions of today and these rules are pretty strict, particularly in the very international nature of the competing teams.'

Quaintly, Commander Fawcett said of the catering for the dinner: 'We deal mostly in inexpensive wines, but we would get in any special vintage for you from Harvey's if you would like us to do so.' A meringue case filled with ice cream and fruit, topped off by a RORC crest was offered to round off the menu. That was politely declined, but Barton & Guestier 1957 Prince Noir and 1950 Quinta do Noval port were considered a sound tactical call for the wine list.

Quite how the series shaped up in the pecking order of the sport as a whole was still open to debate, but J. R. L. Anderson wrote in the *The Guardian* of the 1965 Admiral's Cup: 'To my mind, and I am sure many yachtsmen will agree with me, the Admiral's Cup is a trophy far more worth winning than the America's Cup. The America's Cup has become simply a contest of racing machines sailing around buoys. And the machines are now so expensive that to build and race them almost demands syndicates of millionaires. Victory in the Admiral's Cup calls for seaworthiness in a yacht and seamanship in crew over days and nights at sea in all sorts of conditions. It is a test of men and boats at sea rather than of sailing machines.'

Yet the series was still an adjunct of the Cowes Week, not secure enough to branch out on its own, although the possibility of this happening was widely discussed. 'Whether or not the Admiral's Cup might be better detached from Cowes Week is an open question,' ventured *The Times*. 'When I spoke to the Australian team captain W. Psaltis, he was quite happy with the local sailing conditions. We did not discuss the social aspect but at nine o'clock he was still dressed in sailing clothes and on his way, not to a party, but "to go and see the boys down on the boats".'

Australia's near win had great symbolic value, too, for it was Captain John Illingworth who had given birth to offshore racing Down-Under by instigating the Sydney-Hobart race. That he should have been one of the Admiral's Cup founders, too, and had seen his old protagonists learn so fast, must have been satisfying.

## SHORT TACKS

• Dennis Miller, of *Firebrand* fame, had already raced the Americans earlier in 1965. He came fifth in the Miami-Nassau powerboat race. Asked about the cost of his yachting, Miller replied: 'I make a point of never finding out the cost of a season's racing. If I did, I suppose I'd never do it.'

• Rendall Clarke, father-in-law to Peter Nicholson, extolled the joys of ocean racing, and the Fastnet in particular, this way: 'I don't expect to get my clothes off during the race. You get windswept and soaked in the first five minutes and stay that way for five days.'

• In those days there was a ready reckoner of the cost of offshore racing: about £1000 per ton. *Quiver IV*, for example, at 48ft, displaced twenty tons. Sails, a frightening expense nowadays, cost £150 per headsail, with mainsails priced at £300-400. A season's running costs for insurance, berthing, upkeep and repairs sounded much better at £200.

• Among the faces in *Noryema IV*'s crew was Butch Dalrymple-Smith, later a partner of Ron Holland, one of the top designers of the 1970s.

THE SPACE BETWEEN the 1965 and 1967 Cups was filled by the sound of saws at work. Drastic hull surgery was underway in Britain to *Firebrand* and a clutch of other existing yachts, including Ren Clarke's *Quiver IV* and Arthur Slater's *Prospect of Whitby*.

The reason was a new series in Le Havre, which in the summer of 1965 had attracted fourteen entries. It was the One Ton Cup, a new event with a magnificent old trophy. Frenchman Jean Peytel, from the Cercle de la Voile de Paris, dusted off a huge silver trophy which had first been presented in 1899 for a contest between yachts whose keel weights were one ton. Later, 6-metres had contested the trophy until it faded out in 1962. Peytal revitalised it by offering the trophy to yachts which had the same rating. It was a novel idea for, although the yachts were all different, because they had the same rating they could race without handicap: the first boat home was the winner.

Though using a 22ft RORC rating, they were too small for the Admiral's Cup, but the class became the engine room of offshore yacht design. Dick Carter's *Rabbit* gave notice of how fast for their ratings the small boats could be, a trend that reached a logical conclusion in 1985 when the top teams comprised solely minimum-rating boats.

Split underbodies – where the rudder is moved away from the trailing edge of the keel to hang as a separate appendage – were far from new, but the message of the One Ton Cup was that they worked in boats designed to a rating rule. When the so-called terrible twins, Max Aitken and Bobby Lowein's *Roundabout* and Derek Boyer's *Clarionet*, began to beat bigger boats consistently on the British domestic racing scene, it came as no surprise that hull surgery was carried out to convert old big boat hulls to the same fin and skeg form.

Dennis Miller's *Firebrand* was the first. Even though she had a long keel originally, it was pretty much a separate appendage. 'We were always keen on cutting down wetted surface area,' Rod Stephens explained. 'For this reason we designed *Firebrand* with a very small keel. The rudder was on the back of the keel as usual, but we found downwind sailing very hard, too hard in fact, and no fun at all. So this led us to design for a separate rudder configuration, for us always on a skeg. *Prospect of Whitby* was also altered for Arthur Slater. This started a whole new trend.'

Having got so close to success in 1965, the Aussies came bounding back. Sir Robert Crichton-Brown went to Camper & Nicholsons for *Balandra*, a copy of the 46ft *Quiver IV*; *Caprice of Huon* made a return visit in the hands of Gordon Reynolds, who had been her mate during her glorious 1965 campaign, with the third team yacht being Ted Kaufman's *Mercedes III*, which he co-designed with Bob Miller, a young Sydney sailmaker, who later changed his name to Ben Lexcen and found worldwide acclaim with his wing-keeled 1983 America's Cup winner, *Australia II*.

Nine countries lined up for the Channel Race, Spain making their début with a two boat team and Finland coming in for the first time, making up for the absence of Sweden. The Americans held high hopes, for Bill Snaith had brought *Figaro IV* back with an excellent Transatlantic performance under her belt; Dick Carter was in the team with *Rabbit II*, having won the previous Fastnet and proven his designs in the One Ton competition; while *the* hot boat in US racing, the Cal 40, was represented by Vincent Learson's *Thunderbird*. Like many American CCA rule boats before, her edge was blunted by a cripplingly high RORC rating.

So high was *Thunderbird*'s rating that she sailed in Class I while *Rabbit II*, a full two feet shorter, rated

*Dennis Miller's* Firebrand *was one of several boats converted by designers Sparkman & Stephens from a long keel to the newer fin and skeg underbody (Beken of Cowes)*

close to the bottom of Class II. Not even *Thunderbird*'s hot crew, including designer Bill Lapworth, sailmaker Lowell North and Bahamian Bobby Symonette, could do much with that sort of disadvantage. Likewise *Carina IV*, winner of that year's SORC, had removed her mizzen and shortened the foot of her mainsail to reduce her RORC rating, but only at the expense of speed.

It was Eric Tabarly's huge *Pen-Duick III*, by far the most innovative of an impressive fleet, which rounded the Royal Sovereign light ahead of the rest. She was designed by Tabarly to retain his Singlehanded Transatlantic race dominance and was using the RORC season to work the boat up. A double chined-aluminium hull, fin and bulb keel, tiny spade rudder and ingenious

schooner rig, which not only set a cloud of light weather sails but rated well too, saw *Pen-Duick* packed with ideas. The sail between the two masts was a foresail as far as the RORC rating rule was concerned. It meant that 25 per cent of *Pen-Duick*'s sail area was free. She won the RORC Class Championship with a clean sweep of victories, but her complex sail plain made her less handy inshore.

In a freshening wind, *Pen-Duick* steamed home to win her class and the race overall by almost thirty minutes on corrected time. The Aussies celebrated too: *Balandra* was third in class behind *Pen-Duick*, while *Mercedes III* and *Balandra* took third and fourth. The men from 'Down Under' had worked out a substantial

*Eric Tabarly (Guy Gurney)*

*Norbert Lorck-Schierning's yawl* Jan Pott III *had the ignominy of appeari in the Royal Yacht Squadron's results as* Jampot *(Beken of Cowes)*

lead, with the Americans well down in third place, *Figaro* having spent Friday night with a lobster pot snagged under the hull.

The twenty-six Admiral's Cuppers fought their own battle in the sixty-boat Britannia Cup fleet, with *Pen-Duick* once again in the vanguard. In a dying wind, *Caprice* and *Mercedes* looked like old Solent hands by dodging the tide in and out of the Cowes moorings. One Aussie crewman even explained how the smaller

*Dick Carter relaxes with Edward Heath in 1971 (Beken of Cowes)*

*Mercedes* edged in front of *Noryema* by saying, 'Where *Noryema* went wrong was...' – a sure sign that the visitors had gained 'the knowledge'. *Figaro* spent time aground on Stone Point, just east of Beaulieu River, but it was yet more confusion over the sailing instructions which was the race's distinguishing feature. Twenty boats retired and eight were disqualified.

Several Dutch yachts finished after one round, not realising there were two. Others were disqualified for rounding the distance mark incorrectly and *Rabbit II* was protested by France's *Oryx* for passing through the starting gate on the wrong side. *Oryx*'s protest was dismissed because she had not shown her flag promptly enough but, as a point of honour, Dick Carter withdrew his declaration to say that he had complied with the rules, 'so that I can sleep well at nights, I guess'. Carter's sporting gesture cost *Rabbit II* a three minute win over *Mercedes* and the Aussie lead grew.

Carter's crew could scarcely be blamed for the error. As crewman Sandy Weld recalls: 'To find in the race circular the infringement we were alleged to have made, we looked in the back of the circular under a section called Postponements. This seemed an extremely odd place to find instructions. We were indeed in error; we had passed the offshore mark to port rather than starboard. Not having been concerned with postponements, we were not aware that this marker was part of our course and since the mark was actually quite a large motor vessel it was deemed better seamanship to leave it to windward.'

Wrestling with Cowes Week's sailing instructions had long been the bane of those not familiar with them, though at least this particular oddity was removed from Postponements and put in a more logical location after this incident.

Carter certainly slept well after the New York YC Cup, which was sailed in a fresh Force 5, under blue skies and over a double triangle in the western Solent. *Rabbit II* triumphed again. For her 39-year-old designer, owner and skipper, this meant that in two years three different boats had won the Fastnet (*Rabbit*), the One Ton Cup (*Tina*) and, bar Carter's withdrawal from the Britannia Cup, both of the major Cowes Week trophies.

## DICK CARTER

*Dick Carter showed that outsiders could tackle the yacht design game and win. When he started his studies at Yale after the war, yacht design was a low-key profession with a slow rate of development and was practised in the USA by the likes of Phil Rhodes, Ray Hunt and the Stephens brothers. Carter studied Arts and Letters instead, appreciated sculpture and architecture, enjoyed choral singing and playing the flute and harpsichord. Professionally, he was an engineer in the family paper-converting plant in New Hampshire. However, after racing a Tripp-designed 33-footer in the 1963 Cup, Carter put a deposit down at Frans Maas' yard in Breskens. 'That's not necessary,' the Dutchman told Carter. 'It's not for you, it's for me!' replied Carter, who was forced to design his first boat, Rabbit.*

*The impact of Carter was that he generated an avalanche of ideas. Rabbit had a small keel, spade rudder, mast with internal halyards, a pulpit mounted inside the jib, through mast roller reefing and trim tab. All that in 1965. His 1969 Admiral's Cup offering, Red Rooster, had a swinging keel – extra deep for upwind bite and low resistance downwind.*

*Carter also helped merge the RORC and CCA rules to produce the IOR, a rule with which he rapidly became disenchanted. Though brief but glorious, Carter's design career struck a lasting blow for the revolutionary designers over the evolutionists.*

As if *Rabbit II*'s speed was not enough to annoy her rivals, then having Carter's eight-year-old daughter and wife Polly along for the ride added insult to injury. 'Here we are,' said Graham Newland from the Australian boat, *Caprice of Huon*, 'hard on the wind, everyone amidships and flat on the windward rail. There you are, beating us in a smaller boat with Polly and daughter enjoying themselves in the stern!'

For the British team, there was little to cheer about in the New York YC Cup. 'It seemed like Jutland all

*Dick Carter's* Rabbit II *was one of the first of the smaller, lighter and more easily driven hulls, seen here leading bigger boats round the windward mark (Beken of Cowes)*

*Dennis Doyle's Moonduster from Cork was one of the biggest boats racing in 1967, and part of Ireland first's challenge (Beken of Cowes)*

over again ("There's something wrong with our bloody ships, today"),' *Yachting Monthly* noted, a little testily. Dennis Miller's *Firebrand* hauled herself back to a worthy second but *Prospect* and *Noryema* were thirteenth and twentieth. The Aussies were third, fourth and fifth – a magnificent result.

Forty-four points ahead, Australia took a handsome lead into the Fastnet race for the second successive series. This time they did not squander it. In three races before the 1967 Fastnet, the Australian boats had all placed in the top seven Admiral's Cuppers, a feat they managed to uphold in the 605-mile classic. So consistent were the Australians that *Mercedes*' third, *Balandra*'s fourth and *Caprice*'s seventh in the Channel Race were repeated precisely in the Fastnet Race.

In a race which started as a drifter before building to a mid-race blow, the Australians just powered on. *Firebrand* lost her steering quadrant, lay hove-to for two hours to repair her emergency tiller when that also failed, yet was still the best British yacht. America got into her stride at last, but too late to deny Australia as the second overseas victor in the Admiral's Cup.

During the prizegiving, British captain Ron Amey described the Aussie boats as: '*Mercedes*, a home built something or other; *Balandra*, a design four years behind the times; *Caprice*, sixteen-year-old lump of wood.' He wasn't being rude; Amey was emphasising just how well the Australians had sailed to earn their triumph. It was a victory with a message. The Australians were the best prepared: they had once again studied the Southampton University Solent tidal model, they had gleaned the knowledge from their first challenge, they lived in the same digs and they were sponsored. In short they were keen and competitive.

A royal party was on the cards just prior to the 1967 series to lend it extra cachet. Rear-Admiral Christopher Bonham Carter wrote to Sir Myles Wyatt saying that 'the cocktail party for the Admiral's Cup chaps looks like being alright', despite the racing at Goodwood being a competing interest. A similar party, with *Britannia* alongside at Portsmouth, was envisaged, with the Duke of Edinburgh arriving from Arundel or Goodwood by car and returning smartly for dinner. In the event *Britannia* was not available, the dinner held instead at the Nuffield Club, the United Services club in Portsmouth. For £1 10s. a fine dinner was put on, with the Nuffield offering a 'reliable claret' for consumption. The small scale of the series was betrayed by just thirteen bottles of Château Gazir being consumed by the thirty-five attending, though they did make short work of thirty-one glasses of port, twenty-four of brandy and twenty cigars.

The later Cowes party must have been a bit more of a snorter. Some £209 of drink was consumed, ranging from nine cases of Oranjeboom beer to thirty-four bottles of Scotch. British United Airways undertook the catering, moving the bar stock from Sandown airport on the island to Northwood House. The reason? Sir Myles Wyatt was chairman of BUA.

## SHORT TACKS

• The cost of press releases, telephone calls and postage came to the grand total of £9 7s. 10d. Entertaining the press cost rather more: £47 13s. 3d.

• Typographical errors are not confined to newspapers. Germany's *Jan Pott* appeared in the official NYYC Cup results as *Jampot*.

• *Figaro* failed to shine. Late in the series it was discovered her propeller shaft markings were 90 degrees in error. Instead of being aligned vertically, the big prop was being locked athwartships.

IF ANY INDIVIDUAL was capable of winning a team event on his own, that person would be Dick Carter. The promise of *Rabbit II* in 1967 was brought to fulfilment with *Red Rooster* in 1969. With two firsts, a second and a third, she was the chief breadwinner in the American team and propelled them to an unexpected victory.

What was extraordinary about the US win was that, while the British and Australians chose their teams after tough trials, *Red Rooster* was so new from her builder's yard in Holland that she had never set foot in the US and Dick Nye's *Carina*, a new McCurdy & Rhodes sloop, was selected almost by default, her owner a habitual transatlantic and Admiral's Cup competitor. It seemed that *Carina* had only to be in British waters to ensure a place in the team.

The Australians, by contrast, were even more of a national representative touring team than before. They had three weeks of practice afloat, their coach timing hoists, drops and changes with a stopwatch. Team manager Gordon Reynolds masterminded their whole programme, down to mealtimes and press interviews.

In Britain, the preparations were exhaustive too. Carter's innovative design approach appealed to Ron Amey. His seventh *Noryema* was given the *VGX* suffix, not the *VII* as expected, because she packed so many ideas. *VGX* stood for Variable Geometry Experiment, which denoted a lifting keel, raised by the hydraulic rams more usually seen on the lorries shifting ballast in Amey's road stone business than moving yacht ballast.

Carter had long mused on what it would be like to beat to the Fastnet Rock and then be able to get rid of the keel for the long run back to Plymouth. With Amey's engineering expertise, the seventh *Noryema* was able to lift the entire keel into the hull, whereas *Red Rooster* had a more simple swinging centreboard.

*Noryema VGX* bore the other Carter hallmarks: clean lines, uncluttered decks, big rig with a penalty foretriangle. Though fast, she made only the reserve berth out of twenty-one British triallists. In the British team was the 51ft *Phantom*, owned by one of the Cup's founding fathers, Geoffrey Pattinson. So fastidious was Pattinson that he had his crew in the gym doing physical jerks and Camper & Nicholsons burnishing *Phantom*'s graphite-painted bottom with chamois leathers three times a week!

She was joined by a new S & S-designed *Prospect of Whitby* for Yorkshireman Arthur Slater, and Dave Johnson and Mike Hurrell's Swan 43, *Casse Tête III*. Like the Cal 40, the Swan 43 marked a curious crossover point in technology. While custom-built one-offs were deemed almost essential, glass fibre was competitive with wood and aluminium for a while, especially in a boat of good design that was sailed well.

Australia, honed after a tough season back home, presented a strong team. *Mercedes III* returned, joined by a scaled-up sister ship, Denis O'Neil's *Koomooloo*, and Syd Fischer's S & S-designed *Ragamuffin*. The arrival of Italy, Argentina and Bermuda brought an ever more cosmopolitan flavour to the series.

So how did the Australians, top team in two of the three races before the Fastnet, lose it?

The Channel Race served up a bit of everything: light and strong winds, fog and rain, pronounced windshifts. *Ragamuffin* did the business, just winning from *Red Rooster*, and with *Mercedes III* fourth and *Koomooloo* seventh, Australia seemed on track.

Britain were top team in the Britannia Cup, thanks to Arthur Slater, who took the novel expedient of heading for the mainland shore while beating west to Hamstead Ledge, which is on the island shore. His rivals, who hugged the Wight, ran out of wind, and

*Geoffrey Pattinson was the last of the five founding fathers of the Admiral's Cup [to] win selection to the British team with* Phantom *(Beken of Cowes)*

*Syd Fischer's first Admiral's Cup appearance brought a Channel Race victory to* Ragamuffin *(Beken of Cowes)*

though some of the bigger boats reined in *Prospect* as the race progressed, she was the handy winner on corrected time. As Australia were the second-highest scoring team, they retained their series lead.

The New York YC Cup, sailed in sparkling conditions, saw Dick Carter walking off with the trophy for a second time. The 35 mile course included a long spinnaker run and Carter wound up his keel to reduce draught from 9ft 3in to 2ft 6in and reefed his rudder to the bottom of the skeg to turn on *Rooster*'s booster.

The beauty of *Rooster*'s lifting keel was shown on the run down the mainland shore to Lymington, as the fleet sailed as close in as they dared to dodge the tide. Hans-Otto Schumann's *Rubin* ran slowly aground ahead of *Red Rooster*, finally coming to a complete stop. But

with crewman Taylor Grant lying in the foredeck, taking soundings with the boat hook, *Red Rooster* sailed 200 yards inside the bemused Germans and never touched the bottom, despite the 12ft boat hook landing on solid land many times.

Such was her unfussy progress through the water that her speed was best seen by the company she was keeping. *Red Rooster* was one of those yachts which raced boat-for-boat with larger brethren. Carter's crew was no slouch either: among them were Bill Green, Skip Allan, Jim Anderson and Warwick Tompkins. Not that raising the keel was easy. One person would tire after twenty-five cranks because the gearing was not right, so *Red Rooster* had a keel roster, with people dropping down the companionway and forehatch to relieve each keel man after twenty-five cranks. As this happened when rounding buoys, when sails had to be hoisted, dropped and trimmed, it proved quite a circus.

Before the Fastnet, the USA stood fourth. With triple points, there was a mathematical possibility that they could win, but no one took it too seriously. Australia stood on 317 points, Britain 273, Italy an impressive 250 and the Americans on 244.

America's Cup skipper Bob Bavier was sailing on *Palawan*, Tom Watson's 1964 S & S yacht which was the third boat in the US line-up. Unlike Dick Nye's new McCurdy-designed *Carina*, *Palawan*'s crew had made no attempt to reduce their RORC rating. 'While we had hopes of moving up to second as we entered the final event, none of us, or our team-mates, had any real hope of catching the Australians,' Bavier wrote. 'One reason for our pessimism was that *Palawan* had done poorly in all prior races, with finishes of twenty-sixth, eighteenth and twenty-fourth. Not only was our rating abominable under the RORC rule, but we also had not been sailing as fast as *Palawan*'s norm.'

The course for the Fastnet was the classic route, but with two necessary innovations. First the Fastnet had to be left to port and secondly, cutting inside of off-lying rocks in the Scillies was outlawed. The challenge in 1969 was not the accustomed Fastnet heavy weather, rather completing the course before the wind shut off.

In the days long before electronic aids were allowed, some navigators could not believe their eyes when exceptionally clear visibility and some quirk of refraction allowed them to see the light on Ireland's Galley Head. So it was in 1969. They were tempted to move their DR plot further north than they should, and to bear away for the Fastnet when, in fact, they were already on course.

The Aussies seemed to have the Cup under control. Estimated corrected times at the Rock had the Australian boats holding fourth, fifth and sixth places

## SYD FISCHER

*The least surprising thing about Syd Fischer is the spelling of his Christian name and surname, for even by the standards of the sub-continent, Australians don't come much crustier.*

*A successful property investor, developer and hotel operator in Sydney, he gave up allowing boat builders to create his yachts after his first Ragamuffin in 1969 and had his own Aquacraft and Coordinated Marine build them. He's a man who keeps a tight lid on costs and does nothing fancy with his campaigns, all his energies being devoted to the yacht – a method which has produced an outstanding record. 'Always paid attention to detail and drove the boat to limit.'*

*Fischer sailed in the 1969, 1971, 1973, 1977, 1979, 1981 and 1993 Australian teams, as captain each time. His S & S-designed Ragamuffin won the 1971 Fastnet race and the Aussies took the 1979 Cup. He has sailed in twenty-five Sydney-Hobart races, the vast majority in his own yachts, eventually winning the race in 1992.*

*Fischer is known for his forthright views: 'If it's how you feel, why dress it in fancy words?' Of the designers he's had boats from, he says German Frers was 'good to deal with and sensible', Bob Miller was 'hopeless', Doug Peterson was 'sensible' and the Farr office 'very professional'. Cowes, he reckons, is 'boring and dirty'. To steer ocean racing and the Admiral's Cup out of its 1991-93 lean times, he suggests that owners not yacht club politicians be encouraged to put forward ideas in writing, rather than at open meetings 'where paid hands and jockeys have too much say. If the owners are smart enough to earn the money to buy a boat, they should be smart enough to guide the sport.'*

*He suggests that a new grand prix should quickly be established, that there should be more short inshore races, that Cowes should have more of a village atmosphere with better services for yachts and crews ('must avoid owners being ripped off by marinas, repairers, local merchants') and that professional crews should be limited to three ('otherwise too costly and owners lose interest. Hungry jockeys will kill the sport').*

*Syd Fischer wearing his trademark white hat in 1993 (Gilles Martin-Raget)*

*Dick Carter's innovative lift-keel* Red Rooster *was the Fastnet Race winner amid some controversy over her finish time (Beken of Cowes)*

before the light airs of the final hundred miles changed the entire complexion.

By dint of sailing faster than her size suggested, *Red Rooster* squeezed home before the wind vanished to claim victory. *Carina* was third among the thirty-one boats and *Palawan* placed a respectable, indeed priceless, eighth. No other team got all three boats home in good order, and while *Ragamuffin* was second in the Admiral's Cup, her team-mates were nineteenth and twentieth, and the victory that had looked so secure was lost. The massive 252 points that the Americans reaped in the Fastnet finale gave a total of 496, 14 better than the Australians and 25 more than the British.

There was some bickering at the end over the finish times. *Red Rooster* won by 68 seconds, but Sir Max Aitken's crew found that their finish time was three minutes ahead of the time taken by the keeper on the light at Plymouth breakwater. There was bad feeling all round, and an enquiry was held. Sir Max felt that *Outlaw* was robbed, and protested the race committee, with *Red Rooster* confirmed the winner only moments before the prizegiving.

Colonel Ken Wylie, the RORC vice-commodore, aired his thoughts privately in a club internal memorandum about the future shape of the series, reflecting what many competitors were saying publicly: had the AC outgrown Cowes Week? 'There is some feeling that the races in Cowes Week – the Britannia Cup and New York Yacht Club Cup – may not be ideal for the purpose,' he wrote to secretary Alan Paul. 'The reason for this is that with the very large entries for both these races and the enhanced importance of the Admiral's Cup series as an international event, you get Admiral's Cup boats beginning to become seriously impeded by non-AC boats in both these contests.'

In an eyewitness account, Wylie noted: 'When I was watching the situation at Salt Mead Ledges in the Britannia Cup when *Koomooloo* had already been thwarted once by *Casse Tête*, she was then thwarted twice more by other boats coming in on starboard at the mark when she was having her final go for it on port tack. I believe her tactics were wrong but nevertheless it must have been very infuriating for Denis O'Neil.'

There were no easy solutions concerning a move to other days within Cowes Week: Monday was too soon after the Channel Race and Friday too close to the Fastnet start, while Wednesday was already earmarked as a reserve day for the Britannia Cup. Having separate starts and courses on the Tuesday and Thursday seemed the best solution, though 'it deprives the contestants taking part in these two major trophies. Whether the AC outweighs the joy in winning one of the other trophies is a matter for speculation.'

*Denis O'Neil's* Koomooloo *was part of the strong Australian team which was just pipped by the Americans (Beken of Cowes)*

The Vice-Commodore was also very keen to foster more of a sense of occasion, although there was much conspiring against such atmosphere. Most teams started off in Gosport, as the Channel Race was the series opener, but the Italians stayed there throughout. Arrangements were made to use the first two rows of trots opposite Saunders & Rowe, but teams dissipated, such as the Americans who moved upstream to piles above the floating bridge. With the owners so spread about, attendance at cocktail parties and dinners was not easy to ensure, while clubs such as the Royal London and Royal Corinthian did little to offer facilities to overseas visitors.

Stewart Morris, then Britain's most distinguished Olympic sailor and an influential voice in the sport, had joined the management committee and concurred that the AC boats should drop out of the main body of Cowes Week yachts. 'It was quite wrong this year that members of our team should be shouting to other British yacht competitors to waive right of way or clear their weather. This may not have been confined to our AC team only but it must tend to give the foreign AC entrant the impression that he is racing a very large team!' he wrote to RORC Commodore Buster de Guingand.

## SHORT TACKS

• Qualification requirements for the Britannia Cup were changed from one of waterline (30-60ft) to rating (25ft or above), but as the Cup belonged to neither the Royal Yacht Squadron nor the Royal Ocean Racing Club, permission had to be sought from the Royal Yacht Association to change its Deed of Gift.

• Controversy over *Red Rooster*'s Fastnet finish time, as taken by the Plymouth breakwater light keepers, highlighted races now being won by seconds and showed that the RORC's management had not kept pace. Normal practice was for yachts to take their own finish times. After the RORC appointed Alan Green as assistant secretary with special responsibility for race management, one of his first duties was to create a reliable timing system.

*Italy, Bermuda, Finland and Argentina all made their first challenges in 1969. This is German Frers Sr's Fjord V, whose crew included German Frers Jr. ( Beken of Cowes)*

IN FOURTEEN YEARS, ocean racing and the Admiral's Cup had been transformed. In the 1950s, the numbers who raced offshore could have been put on a pinhead, but the growing popularity of the Admiral's Cup and the sprouting up of the Ton Cups as entry-level classes all served to expand big boat racing.

Outside the sport, however, it was still not big news, beyond the traditional coverage of the royal family at Cowes Week. Sir Edward Heath changed all that. He propelled sailing from the sports pages to the front pages making it big news in Britain and abroad as only a Leader of the Opposition, and then Prime Minister, could.

The then Mr Heath took up sailing at forty-nine, learning on the Kent coast at Broadstairs in a succession of small boats: a North Foreland One-Design, Snipe, Fireball. 'By 1965, the year in which I became Leader of the Opposition,' wrote Sir Edward in his sailing autobiography, 'I was almost fifty, and again I was being told that I could not go indefinitely at the pace I had been living for the previous twenty years if I wanted to carry heavy political burdens in the future.'

Sir Maurice Laing, a prominent figure in the homes and construction business, introduced Edward Heath to the delights of the offshore game aboard *Clarion of Wight* in the Cowes-Dinard race, and he found it so satisfying that Mr Heath bought his own big boat, an S & S 34, the first of five *Morning Clouds*. When she won the 1969 Sydney-Hobart race, the first overseas yacht to do so, the publicity was immense. In quick succession, Sir Edward became Yachtsman of the Year, Prime Minister of the United Kingdom and announced he was building a new yacht to contest the 1971 British Admiral's Cup trials. The press and TV coverage, which started the moment his first *Morning Cloud* tied up in Tasmania, reached a high pitch and maintained it.

The year 1971 was a watershed for another reason. At long last, there was a global measurement for offshore racing, a common currency that meant a yacht built and rated in the US, or Argentina, could have the same rating as if she were a British or Italian boat. The RORC and CCA rules had been amalgamated as the International Offshore Rule, used for the first time in the 1971 series.

The benefits of a global rule were immediate. Entries climbed from eleven to seventeen, with Austria, Belgium, Brazil, New Zealand, Poland and South Africa making their first appearances. Some teams were single yachts, a practice disallowed in 1973. For instance, Dave Allen's *Improbable*, designed by Gary Mull, missed out on the US trials so sailed as the New Zealand team because that's where she was built.

The Channel Race was started, as usual, off the Royal Albert YC's line at Southsea, at the entrance to historic Portsmouth harbour. The previous evening, the Mayor of Gosport had hosted a reception for the AC teams in Gosport town hall. Among the starters, the AC boats were sent away first for what proved to be a fastish and straightforward race, although, unusually, it was an upwind start with a moderate south-easterly blowing. It was something of an omen, for windward work predominated throughout the entire series. Rhumb line sailing was pretty much the order, with *Morning Cloud II* averaging over 6.4 knots.

Yet the winner was her team mate, Arthur Slater's new S & S-designed *Prospect of Whitby* which, at 42ft LOA, rated at the bottom of Class I. *Morning Cloud* was third and another British entry, Bob Watson's *Cervantes*, fifth. The Prime Minister as captain was satisfied with his team's performance, for Britain had the early lead with 270 points, followed by the USA on 234 and the Australians on 216. Argentina were a creditable

*Although American-owned, Dave Allen's downwind speedster* Improbable *was allowed to race as a one-boat New Zealand team (Beken of Cowes)*

## EDWARD HEATH

*'In its heyday, the world knew about the Admiral's Cup. Especially when I was racing, because we had these damned helicopters overhead the entire time.'* Constant attention from photographic boats in the 1973 series allowed Morning Cloud III few favours either. Memorably she ghosted towards the Fastnet finish at Plymouth, for every time her crew coaxed some way on, the press fleet would open up their throttles and create speed-sapping wash.

Such are the special problems posed by the only statesman to have sailed in the Admiral's Cup. Sir Edward Heath's Morning Clouds II, III and V raced in the 1971, 1973 and 1979 Cups, and as team captain in 1971, he was the only British Prime Minister to lead a national team in any international event. The pre-series team meeting that year was held at Chequers, the PM's official country residence. 'The crew always thought that Sir Edward Heath took two hours to wind down after joining the yacht before he was able to cast off the affairs of state,' remembers his navigator, Anthony Churchill.

The security services gave Morning Cloud special radio equipment 'so that if they wanted to get me quickly at any moment they could'. The initial thoughts of those responsible for the Prime Minister's safety after Edward Heath took office in 1970 was that he should give up sailing, or carry two security officers onboard and be shadowed by a Royal Navy vessel with a helicopter permanently overhead. 'When they offered me two large hulking policemen with big boots to stay onboard, I said 'not on your life'. Not after having spent hours saving weight on the boat. Then they offered me two SAS men. So I said are they lighter and can they sail?'

But no close-up measures were used, except during the 1971 Fastnet when few realised they were in place. When the drill to take the Prime Minister off by helicopter was discussed, Morning Cloud's sailing master, Owen Parker, asked : 'What the hell are we supposed to do when all this is going on?' When told that the yacht was to drop her sails and heave to, Parker replied: 'What? And lose precious seconds. Not bloody likely! If you want the skipper we'll push him off in a dinghy and you can pick him up from there while we go racing!' Being able to continue racing was made possible by arranging the diary well in advance and having top class staff ashore and a top-class crew afloat.

Government business did sometiomes keep Sir Edward from racing though. In 1971 he missed the Britannia Cup Race, owing to a House of Commons debate on the fate of the Clyde shipbuilders, while the 1973 Prime Ministers' conference kept him in Ottawa until the Fastnet.

Edward Heath's ship rules were: nothing heard on the boat was repeated ashore; politics were not to be discussed; and no alcohol. Because of his public office, Sir Edward's actions were always scrutinised. 'People used to write to me and say what are you doing sailing at weekends? Don't you realise we pay politicians to work twenty-four hours a day, seven days a week, fifty-two weeks a year? Well, I used to reply, if you think that you're very short-sighted, because the politicians who do that drive themselves into the ground, make ghastly blunders and the people who suffer are you.' Instead, Sir Edward would drive to the Hamble on Friday, stay at the Royal Southern YC, and be aboard at 0800. 'We'd race hard, come ashore, have a bath, enjoy a drink and then I could look at problems again with a fresh mind.'

Sir Edward bowed out after captaining the British Sardinia Cup team in 1980. 'We'd been at the top for over ten years and I didn't want to slowly slide downhill.'

fourth, with a team which included *Matrero*, designed by the up-and-coming German Frers Jr.

Captain or not, Edward Heath returned to Westminster for a Commons debate, leaving *Morning Cloud* in the capable hands of Sammy Sampson for the Britannia Cup race, where she placed fourth. The British effort could have faltered when *Cervantes* was disqualified for a start-line incident, Jock Storrock on *Koomooloo* protesting her for a port and starboard clash, but none of the other leading teams managed to get three boats in the frame either. The USA had Pat Haggerty, the founder of Texas Instruments, in a lowly nineteenth place with *Bay Bea*, which took the edge off the victory by David Steere's *Yankee Girl*, which had placed second in the Channel Race. Australia counted a twenty-first with Arthur Byrne's *Salacia II*, an update of Syd Fischer's *Ragamuffin* which had benefited from much rivalry, and later, speed trials, with her Sydney compatriot.

Shorty Trimingham's *Wizard of Paget* was disqualified, tripped up by the start-line distance marks (a favourite Cowes device for ensnaring the unwary). The same fate befell *Yankee Girl* in the New York YC race, costing her what seemed like a certain win, much to the chagrin of Olin and Rod Stephens who were among her crew.

While the Britannia Cup had been fresh, it blew hard for the New York YC Cup, with gusts up to 35 knots. It was noticeable that the US boats reefed down, while the Australian and British boats persevered with full mains. Whatever, the Solent saw plenty of pirouetting ocean racers as they broached and wiped out in varying degrees of lost control. *Recluta II* had a particularly severe knock-down. Owen Parker, Edward Heath's right-hand man on *Morning Cloud*, was pinned to the lifelines when a winch loaded with the spinnaker guy pulled out its fastenings. Asked by the press if *Morning Cloud* had wiped out more than once, Edward Heath looked Fleet Street's finest resolutely in the eye and said: 'I'm not a one-broach man.'

The Carter-designed *Belita VIII* from the Netherlands won the race after *Yankee Girl*'s disqualification. The Australians clearly loved the rough and tumble of

**ABOVE:** *Edward Heath, British prime minister in 1971, mobbed by spectators' boats (Jonathan Eastland)*
**RIGHT:** *Arthur Slater's* Prospect of Whitby *was second highest scorer to Syd Fischer's* Ragamuffin *and part of Britain's winning team (Beken of Cowes)*

*David Steere's mighty* Yankee Girl *was second highest racing boat in the series and epitomised the American belief in big boats (Beken of Cowes)*

the hard race as their second, third and fourth for *Salacia II*, *Ragamuffin* and *Koomooloo* showed, though the performance that caught many eyes was that of *Improbable*. She was too extreme a solution to the design puzzle to be a dominant all-rounder, but she surfed her way to sixth place. *Prospect of Whitby*, *Cervantes* and *Morning Cloud* were fifth, ninth and tenth. That kept Britain in front, but only just, with 480 points to Australia's 458 and the USA's 419.

Fortunately the strong winds which had dominated Cowes Week throttled back for the Fastnet start. A soft Force 2-3 wafted in from the south–west for the start but, by Sunday evening, had taken off completely. The light winds, especially between Start Point and the Lizard, shaped the race – more than the fresher winds on the way back from the Rock, particularly as a small clutch of boats found a nice breeze between those who went hard inshore and the others looking for gains out at sea. From the Lizard onwards, *Ragamuffin* was the leading boat on the water and on handicap, completing a memorable double.

Spinnakers and halyards popped and broke as crews pushed hard on the ride back from the Rock. Syd Fischer, *Ragamuffin*'s taciturn and tough skipper, loved it. He'd once rowed in a North Steyne and Bilgola Club surf boat and been a top grade rugby league forward (that's the hard man's version, as opposed to rugby union), so that pushing *Rags* hard, sailing her on the edge, was meat and drink to the crusty Fischer.

While her rivals used poled out jibs, *Ragamuffin* was urged to the brink of control and beyond. One cross sea pushed her bow round and Fischer couldn't bring it back. *Ragamuffin* wiped out in a gybe broach and was laid flat for ten minutes, water coursing through the companionway and vents. At one point crewman Doug Patterson said: 'I'm going to release the vang', which cleared the deck fast as others anticipated the boom scything across. From the back of the boat, Fischer said, through clenched teeth: 'Not yet, Doug. Look where your head is.' Sure enough, Patterson was between the mainsheet: releasing the vang then would have taken his head clean off.

Fischer's deeds for Australia were isolated, for in

the depression that brought 32-knot winds on the way back from the Rock, *Ragamuffin*'s team-mates endured gear failures. *Salacia II* broke her steering first, but her crew soon had emergency steering sorted out. Aussie hopes of taking a win off the British were finally dashed when *Koomooloo*'s rudder snapped forty miles from the Scillies. She was out of the race and the St Mary's lifeboat went to her aid.

A second overall for *Cervantes*, backed up by *Prospect*'s twelfth and *Cloud*'s fourteenth, was enough for a British win, with 828 points to the USA's 782 and Australia's 719.

## SHORT TACKS

• 1971 saw the first of the lapel badges, or 'buttons'. In deference to the British Prime Minister, there was 'Ted's Ahead', while *Prospect of Whitby*'s crew sported 'Slater is Greater'. *Cervantes* would have had theirs too, but for the dictates of good taste, 'Up your flue, *Koomooloo*' being the suggested button after their clash ashore and afloat. Following *Ragamuffin*'s Fastnet triumph , 'Rago's arse beats class' appeared. The humour now seems strangely innocent. Today's pro-crews sport advertising logos instead.

*Sir Edward Heath's second* Morning Cloud, *in which he became the first British Prime Minister to lead a representative team to victory in international competition (Beken of Cowes)*

THIS WAS THE NINTH Admiral's Cup. Each previous series had been won by an English-speaking nation: Britain (five), the USA (two) or Australia (one). Now 1973 showed that boats could be fast in other languages, especially German, and particularly aboard Albert Bull's S & S 47 *Saudade*. Her 4-1-1-7 record was outstanding, and she was the only boat in the forty- eight-strong fleet from sixteen nations to finish in the top ten in every race.

By 1973, the Admiral's Cup could not possibly be seen as anything short of a serious enterprise. Whereas twenty-seven yachts signed up for the trials for the British team in 1971, the number had risen to thirty-two in 1973. There was one Angus Primrose design (*Northwind*), a Britton Chance boat (*Perseverance*), one van de Stadt offering (*Spanker*), three Nicholson boats (*Chandanna*, *Yeoman X1X* and *Quailo 111*), three Carter designs (*Frigate*, *Samphire* and *Tiderace*) and no fewer than twenty-three boats from S & S. Another sign of the times was that along with *Spanker* and *Northwind*, many of the S & S yachts were production boats: *Morningtown* was a Tartan 41 from the US, *Whirlwind* was a Swan 48 from Nautor in Finland, while there were eight Swan 44s looking for a team berth: *Superstar*, *Battlecry*, *Matchmaker*, *Synergy*, *Zumbido*, *Chastenet*, *Supercilious* and *Kealoha*.

These were happy days, for although the racing was deadly serious, the boats had not become too specialised to forfeit a dual purpose rule. Few believed a production boat could make it into a top team, though they were capable of a good trials performance and could expect a berth in a lesser team. Yet the custom boats were pushing forward the boundaries of technology just as much as their successors in the 1980s and 1990s. Take Hans-Otto Schumann's 48ft S & S-designed *Rubin* in the German team: her beautiful

mahogany panelling may have looked at home on a cruiser, but it was foam-cored.

The German challenge was centred on the Hamburg YC, who ran the trials off Helgoland and recruited dinghy sailors to bring sensitive helming skills. That saw Hans Beilken steer Dietar Monheim's *Carina III*, with his brother Berend aboard *Saudade*.

The Channel Race proved to be a small boat benefit, with a reaching start in squally conditions, and the main increase in wind strength occuring after the big boats were home. It was offwind sailing the whole way round, with the boats tacking only to turn the Le Havre light vessel. The results tell their own story. First was Jean-Louis Fabry's Finot design *Revolution* (France), an extreme and apparently high rating 'tin dinghy'. She was followed by Robin Aisher and Tony Boyden's Carter 39 *Frigate* (Britain), and Ted Turner's one tonner *Lightnin'* (USA). *Lightnin'* was small, even by low rating standards, so much so that when she was selected she was a full 2.0ft under rating. So the ebullient Ted Turner removed her propeller, upped the sail area and reballasted his boat, modes he switched back from when he took *Lightnin'* to the One Ton Cup in Porto Cervo after the AC.

'The rules say I have to have a motor,' reasoned Turner, 'but they don't say I have to have a propeller!' The trouble with the ploy was that it made docking *Lightnin'* rather an inelegant operation, in which Turner would drop the sails and attempt to glide into the berth. Carrying enough way to make over the tide called for fine judgement, and Turner's twanging Southern drawl was very evident as *Lightnin'*, often much too fast, tried to clear a path through other yachts to her berth. More often than not, the boat would crash to a stop into the pontoon. Unfazed, Turner would brush his hands and step off the boat as nonchalant as you would like. It

# 1973

FATHERLAND
SILENCES
MOTHER
TONGUE

HAMBURG
N.R.V.

*Albert Bull's S & S-designed* Saudade *was top yacht and spearheaded the way to Germany's first victory (Jonathan Eastland)*

*Flamboyant American Ted Turner raised the rating of his One-Tonner Lightnin'
to meet Admiral's Cup requirements by removing the propeller (Beken of Cowes)*

was just the sort of extraordinary thing you expected of the man who had shaken up sailing by converting a 12-metre, *American Eagle*, for offshore racing, livened up the 1974 and 1977 America's Cups and went to build a huge media empire centred on his Cable News Network.

*Lightnin'*'s third was fortuitous. She was protested by *Morning Cloud* and *Saudade*, who claimed they were forced to alter course by *Lightnin'*, without rights, trying to scramble back across the line. That's how it seemed to everyone but the jury, who let Turner's result stand.

The big boats, such as Jesse Phillips' *Charisma* (USA), with Rod Stephens aboard, and Don Parr's three-year-old Nicholson 55, *Quailo III* (Britain), placed a lowly thirty-fourth and forty-first among the forty-eight boats – and that was not a reflection of their ability. To put *Revolution*'s novel shape into perspective, both she and Bob Derecktor's *Salty Goose* on the USA team had matching beams, but the French boat was 18ft shorter.

At last the Admiral's Cup was deemed important enough to extract its races partially from the Cowes Week mêlée, with the AC boats given their own starts. It proved a timely move, for while the Royal London cancelled its programme, the First Inshore (as it was now known) had the AC fleet out racing, albeit well reefed down, oilskin-clad crews wrestling with heavy sails in the driving rain.

The heavy weather clearly suited the bigger boats, with *Charisma*, steered by America's Cup helmsman Bill Ficker, and her US team mate *Salty Goose* making the early running, with *Saga*, Erling Lorentzen's big red S & S 57 from Brazil, first home after some tough beats and rolling downwind legs. She was second when the corrected times were computed, with Germany's *Saudade* the winner by almost six minutes. The Aussies shone in the hard weather, Alan Bond's *Apollo II* (steered by America's Cup skipper Jim Hardy and gold medallist David Forbes), Syd Fischer's *Ragamuffin* (now dubbed 'Fatrags' as her topsides had been microballooned) and Gary Bogard's *Ginkgo* fourth, fifth and seventh. Germany retained their overall lead from Australia, Britain and the Netherlands.

*Don Parr's Nicholson 55* Quailo, *part of Britain's third-place team. Parr later become Admiral of the Royal Ocean Racing Club (Beken of Cowes)*

After such a dusting it was no surprise that Don Parr's *Quailo* was alone among the AC fleet to race in Tuesday's Cowes Week programme, though she ran aground and returned. By Wednesday the wind had eased back, the sun had warmed the Solent's palette of colours and conditions were ideal for the Second Inshore, a double triangle between Spithead and Lymington: a Force 4 south-westerly.

Despite a neap tide, when the rise and fall is at its weakest, and though the race straddled low water, the British boats worked the tide assiduously. It was an example copied by *Salty Goose*, Bob Derecktor's slim white American yacht, for as the AC boats closed on the finish, they ran into the Cowes Week masses similarly tide-dodging in Osborn Bay and around Egypt Point. However, *Salty Goose* picked her tack perfectly just off the Shrape mud to take line honours. *Saudade*, not far behind, won again on corrected time, enabling Germany

to keep a slender lead with 472 points. The points were close though, as *Morning Cloud's* second, *Frigate's* fourth and *Quailo's* eleventh saw Britain in third place with 443, while a 5-8-10 for Australia kept them in second place with 467 points.

The rugged weather that characterised the beginning of the series evaporated in the high that dominated the Fastnet. Indeed, most yachts never set anything smaller than the No.1 jib, with drifters and floaters in frequent use. The USA big boats, *Charisma* and *Salty Goose*, made the early going, electing, like the bulk of the fleet, to go inside the Portland Race to cheat the strong flood tide. This proved to be the only break the smaller boats enjoyed, for the tide had eased when they closed on the Bill.

Light wind and fog dogged the leaders after Land's End. In the days before Decca and GPS, radio direction finding aids and accurate DR were all that the

## SPARKMAN & STEPHENS

*The S & S story effectively started at 0545, July 21 1931. Then, coastguards on the Lizard noted a 52ft white yawl on her way to winning the Transatlantic Race. Her name was* Dorade *and the brothers Olin & Rod Stephens were her skippers.*

Dorade's *win launched the world's most famous and most enduring design office, with Olin a giant in the sport for his design and Rod the perfect counter balance as the seaman and racing sailor who brought a practical approach to their rigs, decks and gear. From the 1930s until the zenith in 1970s, no other design office could match S & S. Their clients ranged from the Aga Khan to Edward Heath.*

*More than 2,500 designs have been created including the last and greatest J class giant,* Ranger *and Bermuda Race winners such as* Bolero *and* Finnistere. *S & S boats pepper the prize lists of the world's top offshore events, were the cornerstone of Nautor's rise in the 1960s and 1970s when they became the Rolls Royce of boatbuilders and underpinned every US defence of the America's Cup from 1937 to 1980.*

*At one time it looked as if the brothers would make their living in the family anthracite business, founded by their grandfather in the Bronx, but having been introduced to small racing by Sherman Hoyt, Olin began sketching some 6-metres. Then Drake Sparkman, an insurance and shipbroker, asked Olin to draw a junior class for the Larchmont YC which lead, in 1929, to S & S being formed.*

*S & S had a distinguished war record, designing small naval craft and developing Rod's pet idea, the DUKW amphibian, which won him the Medal of Freedom. The Korean war also kept the office busy.*

*Olin also played a key role in merging the CCA and RORC rules to the produce the IOR and was a pioneer in the development of the MHS/IMS rule. Both are retired, Olin pursuing his interest in modern art, as practitioner and collector, while the business they founded still flourishes. So do other designers who have graduated from the S & S and set out on their own: Gary Mull, German Frers, Johan Valentijn, Dave Pedrick, Roger Marshall and Scott Kaufman – another measure of S & S' lasting impact.*

navigator could rely on, and as the Fastnet itself had no beacon, the one on Mizzen Head behind it was the key for finding the turn at the Rock. On this occasion, *Salty Goose*'s navigator, with a fine record from the Bermuda, Newport-Annapolis and SORC races, failed to find the Rock. She spent two and a half hours sailing upwind and down, without finding the famous light in the half mile visibility.

Though the small boats, including *Recluta* – launched just before the Channel race and improving in every start – *Frigate* and *Lightnin'*, were well up on corrected times, the wind tapered out on their leg out to the Rock, snuffing out their chances. *Charisma*, by contrast, looked a sure winner until a monumental blunder on closing the Cornish coast, when she mistook a light eight miles to the west of Plymouth and tacked in towards it. When the Americans realised their mistake, it was a long, grim tack out to sea, where they found *Saga*, previously well astern, one mile ahead. *Charisma* still had a chance of saving her time but, cruelly, the wind vanished and she anchored 300 yards from Plymouth breakwater. Bob Bavier described it as 'the most agonising anchor watch in the history of ocean racing', and it must have been acutely frustrating for the young Turks in *Charisma*'s crew, led by boatbuilder Andy MacGowan and John Marshall, president of North Sails. Most of the crew were under thirty and one, aged twenty-six, was sailing his third Fastnet.

*Charisma*'s error assured *Saga*'s win, but the outcome of the AC was anybody's guess. Germany were the first to get all three boats home, and though *Carina* seemed to have jumped the start she did not receive a time penalty, so that the Germans kept the lead generated in the Channel Race right through to victory.

*Saudade* was top boat with *Recluta* second, a result which, coupled with *Saga*'s Fastnet triumph, spurred interest from nations not previously considered First Division. *Recluta*'s form also enhanced German Frers Jr's reputation by no small measure.

Hanging over Germany's win was the suggestion that *Saudade*'s rating was unduly favourable. By one of those accidents of history, *Saudade* had been one of three yachts called for an inclination check before the

*Jean-Louis Fabry (waving) raced in three successive series with his red* Revolution *(Guy Gurney)*

series. Arrangements had been made with the Portsmouth harbour master, but the creek in which the checks were to be made had dredgers at work on the day in question, so *Saudade*'s crew loaded all their gear back onboard, filled the tanks and got ready to race.

The check was therefore never made. Many took great interest when the yacht was sold to a US owner and, re-inclined by American measurement authorities, she rated a foot higher. The idea that German ratings were not quite so gained further currency when *Dorothea*, a sister-ship to Arthur Slater's new *Prospect of Whitby*, ended up with a rating half a foot lower than her British sister-ship because of an unusually advantageous CGF. Olin Stephens, designer of the yachts, was aware of the situation, which the Germans attempted to defuse by offering to have Marcel Leeman of Belgium come and remeasure the German boats. The RORC's commodore, Sir Maurice Laing, wrote to his Rear Commodore, Hans-Otto Schumann, to express his concern privately and in a dignified way, but the matter progressed no further.

The Germans were not to be deflected from their win. 'The main reason for our success, along with our enthusiasm for the sport of sailing, is that we have been able to put recent technological developments to good use. I have been interested in physics and chemistry since childhood and present work continues to keep me abreast of developments in these fields,' said Schumann at the time.

## SHORT TACKS

• The sound of '73 was the Samba. The Brazilian crews enjoyed the series from the moment of their arrival. *Saga*'s Fastnet win was celebrated with bells, whistles, sombreros, gorilla costumes and night long dancing.

• American Ted Turner from Atlanta fully earned his nickname the 'Mouth of the South'. Asked innocently by a journalist if, after three races, the Germans could hold off the USA team, he snapped back: 'The Germans were leading in 1942 too!'

*Designer Bob Miller (white shirt), who later changed his name to Ben Lexcen, checking the finish of Alan Bond's (blue shorts) Apollo II (Beken of Cowes)*

THE FIFTIETH ANNIVERSARY of the Fastnet's inauguration saw no fewer than nineteen countries challenge for the Admiral's Cup. This was the event's zenith, for the 1975, 1977 and 1979 series each attracted nineteen teams to Cowes, a total not equalled since because, as top level offshore racing became more specialised, so the AC has spiralled further away from mainstream racing and fewer numbers were prepared to meet the costs in time and money that it required.

Appropriately for a fiftieth birthday close to the heart of the RORC, Britain won back the Admiral's Cup from Germany. With the growing international fleet came a bigger press pack. This is what Jeff Hammond wrote in the American journal, *Yachting*: 'While the pound tumbled in the international markets and the nation shuddered through one crisis after another, Englishmen all over the country took smug comfort in the thrilling comeback effort of their three-boat team as it regained the Admiral's Cup from the Germans. Publicans in snug hostelries in the forests of Surrey, fishmongers on clammy cobblestone streets in Penzance, bellhops at fashionable London hotels were talking about it. Maritime honour had been regained. Britannia rules the waves once again. Good show.'

The British might not have couched it in those terms, probably taking exception to their country being portrayed as a theme park, but they were pleased enough with the win and, as the top scoring team in all races apart from the Channel Race, deserved the victory.

S & S still designed a dominant proportion of the fleet, being responsible for twenty-four of the fifty-seven yachts, but the tide was turning against them. Dick Carter had begun the charge and Doug Peterson, Ron Holland and German Frers were making up ground fast. Peterson and Holland had already made a big impact in the level rating Ton Cups and in Robin

Aisher's *Yeoman XX* and Archie O'Leary's *Irish Mist* had their first AC boats.

The Germans went to great lengths to mount a successful defence. So much so, that there was a stink over their top seven boats during the Kiel Week trials, redolent of the whiff surrounding *Saudade* when she passed into US ownership. Some ratings went up by 0.5ft and the Germans settled the issue by asking Robin Glover, chief measurer of the Offshore Racing Council (the IOR's administrators), to check the certificates. All the German boats, *Rubin*, *Duva* and *Pinta*, came out at 35.8ft. Glover checked the certificates of the entire fleet, looking for anomalies, and after he asked for the American 54-footer *Charisma* to be re-inclined, her rating dropped by 0.4ft!

All three German yachts were S & S designs, though in the case of *Rubin* and *Duva*, that should have been S & S & S, for *Rubin*'s owner, Hans-Otto Schumann tinkered with the hulls after some tank tests. He pushed and pulled the lines here and there, believing a little distortion would not hurt speed through the water but could lower rating. Thus the forward overhangs were made longer, freeboards went up and the shrouds were brought in to make for closer sheeting angles.

The US used their top domestic regatta, the Southern Ocean Racing Conference, for their trials, though absent was the 1974 Onion Patch star *Scaramouche*. Two boats showed well: Ted Turner's Frers 49 *Tenacious* and Ted Hood's 40ft *Robin*. Jesse Phillips' new S & S 54 *Charisma* got the nod, despite misgivings about her large size and high rating, though Dennis Conner's inclusion in her afterguard tipped the balance. What price would other countries have paid to have had three great America's Cup skippers, Hood, Turner and Conner, in their team?

Fewer boats attacked the British trials, but standards

---

*Archie O'Leary's 41-footer* Irish Mist *was Ron Holland's first Admiral's Cupper. His early commission from Cork-based owners helped launch his international success (Beken of Cowes)*

## ROBIN AISHER

*No family is more closely associated with the Admiral's Cup than the Aishers. Owen entered the trials on many occasions, but never made the concentration of effort to mount a vigorous campaign though his former yacht, as Griffin II, did sail in the 1959 and 1961 teams. His son, Robin, first sailed offshore in 1946, won a bronze medal in the 1968 Olympics and built his first offshore boat after a less than successful 1972 trial. She was Frigate, and among the British fleet was unusual in being a Dick Carter design and the first to use sails from Lowell North – they brought John Marshall from the USA to show how to set them. Like sheet iron, the No. 3 jib could only be rolled not folded.*

*Frigate was a very innovative campaign. 'We were one of the first crews to sail a dinghy offshore,' remembers Robin Aisher. 'The spinnaker poles were stowed in under-deck tubes, the sails were packed in "bricks" to concentrate weight, the crew took minimal clothing, they lived on reconstituted food drinks. We even had a systems analyst, submarine navigator Roger Dobson, on the boat, so that we had charts and data to show what sail needed setting when and how to work up the programme. I think Frigate showed you could race in a different way and would probably have to if you were going to win.'*

*When Robin Knox-Johnston, the first man to sail round the world non-stop, met Aisher at a dinner party, he was signed up. Claiming he liked to get wet, RK-J ended up on the foredeck.*

*Aisher claims to have started crew uniforms and the leg-crossing dance by the crew on the rail. 'Whenever you sail up underneath someone, and your crew cross and uncross their legs in unison, it doesn't half put the other boat off!' So competitive was Frigate's campaign that her crew took the spare halyards out of the mast as she approached the Fastnet to reduce inertia, and they had a rheostat to dim the navigation lights at night to lose the enemy.*

*Though he's 'never regarded sailing as a business venture', Robin Aisher has had numerous marine businesses over the years: North Sails (UK), and marinas on the Hamble and Thames.*

*Aisher misses the commitment of the amateur crews, who squeezed the weekend's racing into busy daily work schedules. One man, Chris Preston, missed the London train and was eventually picked up minutes before the start of an offshore race by stripping off his clothes, putting them in a plastic bag and swimming out to the boat on the Fort Gillkicker start line.*

*Aisher's novel approach followed with the Peterson-designed Yeoman XX. Built from alloy, she was not even painted in her first season, her crew rubbing her with wire wool instead. When it was light and Aisher wanted to unstick the hull, the engine was run. 'The vibrations broke the laminar flow on the hull. We did it a lot, and it always worked.'*

*Yeoman became the only boat to be in a winning Admiral's Cup team twice, in 1975 and 1977. Aisher had learnt a few wrinkles about how to lower an IOR rating: the measurement points were bumped to make the hull appear larger than it was, a Mercury outboard was taken apart and its shaft and gear box used to install a through-keel drive, and as a result the rating went down a foot and the boat went faster.*

*When the Frers-designed Yeoman XXIII, unusually built from glued and riveted aluminum by Newport Offshore, made the 1981 team, it was Aisher's fourth stint and his second win as captain. It was a watershed year: the big-boat ascendancy was ending, small boats with fractional rigs were becoming more effective, and creeping professionalism was making inroads.*

were higher and determination stronger. Tony Morgan, who won a silver medal in 1964 as crew for Keith Musto in the Flying Dutchman class, built a new Bob Miller-designed 49 footer, and Robin Knox-Johnston was poached from Robin Aisher's *Frigate* crew. Despite launching a year early, Morgan did not learn the lesson which was plain to everyone else. *More Opposition* needed more propulsion. The chance to boost the rig during the winter re-fit was missed, with the result that *More Opposition* ended being chartered to the Swiss team and remembered as one of those 'nearly' boats.

Aisher's new *Yeoman XX* had the distinctive Peterson look: deep forefoot, flat underbody and rudder hung right under the counter. She proved exceptionally quick in light and moderate winds and was the one sure selection, looking good in the British fleet, as were her American sisters – *Vendetta* and *Ricochet* – in the USA. The third *Morning Cloud*, from S & S, and Bill McCowan's *Tenacious* sister-ship, *Synergy*, were in the fray, but the selectors plumped for John Prentice's achingly beautiful wooden S & S 47 *Battlecry* and Ron Amey's fast improving Frers 46 *Noryema X*, his fourth boat in three years.

It was Prentice who provided *the* story of the trials, when *Battlecry* rounded the Royal Sovereign Light Tower in the Cervantes Trophy. Helmsman Johnson Wooderson cut it too close, the boat came upright as she lost the breeze and jammed her mast in the tower's platform. The next weekend, not only did she seem faster with her new spar but for good measure, her crew came to the start line with fenders at the masthead!

New Zealand, so close to winning the 1973 Southern Cross Cup, came with a strong team, including *Gerontius*, a wide-sterned, light displacement, stubby-rigged little cruiser racer, designed by Bruce Farr and numbering Peter Blake in her crew. The Carcano-designed *Vihuela* from Italy looked uncannily like *Gerontius* but, unlike Farr, her designer did not go on to greater things.

For the first time, the series was based entirely at Cowes, the new Groves & Guttridge marina fully finished with the AC boats moored in the northern basin. The RORC moved the Channel Race start up from Spit-

head. Not only was it easier, but there had also been a lot of a vandalism of the timing equipment installed on Horse Sand Fort.

No one country managed a good team showing in the Channel Race, raced for the first time over a course set on the day to suit forecast conditions, rather than a pre-ordained track. With the breeze light but unsettled in direction, the results were topsy-turvy.

*Noryema*'s victory was offset by *Battlecry*'s thirty-seventh placing, which dragged Britain down to fourth. Australia, in third place, were the most consistent country, with Peter Kurts' S & S 47 *Love and War* ninth, John Kahlbetzer's Frers 53 *Bumblebee* tenth and Ted Kaufman's 42-footer *Mercedes IV*, which he'd designed with his son Scott, fourteenth. Another third and a fourth for *Robin* and *Charisma* put the USA on the top – despite a twenty-first from *Tenacious*, who went too far offshore on the leg to Royal Sovereign – with the Germans just behind.

Now that the Admiral's Cup had outgrown Cowes Week, the international fleet no longer raced in the Britannia and New York YC Cups but sailed their own

day races, known simply as the First and Second Inshore Races.

In the First Inshore, Robin Aisher in *Yeoman XX* made a peach of a start right on the inner distance mark by the Royal Yacht Squadron, claiming clear air and avoiding the worst of the tide. It was an advantage she did not forfeit, for she finished second on corrected time, by forty seconds, to Bernardo Mandelbaum's *Red Rock III* of the all-Frers Argentine team and sister-ship to *Noryema X*. *Red Rock* was one of four boats, including *Battlecry*, *Bumblebee 3* and the old *Noryema* – now called *Sanumac* as her Spanish owner, José Camunas, repeated Amey's predilection for reversing his own name to create his yacht's name – who made a move to the mainland shore on the leg from Ryde Middle buoy to the Nab Tower.

*Yeoman XX*, spurred on by a keen fight with Ted Hood's *Robin*, lost valuable seconds on the run back from the Nab. After rounding behind *Robin*, she had pulled through, but when she went to drop the spinnaker for the short final beat, it had jammed. Aisher sent David Low aloft to cut through the head with a hacksaw, and though *Robin* was held at bay, time was lost on the clock against *Red Rock III*. *Noryema*'s own sixth and a seventh for *Battlecry* made Britain top team of the day, moving up a place to third.

The Second Inshore was a marathon. As a satisfactory race it had few advocates, and when the Americans complained this was not what they had come for, you could see they had a point. *Yeoman XX*, which won on corrected time, took nine and a half hours for the 33-mile race, and eleven hours after the start only four of the fifty-seven boats had crossed the line. Most finished in darkness, and some only just before midnight: there were still no time limits for the races. Crews were frazzled and strung-out after so many hours of concentration and frustration.

The race started in 5 knots of breeze and for much of the time there was far less. Aisher and his *Yeoman* crew again got it right on the line, starting at the outboard end and lifting all the way up towards Yarmouth. The most frustrating part of the race was its final few miles, when the fleet fell into the void between the

*France's* Coriolan II *(her red spinnaker just behind that of New Zealand's* Gerontius*) marked the only appearance in the Admiral's Cup by five time Olympic medallist Paul Elvstrom, an experience he'd rather forget (Jonathan Eastland)*

original south-westerly and the easterly that was fighting to take its place. That, and a foul tide, explains why progress dropped from slow to nil.

Rather like a bunker guarding the eighteenth green, the yachts had to go round Prince Consort buoy to reach the finish and though it is just off the entrance to the Medina, it has some of the fastest flowing water in the Solent. *Bumblebee* tried three times to crab out around the buoy, which was less than half a mile from the finish line, but she hit it and retired.

Giorgio Falck's *Guia III* (the 1973 *Ginkgo*) was first to finish at 2005, which made up for her pulling out of the First Inshore after fouling *Frigate* (now sailing for South Africa). One jubilant crew member back-flipped off *Guia*'s deck into the water. Six and half minutes later, the suspenseful crowd lining the Parade and path underneath the Royal Yacht Squadron cheered loudly as *Yeoman* slipped over the line. For other crews, there were nearly two hours of kedging and coaxing before they finished. Though *Battlecry* finished thirty-first, all teams counted one or two abysmal results, so Britain jumped into first place with a clear 47-point lead over the Americans.

The Fastnet turned out rather like a longer version of the Second Inshore: light airs and a taxing final stretch. If the wind had vanished off Cowes, then the hole which opened up *en route* to Plymouth can only be described as a vacuum.

The Americans had been doing dandy. After the 354-mile beat to the Rock, *Tenacious* was seventh on corrected time and *Charisma* eleventh; with the bigger boats reaching back to England, they revelled in 30 knots of air with the kite up, looking better and better. That was courtesy of a small depression off Ireland but, after the Bishop Rock, the wind shut down and the fleet concertinaed up behind.

The Germans were looking nicely bunched and menacing, especially so as there was no word of *Yeoman*'s position from the guardship *HMS Achilles*, which was giving some six updates a day.

The Dutch yacht *Goodwin* (Jan van Drongelan) went on to be the top AC boat in the Fastnet. Spotting the parked fleet ahead of her, and in company with

Frans Maas and Piet Vroon aboard *Standfast*, she stood out to sea, something that Arthur Slater had done to great effect two years before. They gave the Bishop a fifteen-mile-wide berth, heading offshore while the others tacked towards the coast, sailing past fifty boats in the process.

The wind hovered between light and nothing, with the fleet leapfrogging up the coast on each flooding tide. Those who stayed further offshore made better gains. *Charisma* was first boat home late on Wednesday night, but the bunch of the fleet reached Plymouth on Thursday. With *Noryema* fifth, *Yeoman* eleventh and *Battlecry* twelfth, Britain took an emphatic win in the most trying of circumstances. Germany were second, a massive 105 points behind, with the USA third and the Netherlands coming fourth, after *Inca*'s disqualification dropped the Kiwis down to fifth. The Dutch had now scored two fourths and two fifths in the past four series. Australia were ninth overall, thanks in part to the disqualification of *Bumblebee 3* in the Second Inshore, and thirtieth in the Fastnet: their worst ever result.

While Hammond applauded the victory of Merrie England, his fellow Americans made rather more barbed comments. Ted Turner showed his more phlegmatic side when he talked Jesse Phillips out of attempting to have the Second Inshore voided. 'Anyone who sails sailboats has to be prepared to accept these sort of things,' said Turner. *Charisma*'s John Marshall, writing in his North Sails house magazine, had still not simmered down weeks after the series. The second day race was a 'catastrophe' and 'the Fastnet race normally is a truly great race... one of the best overall tests of sailing held. This year the wind gods made a mockery of the best efforts of many competitors by rewarding boats which took flyers in the face of long odds.' Marshall even described the RORC's event managers as 'the dregs of nineteenth-century regatta management'.

At the close of the series, hard questions were being asked about whether the AC had finally outgrown Cowes Week completely. The evidence was overwhelming. The sight of the world's best ocean racers

getting wedged in the Sowley outfall, east of Lymington, because the Cowes Week sailing instructions did not prohibit going through the barrier, and of them beating through the ever-expanding moorings off Cowes, made it obvious that instead of enhancing Cowes Week racing, neither the recreational racers nor the AC crews were getting a fair deal. Brazil's *Saga* dismasted one moored boat while others were crashed into as the big boats sought to avoid the 3 knot foul tide. That was unacceptable.

There was talk, too, that rating limits, currently 30.0ft-44.0ft after a drop of 1.0ft at the upper end, should be reduced further. Something that particularly irked overseas teams was the RORC's late announcement of the time allowance. The TMF (Time Multiplying Factor) which converted elapsed times into corrected time results was not announced until February. Ron Amey, for one, left his final decision on *Noryema*'s dimension till he knew the TMF, an advantage not easily enjoyed by overseas teams.

## SHORT TACKS

• Big boys or bloopers, those balloon-like sails that billowed out alongside spinnakers, were banned from Cowes Week racing because the Cowes Clubs were fearful that they reduced visibility and could lead to collisions. Though bloopers were an accepted part of offshore racing, AC competitors were asked not to use them in Solent inshore races.

• Faced with betting in Cowes on the outcome of the series, the RORC's committee felt it 'should be discouraged as much as possible'. Their reason? 'Betting was felt to be unsuitable for a sport which demanded so much on competitors' good faith, was largely uncontrolled and in which it was extremely easy to cheat.'

• Three-boat teams were made mandatory. In 1971, despite the Deed of Gift, the RORC had exercised discretion to allow single boat teams from Austria and New Zealand.

*Dennis Doyle's* Moonduster *sandwiched between the Frers-designed Argentine team yachts* Don Alberto, Matrero *and* Red Rock *(Beken of Cowes)*

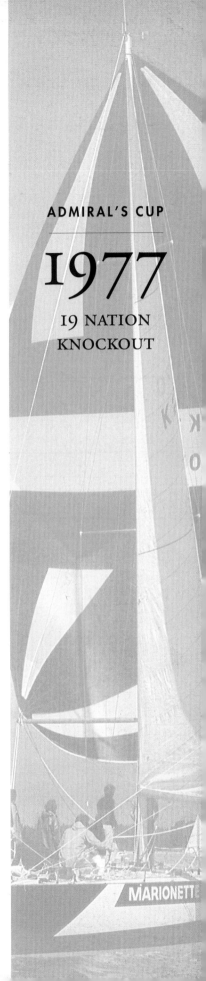

DEVELOPMENT HAD REACHED a dizzy pace and for 1977 there was much that was new. Innovation in the design field – where light displacement and fractional rigs were the norm in smaller race boats, and complicated hydraulics and spindly masts in big boats – was reflected by new introductions to the Admiral's Cup itself.

Not only were there time limits on the inshore races, at long last, to prevent further night-time finishes, but a completely new day race was added to the schedule before Cowes Week got underway. Rating limits were narrowed further, with 30.0ft remaining the floor, but the ceiling dropping to 42.0ft. The days of the giants such as *Saga*, *Bumblebee* and *Charisma* were over, now that 51ft became the effective maximum length likely to meet the rating limit.

Light airs and heavy criticism of the 1975 series had not dampened interest. For the second successive series there were nineteen teams, with the Japanese making their début. Amongst the team was the 54ft S & S-designed *Sun Bird V*, owned by Tatsumitsu Yamasaki, a producer of Soy sauce and other food products and who later led Japan to another debut, the America's Cup, in 1992.

The French even went so far as to hold their own selection trials in the Solent and the Channel for the second time, doing things in a thoroughly British manner: a dinner at the Royal Corinthian Yacht Club and five inshore races run off the Squadron and Royal London Yacht Club lines for their eight contenders. Jean-Louis Fabry's *Revolution* came out on top to make it three ACs in a row. She was joined by Michael Marchais' Peterson 44 *Alexandre* and Jacques Dewailly's Frers 50 *Emeraude*. Over the next fifteen years Dewailly, an industrialist, worked his way up through a 65ft mini-maxi and a full blown 81ft maxi to an interest in the 1995 America's Cup.

Hong Kong also used British waters to pick the best three of their four candidates. Hector Ross's *Uinna-Mara III*, one of Bruce Farr's first big boats, started strongly but was edged out by Chris Ostenfeld's *La Pantera* - a sister-ship to the British *Moonshine* – John Ma's *White Rabbit*, a clean-lined 42 footer which proved to be Dick Carter's last foray into race boat design and David Lieu's *Vanguard*. She was designed by the young Briton Ed Dubois, who had drawn a couple of quick Three-Quarter and Quarter Ton designs and was working with John Oakeley at the UK loft of Miller & Whitworth sailmakers. What set *Vanguard* apart was her 'semaphore' rig, which could be thrown backwards and forwards by hydraulic rams on the forestay and backstay.

As ever, the big threats to Britain were from the USA and Australia.

Eleven boats contested the Aussie trials, with Keith Farfor's Peterson 47 *Superstar*, a development of the American *High Roler*, living up to her name. She broke the traditional Sydney hold on the team, boats from Perth and Hobart excepted, and was the first Melbourne boat in the AC. She was joined in the team by Jim Hardy's *Runaway*, Alan Blackburne's only design ever to make the Admiral's Cup, and Syd Fischer's third *Ragamuffin*, a 47-footer from Frers.

The Americans turned to Florida in January to sort out their team from the results of the SORC. There, the classes had been split by age into pre- and post-1973 boats and no matter how the results were read, Dave Allen's new Holland 40, *Imp*, was the star.

Like Doug Peterson, New Zealand's Ron Holland had pioneered the flat-floored hull form whose ends were symmetrical as sharp bows were matched by pin tail sterns. With *Imp*, he filled out the stern to improve reaching speed. That, coupled with a novel construction

*Chris Dunning's Holland 44* Marionette, *part of Britain's winning line-up (Beken of Cowes)*

method developed by his then brother-in-law, Gary Carlin of Kiwi Boats, made *Imp* one of those boats with a little of bit of magic about them. For under her glass-fibre hull and deck, she had a geodesic alloy space frame. That carried the loads of keel and rig, while skins kept the water out.

48 *Scaramouche* for curtain-rail king Chuck Kirsch.

Britain's defence looked robust. Chris Dunning's new *Marionette* was a Ron Holland 44, built by Joyce Marine and a sister-ship to Ireland's *Big Apple*. She was fast throughout the trials. Edward Heath and David May both tried Holland boats but neither looked con-

*Moonshine, a Peterson 43 built and sailed by Jeremy Rogers, was top boat. Rogers brought dinghy aces Chris Law and Phil Crebbin into his crew (Jonathan Eastland)*

Bill Power's *High Roler*, skippered by Dennis Conner, and as hot a design as *Superstar*, won her class but was rejected in favour of Pat Haggerty's novel *Bay Bea*, a Briton Chance-designed centre boarder, which developed ideas seen in his 1975 One Ton Cup winner *Resolute Salmon*. Rounding of the US team was the Frers

sistent enough, a fault that could hardly be ascribed to Robin Aisher's *Yeoman XX*. Back for a second crack and tweaked and bumped to enhance speed for rating, she was superbly sailed. The same could not be said of Ernest Juer's *Brother Cup*, a Peterson 45 that was fast but erratic. Juer did not make it into the 1977 team, though he was successful two years later, carrying the erratic tag with him.

Joining *Marionette* and *Yeoman XX* in Britain's defence was Jeremy Rogers' *Moonshine*, a Peterson 43 launched in such a scramble that her crew left the food ashore for their first trials race. She was like a floating office for those at the centre of Britain's racing industry. Jeremy Rogers was the builder of the famous Contessa yachts and he shared steering with Bill Green, a Californian who had raced with Dick Carter aboard *Red Rooster* and was now Rogers' right hand man. When Contessa Yachts failed in the mid-1980s, Green started his own custom boatworks, building the Admiral's Cuppers of the 1980s and 1990s.

In the nerve centre of the boat was John Green, who had learned his craft from American spar and rig hydraulics pioneer Tim Stearn and ended up running the Stearn/Sparcraft operation in the UK. Phil Crebbin was one of the three Olympic sailors in the crew, taken offshore for the first time by Rogers. Trimming the sails were Chris Law and Iain MacDonald-Smith who had sailed with Robin Aisher aboard *Frigate* and *Yeoman XX*, having set up the UK loft of North Sails at the start of the 1970s. Jim Pugh, son of Lymington, was also in *Moonshine*'s crew, his contacts with Doug Peterson leading him eventually to San Diego to work for Peterson before starting his own design office with John Reichel.

All this assembled talent had to wait, however. The RORC intended to open the 1977 Admiral's Cup with a brand new inshore race down east in Hayling Bay, but a steadily veering wind saw that plan abandoned in favour of a double triangle course in the western Solent. Even that got away only after two attempts.

Starting fifty-seven ocean racers is no easy feat. First there was a thirty-minute postponement while the limit marks were set, then a recall because so many yachts jumped the gun. There were still gun-happy yachts at the second start, among them Peter Westphal-Langloh's *Champagne* (Peterson 42) from Germany, which failed to return despite recalls broadcast by VHF; a five per cent penalty was subsequently given by the jury.

A light northerly made for a slow first beat, but *Moonshine* was well up, tacking smoothly. *Bay Bea* pulled through to lead at the first mark, followed by *Moonshine*, *Marionette*, *Vanguard* (with John Oakeley steering) and her Hong Kong team-mate *La Pantera*. With *Yeoman* tenth, British prospects looked good.

After a short reach to East Gurnard and a run to Salt Mead, the fleet started a second lap in which *Ragamuffin* and *Superstar* finally got clear of the smaller boats. *Bay Bea* crossed the finish line five and a half

## RON HOLLAND

*It was an eventful path that took Ron Holland from Auckland, where his father gave him a P-class dinghy for his seventh birthday, to Cork in Southern Ireland, where he settled in 1973 to establish his design business. He arrived there via the USA, having sailed across the Atlantic on a John Spencer-designed ultralight, got a job in Gary Mull's design office, and was in Improbable's crew for the 1971 Admiral's Cup, having returned to New Zealand to build the boat. He also had a spell designing with Charlie Morgan.*

*Holland made his mark in 1973 with the Quarter-Tonner* Eygthene, *named after the way the New Zealand tongue slaughtered the word eighteen, then the IOR rating for Quarter-Tonners. She was built in their spare time by Holland and Gary Carlin, who was then working for North Sailors but later went on to found Kiwi Boats.* Eygthene *won the 1973 Quarter Ton Cup and the fast but erratic form of* Golden Apple *in the 1974 One Ton Cup confirmed Holland's arrival on the racing scene.*

*He moved on to* Silver Shamrock *(Half Ton Cup winner 1976),* Manzanita *(Quarter Ton Cup 1977),* Iorana *(Two Ton Cup winner 1978) and* Tilsalg *(One Ton Cup winner 1978), while his Admiral's Cuppers,* Imp *and* Swuzzlebubble, *were top boats of the 1977 and 1981 series.*

*Together with Doug Peterson, Holland signalled a change in the guard in yacht design, which became much more a young man's game. A neat coincidence was that Holland and Carlin helped build and sail* Ganbare, *which established Peterson as assuredly as* Eygthene *had Holland.*

minutes ahead of *Moonshine*, but victory went to Rogers' crew by 22 seconds. A seventh for *Yeoman* and tenth for *Marionette* made Britain best on the day, with Hong Kong a commendable second ahead of the USA and Ireland. Australia fell from their accustomed challenging position, with *Runaway* retired and their big boats in the bottom half of the fleet.

*Runaway*'s fortunes swung right back in the Channel race with an eighth for Jim Hardy's boys, though again the big Aussie boats were not sailing to their rating in a slow light-air race. The course was

**ABOVE:** *Ron Holland in his Irish Studios at Currabinney (Rick Tomlinson)*

from Fort Gilkicker, through the Solent Forts to the Nab, west round the back of the Isle of Wight to the Needles Fairway buoy, across the Channel to Cherbourg's CH1 buoy off Cherbourg, the return leg to Brighton and back into the Solent via the Owers.

Ireland's *Big Apple*, with Harold Cudmore aboard, led on corrected time at the Nab and took the on-the-water-lead from the larger *Emeraude* when she tacked out to sea at St Catherine's. The big shake-up occurred on the leg back from CH1. Some yachts ran out of wind for as much as three hours; others, such as Fernando Pimentel Duarte's *Tigre* from Brazil, snapped a mast.

*Giorgio Carriero's* Mandrake *might be aground but his Italian crew are happy (Alastair Black)*

The Argentine Navy's *Fortuna II* (a Frers 53) was first round Brighton Fairway, closely followed by *Scaramouche*. The American boat was still on her tail at the finish to claim victory and, with *Imp* fourth, the USA moved into the points lead, despite *Bay Bea's* forty-fourth. That put the Americans 16 points ahead of Britain, who had an average race: nineteenth for *Moonshine*, twentieth for *Yeoman* and twenty-ninth for *Marionette*.

The Second Inshore race was postponed a day. Then, by waiting for the afternoon breeze, the fleet got away after a general recall with a beat in the western Solent up to Sconce, beyond Yarmouth, and a run back along the shore. In a carbon copy of the First Inshore, *Bay Bea* again looked good – until that became academic. While the start had been pushed back four hours, the time limit was only one hour later and, in a dying wind, not even *Bay Bea* was going to finish. Given the huge pile up off the Sowley Outfall, with *Mandrake*, *Superstar*, *Moby Dick* and *White Rabbit* so hard aground that they had to be pulled off by spectator boats, many were grateful that the race was scrubbed.

But worse was to come. The Third Inshore was run on its allotted day, with the re-sailed Second Inshore put back to the reserve day on Thursday.

The Third Inshore was a triumph for *Imp*, one of the small boats in the fifty-seven-boat fleet, only three others crossed the finish line ahead of her and the 'smallest' of those rated a massive 4.6ft higher. With *Bay Bea* and *Scaramouche* well placed, the USA were all set to assume the series lead when Pat Haggerty's boat was disqualified for a start line foul against *Pinta*, Willi Illbruck's near sister-ship to *Champagne*. Britain regained their lead, but Friday's lay day before the Fastnet was spent awaiting the outcome of the myriad protests resulting from the re-run Second Inshore from the day before.

Chaos was ensured from the first gun, for instead of giving the fleet an uptide beat, they were sent east to SE Ryde Middle buoy, where the fleet crashed and barged like dodgem cars. So many protests were being lodged over the VHF R/T that RORC secretary, Mary Pera, appealed: 'No more protests until the end of the race!'

*Fortuna* pulled away from the pack with *Big Apple*, and *Marionette* enjoyed another boat-for-boat scrap on the beat to Solent Banks. *Yeoman*, however, was hurting in the disturbed air of a fleet not yet sorted into size order, blanketed constantly by bigger boats.

The wind piped up to 20 knots. *La Pantera* performed a spectacular broach and *Superstar* was laid flat. While *Recluta* was first to finish, from *Emeraude* and *Scaramouche*, she could not save her time from *Big Apple*, *Marionette* and *Moonshine*, the first three on corrected time. There were five disqualifications. Italy had both Giorgio Carriero's *Mandrake* (very similar to *Big Apple* and *Marionette*) and Lorenzo Bortolotti's *Moby Dick* (Peterson 40) penalised, which snuffed out their hopes there and then.

If the 1975 Fastnet had been frustratingly slow, then the 1977 race was positively pedestrian – the slowest since the 1930s, it was claimed. *Moonshine* was the first of the Cuppers round the Rock, but that was at breakfast time on Wednesday when, normally, her crew would have expected to have been sipping beers in Plymouth late on Tuesday night.

British hopes were not buoyant in the opening miles, for the home team was down, while the Aussies and Americans were well placed. But it did not matter, for the entire fleet stopped at Portland Bill in what proved to be the first of many parking lots. The race was never anything but a long, dour and taxing struggle against light winds which, perversely, always seemed to be on the nose. Some boats never set a spinnaker.

As if held by magnetism, *Bay Bea*, *Big Apple*, *Imp*, *Vanguard* and *Moonshine* stayed in contact for days, though *Big Apple* fell out of contention when she went to sniff out a new westerly breeze which never materialised. What wind there was amounted to no more than a few knots of breeze under a high centred on the Scillies and *Moonshine*, with a crew full of able helmsmen, was coaxed round the course. While the British boat rounded the Rock third after the maxis *Ballyhoo* and *Il Moro di Venezia*, they also knew that *Imp* was worryingly close. Being a lower rating boat, she probably held a corrected-time lead.

There was a reasonable breeze on the way back, but The Lizard stood as a hurdle between the fleet and the finish. *Marionette* missed the tide and had to kedge, while *Imp* closed up behind. Some of the bigger boats, *Fortuna*, *Emeraude* and *Moonshine*, managed to get home at breakfast time on Friday, but *Marionette* took four hours to cover the final four miles, all the time aware that *Imp*'s graduated green-striped hull was just astern. *Imp* actually managed to beat team-mate *Scaramouche*, 6ft longer, across the line, to take a memorable win from *Moonshine* by six minutes.

However, *Yeoman* had clung on to *Imp* to give

Britain three boats in the top ten in the high-scoring climax, bringing Britain a seventh win in eleven Admiral's Cups. The Fastnet proved to be the slowest on record for some time. After eleven days virtually all the 330 starters had either reached Plymouth or been among the 60-odd who retired, decisions prompted mostly by lack of water and food. Among the Cup boats, Chris Dunning admitted 'we'd eaten our final meal the night before we finished', while West Germany's *Pinta*

Bay Bea, *a Britton Chance-designed centreboarder was built for the American founder of Texas Instruments, Pat Haggerty (Beken of Cowes)*

was out of food but still had liquids. According to *The Daily Telegraph*, they were able to maintain their ration 'of one bottle of sherry and five pints of beer per day per crew member for "quite a few days"'.

Dave Allen, who first raced in Cowes aboard *Improbable*, saw his *Imp* – dubbed the Bionic Boat – confirmed as Fastnet winner and top-scoring yacht of the series. Allen claimed his crew had never been out of sight of Robin Aisher's *Yeoman* for the entire 141 hours of the race.

Another British win prompted the inevitable dock-side inquisition into whether Britain not only had home-team advantage but was actually favoured by the Royal Ocean Racing Club. After all, the RORC both ran the series and selected the British team. As with any club hosting an event of the Admiral's Cup stature, some believed it favoured the home team. In the America's Cup, it's thought essential for the defender to load the dice against the challenger and no one seriously expects it to be otherwise.

The British team manager did indeed exercise some home advantages. Hugh Wilson, a retired Navy captain from Lymington, was charged by the Club to look after the British team in 1977, and following their emphatic victory, it's interesting to note Wilson's thank-you list. Besides the usual acknowledgement of assistance to the likes of North Sails, instrument makers Brookes & Gatehouse, Groves & Guttridge marina and the Met Office, there was another sent to the Hydrographic Department of the Admiralty in Taunton for the special supply of unpublished information.

One particular navigational worry had been that while the new IALA cardinal system of buoyage was being introduced, largely in the eastern approaches to the Channel, it could take eight weeks for changes to filter through from the French authorities so that their British counterpart could issue a Notice to Mariners. Even if the information leaked to the British team was 'not of any great importance' – in the words of then Superintendent of the Notices to Mariners – it demonstrated a close liaison. The Hydrographer's staff even went so far as to wish the British team good luck, 'although one assumes they will win'.

The inventive Hugh Wilson went to another branch of the Ministry of Defence to see if a few strings could be pulled on behalf of his sailors. Unfortunately, the Army's signal officer in chief was unable to lend short range communications. All equipment was out, either in Northern Ireland or detailed to the Queen's Silver Jubilee celebrations although it had been made available to the team in 1975.

That said, the British had been a well-prepared outfit. There were training weekends at the College of Air Training in Hamble where, for instance, Iain Macdonald-Smith talked about trimming the new North genoas that all three yachts were using, and Dr Frank Newton got the sailors interested properly in training, diet and fitness for the first time. He used the Performance Arousal Cards, developed with the Olympic sailors the year before as means of measuring fitness and improvement, and which must have attracted colourful weather rail banter. Crews comments were bound to be ribald when they scored their themselves on a 1-5 scale on such matters as appetite ('very poor' to 'eat a horse'), fitness ('decrepit' to 'superfit') and libido ('Nil' to 'off the scale').

## SHORT TACKS

• Ireland's *Big Apple* was, rather rudely, dubbed *Apple Crumble*. Due to an error in reading the pilot book, she struck the rocks while entering Guernsey's Beaucette marina, itself little more than a cleft in the rocks leading to an old quarry. Despite her sinking, and requiring the removal of virtually all of her port side when salvaged, Joyce Marine managed a high-speed repair in time for the Cup.

• To celebrate the British victory, Owen Aisher hosted a dinner in Plymouth at the Mayflower Hotel. The menu included Beef Wellington and Bavarois Fastnet.

• Jim Hardy's *Runaway* was a sponsored yacht which slipped past the rule banning advertising, being backed by the Runaway Bay development. Hardy had already scored an unintentional publicity coup when *Runaway* was damaged when being craned aboard the aircraft carrier *HMAS Melbourne*, the Australian Navy having shipped the team to the UK. The picture of the yacht on her collapsed cradle was splashed across the front of *The Australian* and Runaway Bay declared Jim Hardy the PR Champ of Australia.

*Ireland's Marionette sistership* Big Apple *counted designer Ron Holland steering and Cork sailor Harold Cudmore (to Holland's left) in her crew (Beken of Cowes)*

OFFSHORE RACING was thrust on to the front pages and into TV bulletins in 1979 – the year of the big blow, when disaster in the Fastnet Race claimed fifteen lives. It was, arguably, the most significant chapter in the history of ocean racing and is accorded its own chapter in this book (see page 191).

By the time of the twelfth series, as many as twenty-seven countries had taken part in the Admiral's Cup and the only change from the 1977 line up was the replacement of Austria by Singapore. Britain was the only nation to have competed in every series.

Marking the end of an era, there were no new S & S boats in any of the teams. Ruling the roost instead were Doug Peterson and Ron Holland with twenty and sixteen boats apiece, and while there may have been only two Frers' boats – Burt Keenan's American team reject *Acadia* and *Gitana*, recent winner of the Two Ton Cup at Poole – they were given star billing.

Two others signposted the way boats would look in the 1980s. They were Peter Cantwell's Ed Dubois-designed *Police Car* from Australia and the Michel Joubert-designed *Accanito* from France. Both were relatively light-displacement, fractionally-rigged boats that looked like half-tonners scaled up, in a fleet where the look was one of 50-footers scaled down. With the rating limits now closed nearer together at 30.0ft-40.0ft, the British selectors picked a team which represented critical points in the rating band. The idea was to cover the anticipated threat from the top foreigners.

There were plenty of new boats to choose from, including a new Peterson 46 for Robin Aisher, *Yeoman XXI*, which was based on the top US boat, *Williwaw*, but was too heavily optimised towards heavy airs for the light-going trials. The surprise selection was Edward Heath's two-year-old *Morning Cloud V*, his fifth boat and his first from Ron Holland. Although she had

failed to make the 1977 team, much had been done since. The tortured stern was cleaned up, which not only made the water happy but the rating dropped too. The bow down-trim was changed by bringing the ballast aft, which measurably improved control. Larry Marks was added to share the steering with Owen Parker and others in the Old Firm.

While *Morning Cloud*'s crew worked hard to extract her potential, Jeremy Rogers performed his last-minute launch trick once again. *Eclipse*, a 39ft Peterson-designed minimum-rater hit the water the weekend before the first trial, managed only a scant hour's tune-up before she made her first start and then cheekily won the de Guingand Bowl offshore race by ten minutes on corrected time.

For a man who said little and spoke very quietly when he did, Rogers had a happy knack of letting his boats make the noise. *Moonshine* and the 1974 One Ton Cup winner, *Gumboots*, were evidence of that. Besides Bill Tripp from Peterson's office, Rogers had Phil Crebbin and Chris Law from *Moonshine* with him again to share steering duties aboard *Eclipse*, a combination which was to make her the first British Admiral's Cup boat to win the Fastnet since *Clarion* in 1963.

At 51ft, Ernest Juer's *Blizzard* was the largest yacht to have flown British colours in the Cup since *Jocasta* in 1957. She was based on Frers' *Acadia*, which won 1979 SORC in Florida and was sailed for Argentina after the American selectors rejected her. With sterling strong against the US dollar, Ernest Juer had her built in Sturgeon Bay, Wisconsin, by the famous Palmer-Johnson yard. As there was driving snow each time he visited the yacht under construction, her name more or less chose itself.

*Acadia* or no *Acadia*, the Americans still posed a formidable threat. Burt Keenan's Louisiana boat had

*Peter Cantwell's Dubois 40 from Western Australian revelled in the windy conditions of the 1979 series, often sailing faster than her bigger rivals off the wind (Beken of Cowes)*

shown excellent SORC form, finishing second to *Willi-waw* only because Dennis Conner had sailed her down the fleet in the final race, and had won the Bermuda Race the year before. However, she was now thrown out because the American selectors under Chuck Kirsch rescored their results according to their own Time on Distance system as opposed to the British Time on Time method.

Claiming *Acadia*'s place was Mike Swerdlow's Holland 47 *Aries*, joined by the 1977 top boat *Imp* and Seymour Sinett's second Peterson 46 to carry the *Willi-waw* name and bear the familiar electric blue topsides. With Dennis Conner at her wheel and Jim Pugh from the design office in her nerve centre, *Williwaw* was a gentle progression of a proven design sailed exceptionally well.

Her predecessor, now Alan Bond's *Apollo IV*, turned up in the Singapore team, having missed out on Australian selection. That team included Syd Fischer's new *Ragamuffin*, sister-ship to *Williwaw*, and Gerald Lambert's *Impetuous*, which proved that developments (she was based on *Imp*) do not always go better than the originals. Peter Cantwell's *Police Car* from Western Australia, which flew when it blew, rounded off the team. *Police Car*'s crew got endless mirth out of their boat's name and the crew bus was a black London cab with a blue light on the roof.

Argentina continued the 1970s as they had started, with a home-grown team designed by German Frers Jr. *Acadia*, skippered by Frers himself, was signed up to join *Red Rock IV* and *Sur II*, which besides her Two Ton Cup success was equally noteworthy for having been built in twenty days.

Poland were mounting their second bid and had built two new Peterson boats, *Hadar* and *Nauticus*, to join the home grown Hoffman & Siudy-designed *Cetus*.

Japan, too, lodged a second challenge and were not afraid to give their own designers a chance. S Namiki went to Peterson for his *Gekko VI*, but the other two came from the board of Toshio Kihara, who had learned his craft from an internship at S & S, crewing aboard *Bay Bea* in the USA and with Jeremy Rogers in Britain. His *Kamikaze Express* came second when the Quarter Ton Cup was held in Japan in 1978, a pivotal event in Japan's emergence into international yacht racing. Kihara's AC boats were Togo Yamada's *Togo VI* and Teruno Yamaguchi's *Ko Teru Teru II*, which enlisted 1964 British Olympic silver medallist Keith Musto to her wheel. Yamada had found most of his crew through a newspaper advertisement, but they were well coached by New Zealander Robert Fry, who settled in Japan and later became a key part of the 1992 Nippon America's Cup challenge.

Two of Spain's yachts should have caught the eye but didn't. *Yachtsman* and *Campsa* did nothing of note on the race course, but were the thin end of sponsorship wedge. *Campsa* was Spain's main oil company and *Yachtsman* a brand of men's fragrance and, while sponsorship was not banned, Racing Rule 26 still prevented yachts carrying logos or brand names. Canada had made little impact before, but Don Green brought a hot boat to the series. Or at least his C & C designed *Evergreen* was considered hot on the Great Lakes, for she went on to win the Canada's Cup match race against the USA, though she never shed her reputation for fragility.

Hong Kong had surprised many by a third place in 1977 – and but for the Fastnet lottery could so easily have squeezed the mighty Americans out of second place – and were treated as a serious threat by the big yachting powers. Eight boats contested the right to sail for the Crown Colony. David Lieu, owner of the Tsing-Yo island Supercraft boatbuilding company, launched a new Dubois-designed *Vanguard* and Richard Bagnall, who had guided the three-quarter tonner *Golden Delicious* to a memorable overall Fastnet win in 1977, joined Tim Yourieff in the afterguard.

Hector Ross had Supercraft build a sister-ship to *Vanguard* as his *Uin-na-Mara IV*, with Helmer Pederson, a Dane resident in New Zealand, calling the shots. Chris Ostenfeld rounded off a polished team in an unusual way. John Ma's *Mile High*, a Japanese-built Peterson 42, edged Ostenfeld's *La Pantera* out of the third team berth, so Ostenfeld negotiated a swap deal for a boat that was essentially the same design as his, but built some 4000lb lighter by the Chita yard.

Britain's team could have been forgiven for over-looking Ireland's efforts. But that complacency was shaken off by the victory of Hugh Coveney's *Golden Apple of the Sun* in the Solent Points inshore race the weekend before the Admiral's Cup began.

The seeds of a powerful Irish challenge had been nurtured since 1973, the year that Ron Holland arrived on the scene with his Quarter Ton Cup winner *Eygthene*. Then an itinerant Kiwi, he settled in Ireland and got the commission from Hugh Coveney for the fast but erratic one-tonner *Golden Apple*. Harold Cudmore

had by then turned his back on 'proper work', having tried training as an accountant and working for the family firm – and in the framework of Coveney's campaigns, Cudmore started to make big boats go fast and earn a living out of it. He was a trailblazer for the pros that followed.

Through various *Apples* and *Shamrocks*, Holland and Cudmore became a dominant force in the level-rating classes, with Holland's design business becoming an international success. What *Big Apple* threatened as an individual boat in 1977, the Irish now promised to do as a team in 1979.

Cudmore signed up British triple Olympic medallist Rodney Pattisson to steer *Golden Apple*, yet it was

Ken Rohan's *Regardless* which proved the outstanding boat of the Irish trials. She was an *Imp* update, built to even greater sophistication by Gary Carlin's Kiwi Boats in Tampa, Florida, and counting American Ron Love of Sparcraft in her crew.

The surprise was that *Golden Apple*'s sister-ship, again built from carbon fibre reinforced wood/epoxy by Souters of Cowes, was edged out by a boat from Northern Ireland. Though part of the UK in political terms, the north is part of the island of Ireland when it comes to yachting, and from Strangford Lough came

## DOUG PETERSON

*Twenty thousand dollars from Doug Peterson's grandmother changed the face of yacht design. With the money, Carl Eichenlaub built Ganbare, second in the 1973 One Ton Cup to Dick Carter's Ydra, but recognised by all who saw her as a pivotal boat in IOR design. She was smaller, simpler, lighter and more easily driven than any previous IOR design. Her lines had been rushed out on the living room table and the boat built in five weeks. So hectic was the schedule that no blueprints were made.*

*Ganbare's characteristic U-shaped forward sections and pin tail were the result of Peterson's musings when racing on George Kiscaddon's New World, after his Vietnam draft had interrupted a mechanical engineering course. New World's crew numbered Ron Holland, Bill Green (later a partner of Jeremy Rogers), Walter Greene (noted multihull sailor) and Toshio Kihara (noted Japanese designer). Urged by this group to put his ideas into practice, Peterson drew back from the brink of taking a job in the Carter design office in Massachusetts when his family made an offer he couldn't refuse.*

*From Ganbare, Peterson had a string of successes in the Ton Cups classes with* North Star *(Half Ton Cup 1974),* Solent Saracen *(Three Quarter Ton Cup 1975),* Gumboots *and* Pier Piper *(One Ton Cup 1974 and 1975), as well as the dominant Admiral's Cup boats* Yeoman XX, Moonshine *and* Eclipse, *and many others which dominated US and European racing.*

*Like Holland's, Peterson's influence in the 1980s diminished as the design world opened up and Bruce Farr's influence asserted itself.*

surgeon Barry Bramwell and Brian Buchannen in their pale blue *Inishanier*. She was a sister-ship to *Eclipse*, but fitted out more as a Contessa 39.

In July, all had seemed serene on the south coast of England. Sails had scarcely seen a reef, oilskins were collecting mildew and boats such as *Yeoman XXI* and *Marionette* failed to make the British team because their forte, medium to heavy air, had not been tested.

The air of calm was shattered with the very first Admiral's Cup race, held over a Solent course of thirty miles. Even as the fleet was jockeying before the gun, *Sur II* swerved to avoid an impending collision and smartly put her bows through the port side of Brazil's lightly-built *Madrugada*, unzipping her from gunwhale

*Ernest Juer's powerful Frers 50 Blizzard was expected to lead Britain to victory.*
*Instead she is remembered for leading to the wrong mark (Beken of Cowes)*

to waterline. It took three crewmen on the spinnaker pole rigged on the opposite side to stop the Solent from engulfing the yacht. The Brazilians tried to charter the Two Ton Cup winner *Gitana VII*, but eventually plumped for David May's Dubois two tonner *Winsome Gold*, a British triallist. When her mast was damaged in the next race, Brazil's effort was spent.

The new inshore race was given a proper committee boat start near Peel Bank. Conner brought *Williwaw* off the line beautifully, but *Blizzard* soon tramped away on a course that suited power, with long beats against the tide. The Hong Kong pair of *Uin-na-Mara* and *Vanguard* showed well and *Eclipse* kept her nose in front of *Imp*. Impressively, *Blizzard* saved her time to win by over a minute on corrected time, but Hong Kong stood at the head of the leader board for the first time.

*Blizzard*'s glory was short-lived. The blunder she made in the next race is still talked about as one of the great foul-ups of all time, for she went round the incorrect mark while leading the fifty-seven-boat fleet. The great sailor Bobby Lowein was navigator, and sadly was suffering from cancer, from which he died not long after. When you are in front, errors stand out as plainly as lightning in a black sky.

The Second Inshore should have favoured *Blizzard* even more than the previous race: the breeze was up again and the spring tides were running with more vigour. The wind angle was such that the Royal Yacht Squadron's line was used and *Blizzard* immediately got her nose in front on the long uphill climb to the Delta buoy off Lymington. She rounded three minutes up on *Aries* and looked good on handicap before a run back to Hamstead Ledge on the island shore and across to Clipper off Hill Head.

Little by little it started to go wrong aboard the big white boat. The gybe over to the Hill Head was delayed because the wire guy jammed in the spinnaker pole end. That meant *Blizzard* had to squeeze past the west edge of the Brambles bank and she touched several times. On the beat up to Salt Mead, her crew had to switch jibs twice as the tack hooks, securing the jib to the bow, failed. Tellingly, *Acadia*'s more experienced crew had already found out that snap shackles were a better answer on such a powerful yacht design.

'After all these events we were a little rattled,' admitted Ernest Juer. But as *Blizzard* reached Salt Mead on a nicely called tack from the mainland shore, her crew executed a slick spinnaker hoist and Juer's boat powered off downwind. Helmsman Tom Richardson immediately knew something was amiss. 'Why hadn't the press boats followed us as they had on the previous day?', he pondered.

The reason was that the course, taken down at the start, had not been referred to on the beat to Salt Mead, and West Lepe buoy, a short reach across from Salt Mead, had been forgotten. So it was that Britain's lead boat, with old Solent hands Tom Richardson and Bobby Lowein calling the shots, zoomed off at high speed in the wrong direction. The error, from which it took twenty minutes to recover, dropped *Blizzard* from a high place, another win perhaps, to a grim forty-second.

It was a grim day aboard *Inishanier* too, for in the Force 7 winds, the boat broached and Harvey Bagnall, a gentle man recruited for his unmatched knowledge of the Solent, was hit with the full force of the scything boom. No one needed reminding that Tom Curtis had been killed the same way on the American boat *Obsession* seven months previously at the SORC in Florida.

If there is to be luck in such a ghastly accident, then it was Bagnall's fortune to have a surgeon as a skipper. His know-how in the minutes before help arrived and the prompt action by photographer William Payne in taking Bagnall aboard his rigid inflatable, so that the RAF rescue helicopter from Lee-on-Solent could evacuate him free of possible entanglement with *Inishanier*'s rig, prevented the accident becoming a tragedy.

The strength of Ireland was shown by *Regardless* claiming the race with *Golden Apple* second, but overall honours went to the Aussies, with *Police Car*, *Ragamuffin* and *Impetuous* placing third, fourth and ninth. Hong Kong still led, just, but the USA and Australia were breathing down the dragon's neck with Britain fourth.

The Channel Race results were fashioned by the approach to and line taken away from the turning mark of the CH1 buoy off Cherbourg. *Regardless* won again

and the French, feeling more at home, were the top points scorers in the race with Jean-Louis Fabry's irrepressible *Revolution* claiming second spot, with *Accanito* seventh and *Jubile V1* thirteenth. With *Morning Cloud* breaking her rudder and *Blizzard* down the pan, France actually headed Britain on the Admiral's Cup leader board for the first time ever.

The running start to the race denied clear air to the bigger boats and *Blizzard* was only third after ninety miles at the tiny Portobello buoy to the east of Brighton. So inconspicuous was this mark that navigators soon learned to pick it up by finding the famous Roedean girls' school on the cliff above it, a tip not found in any conventional pilot book.

*Acadia* was first round with the light, fractionally-rigged *Accanito* and *Police Car* uncomfortably close astern. On the close reach across to Cherbourg, the loading proved too much for *Morning Cloud*'s new carbon fibre rudder, which snapped. Owen Parker had just taken the helm of *Cloud* and she was beating into the 15-knot breeze when the stock broke without warning between the two bearings. She motored back to Hamble to fit her previous blade with a more reliable aluminium stock and add some trimming ballast, so that the boat floated with the same freeboard measurements.

'Although the designer strongly urged us to adopt this rudder,' said Edward Heath afterwards, 'the crew were always divided about it.

'One group believed that we ought to try new technology; the other said it would be fatal if it went during a race. Although the design of the new rudder appeared to improve the performance of the boat a little, the more cautious members of the crew were, in the end, proved right.' With similar breakages during the SORC, carbon fibre rudders were getting a bad name. Were designers experimenting at the owners' expense?

Gary Carlin and David Kilponen of Kiwi Boats, who had built *Cloud*'s rudder, leaped to the defence. 'The extreme lightness of carbon fibre rudders reduces the pitching moment and allows a rating advantage of saving some 50kg in the very stern of the yachts,' explained 'Fang' Kilponen. *Morning Cloud* had fitted

one as part of her re-vamp. The reason for the breakage, claimed Kilponen, was due to the rudder having been adapted. 'The rudder stock, and aluminium tube encased in carbon fibre, had been machined to enable the old steering quadrant to fit. This reduced the torsional strength of the carbon fibre substantially, causing progressive fibre breakage which eventually led to fracture.'

*Blizzard*'s dismal showing was due to overstanding CH1. She approached under spinnaker a buoy the rest of the fleet laid on a close fetch or beat, which did little to remove her reputation for quirky navigation.

A ninth and seventeenth by *Inishanier* and *Golden Apple* reinforced *Regardless*' victory to give Ireland a sixteen-point lead. As one wag commentated: 'The good news for Ireland is that the team is leading. The bad news is that the crews are celebrating.'

The Irish did not throw it away in the Third Inshore though; *Williwaw* won the race and the prize, which was now the Champagne Mumm Trophy. Dennis Conner became the first of many skippers to win his weight in champagne. With the wind blowing a full gale and the tides running fast, it should have been *Police Car*'s day to show off her much vaunted offwind speed, since the beats were with the tide and runs against them. She did, her crew pumping sheet and guy like crazy as the blue boat hurtled down the Solent in a flurry of spray.

However, the Aussie boat holed Brazil's *Indigo* on the start line, a collision which threw John Mooney into the water, his arm broken. Another photographer came to the rescue, this time Ken Beken, who took the injured man ashore. Two protests then spoiled *Police Car*'s day completely as her fifth became a seventeenth. With Mike Swerdlow's *Aries* backing up *Williwaw*'s win, the USA moved into third place with 625 points behind Australia (626) and the Irish (649).

If there was to be a light Fastnet, many fancied the Irish to claim a memorable victory, while the USA looked good with her big boats if the wind picked up. The points were close, though, and that did not reckon on the storm which shook the event to breaking point.

Two days of gentle sailing took the fleet to Land's

**OPPOSITE:** *Successful steering in heavy air is all about the helmsman's ability to keep the boat under rig, but here the spinnaker of Wicktor Forss'* Midnight Sun *takes charge as the crew prepare to gybe in front of Alan Bond's* Apollo IV (Jonathan Eastland)

*The fresh conditions of the 1979 races reinforced the Australians' reputation for being at home in big breezes. Syd Fischer's* Ragamuffin *charges along under spinnaker and blooper (Guy Gurney)*

End, with the Americans and Irish containing the Australians. After the race, *Imp*'s Skip Allan said his boat had been more in danger at Portland Bill than any other time, the subsequent storm included. 'If you were not there, ask someone who was about this insanity,' he said. 'Starboard tack 60-footers going 10 knots ploughing into a fleet of port tackers going zero knots over the bottom.' Dodging the tide inside the race off Portland had been part of the Fastnet's cruel charm since its inception. 'I'm all for tradition,' added Allan, 'but that's not racing. It's foolhardiness.'

On the leg to the Rock the Australian challenge firmed up. Halfway on the 150-mile leg, *Impetuous* had closed on *Imp*, *Ragamuffin* had got in front of *Williwaw* for about the first time in the series, while *Police Car* was well placed alongside the bigger *Vanguard* and *Uin-na-Mara*.

Even on Monday, there was little inkling of what was to come. The BBC shipping forecast for the Fastnet sea area was Force 3-4, possibly 5-6 later. But events started moving faster than anyone anticipated. The Fastnet lighthouse keepers reported Force 7 southwesterlies by mid-afternoon and the Monday early evening BBC shipping forecast spoke of Force 4-5, later 6 and 7-8 in places.

The lead AC boats were close to the Rock at midnight on Monday, when the full impact of the storm struck. The Aussies kept plugging on, treating the storm trysail as another racing sail – a crewman on *Impetuous* said the whole boat had been three feet under as the Aussies marched on through spray and solid water.

As the first signs of the storm abating came through, the Australian boats' crews cracked on more sail, while their rivals, by and large, remained under storm sails, or bare poles. Syd Fischer on *Ragamuffin* said conditions were nothing to get excited about. The blow in the 1977 Sydney-Hobart had gone on for longer. The most serious accident on *Impetuous* was to Hugh Treharne's thumb, pricked by a needle while he was repairing a sail.

Few would argue that Hobart races have conditioned the better Aussie crews to heavy weather and big seas. As the late Jack Knights, the keenest observer of the racing scene in the 1970s, wrote: 'There was little doubt that the Australian team was better equipped, mentally and physically, to cope with the storm, even if, from a racing point of view, their boats were a degree or two below par.'

*Acadia*, navigated by *Morning Cloud*'s long time tactician Sammy Sampson, was the first of the AC boats home to Plymouth, crossing the line at 0719 on Wednesday, followed some time later by *Red Rock IV* and *Ragamuffin*, which at long last beat her hull sister *Williwaw* by forty-one minutes on elapsed time.

*Ragamuffin*'s team-mates appeared soon afterwards. *Impetuous* and *Police Car* both finished ahead of the much larger *Aries*, quite apart from *Imp*, to ensure Australia quoshed the US threat. With *Impetuous*, *Police Car* and *Ragamuffin* taking third, fourth and thirteenth places on corrected time, the Cup was theirs, Ireland's lead coming apart at the seams as both *Regardless* and *Golden Apple* lost their rudders. *Regardless* was towed in by the Baltimore lifeboat and *Golden Apple*'s crew accepted evacuation by helicopter.

Harold Cudmore, well tutored in the hard school of Irish cruising, was reluctant to abandon *Golden Apple*. His leaning was to nurse the boat to port, but he was persuaded by the argument that the crew would come back when the storm abated to salvage the yacht themselves. Accordingly he left a note on the chart table: 'Gone to lunch. Back soon.' Like General MacArthur, Cudmore did return as promised.

Britain's *Eclipse* shaded the Aussie win with overall victory, beating France's *Jubilé VI* by thirty-five minutes on corrected time. *Eclipse* was west of the rhumb line when the wind began howling, so Rogers' crew were high of the mark when they began to get headed. They

were able to change down to just a storm jib and reach into Cape Clear before tacking and reaching out to the west, and to windward, of the Rock. *Imp*, her arch rival, was low approaching the Rock and, with a broken baby stay, could not set the storm jib she needed to climb up to windward. Once round, *Eclipse*'s crew surfed at a 10-knot average with just a scrap of a sail set. Having the lightest, and probably lightest-built, yacht in the fleet proved an advantage when running back down the vicious seas that were wreaking havoc with the smaller boats making their way to the Rock.

Though no lives or boats were lost from the AC fleet, the big racing boats still suffered from the brutal conditions, no matter how much the victorious Aussies played them down. *Jan Pott* was rolled through 360 degrees. Knock-downs were common. But the loss of the fifteen sailors in six separate incidents and the fact that only seventy-five yachts completed the course of the 302 starters spoke volumes about the severity of the unexpected conditions. The prizegiving was appropriately altered to a 'private' affair, and there was a memorial service afterwards in Plymouth. A special memorial, made from rock, was also erected next to Trinity Church in Cowes in memory of those who had lost their lives.

*Dennis Conner (foreground) burnishes Williwaw's hull with Jim Pugh, then at Doug Peterson's studio before starting his own designing office with John Reichel (Guy Gurney)*

The Fastnet disaster apart, the RORC also considered how to move the Admiral's Cup forward. The difficulties of running inshore races together with Cowes Week races produced a wonderful but confused mix of recreational sailors battling for water with the world's top yachtsmen. To the Club the solution was obvious enough: move the inshore races into the week preceding Cowes Week. But what kept them in check was the well-understood view from many competitors that the series was long enough already and that some of the Cowes Week atmosphere would be lost. Coming from halfway round the world to wrestle with the peculiarities of the Solent's tides and congested waters certainly set the series apart, but for some this was making the Cup a little too idiosyncratic.

Looking ahead to the 1981 series, the Club plumped for holding two of the inshore races in the week before Cowes, while the one race remaining in Cowes Week would start from a committee boat located well away from the baying masses of other competitors. In line with the rest of yachting, alternative penalties were available to the jury to mete out to those who transgressed the rules. This was a practice common with other branches of sailing, from dinghy racing upwards, but the RORC had long recognised the special needs in big-boat racing. As Mary Pera wrote to her fellow jurors: 'The RORC policy over the years has always been to retain the right of disqualification but not to use it – although now and again someone is persuaded to retire.'

A big effort was made to acquaint visitors with the idiosycrancies of the Admiral's Cup, such as 20 per cent place penalties in the offshore races (in which the Channel and Fastnet points were factored by x3 and x5 respectively) and 50 per cent for inshore races, though this would be reduced if the offending yacht carried a *mea culpa* I flag.

## SHORT TACKS

• The Admiral's Cup management committee was expanded to include three non-British members for the first time: Chuck Kirsch, a curtain rail manufacturer from the USA and owner of *Scaramouche*;

Jean-Louis Fabry, from the RORC's French sister organisation UNCL (Union Nationale pour la Course au Large); and Ireland's Dennis Doyle, owner of various *Moondusters*.

• Rating limits were now 300-40.0ft.

• Buoyed up by a run of record entries – nineteen teams – the series savoured splendid isolation. Requests from the British America's Cup challenger *Lionheart* to appear during Cowes Week and join the Admiral's Cup party were turned down as unacceptable. Requests from the Yacht Club Costa Smeralda to give a slide show of its Sardinia Cup series, an imitator of the Admiral's Cup, was also turned down as 'all official functions were committed'.

• A late challenge from Austria, with a team including two chartered German yachts, was turned down.

• Press helicopters were considered a menace during Cowes Week and the inshore races. The Civil Aviation Authority, which was now accustomed to issuing an Information Circular about its low-flying rules over the Solent, went so far as to issue summonses against one pilot, Roderick John McPhaden, who appeared at the Magistrates Court in Newport. This was despite the RORC warning before the series that aerial maroons, which could be dangerous to helicopters flying low, might be used during starts. As Alan Green dryly noted in a bulletin: 'It must be remembered especially, that a helicopter creates considerable noise which can make it impossible for oral instructions to be heard between skippers and crews racing and also between race control staff. When large ocean racing yachts are manoeuvring in good breeze at the start in close quarters, it is quite essential that their handling and control is not hampered in any way.'

• Before the series, Baron Alain de Gunzburg played host to rear-commodore Jonathan Bradbeer, assistant secretary Janet Grosvenor and a pack of press at Mumm's splendid headquarters in Reims.

*Not only was Jeremy Rogers' Peterson 39 Eclipse the smallest and lightest yacht in the Cup, but she was also one of the first composite-built boats. She came throu_ the tough series virtually unscathed (Guy Gurney)*

THE 1981 Admiral's Cup must have seemed some sort of embrocation to soothe memories troubled by the storm-girt 1979 Fastnet and rugged inshore races before it, for it was a light but fluky and frustrating series.

Before it started, there was the whiff of scandal over the ratings of the American triallists and, six months after Britain won the Cup, a full-blown controversy over the rating of the star boat, *Victory of Burnham*, raised the prospect of Britain having to surrender the Cup.

Earlier in the year, off Florida, what should have been a straightforward six-race selection during and after the SORC turned the US trials into a sensation when the top boat, *Louisiana Crude*, was sold from under the selectors' nose to Sweden and then was found to have a suspect rating. So too was the selectors' second choice, *Acadia*, and the third choice, *Williwaw*. This meant the two reserves, *Stars & Stripes* and *Intuition*, were promoted to join *Scaramouche*, whose reputation had remained as white as her topsides.

Although the names were familiar, they were brand new yachts. *Acadia* was at the opposite end of the rating band to her 1979 predecessor, being a 40ft LOA minimum-rater designed by Frers for Burt Keenan. She was built by New Orleans Marine, as a follow-up to yet another *Acadia*, the intervening 1980 model which had been the leading SORC boat.

That design, a Doug Peterson Serendipity 43 type, based on the Dutch *Schuttevaer*, had been developed into *Louisiana Crude*, owned by New Orleans' Tom Dreyfus with Tom Blackaller steering. As for *Williwaw*, she was Seymour Sinett's fourth of that line, identical to her forebears with electric blue topsides and mast, fine red and white cove lines and pale blue decks. Even the driver was identical – Dennis Conner – though designer Peterson had jumped up in size to 48ft LOA.

Just like previous *Williwaws*, this one had blown right through the fleet with good speed, impeccable preparation and smart sailing.

The rating controversy began before the SORC was finished with *Stars & Stripes*' owner Bill Martin protesting *Acadia*'s rating. He was joined by Pat Malloy, owner of *Intuition*, asking for *Williwaw* to be scrutinised. As both were protests, the owner had to be prepared to pay for the cost of re-measurement, carried out under the supervision of Ken Weller, then the United States Yachting Racing Union's chief measurer. As a result, *Acadia*'s rating jumped 1.2ft to 31.1ft and *Williwaw*'s by 1.0ft to 38.1ft. The wrinkle that had been employed was that both boats were fitted with extra-large water tanks to sink the boats during measurement so that they claimed an IOR Mk 111a credit, which was there ostensibly to benefit older, deeper-gutted yachts. In the inquest that followed, the rating of *Louisiana Crude* was declared void, too – although she could not be re-measured because of alterations – a US measurer was struck off and Keenan punished by the USYRU. One effect of the shake-up was that the Americans came with a lower-rating team than the one they had planned.

The problems with *Victory of Burnham* took longer to run their course and, even when the boat's rating jumped a massive 1.4ft, an inquiry could find no evidence of malpractice. Ed Dubois designed the boat for Peter de Savary's America's Cup team to use as a warm-up campaign. Before she ever went to the States for the 1982 SORC, there had been a feeling in the British fleet that her rating was too good to be true, and Dubois had even given the RORC's rating office his predicted values for the hull depth measurements, at the heart of the matter, because her rating was lower than he expected. But the boat was rated and re-rated before the Admiral's Cup and given a clean bill of health.

*Peter de Savary built* Victory of Burnham *as a warm-up for his 1981 America's Cup bid. Top scorer, she headed Britain's Admiral's Cup win, but not before becoming embroiled in a rating controversy (Guy Gurney)*

Dubois had even deliberately bumped the hull to force another complete measurement of the boat, but her 33.3ft rating persisted, despite Dubois' belief that the higher rating of 33.6ft was probably the best that could be achieved, and even that only after careful optimisation from 34.0ft. He felt that 33.4ft as an opening bid just did not seem right.

The warnings were not heeded. Despite Dubois' own concern that the hull depths did not match the lines plan, that the rating was too generous, and that the selectors themselves raised specific concerns over the hull depths, the RORC rating secretary, then Keith Ludlow, asked for another measurer to give the boat a once-over. Incongruously, this did not include specific instruction to check the forward depth station which was the centre of concern.

It was this omission that led to Ludlow's resignation, and that of one measurer, following the RORC inquiry when the case blew up in Florida later. The American measurers came out with the same higher rating after three separate measuring sessions, including one with Dubois and RORC personnel present. It was conceded that the British measurers and their administrators had got it wrong all along.

Fortunately, the recalculated Admiral's Cup scores dropped *Victory*'s contribution to the British winning total by only nineteen points, leaving Britain with a clear 96-point win. However, the *Acadia*, *Williwaw* and *Louisiana Crude* scandal, plus another case of *Tatoosh*, from the winning 1980 US Sardinia Cup team, it was plain that the game had got ahead of those running it. The complexity of the IOR and the competitiveness of the sailors were such that race organisers and the national rating authorities were given a clear warning to tighten their grip on the sport.

Though there were inklings of what was to come, the British trials were not affected too much. Robin Aisher remembered: '*Victory* was the same size as us and not only did she prove tough to beat on corrected time, but we could hardly get past her on the water. Now we know why!'

Aisher was campaigning his new *Yeoman XXIII*, a Frers 45 similar to *Scaramouche* but built like *Intuition*

from Newport Offshore's latest glued and rivet alloy method. Like composites, this new technology was borrowed from the aerospace industry, the plating so thin it would have distorted if conventional welding was employed.

While *Victory* had been top boat of the trials, only once dropping out of the top three places in nine races, *Yeoman* made sure of her place with two victories in the final races to give Aisher his fourth time on the team. *Yeoman* had been designed before the 15 per cent aft overhang limit had been imposed by the Offshore Racing Council and was caught out. It was originally decided to move the girths outboard, rather than shorten the boat, but after watching the water flow exiting the stern, Aisher took the advice of rating consultant Hugh Welbourn to dock 15in off *Yeoman*'s stern. With trimming and other bumping, the rating dropped from 34.1ft to 33.8ft.

At the time, Aisher confessed himself worried about 'the ability of today's minimum-raters to pull out from the pack in inshore races. That was something we were able to do with *Yeoman XX*, but I don't think it can be done anymore.'

The concern was real enough for, as Britain's captain, he had Brian and Pam Saffery-Cooper's Dubois 40 *Dragon* to consider and, tellingly, her best results were in the high-scoring offshore races. It was the first time that the Saffery-Coopers had brought their considerable small-boat experience to bear in an AC boat, Brian Saffery-Cooper having been Britain's Finn class sailor in the 1968 Olympics. Dubois was asked to update his thoughts, which had progressed from *Police Car* to *Sea-u-later* and *Once More Dear Friends*. Being in the timber business, Saffery-Cooper had the Elephant Boatyard at Hamble build *Dragon* from timber he had selected himself.

Ten new boats, plus the yardsticks of *Police Car* and *Impetuous*, lined up when the Aussies chose their team to defend their hard-won 1979 victory, with two Western Australian yachts proving the ones to beat. Both had a British connection. Alan Bond's Peterson 43, *Apollo V*, had been built from composites by Lymington's Jeremy Rogers, while Peter Briggs, owner

*Like the American team yacht* Intuition, *Robin Aisher's Yeoman XXIII from Britain was built from glued and riveted light gauge aluminium (Guy Gurney)*

of the *Acadia*-type Frers 40 *Hitchhiker II*, was an ex-pat. Skippered by 12-metre helmsman Noel Robins, Hitchhiker was the star, counting five wins and line honours in two of the races. Briggs' seriousness was manifest in the German titanium-stocked rudder from Speedwave and the spare Stearn mast ordered for the boat. Not content with dominating the trials, Briggs wanted to improve *Hitchhiker* further. 'Don't touch a thing!' was Frers' advice.

While lying only sixth in the unofficial points table, Syd Fischer made the team yet again with his new Peterson-designed *Ragamuffin*. Though similar in length and rating to *Apollo*, *Rags* was a more moderate, wholesome and rounded shape. Her late-trials improvement, plus the promise of ballast alterations, crew changes and the recruitment of Lowell North for the Cup, won favour with the selectors.

The Kiwis had no qualms about minimum-raters, choosing two in a team that was also remarkable in all having fractional rigs. Ian Gibbs' *Swuzzlebubble* won a tight series from her hull-sister *Wee Willie Winkie*. Both were Holland updates on the *Regardless* hull, with new keel shapes, stern changes and new rigs. They were able to sail slightly faster than the one Farr minimum rater in the trials, *Feltex Roperunner*, in all but surfing conditions. Possibly the Kiwi trials were the last before Farr's second coming in the early 1980s which was to upset the established Peterson, Holland and Frers order.

They were joined by Evan Julian's *Inca*, an S & S *Obsession*-type hull with a fractional rig and similar to Lou Abrams' *Challenge*, which missed Australian selection despite being third on points. *Inca* had Ray Haslar, Chris Bouzaid of Hood Sails and New Zealand Finn champion Tom Dodson aboard. Gibbs, a top Half Ton class campaigner, counted Dodson's brother Rick, an OK class champion, and Andy Ball, a regular from the British *Indulgence* crew with him, while 1977 One Ton Cup winner Stu Brentall was joined by another OK world champion, Peter Lester, as part of *Wee Willie*'s afterguard.

Having come so close in 1979, the Irish were taking things seriously and being taken seriously. *Regardless*

Peter Briggs' Hitchhiker *passing* Prince Consort *buoy off Cowes. The boat came to England having dominated the Australian team trials but she failed to live up to expectations (Guy Gurney)*

was back for the trials, having just beaten the top British boats in two Solent races after being given extra zip by the expedient of adding a new tube to the bottom of her mast, inserting an extra panel in her spinnakers and adding new links to the bottom of the rod rigging. She was top among the five triallists, followed by Dennis Doyle's Frers 51 *Moonduster*, his latest in thirty-five years of offshore sailing. She'd been built from timber by Doyle's own Crosshaven Boatyard and came out so light that she was way above her marks, rating a full

## GERMAN FRERS

*The Frers family of Buenos Aires could very well be yacht racing's first design dynasty, spanning three generations, whereas the likes of the Herreshoffs, Tripps and Nicholsons petered out after two.*

*German Frers Jr's father was a yachting pioneer in Argentina in the 1930s, while his son, German Jr (Jr) studied yacht design at Southampton University as well as working in the Buenos Aires office and Frers' satellite office in Milan. Frers Sr originally raced cars and motorbikes and when he decided to turn to cruising, he designed his own yacht. That was unusual enough, but to build a small yacht and then sail it oneself with just friends and family, rather than be conveyed by the paid skipper, was near revolutionary.*

*Through a succession of boats, Frers Sr ended up racing Joanne in the 1949 Fastnet, while Fjord III won the 1964 Bermuda. His son grew up steeped in the sea and racing against the likes of Illingworth and the Stephens brothers. After studying Naval Architecture at Buenos Aires university, he was offered a job by Rod Stephens in 1965. 'I didn't need to be asked twice,' Frers remembers, for at the time there was no better place, or a better period, to study yacht design. 'Probably their best time ever,' says Frers. 'I went there thinking that Olin would know everything, but he was always looking for ideas to make yachts go faster.'*

*Frers left in 1968 and worked briefly in Manhattan before going back to Buenos Aires. His contacts while racing and when working at S & S ensured he was not cut off, though it was E Korouek's Matrero in the Argentine team which first brought Frers to the Admiral's Cup. He had four yachts in the 1973 series, including the second highest scorer, Recluta. Since then many famous yachts have come from his board: Noryema IX, Acadia, Scaramouche, Yeoman XXIII, Hitchhiker all made an impact in the Admiral's Cup, while for much of the 1980s the maxi class was all Frers' own.*

2.0ft over the 40.0ft maximum. Tony Castro, who had just left Ron Holland's design office to set up on his own, supervised the bumping and re-ballasting, including lead under the deckhead, to bring the mighty *Moonduster*'s rating down.

The third Irish boat was in fact British, *Woolly Jumper*, being owned by London colour printer John Hogan. A Holland 42, she was the last boat out of Gary Carlin's Kiwi Boats in Florida, which was brought down by a cash flow crisis stemming from the construction of Jim Kilroy's maxi *Kialoa IV*, a pioneering composite 79-footer.

The Italian threat was growing, the storm-tossed 1979 Fastnet having dispelled many beliefs about their heavy-air vulnerability. Italy's owners were prepared to spend considerable sums on buying the best – and that included three Californians as their skippers. Not surprisingly, Italy were rather rudely dubbed the American B team, with Congressional Cup winner Dick Deaver at the wheel of G Borromeo's *Almagores*, Tom Blackaller hot from *Louisiana Crude* steering *Brava* for Pasquale Landolfi, and 12-metre sailor Rod Davis at the tiller of Giorgio Carriero's *Mandrake*, her owner's fourth time in Italy's team.

All three Americans were sailmakers for North. *Brava* was the first Italian-designed yacht in the Cup since the wide and flat *Vihuela* from 1975, the product of Rome's Andrea Vallicelli and built from alloy by Minnefords, the New York yard famous for their *Williwaws*. *Mandrake* and *Almagores* were Peterson designs, the former similar to *Intuition* and the latter slightly larger. Both were built with alloy hulls by Chiavari, topped off by composite decks.

One of the periodic tragedies which seem to afflict offshore racing in Japan's rugged waters stopped that country's plans abruptly. Trials were held at the end of May, with *Togo* and *Unschu* looking favourites for the team until storm force winds took out *Unschu*'s rig and put the boat aground. Her crew took to the liferaft. Two men went overboard from one of the other triallists and one was lost, resulting in the abandonment of the challenge.

Germany appeared menacing for the first time since their victory in 1973. Many of the European yachts spent the early season racing in Solent and RORC events to get fully in step with British conditions, and Willi Illbruck's *Pinta* had won the Morgan Cup and *Dusselboot* the Round the Island Race.

The emerging Hanseatic design house of Dutchman Rolf Vrolijk and German Friedrich Judel played a big role in the German effort. *Dusselboot* (another trade name which went unremarked, despite advertising on yachts still being outlawed) was an alloy minimum-rater of medium-light displacement, her tall fractional rig based on a Stearn three-quarter ton section. She'd been nagging away at higher-rated boats all season long, skipper Uli Libor being fond of hitching lifts on the quarter-wave of bigger boats.

Judel/Vrolijk had also revamped *Pinta* and Udo Schutz's *Container*. *Pinta* was a Peterson update of *Eclipse*, but the Germans reshaped the bow, extended the waterline forward by 17cm, shifted the after girth station and changed the keel. This manipulation of key measurement stations saw *Pinta*'s rating go down from 31.3ft to 30.9ft and shed 300kg in weight: both tangible gains.

The surgery on *Container*, so named after Schutz's industrial container business, was much more radical and involved cutting off the entire underbody. Originally based on Peterson's *Yena* and *Love Machine* design, which had proved successful in the Med and at the SORC, the waterline was again pulled forward, the sections flattened and the run aft made fairer. The result was that *Container* became lighter, longer and with a lower rating, though light-air speed was said to have suffered.

And the means to slip along in the softest of breezes was precisely what was required when the series opened with the First Inshore. When the fleet finally got away after a postponement and a general recall at 1245, the 1800 time limit seemed ominously close in the 4-5 knot westerly. *Hitchhiker* got tangled up with *Scaramouche*, Spain's *Bribon III* and *Stars & Stripes* on the line, with the Aussie boat over the line early to double her difficulties.

*Pinta*, with Flying Dutchman Gold medallists Jorg and Eckhart Diesch in her crew, moved nicely in the soft air on the opening leg from the Hillhead start to East Lepe. *Intuition*'s helmsman, Ron Love, made an inauspicious start by going the wrong side of Prince Consort buoy off Cowes. *Pinta* was first round, after nearly an hour, with *Caiman II* breathing down her neck. *Caiman* was Gerry Jeelof's *Apollo* sister-ship, which had been chartered by the Bermudans with Lou Varney of Stearn UK and Jay Hooper of North Sails running things.

*Intuition*'s agonising run against the tide to re-round Prince Consort was a preview of the fretful second leg,

as the fleet tried to sail downwind and uptide to West Ryde Middle. The boats headed for the island shore, with the wind barely able to turn the cups on their masthead anemometers.

Some fancy new sails emerged from turtles, such as the Norcon floater spinnakers set by Lowell North on *Ragamuffin*. Made of transparent plastic and costing some £1500 at 1981 prices, they flew nicely while conventional ½oz nylon kites hung limply from their poles and halyards.

*German Frers Jr (Guy Gurney)*

Just as things seemed to be shaping up nicely for the Italians, Blackaller left a Cowes Week finishing buoy on the wrong hand as he passed the Royal Yacht Squadron and, unable to get back against the flooding tide, *Brava* retired. Third to forty-eighth through being fifty yards too far to one side!

After West Ryde Middle, the leaders took off for the mainland shore and, at long last, the wind filled in at 1730, allowing the back half of the fleet to lay the finish of the shortened course in one tack and for *Caiman II* to scrape inside the time limit.

The twenty-four-mile race had been reduced to nine, but to Tom Blackaller it seemed reduced to farce.

The fleet averaged less than two knots in their five-hour ordeal. Blackaller, who had both jumped the start gun and retired, gave vent to his frustration: 'The is the worst place in the world to sail. San Francisco [his home] is the second. There you have strong currents, but at least the wind always blows!'

Blackaller opened the floodgates. Edward Heath, observing events, opined: 'It is ridiculous to bring the world's top yachtsmen across the world at great expense and then have them race only nine miles.' The following morning's *Daily Telegraph* was in step with the former Prime Minister. 'Few celebrations in calm Solent… yesterday's first race… a near farce.'

It was fortunate that no team could count three good results, so at least everyone felt equally aggrieved. Amazingly Canada – whose line-up was Bruce Kirby's (designer of the Laser) fractional rigged 40-footer *Runaway*, John Newton's Peterson 42 *Pachena* and Jim Plaxton's C & C 46 *Amazing Grace* – were first on points, followed by Germany, the USA and Italy. The British were a lowly ninth.

A decent 12-15 knot easterly arrived for the Second Inshore race, with *Victory* and *Yeoman* taking first and second places. Starting close to West Lepe, twenty-nine-year-old Phil Crebbin shot *Victory* straight out with a perfectly judged run at the line. In fact Crebbin's starts were to become a key feature of her success. His subsequent breakdown, after the 1987 British America's Cup challenge in Fremantle, robbed British sailing of a rare world-class talent.

*Yeoman* tried to help *Dragon* wriggle free of the congested air after the start, but found it difficult to create a gap without prejudicing her own chances. Aisher, as team captain, had already come to *Dragon*'s aid by helping to buy the Saffery-Coopers a new Kevlar mainsail, which was finished only the day before the Cup began.

Beating into the tide, some boats, notably *Wee Willie Winkie*, made determined bids to reach the slacker water on the shore, dipping many sterns to do so. *Victory* made the shore on one hitch and was right up with the Holland 51 *Midnight Sun*, chartered from Sweden's Jan Pehrson by France's Jean-Louis Fabry – who

had retired the venerable *Revolution* from active duty – with sparmaker Tim Stearn steering.

*Hitchhiker* brought a terrific reputation to Cowes, but found it crashing down around her ears. Harold Cudmore joined Noel Robins for the inshore races, and instead of glory the hot Aussie boat could count from two inshore races only two poor starts, one DSQ and an eleven-place penalty in the second race through hitting a mark. Needing to improve from a dismal first race, Robins had approached East Bramble buoy in the second too low, found Spain's *Bribon* in his way and ended up on the buoy.

After two races she had only six points on the board, her chances of being top boat and helping Australia defend the Cup gone. Aussie team manager Gordon Reynolds was not impressed: 'I'm appalled that one skipper can breach the rules two days running, despite continual warnings that in these inshore races it is better to take a lower place than risk disqualification.' Strong stuff.

The race was shaping up to be a big-boat benefit as well as having the only two decent beats of any of the inshore races. *Moonduster* wasted the chance of line honours by picking the island shore on the beat back to East Bramble, leaving *Midnight Sun* to take the gun, followed by *Victory* eight minutes later. The top two places for *Victory* and *Yeoman* were offset by *Dragon*'s forty-second, but Britain moved up to fourth, with the Irish dropping down when *Swuzzlebubble* successfully protested *Woolly Jumper*, causing her to lose twenty-four places. *Scaramouche*'s fifth, *Intuition*'s seventh and twenty-seventh for the small *Stars & Stripes*, steered by 470 champion Dave Ullman, saw the USA ease into first place, as Canada slipped down to fifth.

Crebbin's starting prowess was on show when the Channel Race got away. It was no mean feat to have clear air in downwind start moments after the gun. A strong ebb tide squirted the fleet west down the Solent and all but *Ra Carat* (Sweden), *Inca* (New Zealand), *Hurrycane* (Sweden), *Mandrake* (Italy) and *Almagores* (Italy) chose to thread their way through the North Channel between the Shingles Bank and Hurst Castle on the way down to Poole Fairway.

*Caiman II was owned by Geerit Jeelof of the electrical giant Philips. Aground off Hill Head in the third inshore race, skipper Lou Varney sent the crew aloft to heel the boat off the bottom (Guy Gurney)*

The fleet set off under an assortment of double-headed rigs, with blast reachers and staysails or the regular No 1 jib on the fetch over to Cherbourg's CH1 buoy, an occulting light where the periods of darkness are shorter than those of illuminations, making it very difficult to pick out against the shore lights. Bruce Kirby found *Runaway*'s chart showed two CH1s, owing to the buoy's position having been moved in 1980.

The first boats were around at midnight on Saturday, navigators choosing whether to go along the French side of the Channel before steering for the Portobello buoy off Brighton or aiming for the English shore first. In the 22-30 knot beat into a lumping Channel sea, the rigs tumbled down on *Dusselboot* and Shorty Trimingham's *Flirt of Paget* (the former New Zealand trialist *Spritzer* and a masthead rig version of *Swuzzlebubble*) in the Bermuda team.

Robin Aisher could sense that all was not well aboard *Yeoman*, for the boat was carrying her No. 2 jib above the normal wind range, and it was found she had a bilge pump hose adrift. A ton of water inside the hull had done wonders for her sail-carrying power.

With *Victory* in sight and a fair stream about to run, Aisher realised a good result was brewing for Britain on the final leg from the Nab Tower to Gillkicker. So it proved, with *Yeoman* fourth on corrected time, *Victory* seventh and *Dragon* coming good with a fourteenth – an important placing, as it was bettered among the small boats only by *Swuzzlebubble*, *Vanguard* (a Hong Kong entry sailed by American Dennis Durgan), *L'Emporda* (Rogers 39 from Spain) and *Stars & Stripes*. Britain shot from fourth to first place, 61 points ahead of Ireland. Just one point separated third-placed Italy and fourth-placed Australia. This was despite *Rags* having been seen to collide with *La Pantera* in the Channel Race, with obvious damage to both yachts. Neither protested, and when *Amazing Grace* did so, she was told she was outside the time limit.

Mist and an apology of a wind made it impossible to run the Third Inshore on its allotted day and proved to those still sore that it would not have been possible to re-run the grim First Inshore had it been abandoned. From Hill Head and out through the Forts to Warner in the Eastern Solent, the fleet had a long beat with a fair tide. *Midnight Sun* again led the way but *La Pantera*, Chris Ostenfeld and Irving Laidlaw's Dubois 46 from Hong Kong, was well in the hunt until she fell in a hole off No Man's Land fort and watched the fleet sail past. Dick Deaver managed to squeeze *Almagores* around Warner just ahead of the larger *Victory* as the fleet set off under spinnakers. The course was shortened, though the final beat against the tide did at least allow the fleet to open up a little – but not before *Caiman II*, having successfully dodged the groynes, windsurfers and bathers on the Lee-on-Solent shore, went aground. Lou Varney had the crew up the mast with a kite set to get the boat off in double quick time. Deaver and *Almagores* won, collecting forty-eight bottles of Mumm champagne for their trouble. Italy looked good with *Mandrake* fourth and *Brava* eighth, until *Brava* was protested.

That was her second knock of the series and, with *Dusselboot*'s dismasting, *Hitchhiker*'s failings and the USA's poor showing in the double-point Channel Race, Britain's rivals were making too many costly errors. Going into the Fastnet, British spirits were high. *Victory* and *Yeoman* stood first and second on the points tally.

Few thought of the previous Fastnet, except perhaps the crew of *Regardless*, who had been put out then by a broken rudder and who, after fifty-five hours, rounded the Rock in seventh place on corrected time. Spain's *L'Emporda*, Juan Pla's sistership to the 1979 winner *Eclipse*, might have had a sense of *deja vu* too, for she was the best Admiral's Cup boat at the Fastnet. At last Robbie Doyle and *Scaramouche*'s crew had their boat going well. They'd discovered an 8-degree heeling error in the compass, which partly explained their Channel Race horlicks, but now they were two and a half hours up on *Victory* and *Yeoman*.

*Scaramouche* was leading boat for boat on the way until forty miles from the finish, when the wind switched off and the fleet bunched at the Lizard. 'We watched mast after mast pop up behind us over the horizon like spring flowers,' said Doyle. From being a runaway leader, *Scaramouche* owed the minimum-raters five hours. What promised to be one of the quickest racers in recent years turned into the slowest and the Time on Time system for calculating the results meant that the longer the fleet stayed at sea, the better the small boats looked.

The twice-daily radio skeds (schedules) showed pitiful progress and the real skill was in maintaining concentration. Californian Gary Weisman on *Regardless* would get the Irish boat moving on the faintest of zephyrs, settle the boat down and strive to hold that speed. Then he would try to accelerate again before holding to capture the new gain. And so on. And so on. It was a test to see who had limitless patience.

Weisman's hours of coaxing paid off with a win, with two Rogers/Peterson 39s – *L'Emporda* and *Incisif III* (Belgium) – taking the next spots, followed by a string of smaller boats. Among them was *Dragon* at eleventh. Having been carried by *Victory* and *Yeoman* inshore, *Dragon* scored in the high-point racers to give Britain their eighth win in thirteen series. 'We would have looked quite sick in the Fastnet without her,' said a relieved British team manager Peter Roberts.

*Victory* was fifteenth, and had *Swuzzlebubble* crossed the line ten minutes later than she did, the Kiwi boat would not have leapt up from seventh place to become highest individual points scorer by one point from *Victory of Burnham*. Still, in view of the rating storm that was to break later, that was probably just as well.

## SHORT TACKS

• The format was still not settled. Don Parr, whose Nicholson 55 had sailed for Britain in 1973, took over from John Roome as chairman of the management committee. At his very first meeting he pondered whether the series really needed three inshore races. It was after all, he reasoned, an offshore racing series. But he was swimming against the tide. An extra inshore race had been included largely for the Australians and New Zealanders, who felt that Cowes was an awfully long way to come for just four races. It was the start of a trend towards a more inshore-race orientated series, which still continues.

• The Club prepares against entries rising to over twenty teams by reserving the right to limit entries.

• Nationality rules are tightened up, calling for 50 per cent of crews on each yacht to be nationals or residents.

• Of the forty-eight yachts, thirty-two had been built in the nine months before the AC. Six had raced in the 1979 series.

FTER TEN YEARS, the International Offshore Rule had evolved to the point where a brand new design did not guarantee immediate success. Construction, sails and crew made the big differences in the boat. And for the first time in ten years, the very latest products of Doug Peterson and Ron Holland failed to make an impact in the important American and Australian trials and were not selected. This was in complete contrast to 1977 when Peterson and Holland were the in-vogue designers, with their yachts *Moonshine* and *Imp* the stars of the series.

The stability must have appealed to G H Mumm & Cie, the champagne house from Reims, who had been supporting the Admiral's Cup for some time but now committed themselves wholeheartedly. When they signed a deal with the Royal Ocean Racing Club to buy the full naming rights to the series, the private challenge series of 1957 had matured to become the Champagne Mumm Admiral's Cup.

Cowes, the Solent and the British summer toasted Mumm's commitment by putting on the best series for some time, and exactly ten years after their first win, the West Germans confirmed their status as favourites, winning by a generous 167 points, the biggest margin up to that point. Italy once again were in the hunt, finishing second, after the USA faltered in the Fastnet.

The Germans' meticulous preparation included the commissioning of two advanced sister-ships and concentrated practice in the Solent and the Channel from June onwards. Encouragingly, much of their resources were home grown: designers, builders, sailors and sails.

Despite the high-point Channel and Fastnet Races being slightly chancy affairs, the Germans sniffed out the breeze and mastered the tidal gates which seemed to be a minefield to other teams. Their line-up included two minimum-rating boats, both 'old' boats built in

1980, and Willi Illbruck's larger 43-footer *Pinta*, which rated at 32.7ft. She was one of a pair a sister-ships designed by Judel/Vrolijk and built by Udo Schutz, using pre-impregnated composites. Schutzwerke's normal fare was industrial chemical containers, but they had diversified into the leisure field with Fanatic windsurfers. Building boats helped prove the technology for his other products, so Schutz installed an autoclave to allow curing to take place under pressure and made the plugs, over which the hulls were made, out of steel so that they remained shape-stable when the advanced laminates were cured at high temperature. So thorough was the *Pinta/Container* programme that an entire hull section was built just for destructive testing.

Imagine Illbruck and Schutz's consternation when *Container* failed to make the German team with a fourth in the points-determined trials. Illbruck was furious. 'I want to win this time. With the team the committee has in mind we have no chance. We can only win with *Container*!' he declared, in what turned out to be a mistaken belief. Chairman of the German selectors was Bernie Beilken, who had led Germany to their first win in 1973, and he stuck to his guns. In a more moderate mood in Plymouth at the close of the series, Illbruck said: 'We had good boats and we sailed them well.'

*Container* ended up sailing for Austria with two other German rejects – *Container '79* and *Espada*, a masthead-rigged version of *Dusselboot*.

After the event, Illbruck was to concede that his fractional rig was 'very fast', for Judel/Vrolijk seemed to have come with the solution to making the rig work on bigger boats over a full range of conditions. 'What we have done is give the boats very tall 7/8 rigs, so that they enjoy the benefits of a fractional boat off the wind and the same upwind power as a masthead-rigged boat.

*Udo Schutz's stripy-hulled* Container *was a member of Germany's winning team, 10 years after her country's first victory (Franco Pace)*

We feel designers have been giving fractional boats too full a stern, so we have employed the symmetrical waterplane more normally associated with the "toprigger",' the designers explained.

The British trials were contested by up to twenty-four boats, including six brand new ones and four with hot track records. Inevitably, when top names such as Robin Aisher, with an optimised *Yeoman XXIII*, was left out – along with Peter Whipp's Welbourn 43 *Panda*, whose trim tab on the keel seemed to give her a good edge upwind on the inshore courses, and Larry Woodell's Humphreys 40 *Jade* – the dockside talk was all of the British B team.

Few could remember a time when the entire team was unfancied. The feeling that the 'other' team were better nagged Britain throughout the summer, though only when it was all over, and the results of the Channel and Fastnet Races were compared, could it be shown that the selected team outscored the pretenders 400 to 367 points offshore.

Tactics and crewing, not boatspeed, pushed the British disastrously adrift. At various times in the Admiral's Cup, each of the British team was ahead of the Germans. And to reinforce the point, of *Pinta*'s sister ships *Container* finished twenty-fifth to her fifth, the Dutch *Pro-motion* finished ninth while her twin, *Formidable*, was fortieth in the Japanese team: the British top scorer, *Black Topic*, was fourteenth while her near-sister *Stormbird* was forty-first.

Who was in this vilified A team from Britain? Few doubted that Graham Walker's Dubois 42 *Indulgence* won her place fair and square as top boat of the trials. Walker, a former rugby player who had made a fortune when his in-store tobacco and grocery concession business was bought by one of Britain's biggest grocery chains, had progressed up through the Half- and One-ton classes and, like de Savary before, was one of the first Britons to run an American- or Italian-style big boat campaign: immaculate boat preparation, rockstar crew and lots of style.

She was the first pre-preg-built offshore racer in Britain and, rating at 32.7ft, she was designed to sail in the clear air ahead of the growing pack of minimum-rating boats. The evidence that the smaller boats sailed fast for their ratings prompted Britain to pick two minimum-raters. The first was *Dragon*, back for a second time and with the addition of Soling and J-24 sailor Colin Simmonds to bring some edge to the boat on the inshore courses. A new keel and other changes had boosted light air form.

The other boat was *Black Topic*, or *Black Top* as she was first known until the RORC thought that was too close to her owner's tarmacadam business and possibly open to protest. Dickson Atkinson bought a production boat, a Stephen Jones Oyster 43, whose prototype, *Stormbird*, had almost won the SORC, and walked into the team ahead of others who had spent years of campaigning custom-built boats. No wonder they were sore, but Atkinson had the right-sized boat at the right time and a useful but not outstanding crew. Ironically, if there was any failure in the Cup proper, it was *Indulgence*'s all-star crew.

The first race did not get away on schedule. First the committee waited for the wind to settle in the western Solent and then too many line-jumpers forced a general recall. Peter Kurts, one of Australia's long-standing offshore sailors and a superb navigator, got it wrong, having to come back down the line under spinnaker. Kurts was passed over in favour of Syd Fischer's *Ragamuffin* in 1981, so his Dubois 39, the aptly named *Once More Dear Friends*, was getting a second chance to prove her worth. *Container* was recalled, too, setting off eventually a full half mile behind the pack. Her reputation was justified when she finished ninth over the line.

The US *Scarlett O' Hara* shot off the line in light airs and was the second boat around the first mark, Gurnard, behind Rolf Gustavsson's *Bla Carat* (ex *Acadia*) from Sweden and ahead of the two other Frers 51s in the fleet – Dennis Doyle's varnished *Moonduster* and Wicktor Forss' *Carat* (ex *Retaliation*).

*Scarlett* had been top boat in the SORC, topping the very competitive Class D. She'd also been the runner-up the year before and was one of the venerable Serendipity 43 types designed by Peterson and built by New Orleans Marine. Owned by Monroe Wingate, she been very carefully optimised by sparmaker Chris Corlett and Dee Smith of Horizon Sails.

*Container*'s comeback was due in part to the breeze which swung to the east and strengthened, but not before two large shifts and some pretty big holes had shaken up the order. *Scarlett*'s team-mate *Locura*, designed, built and sailed by Mark Soveral from the famous Florida boat-building family, nipped during one break in the wind from twentieth to eighth but it

was *Hitchhiker* which won the race. Peter Briggs' Aussie boat was trying to make amends for her ghastly 1981 series and the owner had put together a star-studded crew, including Noel Robins, Hugh Treharne, Dave Forbes and American Robbie Haines.

The British had tried team sailing again, with *Indulgence* noticeably holding on to starboard tack off the start line long enough to put other boats about and give *Dragon* a bit more room to breathe in the congested air

*French America's Cup helmsman Bruno Trouble, with Eric Duchemin at his shoulder, steers his Beneteau One Tonner Coyote, named after the Co-Yacht syndicate which owned the boat (Beken of Cowes)*

*Peter Farlinger's C & C 39 from Canada,* Magistri, *was one of the last masthead rigged minimum rating boats. She beat her more fashionable fractional rigged rivals to be top Channel Race scorer (Guy Gurney)*

*Diva, owned by Patrick Faure and Bernard Moureau, become top yacht despite a blemished record. Soon after the Channel Race start, she ran over a mooring off Ryde Sands (Guy Gurney)*

and chopped-up sea. To no avail. The British points score put them at tenth, their worst showing to date in the Admiral's Cup.

The steadier 17-20 knot breeze of the Second Inshore race allowed the bigger boats to break free of the pack. The impeccably sailed *Scarlett* won (and this in a 1979 generation design), with *Locura* second, something that pleased her owner, George de Guardiola, and Ted Turner, who had been enticed out of retirement to be *Locura*'s tactician.

Placing third on corrected time was Neville Crichton's Frers 43 *Shockwave*, a boat that had sent ripples to Europe from New Zealand with talk of much-vaunted speed. She turned the clock back a bit, for she rated quite high at 34.1ft for a 43-footer, Frers thinking that chasing a low rating could be self-defeating if too much of the go-fast factors were given up in the process. Crichton was incensed to have *Shockwave* built beautifully by Terry Cookson and then be told there was no New Zealand team, despite *Swuzzlebubble* having been the top boat in 1981. So he smartly arranged a charter with a Sydney sparmaker, Mike 'Zapper' Bell. Having made sure of a top three place in the Aussie trials, counting five wins and three seconds in eight starts, the boat did not sail the final race. The Aussie selectors promptly ruled her out, so yet again Crichton had a hot boat in need of team-mates.

The boat's potential, and Crichton's outbursts, goaded the Kiwis into action at last, and Ian Gibbs chartered *Wee Willie Winkie* from Ireland (a sister to his 1981 *Swuzzlebubble*), while Whitbread sailor Peter Blake chartered the Frers-designed Beneteau 456 works boat *Lady B*, which came complete with the very useful Eric Duchemin aboard.

The Americans took a knock for, amongst the eight protests in the race, one went against *Shenandoah*, a slightly unfashionable masthead-rigged 40-footer which was essentially a heavier version of Ron Holland's *Regardless* design but with more sail area. The key attribute of William Palmer's boat was the combination of the 470 sailors, Dave Ullman and Steve Benjamin, running the show.

Mac Baxter's C & C 41 *Charisma* (Canada) had a costly race, being given a 50 per cent penalty following a protest from *Dragon*'s Brian Saffery-Cooper, who had seen *Charisma*'s crew offload her liferafts just before the race's start. But for this simple error in not reading the Notice of Race and the Sailing Instructions closely enough, Canada would have taken third place ahead of the USA by the close. Their best ever result was not to be.

The Channel Race turned out to be two events in one, for a dying wind and a foul tide saw the fleet's leaders arrive off CH1 buoy before dawn on Saturday, after the Friday afternoon start, where they were forced to anchor. By the time the stream switched direction and the wind returned, the whole fleet was among them, the small half tonners in the non-AC fleet included. When the Admiral's Cup boats got back home twenty-four hours later, the small boats were to the fore. 'The results looked like the list of ratings in reverse order', said *Scarlett*'s Chris Corlett ruefully.

The return leg across the Channel was much the same, with yachts kedging off the coast of Brighton and similar agonies being repeated at the finish. Many yachts spent forty minutes inching their way up the last half mile.

The winner was Peter Farlinger's C & C Custom 38 *Magistri* from Canada, which had shown great light-air speed, plus a degree of structural fragility, during the previous SORC. She'd pulled out of the Second Inshore with headstay failure, too, yet went on to finish the series a commendable eighth. Germany took the overall lead with two boats in top spots, *Sabina* placing second and *Outsider* fourth.

*Diva*, Bernard Moureau's Joubert/Nivelt-designed minimum rater was twenty minutes behind *Magistri* on elapsed time, much less time than the French yacht had spent tangled up with a buoy marking a dredger. *Diva* picked the cable off Lee-on-Solent, *par erreur*, soon after the start. It produced a wonderful spectacle: sails downed, crew in the water, and the cable firmly lodged between keel and rudder. *Diva* eventually got free by having one crew standing on the buoy, another on his shoulders, both pushing hard. Despite the delay, the unsettled wind allowed helmsman Yves Pajot to work *Diva* back up to fifth by the Nab Tower.

Having given up starts on the Royal Yacht Squadron line and races within Cowes Week and, having added a third inshore race in 1977, it was inevitable that the RORC should now move one of the inshore races out of the Solent so that the course could set free of geographical limitations.

Thus the Third Inshore was the first ever AC inshore where players no longer trod the hallowed Solent turf, and the Olympic triangle in Christchurch Bay, out west beyond the Narrows at Hurst Castle, gave an even mixture of beating, reaching and running, with a more easily understood tidal gradient across the course. *Shenandoah* had added Chris Moody from Swanwick to supply the local knowledge, while the Australians had recruited Warsash-based designer David Thomas for a full Solent briefing.

With thundery black clouds sending squalls off the land, it turned out to be a shifty affair, and the three Frers 51s plus *Shockwave* – steered by FD ace Murray Ross – made the top mark just ahead of a 20° shift. In one leg, the big boats had the race won, for they continued to get the breaks, twice laying the weather in little more than one tack, with *Carat* winning fifty bottles of Champagne Mumm for Vicktor Forss. At the close, with the big boats home, the wind went light, leaving the bulk of the fleet struggling for power in a sloppy chop.

Bruce Tardrew's Frers 41 *Di Hard*, her KP 1 sail number showing the world she was Papua New Guinea's first ocean racer, was holed by Gianni Bassi's *Primadonna*, a Vallicelli 40 from Italy, which tried to dip her stern only to find the mainsail pinned against the leeward running backstay. The lightweight McConaghy Kevlar carbon hull was left with a gaping hole, and *Di Hard* finished the race only by dint of one man pumping below. *Primadonna* flew the I flag to acknowledge her foul and was duly docked 20 per cent of places by the jury, but many questioned the weighting of the penalties, given that *Shockwave* had been given a 50 per cent penalty for missing one of the no-go marks in the First Inshore. With all three yachts in the top twenty, the Americans moved up to second, some 57 points behind the Germans, who added another couple of points to their lead.

The *entente cordiale* in the French team seemed to be evaporating fast on the aptly named *Passion*, a Joubert/Nivelt 42 which had been built for the cancelled Two Ton Cup at Le Havre. Jean-Louis Fabry brought his *Revolution* crew aboard, but owner Alain Forgeot accused the seasoned sailor of incompetence. Blows, verbal and physical, were traded, and Fabry, who was on the committee of management for the 1983

Champagne Mumm Admiral's Cup, quit the boat with the crew following suit.

*Passion* did not race in the Fastnet, the thirtieth, which was sailed in pretty undemanding conditions. In fact, the only hazard which stood in the way of the fleet was a radio warning to watch for a large, dead whale, although none of the boats reported it.

At last *Indulgence* seemed to come good, for Mike Relling fashioned a great start and had Graham Walker's yacht well up with the bigger boats on the way out of the Solent. Navigator Peter Bruce, who had been aboard *Moonshine* and *Eclipse* in the 1977 and 1979 British teams, was concerned about running out of wind, as the weather picture gave little promise of a decent breeze.

Past Portland Bill, *Indulgence* was leading on corrected time until she made an LTO, the crewman's slang for Long Tack to Obscurity. By going in to Lyme Bay to keep the breeze, *Indulgence*, in fact, sailed right out of it. She spent four hours kedged while the fleet, to seaward, sailed by. Twenty-four hours into the race, the radio sked showed the awful truth. *Indulgence* was forty miles behind the leaders and out of it. Graham Walker admitted: 'Well, yes, our tactics were rather questionable. We seemed to put ourselves in positions where there was no wind.' All this on a boat with the likes of Johnson Wooderson and Peter Bruce, whose combined Fastnet experience would be the envy of the majority of the fleet.

Pasquale Landolfi's Vallicelli 44 *Brava*, back for her second Admiral's Cup, found a lane of breeze which she rode from Land's End to the Rock, where she was first boat round, a full four hours in front of the 50ft *Bla Carat*. Skipper Lorenzo Bortolotti and Australian navigator Phil Wardrop must have been chuckling into their beards.

But as on the way out to the Rock, so the Land's End/Lizard area shook up the standings on the return leg. Harold Cudmore on Frank Wood's *Justine IV* virtually match raced *Diva* round the 605-mile course and showed the French boat the way to the Rock. 'Don't forget I have sailed around this area for a long, long time in engineless boats,' recalled Cudmore of his cruis-ing days. 'So I knew where the favourable tides ran and where the wind could be found.'

*Diva* rounded the Rock minutes ahead of *Justine* and on the run back, when the wind piped up to 30 knots, *Justine* lost track of the French yacht's navigation lights and Yves Pajot's crew got back to Plymouth an hour ahead of the Irish. Cudmore was not impressed. He knew he'd been sold a dummy by the French crew, for switching off your navigation lights to slip away from an opponent was all part of the hard school of Ton Cup sailing.

Cudmore successfully protested *Diva*, who maintained that her lights were faulty. Even with a 5 per cent penalty, *Diva* was top boat of the series, while a fourth for *Sabina*, sixth for *Pinta* and eleventh for *Outsider* reaped yet more points for the Germans, who won with a staggering 847 points over Italy's 680 and the USA's 655.

## SHORT TACKS

• *Sabina*'s owner, Hermann Noack, was a sculptor. Among the things he was responsible for was the restoration of the sculpture on top of Berlin's Brandenburg Gate. He cast much of Henry Moore's work in his foundry.

• Denis O'Neil's *Bondi Tram* had her home port shown on the transom as King's Cross, once Sydney's red light district and still pretty colourful today. Asked about the name, an Australian explained: 'You must've heard the expression "she goes like a Bondi tram"?'

• Crews spotted a rare sight at the Bishop Rock: the lighthouse keeper jogging around the platform.

• At one point the Americans intended to send over seven boats to Cowes to give owners experience of English conditions. That fell flat, though the very fact that it was contemplated says much for the Admiral's Cup's drawing power in the early 1980s.

*Tilmar Hansen's* Outsider *raced in 1981 as* Dusselboot. *A shaft of sun picks her out of a black sky alongside* Diva *(Beken of Cowes)*

THE 1985 RESULTS looked like a a re-run of 1983, with the German team winning by an even more substantial margin – up from 167 to 280 points. Again there was no magic involved, with their boats, *Outsider*, *Rubin* and *Diva G* placing second, fourth and eleventh against the second, fifth and seventh form of their predecessors, to give solid top ten results. None of their boats won a race outright, but again, none of them went anywhere near the protest room or received a penalty for rule infringement.

What was remarkable was that the victory perpetuated an astonishing run of form in Germany's offshore yachting, in which they were Champagne Mumm Admiral's Cup winners in 1983 and 1985, Sardinia Cup winners in 1984 and SORC top boat in 1984.

All three boats were designed by Judel/Vrolijk with German sails and German spars from Reckmann, which were mechanically milled down to give superior results to chemical etching in the quest for a lighter, stronger spar. In design terms, though, the boats were more different than was apparent. Such was the confidence in the German camp that not one of their boats was in the winning Sardinia Cup team the year before. Those boats which did not make the German team took up their accustomed places in the Austrian line-up.

Willi Illbruck's second *Pinta* off the J/V 42 mould, a follow-up to his 1983 boat, was among those sailing for Austria, as was *Container*, Udo Schutz's Mk II version of this design, the main change of which was lightness and a switch to tiller steering. In *I-Punkt*, Thomas Friese had a Mk III type, lighter still with reduced freeboard and sail area, which completed the Austrians' team.

For Germany, Tilmar Hansen's new *Outsider* and Hans-Otto Schumann's *Rubin VIII* were One-Tonners,

which had sailed a patchy series at the One Ton Cup in Poole the month before the Champagne Mumm Admiral's Cup, but had managed a win and a second among the five races. *Outsider*, the lighter of the two, was steered by Star class Olympic silver medallist Achim Griese. Winner of the German trials, she was a narrow boat overall and on the waterline, though markedly bumped around the measurement points.

*Rubin* was a smoother shape, built from pre-pregs by Schutz. In keeping with Hans-Otto Schumann's fascination with the technology of fast boats, he fitted a shark's fin keel, based on concepts from Dornier Aerospace which had been tested at Heidelberg University. *Rubin* was a better all-rounder, less cranky in fresh offwind conditions.

So strong was the performance of this pair that the Germans were not unduly hurt by *Diva G*, Freddy Diekell and Peter Westphal-Langloh's 44-footer steered by Jorn Bock, in a series where small boats completely dominated the proceedings.

The 1985 season was also remarkable for the number of accidents that befell the top names in the sport during the trials. There was no bigger fall from grace than that of Dennis Conner, who was sailing Roger Livingston's Reichel/Pugh designed 42-footer, *Lobo*, in the US trials, held for the first time in Newport, Rhode Island, in place of the SORC. That should have been an advantage to Conner, for he had his two-time America's Cup navigator Halsey Herreshoff with him who, as the grandson of the legendary Nathanael Herreshoff – 'the Wizard of Bristol' – knew the Newport waters like his own backyard. Except that Conner wanted to dodge the tide soon after the start of the final race and headed between rocks known as the Dumplings, through a gap which looked closed on any chart. Tactician Tom Whidden muttered: 'This is the stupidest thing I've ever been involved in,' moments before the impact at a full six knots. Livingston called it a 'dumb stunt', for it cost *Lobo* a team place.

In England, Harold Cudmore and Eddie Warden Owen took Graham Walker's fourth *Indulgence*, a Daniel Andrieu-designed One-Tonner, out for her first

*Germany's defence was very thorough. Here Freidrich Judel, of the Judel/Vrolijk design partnership and rating secretary of the DSV national sailing authority, studies satellite weather pictures in the team office (Jonathan Eastland)*

offshore race, the RORC's De Guingand Bowl, and again were sailing in shoal water to get out of a foul tide. The final tack round the back of the Isle of Wight and out to the Nab Tower was thought to be the race's key move, which would sort out the order of a closely bunched pack of even-speed boats. *Indulgence* was near Bembridge Ledge at 0300 when she hit what later

proved to be *Empress Queen*, a paddle steamer wrecked on the Ring Rocks in 1916. All seemed well until half an hour later when a crewman, going below to fetch a spinnaker up on deck, found water filling the boat fast.

*Indulgence*'s crew were taken off the sinking yacht by other competitors and Cudmore left to make 'the Dear Graham phone call' to the owner, who had not been on board. The boat was a write-off. Walker swiftly arranged to charter another British one-tonner, a Fauroux/Finot/Berret design from Beneteau, which was renamed *Phoenix*. With such a name she could scarcely fail to go on and be top scorer in the AC.

Robin Aisher's new Tony Castro-designed one-tonner, *Yeoman XXV*, which was short on sail area, hit the same wreck three weeks later but she was patched up and chartered by the Irish, who named her *Yeoman of St Helier*.

The British selectors had made a wise choice in picking three One-Tonners: *Panda*, *Jade* and *Phoenix*. Each was well sailed and together they had different but complementary characteristics. Each managed to win a race in the Admiral's Cup, but Britain forfeited any chance of beating the Germans through protests and penalties. Britain went into the Fastnet 60 points adrift of the German total, having already thrown away 84 in the protest room. Then *Jade* lost her mast in the Fastnet and the team that could have won, indeed should have won, still managed to come second by humbling sixteen other nations.

It started to go wrong for the home team in the Second Inshore race when *Panda* and *Yeoman*, sailed by Mark Mansfield for Ireland, ended up in the protest room for a mark-rounding incident. There was real brittleness in the jury room, for the crew of Peter Whipp's *Panda* called one of the *Yeoman* crew as their witness – and immediately regretted it when his evidence did not take the form they expected. *Panda* was docked 52 points, even if there had been no collision.

Larry Wooddell's *Jade*, the One Ton Cup winner, took a 20 per cent penalty when she acknowledged an error against New Zealand's *Canterbury* in the Third Inshore. That, plus *Jade*'s dismasting in the Fastnet, in which she would have faced yet more protests had she finished, sealed Britain's fate. To many it was a tragic waste. *Jade* was a Rob Humphreys design, small and clean, steered by triple Olympic medallist Rodney Pattisson and skippered by David Howlett, an Olympic Finn and Star class sailor and one the best speed and rating technicians about.

She was owned by an American working in London, as was *Phoenix*, whose Lloyd Bankson was employed by Citibank and shared time on the boat with its charterer, Graham Walker. Cudmore had put together a strong crew, signed up new British J-24 champion Eddie Warden Owen as his driver and used the experience of the One Ton Cup to 'finesse' the boat – trading some

upwind speed for better reaching and running form and tinkering with the ballasting, deck gear and sails.

Peter Whipp made the British team at his third attempt, plumping for a Philippe Briand-designed one-tonner on the strength of *Passion 2*'s showing the year before at the One Ton Cup and Sardinia Cup. Where *Dusselboot* pointed the way to minimum-raters in 1981, *Passion 2* surged development forward by turning 40-footers into true offshore dinghies.

Whipp had signed up Lawrie Smith, probably Britain's most outstanding sailor. Oozing talent and outstandingly competitive as soon as the ten-minute gun is fired, Smith seemed to find winning so easy, he

*Larry Woodell's Humphreys-designed* Jade *won the One Ton Cup immediately before the Admiral's Cup but along with her British teammates, failed to fulfil their status as favourites (Guy Gurney)*

rarely put in the hours of slog that others require and, arguably, had sold himself short because of it. Then, and now, it is a Smith characteristic which his peers find at once endearing and infuriating. With Tony Gale as relief helmsman, the selectors slotted in Iain Macdonald-Smith from *Yeoman* to add experience to an

Tonner line up. Thirty-four of the fifty-seven boats in the fleet were rated at or near the 30.0ft minimum. The way the Time Multiplication Factor curve was drawn seemed to be favouring the small boats, while their very number meant that they had been brought to a high state of tune, boosted by the One Ton Cup.

*Graham Walker hastily chartered* Phoenix *from Lloyd Bankson after Harold Cudmore sank* Indulgence *in the British trials. She rose to her name to be top boat (Guy Gurney)*

essentially young crew, while Cudmore followed suit by adding David Arnold as *Phoenix*'s navigator.

The message that small boats were required was well understood. The Americans, who liked big boats, had imposed a 33.7ft rating ceiling on their team, while Denmark, France, New Zealand and Papua New Guinea joined the British in selecting an all One-

Sixteen other countries set out to prove that the series was not a contest solely between Britain and Germany when the First Inshore race got underway in medium airs. A flooding tide and south-westerly wind required short tacking up the island shore. Bill Power's Nelson/Marek 43 *High Roler* was skippered by Gary Weisman who, having sailed for Austria (*Iorana*

1977), Brazil (*Indigo* 1979), Ireland (*Regardless* 1981) and Italy (*Brava* 1983), had made it at last into his own American team. His boat was going slowly until the crew discovered the prop was not aligned correctly.

Lowell North's *Sleeper*, another Nelson/Marek 43 though this time with a fractional rig, found an even better way of going slow when she went aground for fifteen minutes on Mussel Bank near Newton Creek. She had been up with the front runners, such as Peter Kurts' Farr 43 *Drake's Prayer*, which was being steered by six-time 18ft skiff world champion Iain Murray.

By the time North's crew had punted the boat off with the spinnaker pole, she arrived at the weather mark to find herself amongst a flock of one-tonners and clipped one of their sterns. The Americans had already suffered a dismal start, with *Sidewinder* hitting Canada's venerable C & C 47 *Amazing Grace* when the tiller came apart in Steve Taft's hands as he tried to duck *Grace*'s stern. Both *Sidewinder* and *Sleeper* ended up with a 50 per cent penalty. Sidewinder was Jim Pugh and John Reichel's debut boat – they had left Doug Peterson to branch out on their own – and Randy Short's first boat of any sort after he had sold his supermarket business in Australia to Safeway. Taft had also brought along another *Imp* shipmate, Skip Allan, as well as Paul Cayard.

The first beat over, a change in the tide and the course configuration tended to produce short beats with the stream and long runs against it, which suited the smaller boats nicely. Mike Clark's New Zealand Farr one-tonner *Exador*, and Ib Andersen's Niels Jeppeson-designed X-1 Ton *Euro*, from Denmark, were the corrected-time leaders at the mid-point. Each had won one of the previous weekend's Solent Points races, used by many foreign boats as a warm-up.

That's how they finished, split by only a second on corrected time, after a run past the Cowes Green to the Squadron line. It may have frustrated some crews to be bunched right up on the beach instead of having a committee boat finish, but it created one of the most stunning sights from any Admiral's Cup: crowds on the shingle shore, blue skies, white clouds, hard sun, and the world's top ocean racers cheek-by-jowl as they trickled down past the Squadron under spinnaker, the airs full of skippers calling for and denying rights of passage.

A fourth and fifth place from *Phoenix* and *Jade* put Britain ahead of New Zealand by 31 points, with the Germans just behind in third slot.

In the Second Inshore race – sponsored for the first time by Swiss watchmakers Corum – positioning was more important than speed, for the race run in the mid-Solent area saw the fleet split in two after the gun, with the majority taking the mainland shore from the start near Wootton Creek to a mark off Hill Head. *Sleeper*, *Sidewinder* and *Jade* looked good on the Island shore, but no sooner had they struck out to cross to the north side of the Solent than the breeze tapered off in preparation for the sea breeze's arrival.

The two leaders, Vicktor's Forss' Frers 51 *Carat*, from Sweden, and Bill Power's *High Roler*, slipped around ahead of the failing breeze, while the bunch on the mainland shore sailed down the second leg, passing those who had taken the island shore.

*High Roler* went on to win by two minutes on corrected time, with *Euro*, steered by Jens Christensen, runner-up for her second successive race. When she placed equal fourth in the Third Inshore, it made her top scorer in the day races, though not before the dockside mutterers had cast aspersions on *Euro*'s rating for her mid-depth measurement point being bumped beyond a legal radius of curvature. However, no-one lodged a protest.

With *Phoenix*, *Panda* and *Jade* fifth, twenty-ninth and thirty-fifth in the race, a situation created partly by *Panda* having been docked points after meeting *Yeoman* in the protest room, with the jury deciding she had not given buoy room – Britain slumped to fourth with the new leaders, Germany, 40 points ahead of the Kiwis, followed by the Danes.

The Channel Race was bumpy from the very outset and, unusually, there was an upwind start, with the fleet sent west through the Hurst Narrows. With 40 knots across the deck, Lou Abrams, who had made the Australian team at long last in his Frers 43 *Challenge III*, didn't even make it out of the Solent when a spreader failure saw the Zapspar mast crumple. It was a cruel blow for one of Australia's most ardent offshore campaigners, who seemed to have turned the corner and found longed-for success. Abrams had just won the Sydney-Hobart race at his twentieth attempt and had twice been pipped for an Admiral's Cup team berth prior to 1985.

Portugal's *Bigamist*, the old Castro one-tonner *Justine*, also lost her rig and ran into further difficulty when she was offered a tow. Having agreed a price, the launch's owners then claimed salvage and had a writ attached to the boat's mast. The dispute meant *Bigamist* failed to complete the series.

Those boats which held together had a very fast race, whose course incorporated a small triangle on the French side of the Channel. But with a run against the tide, and reach all the way back, the small boats revelled in the fresh going. In a 200-mile race, there were only fifty miles of beating and running, the rest was reaching. On the leg over to France, *Sidewinder* watched a One-Tonner hitch a lift on her quarter wave for a free tow but then break off to sail on her own – faster. *Sidewinder*, rating a full 2.5ft higher, promptly latched on to the quarter wave of the smaller, faster-moving boat! The British made amends with first, second and eighth for *Jade*, *Panda* and *Phoenix*, which hauled them back to second place, still 15 points off the German lead.

Once again the Third Inshore was in Christchurch Bay, and with the moderate north-westerly blowing over flat water and the worst of the tide left behind inside the Solent, it proved to be a great leveller. The Americans were able to give their bigger boats their head to be top team on the day by a full 50 points over the Germans. *High Roler* was third, *Sleeper* fourth and *Sidewinder* sixth, proving that the designs, sailors, sails and hardware which had made the USA the powerhouse of ocean racing in the 1970s and early 1980s was still very much alive in 1985.

There was no keeping the good small boats down, with Cudmore and Owen fashioning a win for *Phoenix*, and the young Cees Barnard bringing Geerit Jeelof's *Caiman II* to a well-earned second for the Dutch team.

**OPPOSITE:** *Brazil's* Indigo *(formerly Bert Dolk's* Pro-motion*) leads Irvine Laidlaw's* Highland Fling *from Hong Kong and Tilmar Hansen's* Outsider *from Germany (Franco Pace)*

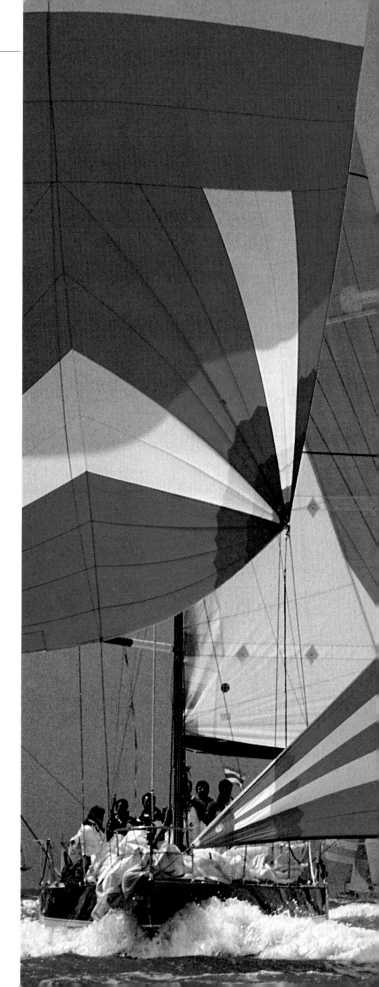

If the Channel Race had been breezier, then the Fastnet was more robust. The attrition rate was astonishingly high, with only three of the eighteen teams bringing all three boats to the Plymouth finish: Ireland, Australia and, of course, Germany. Of the entire RORC fleet, only 84 yachts finished out of 222 starters.

Peter Kurts' *Drake's Prayer* broke her main halyard soon after the start but, in true Aussie battler fashion,

*Pasquale Landolfi's Vallicelli-designed One-Tonner,* Brava, *heading east into the setting sun after the Channel Race start (Franco Pace)*

the halyard was repaired and *Drake's Prayer* put to sea again. You could almost hear Kurts utter the name of his last boat: *Once More Dear Friends*.

That combative spirit was lacking in the US team. The wind gradually backed during the first night at sea, giving a fast reach down England's south coast, before a front came through the next morning, the wind piped up and the seas built. *Sidewinder*, chock

## PIET VROON

*The record of Dutch shipowner, broker and manager Piet Vroon is matchless. He has competed in thirteen successive Admiral's Cups between 1963 and 1987 and – with the exception of 1985, when* Formidable II *was dismasted in Plymouth Sound, within sight of the Fastnet finish line – every race in the every series has been completed.*

*For the first fifteen years of racing, Piet Vroon raced yachts designed by Frans Maas. Maas was the helmsman on Vroon's boats and a boatbuilder from Vroon's home town of Breskens on the Schelde estuary. He designed* Tonnerre de Breskens *(1963, 1965, 1969 and 1969), plus three different* Standfasts *(1971-1977). In 1979, Vroon bought Chris Dunning's Ron Holland-designed* Marionette *and raced it in that series as well as 1981. For his last three Cups (1983-1987) he campaigned* Formidable, *a Dubois 44 which was built as one of a pair of sister ships, the other for fellow-Dutch shipowner Bert Dolk. Apart from 1983 and 1987, Vroon has always raced for the Netherlands and competed in three Onion Patches in the USA and three Sardinia Cups besides his Admiral's Cup campaigns.*

*He is an unashamed member of the old school. 'Since the change from amateur sailing to professionalism, the event has lost a lot of interest for the Corinthian competitors. I believe in a new form it could be revived, although it might take quite some time before it reaches the interest we used to have.'*

full of stars such as Skip Allan – who'd done four Admiral's Cups on *Improbable*, *Red Rooster* and *Imp* – decided enough was enough. The US were not going to win, so why battle for another 500 miles? They retired to Plymouth.

Paul Cayard did not sail the Fastnet, because that weekend he was due to marry Icke Petterson, daughter of the famous Volvo P1800 car designer and America's Cup skipper. 'When we struggled to put the marquee up in the garden I thought, those guys in the Fastnet are going to get a real blow,' remembers Cayard.

Lowell North needed no excuse as *Sleeper*'s mast broke, annoyingly, when she was lying second. It seemed the wire seizing on the spreader tip had worn through and the shroud jumped off, leading to catastrophic loss of lateral support. *Jade* lost her rig too, when a rigging terminal broke, while the New Zealand *Epic*, sailed by Peter Walker and Peter Lester, dropped her rig in a squall near the Rock. That left the poor Kiwis with the dubious distinction of having lost the

rigs on all three of their boats during their visit to England for the One Ton Cup and the Admiral's Cup.

*Panda* was one minute behind *Outsider* at the Rock, but the Briand boat loved the blast reach back to the Bishop to finish thirty-three minutes ahead of the Germans, and eleventh boat over the line to win the race overall. It was tough going, though. Gary Weisman reported that on *High Roler* they must have dropped reefs in and shaken them out at least thirty times, with five or six sail changes per four-hour watch in the squally Irish Sea section.

*Outsider*'s second, *Rubin*'s fifth and *Diva G*'s ninth meant that the toast in Plymouth was 'Prost'!

## SHORT TACKS

• Among the AC boats, Peter Kurts' *Drake's Prayer* was the first Fastnet casualty when she limped back with snapped main halyard. It just wasn't the pale grey boat's series. She'd been holed, too, before the start of the series by colliding with a buoy whilst out tuning and had broken a shroud in the Channel Race. Little wonder she'd been dubbed *Drake's Repair*.

'EH' IS A KEY WORD in the Kiwi vocabulary. Its one syllable and two letters are full of meaning and can be used in every conceivable circumstance. So when Brad Butterworth muttered 'We won, didn't we, eh?' from behind mirrored sunglasses and underneath a baseball cap, you knew he was over the moon. For 1987 was the year when the New Zealanders achieved what they had long threatened since their first challenge in 1971: the double – the Cup and the top-boat slot with *Propaganda*, sailed by 'Billy' Butterworth and his boys.

Their effort was uncommonly like the German bids of 1983 and 1985 – a home grown-effort based around a small group who had all the right skills. New Zealand yachting was, and remains, an illusion. Although in the 1980s the Kiwis won virtually everything worth winning, this giant in sailing is actually a country of only three million people. And while the Kiwis are boat-crazy, having one of the highest per capita ownership rates in the world, there is scarcely any grand-prix IOR sailing at home to speak off.

On a roller-coaster of success, the Kiwis had won the World Youth Championships, five medals at the Los Angeles Olympics, had made the Whitbread Round the World Race their own, won the Kenwood Cup and made an indecently impressive debut at the America's Cup.

In 1987 at Cowes, they beat the Germans and twelve other nations at their own game. They came with the best-prepared team; their boats had excellent speed and the sailors were good enough to sail a textbook series which minimised risk and maximised points. Only *Propaganda* seemed to have an extra cutting edge with her phenomenal upwind form.

Don Brooke, the team manager from the Royal New Zealand Yacht Squadron, was not exaggerating when he said: 'We believe we won the Cup twenty-four months ago. We sat down and got contributions from everyone who had been involved in the Champagne Mumm Admiral's Cup and had monthly meetings at the Squadron. Our big job was to change the triallists from enemies into friends.'

So the Kiwis put in a full twenty days practice in Auckland's Waitemata harbour before coming to the UK, and then had another twelve days sailing in British waters, with video analysis to bring crew technique and sail shapes to race-readiness. They even sailed a practice overnight race in the Channel, something few teams had contemplated before. The squad were coached by Californian Rod Davis, who by then had put his roots down in New Zealand through marrying the sister of ace sail designer Tom Schnackenberg. He prepared their programme, advised on sails, suggested new gear and moved crew around. John Clinton, the sail designer for the *KZ-7* 12-metre, came over to England to re-cut the sails, though Rick Dodson thought the Kiwis had anticipated British conditions pretty well. Dodson, who had been *Swuzzlebubble*'s mainsheet trimmer when she'd been top AC boat in 1981, was now skippering Mal Canning's Laurie Davidson-designed one tonner *Goldcorp* (ex *Mad Max*).

No mean sailor himself, with five America's Cups and an Olympic gold and silver medal to his name, Davis was worth listening to. 'I am the catalyst to help them figure out how to do things. You win the AC by putting three boats in the top ten or twelve places in every race. You do that by not breaking anything, by not doing anything stupid and by staying outside the protest room – no bogies, no double bogies, no sand traps!' Admittedly, Davis had good ingredients with which to work. *Goldcorp* had been re-vamped and stripped out by Dodson and Davidson, to be turned into the winner of the New Zealand trials.

*Brad Butterworth, Peter Lester and Bevan Wolley guided the Farr one-tonner* Propaganda *to the top slot in New Zealand's first, and only, Admiral's Cup win. Racing here in Christchurch Bay, she leads Spain's* Anquin's Too *(Guy Gurney)*

She was joined by *Propaganda* which, as a new boat, had struggled to make the team. Terry Cookson had built the boat lighter than anticipated, with the effect of making her too stiff. Normally this is desirable, but as a speed-producing factor it is penalised under the International Offshore Rule, so that *Propaganda* rated 31.2ft instead of the 30.5ft objective. A hasty bit of keel surgery was required to get the rating down and the boat into the team, for it was clear the potential was there. *Propaganda*'s sister ship *Fair Share* failed to win a berth, so her skipper, Peter Lester, joined *Propaganda* as helmsman to free Butterworth as tactician, the job he'd done on *KZ-7* in Fremantle.

So 1987 was really a trial between the three Kiwi boats and three British. Each pushed the other to greater levels of competition, shown by the fact that all six boats in the two teams were among the nine highest points scorers when it was all over.

In the first race, both teams scored the same points, to lie sixth on the leader board. Britain came out top in the Channel Race, though *Propaganda* was overall winner. The Kiwis turned their deficit into a lead after the Second Inshore had left them one point behind Britain. Britain failed badly in the Third Inshore, leaving the home country 109 points behind before the Fastnet. Despite careful cover, Britain were the top scorers in the series climax, but could only take 25 points off the Kiwi lead. It had been a classic battle.

They were closely matched teams. Alan Gray's Farr One-Tonner *Jamarella* was much the same as *Propaganda*, aboard which Lawrie Smith and Rodney Pattisson made a powerful team: Smith's virtuosity combined with Pattisson's matchless powers of concentration. Pattisson's ability to keep a boat in the groove, especially at night, is legendary. In the Fastnet Race the boats rarely lost sight of each other, trading tacks, gybes and sail changes for more than 600 miles, *Jamarella* enjoying an edge offwind, especially when it was light, and *Propaganda* looking the sharper on the wind.

The Kiwi big boat was named *Kiwi*. She was run by a group headed by Peter Walker, who had been an associate of designer Bruce Farr when his office was still in New Zealand. Compared with previous Farr

**OPPOSITE:** *This knock-down in the Irish trials shot Richard Burrows' One-Tonner* Jameson Whiskey *straight into yachting magazines around the world before the Admiral's Cup even started (Rick Tomlinson)*

44s, such as *Drake's Prayer*, *Kiwi* was longer, heavier and had a much less distorted hull. She also had lower freeboard and a noticeably less pronounced coachroof. In comparison with her near sister from Australia – Peter Kurts' new *Madeline's Daughter* – Walker claimed his boat was heavier and stiffer, yet was pitched more towards reaching and running. In her 'brains trust' was Rick Dodson's brother, Tom, and Tom Schnackenberg.

With five boats in their trials, none of them comparable to *Kiwi*, the boat was worked up in a vacuum. 'We used the velocity prediction program supplied by Bruce and George Hazen. We knew they were good and we had faith in them,' said Walker, adding a new element to the 1980s' offshore vocabulary: the VPP, or the designers predicted speeds for the boat on different angles of sailing in different wind strengths.

Lined up against *Goldcorp* was Mike Peacock's *Juno III*, a Rob Humphreys design that sought to retain *Jade*'s staggering two-sail reaching speed while adding some upwind poke. Peacock had been the launch controller of the BBC 2 TV channel before starting his own video film making business and his partners

included *Monty Python*'s John Cleese, and Anthony Jay, who scripted the popular *Yes, Minister* and *Yes, Prime Minister* comedy shows.

For his third time on the British squad, Graham Walker had built a 44-footer, using the same French designer and builder – Daniel Andrieu and B et B of La Trinite – as had produced his doomed 1985 one-tonner which had sunk in the trials. Cudmore, Warden Owen, Arnold and the others were back in a light boat with a modest sail area. With fair lines and rounded entry, *Indulgence* was a great reaching boat, but made her crew work hard to get her upwind. For this group the Champagne Mumm Admiral's Cup was gentle therapy after the Fremantle America's Cup, where they had campaigned *White Crusader*.

Though the number of the teams had dropped to fourteen, there were some outstanding boats in the fleet and others that were, well, interesting. Take Belgium's *Val Maubuee*, a 44-footer which had failed to make the French team, despite Yves Pajot's best efforts and odd flashes of great speed. Some thought her the ugliest Admiral's Cupper ever – high-sided, angular, ungainly, scalloped in the area of maximum beam and featuring an odd little ledge on her transom to carry the backstay. She was the work of Guy Ribadeau-Dumas, designer of Philippe Jeantot's 60ft *Credit Agricole I* and *II* in which he'd twice won the BOC solo round the world race.

New designs and sponsors' largesse were no guarantee of success. Compare the success of the Kiwis who, apart from shipping assistance, enjoyed relatively little backing, with the relatively poor showings of France, Denmark and Germany.

Denmark came with an all X-Yachts team, designed by Niels Jeppesen and built by his company. The One-Ton design, which originated in 1984, was given its latest tweak and built from epoxies to appear as *Andelsbanken*, sponsored by the Andels Bank and owned by Denmark's main BMW dealer, Victor Greulich. With a lighter construction, which meant that she had more sail area and a smaller keel area, she was guided by helmsman Peter Kampmann and tactician Jens Christensen. At the series' end, Greulich was unsure whether

*Jean Pierre Dick's* Centurion *and the Italian Navy's* Merope *are balked after the start of the First Inshore race by press, marshall, TV and the French team support boats (Rick Tomlinson)*

the new epoxy boat was any faster than his polyester 1986 One Ton Cup winner.

She was joined by Poul Jespersen's replacement for X-1 Ton *Krone*, the new Two-Tonner *Original Beckmann Pletfjerner*, sponsored by a German stain remover for whom Jespersen was the Danish agent. It seemed that this sponsorship had done wonders for sales of such an unglamorous product. Both Niels and Lars Jeppesen were aboard, along with Ib Andersen, the man who had guided *Euro* the series before.

Jens-Erik Hoest won his team berth with the old Judel/Vrolijk 43 *I-Punkt*, chartered from Germany, but the selectors gave the nod to build an *Andelsbanken* clone, called *Stockbroker Lief Jensen*, to keep the team's aggregate rating down. While the Two-Tonner looked good inshore, with devastating upwind speed, the One-Ton boats suggested that a shape which was more pinched around the rating points than newer designs had had its day.

The French, too, had shaped a strong challenge, with the backing of a group of sponsors headed by TV and audio manufacturer Tompson ECF and dubbed 'Objectif Admiral's Cup '87'. The French got rolling with early training, points-only selection in both British and French waters, and a full support team that was the envy of many others. Yet despite the success of French sailors in the smaller Ton Cup classes and several new boats sailed by factory works teams, their One-Ton boats were old faces from 1985. Bruno Trouble was back with his old Beneteau One-Tonner *Coyote*, renamed *Xeryus*, while Jean Pierre Dick had bought the former *Jade*, renamed her *Centurion Musclor*, installed Laurent Delage as skipper and won the French trials by a clear

## I-PUNKT CHEATING

The 1987 series was sullied by revelations that the German One-Tonner which sailed for the Japanese team, Thomas Friese's I-Punkt, made illegal use of water to boost her stability, and hence her upwind speed.

The Australian, Andrew Cape, blew the whistle on I-Punkt during the One Ton Cup in Kiel, a few weeks after the Admiral's Cup. The boat's paid hand, Tom Swift, arranged the electric bilge pump so that it could draw in water rather than expel it, an elegant means to pick up water which others were doing more crudely. His idea was to fill collapsible water containers and stack them on bunks on the weather side; the bags could be knifed and disposed of before the finish and a possible inspection. Their 250kg was equivalent to three extra crew on the rail and was used in the Channel and Fastnet Races during the Admiral's Cup and the first race of the One Ton Cup. Cape first realised what was happening when he heard the pump running at the leeward mark in the Channel Race. 'I asked what was going on and the crew told me. It happened in front of me.'

The effect was devastating. A mediocre boat gained 0.2kt of speed. 'We came from pretty much last one-tonner to second in one leg,' remembers Cape. New Zealand skipper Rick Dodson remembers his Goldcorp being passed. 'It was extraordinary – a performance never repeated in the inshore races!'

A ban was imposed on Friese, Cape and Swift by British, German and Austrian authorities, on the basis of clear violation of the International Yacht Racing Rules. But twenty months after the whole sordid affair, Friese retained a Liverpool solicitor and commenced civil proceedings against the Royal Yachting Association to take them to the High Court.

His case was that the RYA's hearing into the I-Punkt's use of water ballast did not comply with the required standards of natural justice. The incident still turns stomachs amongst Britain's yachting administrators, for Friese's contention was not that he was innocent of the charges, but that he had been called to the hearing at such short notice that he'd had insufficient time to take counsel and prepare his defence, that the offending water pump was installed by the builders of the yacht and that the RYA's ten-year ban was plainly at odds with the eighteen-month ban imposed by the DSV, his own national authority.

Cape does not blame Friese. His paid hand presented him with the idea to get even with other boats doing the same or which were crewed by expensive stars. In a culture of 'if the other guys are doing it, it must be OK', it may have been an easier choice than sanctimonious critics declared.

The alarming point is that this boat was found out. Ever since the 1974 One Ton Cup, crews have been moving heavy objects to windward side, and tacking the sails below decks was almost a common practice. At the time of I-Punkt, and even afterwards, paid hands who knew exactly what was going on maintain that several prominent European team yachts used jerry cans of water to boost sail-carrying power.

It cost Cape a lot in solicitors' and barristers' fees to prevent the RYA from slapping a ten-year ban on him, as well as in potential earnings. 'Those who know think it was a honest thing I did, but a lot of others still label me a cheat,' says Cape. For exposing a malpractice he did the sport a service, but was offered no immunity from prosecution, yet the following year, indemnities were offered in an offensive against cheating. 'But there's no doubt it improved the sport a lot,' says Cape. 'It's much cleaner as a consequence.'

The ramifications of the case were profound. It demonstrated to the IYRU that, if violation of its rules were proven, it did not have a mechanism in place to impose a binding worldwide ban on offenders. That drove the Union to create such a body, though it took considerable time while they considered questions of liability should an athlete bring civil proceedings against the Union. For that reason, the term Disciplinary was removed and Tribunal inserted in the new commission's title, and the Union took soundings from other international sports federations to ensure the sailors understood the contract: if they competed in yachting under the IYRU rules, then they agreed to be bound by those rules, with transgressions open to agreed review and sanctioning procedures. Given the quick resort to the courts by Olympic athletes banned for alleged drug abuse, the IYRU's caution in creating a means to deal with its own offenders is understandable.

**ABOVE:** *Thomas Friese (white hat) was banned from racing after revelations of using water ballast to boost performance of the his 1987 One-Tonner* I-Punkt *(Gilles Martin-Raget)*

margin. The one no-holds works project which did make it was *Corum*, a Philippe Briand Two-Tonner developed jointly by Beneteau and Swiss watchmaker Corum. Yet for all this effort, the French were to end up eighth overall and *Centurion* maintained her form to be their best boat.

No fall from grace, however, was bigger than that of the Germans, victors in 1983 and 1985, but a disappointing fifth of fourteen in 1987. At 1642 on 5 August, their hopes foundered in Christchurch Bay. The fourth weather mark of the Third Inshore was the problem area, for *Diva*'s helmsman, Bernie Beilken, found the path to the layline blocked by Austria's *Pinta*, *Original Beckmann* and Italy's *Marisa Konica*. Beilken tried to tack underneath and squeeze up to the mark, attempting to extract height out of a low-area/high-lift keel before it was working efficiently. He failed.

When the German One-Tonner, *Saudade* came up to the same mark a few minutes later, she too pressed the self-destruct button. Helmsman Uwe Mares underestimated the tide carrying boats on to the mark so that *Saudade* brushed it, and when Mares rerounded he managed to baulk other yachts. That evening, back at the jury room in Cowes, *Diva*'s indiscretions dropped her from sixteenth to twenty-fourth place and *Saudade*'s fall from grace was from twenty-sixth to forty-second place. Germany had committed the cardinal Admiral's Cup sins: risks, mistakes, protests, penalties.

Fortune's wheel had started to turn backwards for the German *wunderteam* long before all this. Those with any sense of fate could have said months previously that the Germans were not going to win. Peter Westphal-Langloh's *Diva*, for instance, had made the team with only a few weeks in the water before the trials. Did this point to blazing speed against the fully worked-up *Rubin X* and the new *Pinta*, or had the J/V big boats run their course and now required a re-think?

*Diva* then picked up debris in her propeller while passing through a narrow channel *en-route* to England, ran aground, and spent a night on the sands off Helgoland as a consequence. Her keel was straightened back to true with hydraulic jacks, but she was not 100 per cent right. Nor was Beilken, who was ill for the

*The Fastnet race finish moved from Millbay Dock to the Royal Western YC's new home in Queen Anne's Battery in Plymouth (Rick Tomlinson)*

first race, and the aggressive style of Achim Griese, hastily recruited to the cause, did not sit well with the rest of the crew.

The other boats, ironically, were undone by their preparation. Albert Bull had wintered *Saudade* in Palma, Mallorca, which gave her great speed in 15-20kt conditions. *Container*, a new style of J/V One-Tonners, had experience of 5-10 knot and 25-30 knot breezes only from the German trials, and it took her crew until the middle of the third Admiral's Cup race to get their VMG (Velocity Made Good) numbers right.

Helmsman Gerd Eirmann liked plenty of weather helm, something that did not match the keel's characteristics. The crew finally found that by easing the running backstay, the rig was de-powered, the keel working better and the VMG came up to target by jumping a full three-tenths of a knot.

'Our problems were experience,' claimed Rolf Vrolijk, sailing aboard *Container*. 'The conditions in England were not normal. We are still amateurs in Germany and it shows. We have normal jobs to go to and when we reach a peak with our boats we forget about the basics. Sailing as amateurs doesn't work any more in competition this intense.'

Intense would be the wrong word for the First Inshore. As if by tradition, there was a hold-up for the wind to settle. A new departure was a committee boat line, with beats to start and finish the race, so that bunched finishes off the Squadron were now a thing of the past. Of the fancied teams, only the Danes acquitted themselves well over the twenty-four-mile course sailed in a 6-9 knot north-westerly.

As they sailed in mid-Solent close by the Bramble Bank, the flat water and light air suited the big rigs on the Jeppeson boats to give the Danes the opening day's lead. *Beckmann* was top boat on what was largely a big-boat day, given the amount of uptide work. The Kiwi *Goldcorp* was over the line at the start and suffered ghastly chop and disturbance from the spectator fleet. *Full Pelt*, a proven Dubois light-air design which had been chartered by the Irish, placed thirteenth with *Jamarella* the other top one-tonner at fourteenth.

*Indulgence* covered herself ingloriously by taking a

flyer whilst lying ninth on corrected time. Splitting from the pack who were hugging the mainland shore on the spinnaker run from Kemps, she looked for a freshening and freeing wind. Instead it backed and lightened. 'There's no logic to it,' Harold Cudmore was forced to admit.

But Walker, Cudmore, Owen, Arnold and Co redeemed themselves in the Channel Race, which had been turned into a multi-leg zig-zag course specially with the Champagne Mumm Admiral's Cup in mind. The fleet headed out of the Solent through the Hurst

*Lawrie Smith aboard Alan Gray's* Jamarella *had a series-long duel with New Zealand's* Propaganda, *outscoring her Kiwi rival in the First Inshore race and Fastnet finale (Franco Pace)*

Narrows to the west, past the Needles to Poole Fairway, before heading back east past the bottom of the Isle of Wight and completing two small triangles using the Nab Tower, Owers and mid-Channel EC2 buoy and heading back into the Solent from the east.

The aim was to give a good mix of conditions, making the Channel Race less of a small-boat benefit, but a breeze veering to the west ended up giving plenty of reaching, much to the One-Tonners' delight. *Indulgence* was down on speed when weed tugged open her

*Italy's* Merope *leads the Danish X-1 Ton Stockbroker* Lief Jensen *round the weather mark during a Christchurch Bay race* (Franco Pace)

propeller at night, but the Andrieu design came into her own on the way back from EC2 for the second time, surfing happily under spinnaker for minutes on end. In a leg less than two hours long, she took a staggering fifteen minutes out of the larger Reichel/Pugh designed *Sidewinder*, which John Bertrand sailed superbly for the American team. *Indulgence* was the only big boat in the top twelve, with *Propaganda* and *Jamarella* taking first and second, split by just sixteen seconds.

*Sidewinder*'s team-mate, Bob Towse's *Blue Yankee*, was last boat home, despite being a Judel/Vrolijk 43-footer. She finished under trysail and No. 5 jib after Steve Benjamin and Dave Ullman, the combination from *Shenandoah* in 1983, struggled along with only the top of the rudder remaining. The rest of the blade, built by Germany's Rudi Magg, split open and fell apart.

With *Jamarella*'s second, *Juno*'s seventh and *Indulgence*'s eighth the British team moved up from sixth to first. *Juno*'s result was commendable, for she'd been

hampered by ankle-deep water on the surfing spinnaker run back from EC2, owing to a failed gasket around the engine strut drive.

The Second Inshore was the first of two races out in Christchurch Bay, but the wind blowing off the hot sandy heathland was patchy. The Kiwis turned in a top team performance, with *Propaganda* taking another win, backed up by *Kiwi*'s third and *Goldcorp*'s tenth. *Propaganda* was starting to establish herself as something a little special. She was deliberately more upwind-orientated than other Farr One-Tonners, but the way she lifted clear of the pack marked her out. *Jamarella* and *Juno* had a middling race, simply by being part of the pursuing pack and being forced to go round the outside of the bunch at the gybe between the reaches.

Amid all this assembled talent was *Ritec Poinciana*, the same 1985 Briand one-tonner sailing in the same, lowly, Belgian team. She earned her place in dispatches by dint of hopeless leeward mark rounding: not only did her crew manage to lasso the buoy when they dropped their spinnaker, but one of them slipped overboard.

In the Third Inshore, Britain's *Juno* came a cropper at the same mark that had already been the undoing of Germany's *Diva* and *Saudade*. With a moderate sail plan and small keel, *Juno* had been hampered by getting into the pointing contests with the Farr and J/V boats, but at last Andrew Hurst and Tony Gale bit the bullet and ducked past a few sterns to claim some clear air.

Unhindered, *Juno* had started to move, until Hurst and Gale got into a push-me-pull-you tussle with the tiller. Hurst was down to leeward and called for Gale to duck under *Stockbroker* as they went into the mark, but Gale wanted to tack underneath without realising *Centurion* was sailing in the Danish boat's wake. With Gale trying to push the helm down and Hurst forcing it back up with his foot, *Juno* T-boned *Centurion*, which was rather ironic really, since *Juno* was *Centurion*'s spiritual successor in design terms, and the French boat, as

*Jade*, had already been T-boned in a matching place on the opposite side in the 1985 One Ton Cup. *Juno* took a 20 per cent penalty.

It was an unhappy race for the British team, for they started at the right hand end of the line and sailed for the beach, confident in their knowledge of the waters where many of the trials had taken place. It was a disastrous move in the unstable conditions. 'We couldn't believe when all three boats went for the right hand corner,' said *Kiwi* skipper Peter Walker, for clearly there was no scheme to cover the New Zealanders. Alan Gray was forced to admit that it wasn't until the Fastnet that the British had a game plan. 'We had been trialling in Christchurch Bay and therefore we all thought we could win the race individually. It was a coincidence we all went right, for although we had frequent team briefings there were no team tactics.'

It was another big-boat day, sailed in an 8-16 knot south-westerly, which resulted in only two one-tonners

*Randy Short's Reichel-Pugh-designed* Sidewinder, *unmistakable with her flouro-pink spinnaker, was the most consistent of the higher rating boats along with Peter Walker's Farr 43* Kiwi, *racing down towards the Needles (Kaoru Soehata)*

making the first ten. They were, of course, *Propaganda* at sixth and *Goldcorp* eighth, getting there thanks to their upwind edge.

The USA took a 1-2, with Dean Tank's masthead-rigged Nelson/Marek 45 *Insatiable* sailed into top spot

The Irish Sea section of the race was the vital part, for approaching Land's End the wind was still out to the north-west, indicating a long slog upwind to the Rock. But a front was forecast to bring more breeze and take it round to the south-west, tempting some boats to sail

*Wet, exhausted and drained, the Kiwis emerge victorious at the end of the Fastnet (Gilles Martin-Raget)*

by Gary Weisman, followed by Randy Short's 45ft *Sidewinder*, notable for her shocking pink spinnakers and 'lamb chop' keel profile. The Kiwis scored a massive 220 points for the day to lead the British by 109 with just the Fastnet remaining.

low. As it turned out, being on the rhumb line, or slightly right of it, paid off because, for once, the best way to the next mark was to sail straight towards it.

*Irish Independent/Full Pelt*, steered by Tim Good-body but still with the bulk of Stephen Fein's British crew on board – including Ed Dubois, Jo Richards and Graham Deegan – two-sail reached to the Rock while those who went to the west looking for the shift sailed needless additional miles. Being able to sail fast on the rhumb line was a right and proper home advantage, the Irish in *Pelt*'s crew reckoned. They went on to win, but since the main prizes were not yet awarded to sponsored yachts, the Fastnet Trophy went to second-placed *Juno*.

By clamping a tight cover on the British boats, the Kiwis ensured their win, despite the British being the heaviest scorers in the race. Even so, Britain only marginally narrowed the gap on New Zealand to 84 points.

The loser was undoubtedly Italy's *Marisa-Konica*, who was dismasted on the return leg by a shroud failure. She had been lying second on corrected time at the Scillies and could have finished fifth boat overall in the series but for the accident.

## SHORT TACKS

• To swing the balance back towards bigger boats, the RORC adjusted the Time Multiplication Factor curve used to generate the time allowances, which converted elapsed times into corrected time results, and imposed a 95ft aggregate rating for the three-boat teams. This snuffed out the fast-growing trend towards teams consisting solely of One-Tonners.

• Kiwi team manager Don Brooke said of his team's victory : 'It was dedication which brought us this win, along with the support of three million people and sixty million sheep!'

• So serious was the New Zealand effort that non-alcoholic beer was served at their pre-Fastnet barbecue.

• The contentious Rule 26, banning sponsors' advertising, was relaxed, with the result that many brand names appeared on hulls.

*Lawrie Smith (Rick Tomlinson)*

It was in 1989 that the Champagne Mumm Admiral's Cup reached its zenith under the International Offshore Rule. The fourteen-team entry was of exceptional quality, the racing was superlative with just 18 points dividing the Danes from the winning British team, and the decline which was beginning to affect parts of IOR racing had not shown itself among the Admiral's Cup fleet.

An important change for the British was to place one of their best sailors ashore. Harold Cudmore had been a leading light since 1975 for various Irish and British yachts from *Irish Mist* to *Indulgence*, but for 1989 he was given the budget and power to mastermind things from the dockside. 'For 1989, the relative sizes of the three boats were going to be decisive, because of the combination of the development of the bigger boats and the changes to the TMFs,' Cudmore explained.

So it proved. To curb the ascendancy of the one-tonners, the RORC shifted the TMF curve again in favour of the larger sizes, because the minimum-raters still appeared to be enjoying a disproportionate level of success. In 1985 it was obvious that an all one-ton size was the way to go. For 1989 the balance of power had shifted so much that an all-50ft team was the ideal combination, but few appreciated that fully before the series – except perhaps the Danes, who fielded two of them in their team.

At first the changes seemed slight. The redrawn TMF curve would give a 50-footer an extra forty seconds per hour over a one-tonner compared to the 1987 values. These would work out at something like an hour during a four-day Fastnet race, whereas in 1987 the top one-tonners had beaten the best 50s by about four hours.

The British team was chosen only after the most acrimonious of selections. It was thought all along that the team would comprise Graham Walker's Andrieu one-tonner *Indulgence*, Mike Peacock's Castro 45 *Juno IV* and Alan Gray's Farr 50 *Jamarella*, for these were the only new, specially built boats and the calibre of the alternatives was moderate. But in reaching the point where the team was named, Cudmore travelled the bumpiest road imaginable.

Gray built *Jamarella* expressly to try out the newly established 50ft World Cup circuit and because he felt that the TMF changes could produce a 50-footer which was not just a useful team yacht but potential series top scorer. 'Bruce Farr, Morgens Brinks (the Danish manager) and myself were the only three people in the world who thought a 50 could do it,' claimed Gray, a London haberdasher, at the end of the series.

Peacock was drawn to the mid-size because it was the vacant slot, for beneath him Graham Walker already had a well-advanced plan to try to win the One Ton Cup in Naples. It was a case of unfinished business for Walker, who had been twice runner-up and once third in the event. Absences in France for tuning up with her hull-sister *CGI* and for the Italian event meant that *Indulgence VII* was unavailable until very late in the UK trials.

The selectors told Walker this was risky, but that if *Indulgence* finished in the top three of the fourteen-nation, twenty-eight-boat One Ton Cup fleet she would probably have earned her place. This caused much hue and cry over supposed secret deals. With Cudmore and Walker close from America's Cup and Admiral's Cup campaigns in the past, it was the simplest charge to level but the hardest one to answer. If people chose not to believe the denial, there was nothing Cudmore felt he could do about it.

Foremost among the angry brigade was Andrew Hurst, skipper of the 1987 *Juno* and now running

*Guided by the two lights denoting the transit on the Royal Yacht Squadron's line, Mike Peacock's*
Juno IV *counts down the final seconds before the Channel Race start (Beken of Cowes)*

*Hitchhiker II*, Peter Briggs' one-tonner which was a strong fourth in the Australian trials. As the old 1987 *Jamarella*, which had been successfully updated, she made a late but convincing case for inclusion.

Matters came to a head in June. Few overseas boats came to the UK, so the selectors realised late that they had better send their boats to Kiel Week, the last part

*King Harald of Norway's* Fram XI *heads the one tonners' charge from Jockey Club,* True Blue, Propaganda *and* CGI *(Beken of Cowes)*

of the German and Danish trials, to measure them against the opposition, a reversal of what had become the norm in the 1970s and early 1980s. The new *Jamarella* was showing exceptional if patchy potential and her selection was never in doubt – especially when Lawrie Smith was released from his obligations to the Rothmans Whitbread Round the World race maxi to

join the young Irishman, Gordon Maguire, at the back end of the boat. *Jamarella* had a great crew, with the likes of Lou Varney in her aftergaurd, and Smith brought an extra edge.

Gray was determined to make an impact in his second Admiral's Cup campaign. Not only had he chosen the biggest class to build, but had hired professionals to sail. He formed British Performance Sailing, which had many of *Jamarella*'s crew on the payroll. Some even had company cars. It was only a small step from there to organise a pre-Admiral's Cup warm-up event, the BPS Regatta, whose four days racing in the western Solent and Christchurch Bay was universally enjoyed.

Though the selectors had said they favoured *Indulgence* and *Juno IV* to join *Jamarella*, *Hitchhiker II*'s crew were gunning for either of their berths. *Indulgence* did not go to Kiel, being back at the B & B yard in La Trinité for alterations from her light-air Naples trim to British mode. *Hitchhiker*'s crew were making more and more vocal jibes, and they seemed to have a case when *Juno IV* finished last of the main British trial-lists in Kiel.

*Juno IV*, launched late, had looked good in a breeze but slow elsewhere. A keel-swapping exercise reduced the boat's stiffness and rating, but also made her seem slow against the German 34-raters in Kiel. Yet Cudmore stuck to his guns and selected her, as well as the absent *Indulgence*. 'Going to Kiel proved to be a pivotal decision that contributed to the success of the team,' said Cudmore, 'because there the contenders quickly realised their problems.'

He picked *Jamarella* and discarded the claim of Robin Aisher's older 50-footer *Yeoman XXVII* (ex *Great Expectations*), because with only four or five more 50s expected to turn up in Cowes, any races which favoured small boats would disadvantage a team with two 50s. *Indulgence* was selected because of her top three results in Naples but, as only a single One-Tonner was sought, the nod went against *Hitchhiker II* to the apparently mediocre *Juno IV*.

'The third boat was a difficult choice and the selectors were in a quandry,' admitted Cudmore when he justified his team choice, 'as the bigger boats were proving to be more successful with the new TMFs. Within the mid-size category, *Juno*'s performance had been disappointing. *Hitchhiker* was a proven boat with a proven owner. *Hitchhiker*'s performance at Kiel was good. *Juno* was in extreme rating mode, more similar to the smaller Kiwi boats, which was wrong for Kiel and wrong for the Admiral's Cup. Whether in correct rating mode she would be more competitive·was unknown. Size was the deciding factor, and *Juno* was selected.'

The *Hitchhiker* and *Yeoman* crews remained bitter, especially having been asked to prove themselves, which they did by beating *Juno*. RORC commodore Jonathan Bradbeer, himself a seasoned Cup campaigner from *Moonshine*, *Eclipse* and *Indulgence III*, had already intervened once to calm the selectorial waters. Now he found that once the team had been named, past commodore and team captain Robin Aisher approached him directly to have the selection overturned.

To 'Brad' this must have been distressing, for a kinder-intentioned man would be hard to find. At a crisis meeting of the UK flag officers it was noted that 'the main problem was that plans for selection changed as the season progressed. Unfortunately not enough notice had been given about the changes, or not everyone had been thoroughly consulted in order to ensure that short-term changes would be acceptable.'

The flag officers listened to the allegations of *Indulgence* being indulged, but could find no sign of a 'special relationship' between Walker and Cudmore, and felt 'it would be wrong to take action without evidence'.

As was so succinctly noted in the final minute of the meeting which investigated the acrimonious trials: 'This last issue might be looked at as choice between the maintenance of confidence, trust and respect on the one hand, and the philosophy of winning is everything, losing is nothing, on the other!' For effect, an exclamation mark was added. There are not many of those in the minutes of the Royal Ocean Racing Club.

The net result was that the British realised they had only a month to tweak their boats. Tony Castro planned a longer, lower boom for *Juno* to increase sail area by 5 per cent, as well as the removal of 200kg of internal ballast to reduce stability, plus further bow-down trim to offset the consequent rating increases.

In the German camp things were little better, for they had long stuck to a strict points format for their

*Graham Walker's Andrieu-designed One-Tonner was at the centre of a contentious British team selection, but victory healed any wounds (Beken of Cowes)*

trials to avoid the comebacks of a subjective system. Two 44-footers, the Judel/Vrolijk-designed *Rubin XI* (Hans-Otto Schumann) and the Reichel/Pugh-designed *Pinta* (Willi Illbruck) garnered the right amount of points, but Udo Schutz's new 50ft *Container*, another Reichel/Pugh design, was disqualified

Andelsbanken's crew had to put behind them the disappointment of a broken headstay during the long inshore race in Christchurch Bay. Until then, the Danes were on track for their first-ever win (Gilles Martin-Raget)

from the last race as a premature starter, leaving *Beck's Diva*, another J/V 44 owned by Peter Westphal-Langloh, to claim the third place.

Everyone knew that it was an inappropriate team, simply because it comprised three 34-raters. It was an all-the-eggs-in-one-basket approach at a time when not one pundit had suggested that the two-ton size was the right basket. When they got back to the dock, the owners took a straw poll which indicated that *Container* was favoured for the team – but the results sheet could not be not overturned by the DSV.

Germany's loss was Denmark's gain, as the Danes welcomed *Container* into their team. They already had two One-Tonners in their line-up, *4K* and *Stockbroker*. *Stockbroker* was a new Jeppeson boat which placed third behind *Indulgence* in Naples, yet now she was discarded. Henrik Soderlund, a member of the Diamond Sails' triumvirate with Ib Andersen and Jens Christensen, switched to *Container*, along with Christian With. That left *4K*, a classic Farr One-Tonner, which was steered by Poul Ricard Hoj-Jensen, head of the Danish North Sails loft and a superb Dragon, Soling and quarter-ton competitor.

While the Judel/Vrolijk grip on the German team faltered momentarily, the X-Yachts/Diamond Sail combination, which could already count several Three-Quarter Ton Cup wins and a One Ton Cup victory

through the mid-1980s, manifested itself in a new 50ft *Andelsbanken* for Victor Greulich. Jens Christensen skippered the Nomex, carbon fibre, epoxy hulled boat, which was post-cured in an oven – the Danes' most ambitious project to date.

Australia and New Zealand had put together useful teams. Having last won in 1979, the Aussies were hungry to turn a run of reasonable teams into one capable of victory. Peter Kurts returned with *Madeline's Daughter*, his Farr 43 from 1987 which had been sailed in the trials by Peter Gilmour but was skippered in the Cup by Iain Murray. Kurts' boat had been well ahead on points in the first set of trials in Australia, along with John Calvert-Jones' Farr 50 *Great News*, the design successor to *Great Expectations/Yeoman XXVII*, but the light second series saw the flock of eight-tonners dominate the points. *Great News* was discarded, picked up by a grateful American team, leaving Lawson Klopper's *True Blue*, another Farr 40, skippered by Gordon Lucas and counting top New Zealand match racer Chris Dickson in her afterguard.

Ron Elliott's Farr One-Tonner *Joint Venture III* featured another Kiwi in her crew, with 1984 Finn class gold medallist Russell Coutts joining Colin Beashel, who had sailed on the *Australia II* and *IV* 12-metres for Alan Bond. Coutts was signed up late from the Kiwi team, where he'd been named as reserve, because *Joint Venture III* was widely regarded to have underperformed in the Naples One Ton Cup.

From next to nothing in the way of a domestic IOR fleet, the Kiwis had to conjure up a world-class team to defend the trophy won in 1987. Luckily they had *Propaganda*, which after being top boat in 1987 seemed simply to carry on getting better by winning four out of five races to take the 1988 One Ton Cup in San Francisco. Her sister-ship, *Fair Share*, which missed selection in 1987, was dusted off and the pair engaged in an America's Cup-style two-boat sail, rig and appendage testing programme that showed considerable potential. *Propaganda* was owned now by Tim Bailey and the two-boat programme was made easier by having Rick Dodson steer her while his brother Tom ran things on *Fair Share*.

Michael Fay and David Richwhite – merchant bankers who started off by being sub-sponsors to Peter Blake's *Lion New Zealand* Whitbread boat in 1981-2, before backing three Kiwi America's Cup campaigns – answered the call for a third boat by building a new Farr 43. She was called *Librah*, after their wives Sarah and Libby, and during the BPS Regatta in Lymington had looked formidable in the hands of Peter Lester and Rod Davis.

While this was a creditable team from tiny New Zealand, all momentum had expired in the USA. The sometime world's greatest yachting nation seemed to have lost all interest in the IOR, bar the exclusive and expensive 50ft and maxi circuits.

The American team had all the hallmarks of having been scraped together. Randy Short maintained his interest by chartering *Great News* from the Aussies and signed on Tom Blackaller to be her skipper. Irving Loube had got back into the frame by building a Farr-designed *Bravura* for the 1988 One Ton Cup in San Francisco, a boat which still looked sharp in Naples in the hands of Robbie Haines, the man from the North Sails' Huntington Beach loft, with whom Rod Davis and Ed Trevelyn had won the Soling gold medal in 1984.

The First Inshore was the only Solent race in the programme. Eddie Owen made a blinder of a start with *Indulgence*, bravely coming into the line on port and then tacking round with under a minute to go. This kept his speed on and allowed him to clear the line ahead of boats stacked up above him, as *Indulgence* made for the island shore against a young flood tide. After a leg over to Yarmouth, the course brought the fleet back to the mainland shore. It wasn't until the end of the first triangle that the fleet spread out according to rating, the Two-Tonners taking a noticeably long time to wriggle free of the smaller boats.

However, a break in the wind late in the race overturned the big boats' good deeds. *Joint Venture* sailed a remarkable race, having been eighth boat round the first mark, and still held the corrected-time lead when the wind vanished. *Jamarella*, which had led the whole way round, managed to cling on to take the race by nearly two minutes from *Librah*. Owen performed his second

piece of cheek in the day by wriggling free of the One-Ton pack, when the breeze failed, to take third place.

Australia topped the table with a fourth, tenth and thirteenth for *True Blue*, *Joint Venture* and *Madeline's Daughter*. Britain were three points behind, *Jamarella*'s and *Indulgence*'s first and third offset against by *Juno IV*'s twenty-sixth. Skipper Mike McIntyre, frail on a

*Bruce Farr (right) and his engineering partner Russell Bowler (Rick Tomlinson)*

### BRUCE FARR

*In the words of Sir Michael Fay, a patron through three America's Cup campaigns: 'I believe Bruce Farr will be seen as one of the dominant, if not the dominant designer of the century, as great in the twentieth century as Herreshoff was in the nineteenth century.'*

*High praise indeed. By the late 1980s and early 1990s, Farr had the lion's share of the IOR boat market, the Whitbread business and the winner's titles, and was in huge demand by production builders and America's Cup groups. He was as big as S & S in the 1960s and 1970s. In particular, he'd made the One-Ton class his own, winning the 1987, 1988, 1989, 1991 and 1992 titles. Only in the 50ft class and the America's Cup class has the Farr hegemony been dented and only then, argue some, because of the strength of individual campaigns rather than design. As the IMS becomes the de facto grand prix rule, Farr's boats are in front again.*

*All this from a man who walked away from race boat design in the late 1970s. By then, he'd already taken the Quarter Ton Cup with 45° South (1975), the Half Ton Cup with Gunboat Rangiriri (1977), the Three Quarter Ton Cup with Joe Louis (1977) and the One Ton Cup with The Red Lion (1977) which, added to Larouge's 1991 Two Ton Cup win, makes Farr the only designer with a full house of Ton Cup titles.*

*What incensed Farr were rule changes made by the Offshore Racing Council. Only the Farr style of distorted sterns were clipped for the 1978 season, but the following year centreboards and his light and long approach were curbed by a displacement:length factor. His One-Tonners shot up by 2ft of rating overnight. 'What the hell are we going to do?' he asked himself at the time.*

*The answer was a walkabout. Farr all but stayed away from IOR design for four years. A sailor since childhood on the north shore of Auckland's harbour and a teenage prodigy in the skiff class, he now concentrated on production boat design and setting up a new base in Annapolis, Maryland.*

*In 1982 he stamped his authority all over the race boat world once more with the One-Tonners Pacific Sundance and Exador in the vanguard. They proved that Farr had been right all along, that the fractional rig which he'd put on Titus Canbe back in 1971 was right for IOR boats, as was light displacement and a skiff-like approach to construction, gear and weight saving.*

*Disenchanted once, Farr is now in the thick of rules administration, sitting on the ORC's International Technical Committee and a speaker of forceful delivery and undoubted influence. 'The problem is that the administration is deciding a course which isn't popular with the people for whom it is intended,' said Farr of his long-running battle to get the rule-makers in step with the owners of race boats.*

*His impact on the Admiral's Cup simply reflects what his boats had done elsewhere: top boats in the 1987 (Propaganda), 1989 (Jamarella) and 1991 series (all three class winners).*

*British triple Olympic medallist Rodney Pattisson joined fellow Olympian Robbie Haines*
*aboard Irving Loube's American One-Tonner Bravura (Gilles Martin-Raget)*

congested start line, was boxed in and never recovered.

It was not a happy day for Tony Castro. *Juno IV* was his only new boat in the series and no designer wants his creation at the centre of the wrong kind of attention, as *Juno* had been in the trials. He hoped she'd redeem herself once the racing began. Never afraid to speak his mind, Castro had described the criticism of *Juno*'s selection as disgusting. 'I think the people who used to go hare coursing now chase sailors and designers. It affects the crew's performance. You can rubbish a racehorse and it just goes on eating hay, but these guys read newspapers. If you get labelled a dog boat, it has a very bad effect on everyone.'

Questions over the rating of some boats, particularly the Kiwi One-Tonners *Fair Share* and *Propaganda*, blew up between the First Inshore and the Channel Race, when the Australian team lodged a complaint against them as well as *Full Pelt* and *Turkish Delight*. A technical protest, it centred on the update to hulls aft which did away with sloping transoms in favour of a more upright profile. Old boats without the feature made alterations so that they could carry their crew further aft, but did so in the belief that this would not affect their 'hull date'.

In the four days the fifteen-strong measurement squad spent checking the yachts before the series, they knew of the Australian concerns over alleged alterations to the Kiwi boats' working decks. RORC chief measurer, Tony Ashmead, wrote to the jury: 'After lengthy investigation and discussion, their objection has been reduced to the two New Zealand boats. Both yachts submitted valid certificates from their national authority to which they have been check measured and a facsimile letter has been received from the New Zealand chief measurer stating that the after decks of both yachts were altered prior to 1/1/89.'

But the matter did not end there. National Rating Authorities around the world had been giving different interpretations to hull dates and it needed the International Jury to ask the deputy chief measurer of the Offshore Racing Council, who administer the International Offshore Rule, to make a ruling. Keith Ludlow was categoric. 'IOR 110.3 prohibits voluntary changes to the hull other than to the keel, skeg and rudder without the allocation of a modified hull date.[1] This meant small increases in rating for the yachts concerned and a rescore of them in the results.

Tony Castro must have been relieved by *Juno*'s form in the Channel Race for though twenty-fourth place was not outstanding, it was enough, for coupled with *Jamarella*'s third and *Indulgence*'s seventh, the British boats harvested enough points to be second best in the race and move into the series lead.

As in the First Inshore, the 34ft-raters found themselves in the no-man's-land between the one-tonners and 50s, and *Juno* worked hard to take thirty-eighth place among forty-two boats in the first half of the race. The Danes were top team with *Andelsbanken IV* second, *Container* fourth and *4K* fifteenth.

*Jamarella* had led the 50s down to Poole Fairway, but lost time when an hour was spent prodding weed off the rudder blade. Crucial to the 50s' dominance was that every tidal gate was open in their favour. After they'd pulled clear of the start, they didn't see the rest of the fleet until they headed for EC2 for the second time, having rounded the Nab Tower and the Owers.

The race winner was Ryouji Oda's *Will* from Japan, a boat so new she was sailing in only her sixth race, while the Kiwis and Aussies took knocks in the protest room. *Fair Share* lost 12 per cent of places for failing to keep clear of *Jamarella* at the start, while *Joint Venture* received a 48 per cent penalty.

British corporate strength was displayed in the Second Inshore, sailed in moderate Christchurch Bay conditions. They moved further ahead with 99 points, one point more than Argentina, at the bottom of the table, had managed in all three races thus far. *Jamarella* also moved to the head of the individual points table.

Three general recalls were needed to get the fleet away, with Rick Dodson getting the best in the start that counted. *Propaganda* was round the first mark in twelfth place and was still snapping at the heels of the 45ft *Pinta* after three hours of racing.

The Germans again had mark-rounding difficulties in Christchurch Bay, perhaps a flashback to two years before in another *Diva*, while *Pinta* also managed

to round one leeward mark with her headsail half up and spinnaker streaming aft. After they had finished last in the opening race, the German effort looked psychologically crushed.

*Juno IV* scored her best result so far when 1988 Star-class gold medallist Mike McIntyre took over the helm from Falmouth sailor Jonathan Money to perform the jobs of both helmsman and tactician. *Juno*'s eleventh, which split another second for *Jamarella* and seventeenth for *Indulgence*, was a good result considering the time she'd lost on the last run. Trying to shake off

*The Admiral's Cup fleet beat west out of the Solent in the Fastnet Race finale (Guy Gurney)*

*Librah*, the crew attempted a gybe set but managed to get the main boom tangled in the running backstay. The ensuing broach tore the kite and *Juno* was bareheaded while a new spinnaker was fetched up from below decks and hoisted.

The British were looking good at the halfway stage, as was *Jamarella*'s dominance. That's how it stayed, despite British humiliation in the Third Inshore, in which *Jamarella*'s third was the exception. *Juno* was twenty-first and *Indulgence* twenty-seventh. There were mitigating circumstances, for a too-short delay for the breeze to fill in saw a massive shift on the first beat, which meant that the first triangle was not correctly orientated at all. The information coming back from coach boats up at the windward mark made it obvious that the race had been got away prematurely, their wind readings at 30° variance to the committee's. Worse still, down on the start line the spectator boats had not been moved when the gun went.

The day developed into a classic Christchurch Bay sea breeze to show what might have been a day later. The Philippe Briand-designed *Corum* from France and her sister ship *Mandrake-Krizia* from Italy placed first and second, owing largely to having clear air for much of the race. It was the only time the Two-Tonners topped the results in a series where the 50s were taking it in turns to win.

It seemed inevitable that the Danes would eventually take a first and second with *Container* and *Andelsbanken*. What better place than Hayling Bay for the new Long Inshore? This was a forty-miler, made all the more interesting by a mid-beat gate and Z-shaped reaching legs, which served to keep the fleet together and give crews plenty of work to do at the corners.

Sure enough, the Danish threat materialised, with *Andelsbanken* leading through the gate, pursued by *Container*. In a building sea breeze and the fleet sorted into rating sizes, there was every indication that the Danish thrust had come. But near the end of the second beat, *Andelsbanken*'s forestay failed at the top. Unknown to the other yachts, her crew had already stabilised the mast with two halyards forward and the boat bore off down the run. That gave Christensen, Jeppesen and Greulich thinking time, but the inescapable conclusion was that to beat back upwind would risk losing the whole mast, with no chance of repair or replacement before the Fastnet. So, instead of rounding the leeward mark, they carried on back into the Solent, to Cowes, and retirement.

But for that, Denmark would have gone into the Fastnet just 14 points behind Britain and, as the results turned out, quite possibly could have won the Champagne Mumm Admiral's Cup, as they had promised to do several times before. *Andelsbanken*'s break worried the other 50s to check their forestays and, indeed, similar problems were found – time bombs waiting to go off. The problem was the terminal fitted at the top of the stay was not articulating properly, the fitting not having been designed for the pronounced mast rake and high runner loads that the 50s were now putting on. Several of the fittings on the other boats were discovered to be so fatigued they would not have lasted the Fastnet.

The concluding Fastnet was shaped by two of the great names in the sport: British triple Olympic medallist Rodney Pattisson, who had signed on to the American One-Tonner *Bravura*, and Californian Tom Blackaller, the man with the movie star looks who loved fast boats, fast cars, fast talking and a few more of life's vital ingredients.

Pattisson told his American team-mates that two times out of three it pays to give Portland Bill a wide berth. It certainly did in 1989, for while the fleet was kedged behind the headland, waiting for the ebb tide to run, Blackaller and *Great News* were making hay offshore, going out sufficiently until they could tack back and lay Lyme Bay. *Great News* had a good story: she'd gone out on lift and come back to the coast on another lift. Worth twenty miles, Blackaller reckoned.

While the position reports came in over the radio, the progress of *Great News* and *Sagacious* did not trouble the fleet. The USA were not even considered contenders, yet those whiling away their time in the media centre worked out that the Americans could actually win if *Bravura*, then the leading one-tonner after four races, could score another good result.

As the bulk of the fleet cleared the Lizard, so they left behind them the light and shifty breeze. Going across the Irish Sea to the Rock, the wind built as did the sea, and the crews changed down to smaller headsails. The race become less tactical and more one of preserving boat and sails. The wind piped up to 45 knots and the two-sail straight-line reach down the 145 miles back to the Bishop was wet and miserable. Water was all over the deck, with rain squalls offering no relief to crews perched on the rail.

GREAT NEWS
FASTNET 1989
Tom Blackaller

## SHORT TACKS

• The small-boat hegemony was curbed by changes to the TMF curve, the addition of a fourth inshore race and a reduction in the points loading on the Channel and Fastnet Races.

• *Will*'s owner, Ryouji Oda, was in the textile business. Among the futons he supplied were those to the Japanese Imperial household.

*Polaroid autographed by Tom Blackaller moments after winning the Fastnet Race with John Calvert-Jones's* Great News. *Blackaller died of a heart attack a few weeks later*
*(Jonathan Eastland)*

The small boats were accelerating down the waves to the extent that their mainsails were taking a hammering on the leeward shrouds. Reefed down, they were snapped full of wind one moment and feathering the next as the apparent wind jumped about. *Indulgence*, which had been set the difficult task of covering the Kiwi One-Tonners, used a trysail to save the mainsail from its battering.

From the Bishop, the fleet bore away and roared all the way home. First into Plymouth was *Great News*, giving Blackaller a memorable victory which was made poignant by his death just six weeks later when he suffered a heart attack while motor racing. *Jamarella* was fourth, to become top boat, while Alan Gray, as team captain, had to wait ten hours for the One-Tonners to finish to determine if the Danes had unseated the British. With *4K*, which had sailed without a watching cover from the British, placing tenth, *Indulgence* had to be no worse than twenty-fifth for Britain to win. She made it to take twentieth place on corrected time. 'This time it all worked,' said a relieved Cudmore, his plan having won the game.

*S*TATISTICS TELL THE whole story of the first series in the 1990s. The number of countries entered was the lowest since 1965. Of the twenty-eight overseas countries who had competed in the Admiral's Cup only France, the Netherlands and the USA had sailed in all but one of the seventeen series to date. At their seventeenth attempt the French finally savoured victory.

At first it seemed a gloomy prospect. The Dutch were absent, their line of attendance since 1959 finally broken; the Kiwis could not come to try to regain their crown; and the failure of Sweden and Ireland to raise teams made it seem like a party without old friends.

In one of those conundrums for which the fragmented sport of sailing is famous, the RORC had chosen a new team format for 1991 which actually made it more difficult for countries to assemble their teams. Hatched on the back of the fourteen-strong 1989 series, where the fleet had naturally coalesced around the One-Ton, Two-Ton and 50ft bands, the RORC decided that the event would be better served by requiring teams to field one boat in each rating band.

At a stroke this introduced level rating into an event traditionally built around teams of mixed handicaps. It made racing more exciting for competitors and more easily understood by observers, simply because the order in which the boats stood on the water would be the order in which they would appear in the results. No more conversion of elapsed times into corrected times, no more trying to figure whether or not a boat was saving her time in mid-race. At any time, anywhere, it would be obvious how the fleet stood, and, by adding each of the three boats' placings, any team's progress could be totted up in seconds.

The flaw in the plan was a major one, and it remains a moot point whether the RORC's Admiral's Cup committee of management could have foreseen the declining

interest in IOR boats, which then coincided with a world economic slump. The RORC had grown accustomed to the fact that their event was one of the very few for which owners still launched boats. At the end of the 1980s, only the One Ton Cup and the 50ft World Cup had that sort of drawing power, and even then many boats had a second Admiral's Cup purpose in mind.

Fortunately, quality made up for the shortfall in quantity. Indeed, even in the heyday of nineteen teams in the 1970s, the series was decided amongst a handful of teams. Having just eight teams was the logical outcome of survival of the fittest.

When Australia, Denmark, France, Germany, Italy, Japan and the USA joined the fray with Britain, it seemed that only the Aussies and Japanese could be said to lack three top-drawer yachts. The Danes and the Italians, in particular, were seen as the ones to beat.

Italy set out with a clear game plan by giving the nod to three owners, whose places in the team were confirmed twenty months ahead of the Cup. All three went to Bruce Farr for their designs and had the boats built in New Zealand by Terry and Mick Cookson's yard. In a throw-back to the early 1980s, the Italians bought in expertise to bolster their campaigns.

Pasquale Landolfi had become the top One-Ton owner in Europe, winning the One Ton Cup in 1989 and placing second in 1991. Francesco de Angelis was *Brava*'s regular helmsman, while her crew also numbered the Brazilian, Torben Grael, Olympic bronze medallist in the Star class.

Christian Democrat politician Giuseppe Degennaro launched *Larouge* to fill the Two-Ton spot and had Robert Ferrarese steer the boat, with Lorenzo Bortolotti, who had been at the centre of Italian offshore racing for the much of the 1970s and 1980s, running the show. They had secured New Zealander Brad Butterworth

*Victor Greulich's Two-Tonner* Unibank *punches her way out of the Solent (Gilles Martin-Raget)*

to call the tactics, while on the team's 50-footer, Giorgio Carriero's *Mandrake*, American John Kolius had been signed up. Kolius had been with the 50ft World Cup tour from the very outset and had won the world title with *Abracadabra*. He was a terrific big-boat sailor, counting two America's Cup campaigns with *Courageous* and *America II* in his sailing CV.

As part of their preparation, his Italian team walked off with the 1990 Sardinia Cup, winning with a day to spare. Given the stability of the IOR rule, where gains from new designs seemed to be getting infinitesimal, having the Italian team on the water nine months ahead of the Champagne Mumm Admiral's Cup was seen as a huge advantage. Helping to work the team up to a fine pitch was American Rod Davis, who had sailed *Mandrake* for the Italians in 1981 before the rules banned non-nationals from steering in the inshore races.

The Italian status as favourites looked more secure when *Larouge* won the Two Ton Cup in Kiel, *Brava* was runner-up in the One Ton Cup at Nieuwpoort in Belgium and *Mandrake* lay third on points throughout the 1991 50ft World Cup tour.

The Danish effort emphasised what was obvious from the Italian team: the top of the sport had shrunk to the point where it was supported by a tiny band of owners. There were probably no more than thirty of them keeping the world's top designers, builders, sail makers, spar makers, equipment suppliers and professional sailors busy in the IOR field.

Like the Italians, the Danes knew their line-up more than twelve months ahead of the Cup. The Danes moved away from their long-standing relations with Niels Jeppesen and his X-Yachts and gravitated towards Judel/Vrolijk. Jens-Erik Host was charged with filling the One-Ton slot. His *Zurich Forsikring* was built by Solution Composites in Cowes, the bare hull and deck weighing in at just 400kg. Crews had the unexpected chance to inspect her construction at the One Ton Cup in Nieuwpoort, when she was involved in a major collision. Retired from the series, she looked to be the best of the fleet chasing the sharp-looking *Brava* and *Vibes* designs from Farr.

Victor Greulich was back, continuing his association with Andels Bank, though as a result of mergers and acquisitions his new Two-Tonner sailed under the colours of Unibank. Sailed by Jens Christensen, she was second to *Larouge* in Kiel at the Two Ton Cup. She'd spent much less time in the water, but seemed to be getting closer and closer to the Italian boat's form in every race.

Ib Andersen rounded off the team. When Tuborg put some kroner in his pocket, enabling him to pick an existing boat to fill the 50ft berth, he chose *Container*. She had served the Danes well in 1989, proved competitive against newer boats during the 1990 World Cup season, and having been pre-pregs built, had not really been overtaken in construction terms. In view of the manner in which *Andelsbanken*'s broken forestay cost the Danes the Cup in 1989, *Container* came with the added advantage of being proven durable.

It was ironic, therefore, that the boat suffered a collapsed mast step. Andersen's crew knew something was amiss when Tuborg could not achieve the same runner tension and pointing angles she had been demonstrating in the Oracle Lymington Regatta, a warm up event two weeks before the Cup. Andersen got to the root of the problem only halfway through the series. 'We know we haven't been able to find our numbers and our trim,' he admitted.

The American potential was underestimated, not because of *Vibes*, David Clarke's impressive new Farr One-Tonner, but because of the other two boats. *Champosa VII* was a Reichel/Pugh 50, owned by Japan's Mark Morita, who had long run much of his business and all of his yachting out of the USA. She was an update on *Abracadabra*, double 50ft world champion, but despite the best efforts of John Kostecki, she was never to reproduce *Abracadabra*'s form or that of the top Farr 50s.

Irving Loube's new Farr Two-Tonner *Bravura*, looked like a non-starter owing to her owner's illness. At first the original skipper, Robbie Haines, seemed to be getting a charter together, but then along came Steve Benjamin, having done a deal with Bob Towse, whose *Blue Yankee* had sailed for the USA in 1987. Benjamin made a smart recruitment of Dave Howlett from Britain, while his cohort Rodney Pattisson, with whom he'd taken *Jade* to her One Ton Cup win in 1985, was already signed on to *Champosa*.

The undoubted star of the US line-up was *Vibes*. By the late 1980s, Farr had beyond question become the dominant race designer. Curiously, the numbers of his boats in the various Admiral's Cups did not mirror the truth elsewhere: that Farr had a lion's share

boats sailing that each design change could be judged in what amounted to full-scale, real-life tank testing. Just when Judel/Vrolijk seemed to be threatening the Farr hegemony in the One-Ton class, so Farr produced *Vibes*, commissioned by the man who ran the US arm of Hanson Trust, Britain's largest private company.

Shipped straight to England from Cookson's in New Zealand, she was fast out of the box against the English

of the market and his boats were winning more of the big prizes than those of other designers.

Farr underpinned his designs with a huge amount of research and sheer effort, but there is no doubt that he enjoyed the twin benefits of having Geoff Stagg from the Farr office's sales organisation to feed back information from the race course, and of having so many

One-Tonners, and just as fast when lined up against the best Europeans in the One Ton Cup. With Stagg and past J-24 world champion Jim Brady running the boat, she had the unmistakable air of a winner. The Germans seemed back on song after re-evaluating their poor 1987 and 1989 campaigns. Udo Schutz's new *Container* was scarcely different from the old 50 footer, though she

*Bouwe Bekking steered Udo Schutz's 50ft Container, a First in class during the Second Inshore race being by far her best result (Rick Tomlinson)*

grew a little in length to suit the new 40.50ft rating which the 50ft class allowed for 1991. She got straight in the swing of things when she joined the class, one change made for the Admiral's Cup being the loss of Jens Christensen to *Unibank* in the Danish team, though her Kiwi tactician and skipper, Peter Lester, remained.

When the RORC failed to agree terms for Harold Cudmore to direct the British team as he had in 1989, the itinerant Irishman joined the German boat, having already had a taste of what was to come by sailing Willi Illbruck's *Pinta* in the 1990 Sardinia Cup.

Hasso Plattner appeared in the German team for

*Britain's One-Tonner* Port Pendennis *(K 518) jumping the start gun during the fourth race of the series, a triangle in Christchurch Bay (Gilles Martin-Raget)*

The cosmopolitan flavour stayed with Hans-Otto Schumann's two-tonner, *Rubin*, the twelfth boat to bear the name and the famous red band around the white hull. Or should it have been *Rubin XI½*? For Schumann retained the deck, winches and mast of the 1989 boat, putting it on a new hull modelled after *Unibank*.

the first time, once Albert Bull pulled *Saudade* out of the One-Ton slot so that he could concentrate on business in the newly united Germany. Plattner's *ABAP/4* – named after one of his company's software products, Advanced Business Application Program/4 – was pretty much identical to *Zurich*.

Illbruck's *Pinta* turned up in the Japanese team which, like the Australian effort, was a rag-bag. However, the Japanese team did contain Ryuoji Oda's new *Will*. Even as she was launched she was being marked down in the chronicles of yachting as the finest and the last big IOR racing yacht outside of the maxis for the 1993-94 Whitbread Race.

*Will* was *the* carbon fibre boat. Seemingly everything was made from the black, magic material: the winch grinding pedestal, the steering wheel, the stern light bracket, the mast collar, the guy blocks, the companionway ladder, the bunk frames...

In the $700,000 yacht, even the kitchen sink was made from carbon. Not that it was ever going to be used. 'Sure there's a lot of carbon,' admitted project manager Andy Ogilvie, the big Australian who had looked after the previous *Will*. 'But the boat was a fixed price contract and McConaghy was set up for it. It was just as easy for him to make the items himself from carbon as it was to buy them in.' But even Andy Ogs, battle hardened from years on the ocean racing circuit, admitted that Sydney's John McConaghy 'had lost the plot' when he built a carbon fibre fuel tank.

*Will* was one of the very first boats to be built from T800 carbon fibre. This made her no lighter but some 25 per cent stronger for an added material cost of some $50,000. The gain those dollars bought was a stiffer structure, allowing 16-17,000lb to be loaded on the running backstay – instead of the normal 12,000lb found on a 50-footer – to produce a straighter headstay for better upwind pointing.

Britain's team served as an indication of how fast the pool of Admiral's Cup boats was slipping away. Only Mike Peacock's new Farr 50, *Juno V*, was the old style of yacht: owned by a private individual and sailed by pretty much a Corinthian amateur crew, headed in this instance by Mike McIntyre.

Her team-mates were of unusual provenance. The one-tonner, *Port Pendennis*, was actually owned by Bulent Attaby of Turkey, although the designer, Ed Dubois, had arranged a deal whereby a British crew, under Lawrie Smith, would race the boat in the One Ton Cup and Admiral's Cup before the boat's owner

took delivery. What he would get then would be a fully cranked-up grand prix boat. But *Port Pendennis* did not seem to have the pace, particularly the pointing, of the new Farr boats or the J/V boats, and Smith and his excellent crew sailed their hearts out to score a third in the One Ton Cup.

The Two-Tonner also pointed to a future in which grand prix boats were owned by sponsoring companies and not private owners. The money, and there was lashings of it, came from Oracle Software, a business that had come from zero to billions in a few short years and wanted to give their corporate identity a boost. They put their toe in the water by sponsoring the Royal Air Force Sailing Association's Sigma 38 one design cruiser-racer, which, during the 1990 season acquitted herself well in club level racing.

However, Oracle put RAFSA in charge of a new Farr Two-Tonner and straightaway were told that their lack of experience would catch them out. The Oracle saga preoccupied the British newspapers for six months. The specialist yachting magazines chimed in, anticipating that if it went wrong, it would be a terrible waste to see a new sponsor, from a young and vital sector of the economy, come into the sport and walk away because they felt yachting had not served them well.

What preoccupied the press was that anyone with an opinion had advised that serving RAF personnel would be deficient in world-class grand prix racing. Oracle came close to signing Eddie Owen, who had sailed three Admiral's Cups, but the company never took the plunge. Some suggested there was a hidden agenda, linked to Oracle's software supplies to the RAF.

No one accused the boat of being weak. She was built by Green Marine and, like *Bravura*, was an improvement on *Larouge*. When *Wings of Oracle* underperformed in the Two Ton Cup, the call for crew changes was less clarion and more klaxon. Geoff Stagg stepped briefly into hot water when he described the boat's tactics as 'requiring not so much brain surgery as a total lobotomy!' It was an off-the-cuff comment about a client, which was picked up by the British newspapers without Stagg realising it would be repeated. Even Rod Davis, who was to spend nine months coaching the

*Giorgio Carriero's 50ft* Mandrake *leads* Wings of Oracle *and France's yellow* Corum Rubis *up the Solent (Rick Tomlinson)*

Italian team and who never has a hard word to say about anyone publicly, was forced to admit that *Wings of Oracle*'s tactical performance on the race course was 'er, interesting, to say the least'.

The message could not have been written bolder, yet summit meetings between Oracle's men in suits and Group Captain This and Air Marshall That only saw them nibble around the edges of the problem. A few civvy trimmers were brought on board and eventually, just three weeks before the Cup, Flight Lieutenant John Best was replaced as skipper by Stuart Childerley, a 24-year-old Finn sailor, who was in charge of a big boat for the first time.

He admitted after the Admiral's Cup, in which the boat was once again lacklustre, that: 'I felt, as did some of the crew, that every time we did something there was someone to kick us in the face.' Once an unhappy boat, always an unhappy boat?

The First Inshore start was set in Thorness Bay in the Western Solent, and amazingly, given the feeble breeze and spring tide, the fleet got away first time. Some boats, though, were caught too far from the line and struggled to make up over the tide – most noticeably France's One- and Two-Tonners, *Corum Diamant* and *Corum Rubis*, who eventually crossed three and a half minutes late.

Specially laid marks allowed a practical course to be set within the confines of the Solent: an uptide beat, downtide run and some reaches saw Flavio Favini, steering in place of John Kolius because of the nationality rules, take *Mandrake* to a gun-to-gun win. *Juno* was in close pursuit, but never managed to cross the bows of the big Italian boat.

The Italians were the top team, with *Larouge* hauling back from a grim start to take fourth among the Two-Tonners and *Brava* top in the One-Ton pack. Britain was the second-heaviest points scorer, with thoughts that *Wings of Oracle* might have turned over a new leaf prompted by her second to match that of *Juno*. Lawrie Smith had a disappointing day, though: fifth among the One-Tonners, he had gone aground while hugging the mainland shore on the long beat and then lost a place to *ABAP/4* on the long, trickling run, a point of sail which had been the boat's forte. Weed was blamed. Most yachts carried long prodding sticks or knotted ropes which could be dropped over the bow and run aft under the boat to cope with the weed, which had proved a problem all summer long.

The demon weed struck in the Channel Race. Its effect was especially noticeable given that only a 4-13 knot breeze was available to propel the twenty-four boats around the 187-mile course. *Wings of Oracle* led the Two-Ton pack early, until being struck down by the dreaded weed, having already been fouled on the start line by *Unibank*, who sailed round the course with an I flag on her backstay, accepting a 20 per cent penalty.

The Danes may have had good reason to believe this was not going to be their year when *Zurich* found herself baulked several times by Teddy Turner Jr's former Whitbread maxi *Challenge America* after the start. (Turner is son of Ted Turner of *Lightnin'* and *Tenacious* fame.) *Unibank* struck her second mishap when she picked up weed. In the dark and with the wind very patchy, it wasn't immediately obvious to the Danes why their speed was down; then sticks, ropes, even sailing backwards would not dislodge the weed, so a man was sent over the side.

*Port Pendennis* won the small-boat division by taking the lead when *Vibes* overstood the EC2 mark. *Pendennis'* navigator, Mark Chisnell, predicted precisely the amount that the tide would shift the wind to the south-east and picked a perfect layline, Smith hanging on grimly to keep the faster boat behind. The race was a marathon of concentration. 'The only good thing about it was we won,' admitted Smith.

*Mandrake* won the big-boat division which, coupled with *Larouge*'s third and *Brava*'s fourth, extended the Italian lead, while Britain dropped back, unusually putting up a poor show in a race in which the home country normally scored well.

Both the Second and Third Inshore races were sailed in similar conditions in Christchurch Bay, with a pleasant 14-19 knots blowing across the deck. But the south-westerly wind direction and the need to set three-mile beats placed the leeward mark in shallow water, which meant the right-hand side of the course

was the only way to go. With spring tides running and the breeze holding steady, it was a simple choice to work the slacker water inshore. Although this had long been understood, crews now could read the tide effect with uncanny accuracy, thanks to Global Positioning System satellite navigators interfaced with their tactical computers.

Christchurch Bay also proved to be a place of injuries and breakdowns. Bruno Finzi, *Brava*'s mainsheet trimmer, pulled his back muscles just before the gun and *Vibes* crossed in front, having had a near miss. 'Our trimmer said, "I don't think anyone's looking. They haven't seen us yet,"' recalled skipper Jim Brady. 'So we hollered "Starboard!" real loud, and they crash tacked in all sorts of mess. If we hadn't shouted, they'd have gone straight through us.'

The damage among the boats was high. Australia's One-Tonner, *Shardana*, retired when skipper Gordon Lucas pulled the boat out after her spar kinked. *ABAP/4* broke her spinnaker halyard and was bareheaded for a while and *Will* had her spinnaker halyard jam on the second reaching leg so had a man up the mast. The 50ft *Corum Rubis* rippled her mast as well, when the titanium padeye anchoring the end of the mainsheet broke, sending a whiplash up the spar.

While that mast remained standing, and the French raced with it, kink and all, the next day, the stick on the Japanese *Carino* (*Pinta*, chartered from Germany) came down soon after tacking. Failure of the lower diagonal was suspected.

Britain were the top team in the Second Inshore by just 0.25 points from Denmark, who had *Container* and *Unibank* win their classes. The Americans dominated the Third Inshore with a 1-4-3 score from *Vibes*, *Bravura* and *Champosa*.

The British had a grim time on the start line. Stuart Childerley took *Wings of Oracle* back, even though she had not been recalled. 'I made the judgement that we were over the line early and as there was an opportunity to return we did so.' *Pendennis* got called back, as did *Mandrake*, *Container* and *Zurich*. 'Zurich carried us up the line, so what do you do? If there's a charge on and you are conservative you'll be left for dead. If you go with them there's a chance you'll be caught and today it was our turn,' said Smith.

*Oracle* went on to claw back two places, only to get a 20 per cent penalty when the spinnaker flicked the second weather mark when it was set.

Just as in 1989, the Long Inshore, race five of the series, was guilty of misrepresentation. Out beyond the Nab Tower, it could not be said to be inshore and – shortened to 24.4 miles, from the 40 in the programme – it was not long either. Cut back in length due to the very late arrival of the sea breeze, it turned out to be shorter than the races in Christchurch Bay.

Under a cloudless sky, the remains of a north-east-

erly was locked in a battle of wills with the young sea breeze. It was plain that the sea breeze would fill east of south and march around the horizon following the sun. What was not clear was how quickly the sea breeze would establish itself and at what strength.

The start was delayed fifty minutes, but that was not nearly long enough. As early as the second leg of what was meant to be a twelve-legged race, it was apparent that the new breeze would turn the race inside out. The fleet had scarcely trickled round the first three and a bit legs, when the water darkened to seaward and the sea breeze arrived, reaching the tailenders first.

Then the French did something which puzzled all those watching. First their 50, *Corum Saphir*, tacked in towards the cliffs at Tennyson Down, into what seemed like a wind shadow. Then the Two-Tonner, *Corum Rubis*, followed suit and, without anyone particularly noticing, the French sprang from nowhere to score a 1-1-6. It moved them up to fourth overall, dislodging the Germans, and placed them just 2.38 points from the third- and second-placed teams from the USA and Britain. Italy, who had led the series from the outset, were clear ahead by 20 points and concerned only to cover the British and American boats.

Though it was unrecognised at the time, the French had played their joker for the first time in the series. Their strength was their highly cohesive team work, an *esprit de corps* generated in large measure by the meticulous planning Luc Gellusseau had put into the Corum Sailing Team, which was jointly financed by Corum and the French national federation, the FFV.

The team was not considered a real threat by the other countries because the French boats seemed to have only patchy boatspeed at best. What they had in abundance were excellent navigators, foremost of whom was Jean-Yves Bernot, a world leader in the esoteric art of weather routeing and the man behind many of the big French trans-ocean multihull and solo round-the-world successes. He treated the weather like a war game, and the French boats were all aware of numerous scenarios and how different elements could point to one of several outcomes. This is how they read the Hayling Bay race so well. They had done their home-

*Skipper Jens Christensen brings* Unibank *right up the Sowley outfall whilse dodging the Solent tide in the first race of the series (Beken of Cowes)*

work and studied the sea breeze in Sandown Bay for several days ahead of the race.

For some, this explanation was too pat. Did the French have a spotter on the shore? 'How did they have two boats in winning positions?' challenged Giorgio Carriero of *Mandrake*. 'They tacked to what seemed like a no-hope situation out to the right under the cliffs. I was sure they would come back. When they didn't and it looked worse for them, I was suspicious. Then when they picked up wind and got two wins, well, I was confused.'

Rodney Pattisson was bemused by the formation yachting, despite his years of experience. 'I'd love to know why they all went right together. Maybe a good weather man could have known where the breeze was coming from. It may have been team orders to follow

the lead boat in light shifty conditions. Bernot was on the big boat, so he was in front of his team-mates – perhaps out of respect for his experience they all followed his lead.'

If the Italians were rattled, then worse was to come in the Fastnet, for there the French mounted one of the best ambushes ever seen in offshore racing. They came from fourth to first and snatched victory from under the noses of the Italians by just 0.62 of a point.

The light airs persisted for the Fastnet, which for many was just as well as the 50s were considered frail. Specialised for their upwind/downwind inshore courses of the 50ft World Cup circuit, there had been considerable speculation about how they would deal with a heavy offshore race. Everything on a 50 was pared to the bone, like the forestay. They operated on only a

*The 50ft* Corum Saphir *orchestrated France's first-ever win by spearheading the team's weather strategy (Guy Gurney)*

15 per cent safety margin, for any more than that means a bigger stay size, which requires a bigger headfoil and which in turn equals more weight and windage.

*Champosa* and *Tuborg* almost came to grief beating out of the Needles Channel, when they looked for the tide push down the Shingles Bank, but found themselves instead drawn by an invisible hand as the undertow all but dragged them on to the bank.

Italy added Rod Davis to *Brava's* crew, sensing the One-Ton battle might be the tightest in the race and crucial to the outcome. 'The *Brava* v *Vibes* v *Port Pendennis* battle is very important to us,' Davis admitted. 'We see our chances improved if we stack the boat with helmsmen.'

While cover and counter-cover moves were pre-occupying the Americans, British and Italians, the French were sailing in their own sweet way. Bernot had studied more than a hundred different weather situations before the start, had selected the probable ones 'and rehearsed his team's responses. It was to clinch the issue.

No matter what dark thoughts were expressed over the French team's weather information, there is no doubting Bernot's credentials. 'We had a situation develop identical to that when Philippe Poupon won the 1988 C-Star by a hundred hours,' said Bernot, who had long been Poupon's *routeur*. 'It was obvious what we should do from the weather fax,' he added. Other boats also carried faxes, but did not use the charts to prepare anything other than one move at a time.

*Corum Saphir* sailed an extra fifteen miles to the north of the rhumb line after rounding Land's End to skirt round a secondary high pressure area and then judged her line into the Rock nicely. On the way back she set a spinnaker and sailed well south of the rhumb line, while her rivals stayed high under jibs. The big *Corum* avoided the area of calm the others sailed into. By the time *Corum Saphir* had reached the Lizard she was a full four hours clear of the second 50, *Will*. But the breeze died as the tide turned, and the French spent an anxious time kedged as the fleet closed in.

In climactic denouement, *Corum Saphir* beat *Will* home by twenty minutes after ninety-nine hours at sea. In the final scramble to finish, the fleet order went haywire, the One-Ton *Corum Diamant* being seventh boat home and beating all but two of the mid-size boats. Those in Plymouth started totting up the points and the French were the first to realise that an extraordinary win – one they had waited 34 years for – was possible.

As Rod Davis had predicted, it all came down to the One-Tonners. *Pendennis* was the second One-Tonner home, but two sevenths from *Oracle* and *Juno* put the British out of the frame. *Vibes* needed to be third or better for the Americans to win, so her fifth placing gave the Cup to the French.

## SHORT TACKS

• A new level-rating format was tried for the first time. The fleet raced in three rating bands – the one-ton, two-ton and 50ft divisions – with no time allowances.

• *Carino's* dismasting in the Second Inshore threw up a curiosity in the scoring system. *Carino* scored more points by remaining tied to the dock in the remaining races than if she had gone racing. This was due to a high scoring system. In the first two races, *Carino* had finished last in the Two-Ton division and received a penalty for a foul, so that she scored zero points instead of the one due to her eighth place. When she didn't race, she still got one point as an entrant so that by the end she'd scored 5.5 points!

*Ryouji Oda's Farr 50, Will,
rounds the famous Fastnet Rock
lighthouse (Kaoru Soehata)*

AFTER TWENTY-THREE glorious years the sun set on the International Offshore Rule as the single currency for racing around the world. As a swansong, the 1993 Champagne Mumm Admiral's Cup was keen, tight and incident-filled. Outsiders before the start, the Germans clinched victory seven races later by the narrowest ever margin: 0.25 points. It was a slimmer victory even than that of the French two years previously.

It was an appropriate reward for the Germans, winners of the series in 1973, 1983 and 1985, especially as Willi Illbruck, owner of *Pinta*, and Hans-Otto Schumann, on his twelfth *Rubin*, had supported the event for three decades. Schumann was part of the 1973 and 1985 winning teams, having started his run of twelve Admiral's Cups as far back as 1963. Illbruck was a member of the 1983 line-up, and for 1993 he built his smallest *Pinta* for a long time, a Judel/Vrolijk One-Tonner which had already won the 1993 One Ton Cup in Cagliari, Sardinia, before coming to Cowes. Save for Australia's Syd Fischer and Peter Kurts, and Italy's Giorgio Carriero and Pasquale Landolfi, few other yachtsmen have put so much into the Admiral's Cup for so long.

The last IOR series it might have been, but it was brimfull of drama even before the climactic finish. Harry Cudmore sank Ireland's One-Tonner, which had been chartered from King Harald of Norway, and two more yachts were severely damaged.

The similarities with the 1991 Cup were uncanny. The Italians brought immaculately prepared boats, packed full of talented sailors who were housed and fed (by a chef flown in from Rome) in considerable style. They led the series from the second race onwards, building up considerable momentum, so that a much deserved prize seemed to be theirs until it all fell apart at the end.

The race programme was changed to replace the Third Inshore race, normally the long race, with two twelve-mile windward/leeward races. In the first, Giorgio Carriero's 50ft *Mandrake* was dicing with Bert Dolk's *Pro-motion* from the Netherlands. Crossing bows and dipping transoms with inches to spare is meat and drink to the crews of the 50-footers, but this time it went spectacularly wrong. Approaching the weather for the second time and just a hundred yards short of it, *Mandrake* approached a line of starboard tack traffic, apparently about to slot in behind Britain's *Indulgence* (Mike Peacock's old *Juno V*, which was bought by Graham Walker) and *Pro-motion*, but ahead of France's *Corum Saphir*.

*Mandrake*'s helmsman, Francesco de Angelis, was perched high on the weather side, waiting for tactician Torben Grael to talk him through the crossing. Grael and Giorgio Carriero could see *Pro-motion* approaching; the two 50-foot yachts were closing at right angles at a combined speed of about 13 knots. In the time Grael had decided not to tack underneath *Pro-motion* but to cross her stern, the moment to avoid collision had gone. 'There was a collective black-out,' said Carriero.

The crash was ear shattering. *Mandrake* speared into *Pro-motion*, penetrating her starboard side deep enough to dislodge a primary winch. Bouwe Bekking, taking a break from Dennis Conner's Winston Whitbread campaign to steer *Pro-motion*, dislocated his thumb when it was jarred against the steering wheel, though, mercifully, there were no other injuries.

For a full five minutes the yachts were locked together like rutting stags. When they disengaged, it seemed one, or both, might sink. *Pro-motion* was holed to below the waterline, but stayed afloat, just, by dint of sailing heeled right over on starboard tack straight into Chichester Harbour. 'We bounced the

*Harold Cudmore (second right) sank* Jameson I, *chartered from King Harald of Norway, by striking Gurnard Ledge on the second leg of the first race. Other One-Tonners clipped the ledge but while they dented their keels,* Jameson's *keel ruptured the hull (Gilles Martin-Raget)*

boat over the sands and went aground three times, twisting the keel, just to get her into the boatyard at Hayling,' said Bekking.

*Mandrake* looked imperiled too, the front four feet of her bow missing. Only the huge amount of pre-bend put into it stopped *Mandrake*'s mast from springing out of the boat when the forestay broke. With a sail wrapped over the bow, *Mandrake* was towed gingerly back to Cowes. With welling eyes and choked throats, Grael and de Angelis found it hard to explain the crash

*Bow-less, Mandrake was an irresistible attraction to the West Cowes Marina crowds (Heinrich Hecht)*

and the depth of their sorrow was very evident.

Down to two boats, Italy took just a two-point lead into the deciding Fastnet Race. De Angelis was put aboard Pasquale Landolfi's One-Tonner, *Brava Q8*, because the Italians knew they had to drive the heart out of *Brava* if they were to stand a chance. With Paul Cayard as skipper, Rod Davis at his shoulder, Flavio Favini as alternate helmsman and Stevie Erickson on mainsheet, *Brava* lacked nothing for talent.

Yet their deeds counted for nothing when, on the

third morning of the Fastnet, Italy's Two-Tonner, Giuseppe Degennaro's *Larouge*, dropped her rig over the bow forty miles to the north and west of the Scilly Isles on the way back from the Rock. Officially, the rig failed because the running backstay broke, but one crew member confided that the runner tail had not been put in the winch's self-tailer jaws properly. What-ever, it was the end of the Italian dream. As Rod Davis, coach to the Italian team, had uttered with considerable prescience on the Fastnet's eve: 'Whatever you do, don't call us favourites!'

The very strong Ausssie challenge missed a beat in the Fastnet too. John Calvert-Jones' Two-Tonner *Great News II* (the former British yacht *Wings of Oracle*, still a bad luck boat) lost her rig twenty-four hours earlier than *Larouge* because of shroud failure. The Aussies were not out of the reckoning, but their odds had lengthened. Four years previously, Calvert-Jones, brother-in-law of Australian media magnate Rupert Murdoch, had won the Fastnet with his 50-footer skip-pered by the late Tom Blackaller. 'I have no illusions about the law of averages,' said Calvert-Jones before the Fastnet. 'Two wins from two starts is not in my book, but two starts and two good places is.' It proved an empty prophecy.

While the focus was on the Australians and Ital-ians, Germany had attracted little attention. But by the time the Fastnet had run two-thirds of its course, the Germans were the only real contenders with all three boats still sailing.

When Graham Walker's British team yacht, *Indul-gence*, led the 50ft class home at the close of the Fastnet, crossing the line just two boat lengths ahead of Syd Fischer's *Ragamuffin* from Australia, with France's *Corum Saphir* in tight line-astern formation just behind, the series still looked good for the Australians. *Indul-gence* held on to her lead on corrected time, with *Ragamuffin* seemingly a safe third in fleet (after *Corum Saphir* edged in ahead her on corrected time).

Steady moderate to fresh winds had allowed the bigger boats to stretch their legs, more especially as the 50s laid the Fastnet from Land's End, while the One-Tonners were forced to tack along the Irish coast.

Given that *Ragamuffin* had failed to pip *Indulgence* in the 50-footer fleet and that Germany's *Container* was placed fourth, it came down to the One-Tonners to decide the issue.

In a freshening morning breeze, Germany's *Pinta* came home first ahead of *Brava Q8*, but corrected to seventh overall in the fleet, scoring priceless points. The door was prised open for a German upset by *Pinta*, winner of the 1993 One Ton Cup, devastatingly fast in a breeze despite having no new sails for the AC and superbly sailed by her twin Gold medallist skippers, Jorg Diesch and Kiwi Russell Coutts. Australia had looked certain Cup winners throughout the Fastnet and, to make sure of it, *Ninja*, the one-tonner chartered by Peter Kurts, who raced aboard at the grand age of sixty-nine, had to finish within six places of *Pinta* overall on corrected time.

In fact she finished seventh, pipped by the British One-Tonner *GBE International* (ex *Port Pendennis*), who beat her by 1min 58 sec, unwittingly giving the Cup to Germany. This was a good result for the British One-Tonner, especially as she had a young crew. Apart from designer Ed Dubois, who had sailed his first AC in 1977, and two-time Whitbread sailor, Ed Danby, few of the crew had tasted the big-boat big-time.

Skipper Glyn Charles made consistent good starts and the One-Tonner acquitted herself well. Charles owed his place on the One-Tonner to the unusual source of the British team. The root of the problem was that IOR racing was all but dead by the time of the 1993 Admiral's Cup, save for a few pockets of interest: the One Ton circuit and 50ft World Cup. When Graham Walker bought the old *Juno V* as his eighth *Indulgence*, he also took it upon himself to line up two team-mates. It was the first, and almost certainly the last time that the RORC let control of the British team slip from their grasp. Walker's *chef d'equipe* Peter Morton procured a One- and Two-Tonner from Turkey, chartered from Ergin Imre and Bulent Attaby: *Provezza Source* was the old *Unibank*, carrying some Turkish crew and with Kiwi Chris Dickson joining skipper Stuart Childerley.

The problem with the Turkish deal was that the British took control of the One- and Two-Tonners only

days before the Champagne Mumm Admiral's Cup started. Other sailors who had been active in One-Ton and 50ft racing in Europe earlier in the season were much sharper, and it showed.

*Indulgence* did not get into her stride until the series was already half over. The decision to move Eddie Warden Owen sideways and bring in Chris Law, who flew from Australia seventy-two hours before the first race, demonstrated that Graham Walker knew things were not right at the back of his boat. Walker can't

*Gold medallists Jorg Diesch and Russell Coutts, and the crew of Willi Illbruck's One-Tonner* Pinta, *struggle to keep on their feet in Hayling Bay (Rick Tomlinson)*

have enjoyed the series. Praised for saving Britain's bacon by producing a team when it seemed there might not have been one, he was also held to account for its early failings. 'We started too late, you can see that, but we improved,' he said at the close.

For sheer frission, nothing topped Ireland's attempts to bring in a replacement for their One-Tonner *Jameson I*. The jury, consulting regatta rules, declared that substitution was not possible after the first race unless the Irish won support of all the competitors. The Irish played the injured party role perfectly, even though their loss was due to plain crew error. The most competitive sailors were against the swap, for as Paul Cayard pointed out: 'If the Irish do it, what's to stop us putting *Mandrake* aground in the sixth race and bringing in a much better-reaching boat, the *Capricorno*, for the Fastnet?'

Other highly placed sailors felt the same, especially as in the First Inshore and the Channel Race, the One-Tonners did not score points, so Ireland had not paid any price for sinking a boat because for the first time the RORC decided to count only the best two scores in each team. The Italians, craftily, refused to support the Irish unless all countries agreed, which left it to the French to say 'non'. Not surprisingly, Irish disappointment was heaped on the French.

The incident was not without its ironies. Had Ireland got the go-ahead, they would have used the German *I-Punkt*, a much faster boat and the one Cudmore tried to get for his team in the first place. And had they been allowed to do that, Italy would have

been free to bring in *Capricorno* when *Mandrake* crashed out and, possibly, gone on to win...

A miserable, grey and rainy day for the First Inshore, a twenty-nine-miler, was a far cry from the glorious evening reception on the Royal Yacht Squadron lawn which formally opened the series. The day was made worse by the loss of Ireland's *Jameson I* (ex *Fram XI*). A lop-sided beat favoured those boats which started on the right-hand end of the line, who were able to all but lay the first mark, a buoy on the Island shore between Gurnard and Hamstead Ledges.

On the run back west, *Jameson I* clobbered Gurnard Ledge. Skipper Harold Cudmore talked of a 'glancing blow', but others saw *Jameson's* bow dip sharply. Killian Bushe, a builder of repute, looked below and said 'Beach!', whereupon *Jameson* headed inshore fast, sinking fifty yards off Gurnard and losing her keel.

There were no injuries; only dented reputations. Cudmore's crew was packed with Solent specialists, so familiar with passages around the ledge that they scarcely gave it thought. More concerning was that when the Cookson-built boat was hauled out, it was obvious that the keel had pulled out of the hull which, in place of solid laminate, had Nomex honeycomb floors, which turned a simple grounding into a catastrophe.

This made many question the ABS Scantling Rule which allowed such practice. The point was made forcibly when five other One-Tonners clipped the same ledge on the second beat. *GBE International* knocked her wooden keel shoe clean off; *Pinta* did the same, and split her rudder tip, and yet neither incident caused serious damage to the hull/keel joint.

Willi Illbruck was outraged at the course, even if the 50s and Two Tonners managed to avoid grounding. He threatened to pull *Pinta* out of the event and only through-the-night repairs and effective pleas from *Container's* skipper, Jens Christensen, averted Illbruck's withdrawal. 'I've been racing here for twenty-five years and they set a course over the rocks; it's crazy!' said Willi Illbruck. His blood boiling, he added: 'The race committee sit around green-covered tables and don't race themselves.' Other sailors had the same message, if expressed more colourfully.

*The boats may rest between races, but crews continue essential running repairs (Yachting World)*

The RORC race director, Alan Green, tried hard to set a good course but faced constraints, amongst which was the requirement to use the big inflatable sponsors' buoys. This had two effects: in the fresh 20 knots they could be anchored successfully only in good holding ground; and he was denied use of the fixed Solent racing marks out in deeper water. In addition, a prohibition on anchoring in the central Solent area made it difficult to lay the course short of the troublesome ledge.

Australia came out on top in the race, with Peter Gilmour taking *Ragamuffin* past *Indulgence* at the top of the second beat to claim line honours, backed up by a fourth from *Great News II*, who headed right from the start to gain an advantage she clung on to.

The controversy over the course was a shame, for all the ingredients for a great Solent race were there: strong tidal influence, a nose-to-tail spinnaker run past Cowes Green and short tacking just off the beach. Only miserable weather and the dubious placing of the start and weather mark turned it into a grizzly affair.

By contrast, the 206-mile Channel Race started in sparkling weather which turned the Solent silver. A short beat west from the Squadron line to East Lepe set the fleet up for a long spinnaker run to the Nab Tower, a reach south to the EC2 buoy, a beat to Poole Fairway, a long run south-east to EC2, a reach north to Rustington buoy off Littlehampton and a beat back into the Solent via the Owers and Nab. It was a Two-Tonner benefit, with Germany's 50ft *Container* the best of the rest in seventh place, while top honours went to Italy's double Two Ton Cup winner *Larouge*.

France, joint-favourites with Italy, displayed impressive self-destruct qualities, notably when their 50ft *Corum Saphir* tried to barge underneath *Container* and *Jameson 3* – Warren Johns' Australia 50 *Heaven Can Wait* which had been chartered by the Irish – at East Lepe. Being low of the lay line and squeezing hard for buoy room might work in the 50ft class, but not in the Solent with the tide running hard past a large red steel Admiralty buoy.

It was one of those fascinating and frustrating Solent moments which have variously annoyed and enthralled visiting crews over the years, as misjudgement by helms-man Pierre Mas saw the big *Corum* wrapped around the buoy. Neither the mainsheet nor the backstay snagged the structure, fortunately, and *Corum Saphir* wriggled free. To complete the entertainment, tactician Bertrand Pace looked at the buoy and then Mas, and threw his palm up against his forehead in disgust.

Processional it may have been, as the beats were not true enough to force the boats to tack, but the race was not without excitement. Approaching the Nab Tower, *Great News II* pounced into a gap left by Japan's *Swing*. Aussie skipper Colin Beashel said he was waiting for *Swing* to bear away in the lee of the tower, but *Swing*'s crew were amazed there was not a serious crash between both yachts and the huge tower. Certainly those sitting on the side deck with their legs over the side had to move them quickly. *Swing*'s tactician, American Ed Baird, reckoned 'it was the scariest moment I've ever known, and I've sailed a lot of miles'. The jury dismissed *Swing*'s protest.

Outscoring the Germans by 0.38 points, Italy moved into the series lead over Australia and Germany with *Larouge* first in fleet, Pasquale Landolfi's *Brava* ninth and *Mandrake* thirteenth. Britain were second-lowest scorers, remaining seventh on the leader board. In what was a big-boat race, Britain discarded *Indulgence*'s score in favour of *GBE*'s seventeenth place.

When the breeze picked up from 15 to 25 knots, the complexion of the twenty-seven-mile windward-leeward Corum Trophy Second Inshore race changed with it. For a while, it seemed a decent British result might be on the cards, for halfway through the seemingly interminable three-and-a-half-hour, four-and-a-half-lap race, *Provezza Source* and *GBE International* were second *behind* Japan's *Swing* and *Nippon* in the Two- and One-Ton divisions, with *Indulgence* fourth among the 50s.

The short, whipped-up seas, off the shoaling water near Selsey Bill, made the 50s hard to handle on the run. The smaller boats seemed to fit the wave pattern better, but the third run saw spectacular wipe-outs for the 50s. Japan's *Champosa VII* finished the leg under jib because all her heavy kites were shredded. *Indulgence*, whose principal trimmer Jerry Richards was hampered by a ricked back, careered round in one huge broach because Richards simply could not pull in the armfuls of sheet at the critical time. Minutes later, *Indulgence*'s spinnaker pole end failed to open after a gybe leading to another broach and she lost five minutes bare headed sailing as a snatch block was fitted to the pole.

Paul Cayard, *Brava Q8*'s skipper, will be the one most wanting to forget the race, though. The start was delayed because, as Cayard sailed down the line to

*Brava's torrid series included one dismasting, one buckled rig and, in a rare error, helmsman Paul Cayard (white cap) sailing over the start line buoy. Steve Erickson was sent over the side to free the rudder from the tangle (Gilles Martin-Raget)*

assess it, he misjudged the tide and *Brava* tangled with the pin end buoy, becoming firmly anchored to it. Steve Erickson went over the side, but could not free the boat. The buoy was cut from its ground tackle and when *Brava* fired up her engine, more ropes fouled the prop, whereupon Paulo Massarini and Lorenzo Mazza were also sent over the side and *Brava* eventually started two minutes late. Despite this, and a rudder cut up badly by the buoy's chain and slowly filling with water, Cayard fought back to second in class. If he breathed a sigh of relief that the worst was behind, he was mistaken.

Some hundred yards upwind from the final leeward

mark, the mast crumpled over the side. Rod Davis, surveying the mess, said: 'We've got the spreaders and we've got the rigging and neither is broken.' Why the mast failed is not clear. Another One-Ton crew close by reckoned the runner was not put on in time, which would be remarkable if true, given the calibre of *Brava*'s team.

As it was, *Brava*'s trials and tribulations counted for naught. It was another big boat day, with *Mandrake* winning, and teams did not need to count the One-Ton scores. *Larouge* was eighth, but dropped six places for a finish-line incident with Ireland's *Jameson 2*, which made Australia top team on the day, with Germany second and Italy's series lead cut to 0.5 points.

The next day saw a similar course for the Champagne Mumm Race, but with the addition of two reaching legs between the first and second beats. Italy stretched their lead to 3.5 points as *Mandrake* took her second successive win, with Australia's *Great News II* and Germany's *Pinta* winning the smaller classes.

'We were able to establish a lead as Peter Gilmour in *Ragamuffin* had to fight back from being fourth at the first mark,' said *Mandrake*'s tall, polite helmsman Francesco de Angelis. *Indulgence* was in the wars again, with the replacement pole end playing up. 'We had the pace to be second but had three major errors,' said navigator Peter Morton. First, a jib sheet broke minutes off the start line. Next, helmsman Chris Law hit his head on the boom three-quarters of the way up the first beat, and was felled to the cockpit floor. Then as bowman Tim Haynes was trying to sort out the pole end, he was launched into the sea as the kite snapped full of breeze. He hung on and was hauled back aboard, but not before a £3,000 spinnaker was lost over the side. Britain's flagship was flagging badly.

Place changes were modest, and the confidence of the Italian effort was shown by a superb one-man gybe aboard *Mandrake*. In a 20-knot breeze and with a useful lead, a conservative two-man gybe could have been attempted. Yet *Mandrake*'s bowman tripped the pole himself as he walked forward, picked up the lazy guy and snapped it into the pole end as it swung in from behind him.

There was one dent to the Italian effort, when *Brava* rippled her replacement mast. The damage occurred in the same place as the previous break, seven feet above the deck, but this time the spar remained standing.

In place of the long inshore race, the RORC instituted two twelve-mile windward/leeward races for the Kenwood Trophy, an innovation welcomed by all crews, even if they were growing tired of the three-hours-each way journey to Bracklesham Bay, some seventeen miles from Cowes. although it was about the same distance as Christchurch Ledge. The demand to move the inshore races outside the Solent was strong in the 1980s, but the 1990s were emphatically a time of short, ninety-minute day races close to the shore, as exemplified in the One-Ton and 50ft circuits, and the 1993 Admiral's Cup was clearly out of step with its customers on this.

Even the worst crash in Admiral's Cup history could not dislodge Italy from the leader board. Inevitably *Mandrake*'s collision with *Pro-motion* overshadowed the double windward/leeward races, which, with short two-mile legs, demonstrated just how futile the previous long inshore courses 1991 and 1993 had been.

Britain, finally, put up the sort of performance expected of their boats and crews. In the first race, *Provezza Source* and *GBE International* won their divisions, with *Indulgence* fifth among the 50s. The day belonged to Syd Fischer's *Ragamuffin*, counting a first and second in the fleet, with *Larouge* third and fourth. Germany were the day's heaviest scorers, closing right behind Australia and Italy with just the Fastnet to come.

With the Fastnet shaping up to be a big-boat race, and the freshening wind likely to strike the smaller boats while they were still slogging out to the Rock, Italy knew they just had to make *Brava*'s score count. Amazingly for one so prominent in the sport, this was skipper Paul Cayard's first Fastnet. Francesco de Angelis, from the bowed-out *Mandrake,* joined Cayard, Rod Davis and Flavio Favini as *Brava*'s fourth helmsman, knowing full well they'd have to drive the heart out of the boat to keep Italy in with a sniff of a chance.

Syd Fischer's *Ragamuffin* made the running for much of the race, though at Land's End, on the way

*Fastnet Race start, with two boats recalled for jumping the gun (Daniel Forster)*

out the Rock, France were looking strong, their 50ft
*Corum Saphir* up with *Ragamuffin* and the Two-Tonner
*Corum Rubis* well placed. On the lumpy beat out across
the Celtic Sea, *Indulgence* assumed the lead, but *Rags*
led round the Rock, only to be overtaken by *Indulgence*
between Bishop Rock on the Scillies and the Lizard.

The dramas were in her wake: *Great News II*'s dismasting as the spar snapped without warning at deck
level, *Jameson 3*'s retirement when her boom broke at
the mainsheet attachment, and the Japanese One-
Tonner, *Nippon*, heading back to Plymouth, her crew
chastened by a man-overboard incident.

It occurred at 2300 on the second night at sea. A
20-knot wind, fog and lumpy sea made classic ingredients for tragedy as a large wave swept bowman
Kazuhiko Sofukyu over the side. He had no harness on,
but did have a torch. This, and the man-overboard panic
button on the GPS satellite navigation system, allowed
*Nippon*'s crew, headed by Manchester-born Kiwi John
Cutler, to retrace their steps under power. Just as *Nippon*
approached Sofukyu, his torch went out.

A grid search was begun and mainsheet trimmer
Chris Mason fired off red flares to alert other yachts
and provide some illumination. Ten minutes with no

sign of Sofukyu prompted Cutler to extend the search and, just as the fourth parachute flare was about to burn out, the crewman was sighted. Cold, shaken but with the presence of mind to have shed his heavy and sodden thermals and oilies – which is how he dropped his torch – Sofukyu managed to stay afloat for nearly twenty minutes. Faced with a 180-mile beat to the Fastnet or the chance to get his crewman warm and ashore, Cutler made the sensible choice of returning to Plymouth.

Calculations as the leaders approached the Lizard still had the Aussies poised for victory. On finishing at 2108 on the fourth night, *Ragamuffin*'s Peter Gilmour wisely declined to celebrate prematurely. 'Wake me up when it's certain,' he said before heading for some sleep. It was just as well he waited, for by breakfast the Germans had stolen the series.

## SHORT TACKS

• There was a consensus that the aggregate crew weight limit was too low for sailors of normal height and build. The result? Diet drinks, dehydration treatments, sauna sessions and so forth. France's *Corum* team were regularly seen jogging in their drysuits. Many sailors reported loss of strength, light-headedness and susceptibility to colds and sneezes resulting from starvation diets, which was a farcical situation days before a tough regatta with two demanding offshore events.

• There were several try-ons in the weighing-in room. The Italians and French sought to impress with freshly applied aftershave. One Italian crew had brought one pair of deck shoes, with the soles cut out and laces removed, which they passed down the line as each man was weighed.

• In 1993 the three-class level-rating scoring, which had proved so successful in 1991, was dropped. Elapsed times had to be corrected not just into class order, but fleet order too. Age allowance made a comeback too, and, worst of all, only two scores from three boats counted. This expediency was introduced when it was feared that the series might fail, so two-boat teams were permitted for the first time. As it was, only

the Dutch failed to field three boats, and their One-Tonner, *Ace*, patently did not belong in a fleet of Admiral's Cup calibre. All of which meant it was impossible to tell the state of play while racing was underway. Worse, as the windiest series for a long time, it favoured the higher-rating boats. That meant some crews sailed their socks off, but were rewarded with no points. Germany's *Pinta*, the year's One Ton Cup winner, was scored in only two out of seven races, which was hardly satisfactory. The 50s *Ragamuffin* (Syd Fischer), *Container* (Udo Schutz) and the two-tonners *Corum Rubis* (Michael Kermarec) and *Larouge* (Giuseppe Degennaro) were the only four boats, the Dutch team excepted, to score in all races. Without the discard system, Germany's score would have been even higher, so at least the 'right' country won under the 1993 system. *Ragamuffin* was the highest individual points scorer, though there were no prizes.

*American Rod Davis sailed for Italy in 1981, New Zealand in 1987 and Italy again in 1991 and 1993 (Kos)*

IF IT WASN'T for a yacht race, the Fastnet Rock would probably have remained nothing more than a useful marker and staging post for the Atlantic's regular users. Instead, it can realistically be described as the site of the world's most famous lighthouse.

The Fastnet Rock is just four miles south of Cape Clear, the most southerly of the fingers that slant out into the Atlantic on Ireland's south-west corner. The mainland is a stone's throw away and, besides Cape Finisterre and northern Newfoundland, there is nothing to the south and the west of the Rock besides America, and that is some 2000 miles away. And remember, this is the country where mythical giants can pull up swathes of land and fling them into the sea to create new islands.

Consequently, the Rock was the principal point of departure or landfall for navigators involved in transatlantic trade. The Fastnet, however, was not the first light to be established on Ireland's south-west corner. Before it came Loop Head at the entrance to the Shannon and the Skelligs to the north, followed by the nearby Clear Island and the Old Head of Kinsale to the east.

Clear Island was obscured by a shroud of mist and, apart from anything else, was inshore of off-lying dangers such as the Fastnet Rock itself. So, in 1848, the Corporation for the Preserving and Improving the Port of Dublin extinguished the Clear Island light and set one on the Fastnet.

It was designed by George Halpin, engineer to the port of Dublin. The tower's toe-hold on the Rock was tenuous and despite thirty-two bolts sunk two feet into the highest point of the Rock, the cast iron structure, plated up like an iron-clad ship, wobbled and juddered under the impact of the Atlantic. Having cost £17,930 to erect, the Tower made a noble effort of producing a 38,000-candela light which flashed every two minutes. The keepers lived in a brick block-house a few yards away, but frequently found themselves unwilling to dash to the tower for fear that the sea would take them.

As with many a lighthouse standing sentinel over an exposed coast, the power of the sea is not fully appreciated except by those who live in it and experience the full range of its moods. Hydraulic pressure can be as much as 16 tons/ft$^2$. For the old iron tower, this meant the equivalent of having three-ton rocks hurled at it, and on one memorable occasion a 60-gallon water butt was plucked clean off the tower's exterior, despite its being lashed on 130ft above the high-water mark.

Even today, the wave action nibbles away at the Rock, sometimes biting viciously to remove chunks. Coping stones just disappear. Heavy-gauge steel doors on the store rooms have to be straightened with sledge-hammers, while H-section girders are twisted as easily as if they were made from lead, rather than heavy-gauge steel.

The Rock itself has fallen victim to the sea, for it is not one, but two, with a chasm running through the heart of the Fastnet. This is because much of the south-west Cork coast is slate, which fractures easily into great serrated teeth. That is why seafarers have long dreaded this shore, its reputation for claiming ships being well justified.

In a long battle of attrition with the Atlantic, attempts were made to make the tower more durable, with the addition of masonry and concrete to strengthen the tower's foundations on the Rock and the addition of an external petticoat to the tower's base. But the sea won. When a storm in 1881 took the top of Calf Rock lighthouse clean off, despite its having had a similar petticoat, the Commissioners for Irish Lights, who had succeeded the Port of Dublin authorities,

*Ryouji Oda's 50ft* Will *from Japan rounds the Fastnet Rock in rain and twilight during the 1991 race*

189

reached the inevitable conclusion that something newer and tougher was needed on the Fastnet. Trinity House's Elder Brethren in London – who were ultimately responsible for lights around the British Isles – agreed, sanctioning the new light in December 1891.

The task was entrusted to William Douglass, whose first job was to survey both halves of the Rock – the 340ft x 180ft Fastnet and the 240ft x 60ft Little Fastnet, which are separated by a 30ft channel. The surprising outcome of this was that Douglass chose not to build the new light on the top of the main Rock but on its base and on the seaward side, open to the south-west weather. His reasoning was that the waves would wash around the tower before exploding on the higher mass

*Vertical Section of Rock and Halpin's Lighthouse, 1854 (Commissioners of Irish Lights)*

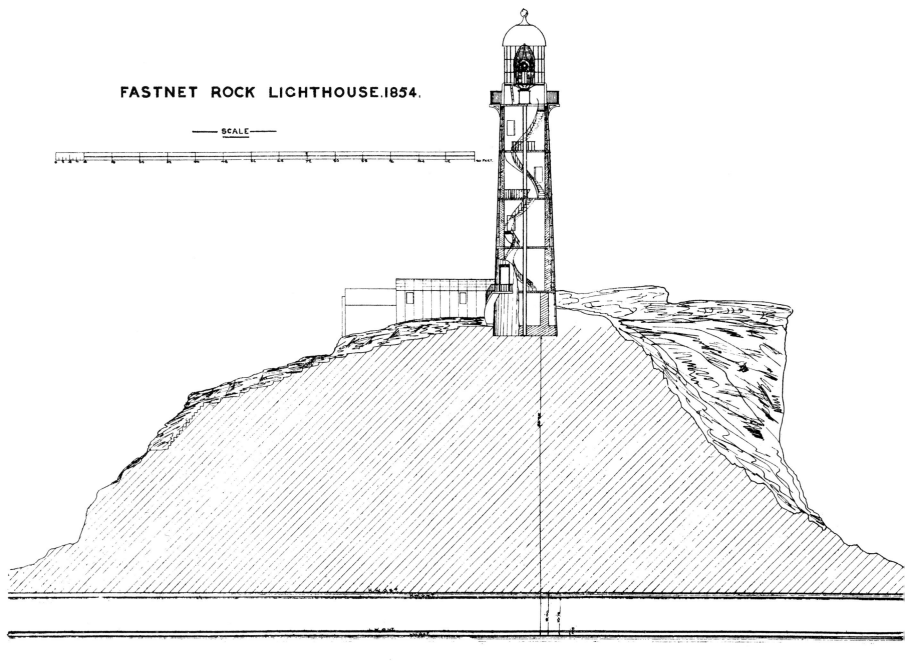

FASTNET ROCK LICHTHOUSE.1854.

—— SCALE ——

PLATE I.

behind it. Besides, the Rock's western tip was made up of the hardest Lower Silurian slate.

The immensity of the task is belied by the eight years of work it took to build the new tower. It was one of many such feats that have made Victorian engineers so revered. To make sure the new light was for keeps, the channel between the two rocks was filled, then the main rock was cut into, so that the first ten-part rings could be built, ready to accept twelve courses of the tower. To make the job easier, a landing pier was built, complete with causeway, some 30ft above the high water mark, along which trams ran materials from one end of the Rock to the other.

Douglass was the complete engineer. He planned the tramway, an on-site foundry and the building of the 126ft twin-screw steamer, *Irene*, which carried the stone to the Fastnet, as well as designing every detail of the tower itself. Some 4300 tons of Cornish granite, chosen for its hardness, was used and, although only a handful now had the chance to inspect the tower close-up, its stones were as bright, as evenly marked and as free from flaws as any architectural landmark building designed to be admired by the masses ashore. If the extra materials used to fill in the foundations are counted, then the total landed on the Rock was 4633 tons.

To transfer the granite stones, Douglass drew up a five-point mooring for the *Irene* which, thanks to 50 fathoms of heavy chain and half-ton sinkers, kept her on station. The stones were rolled off her port side and hauled out of the water on to the tramway using a derrick on the Rock. In the centre of the tower was another small crane, mounted on ball bearings, which lifted each stone up to its correct course.

Douglass had an equal in the stonemason James Kavanagh who, over a four-year period, set each and every one of the 2074 stones himself. On 22 September 1899, twenty-two stones were landed, hoisted and set in the best day's work in the entire 48-month period. The triumph of Kavanagh's toil and Douglass' vision was that when the tower was completed, no course deviated from the drawings by more than 1/4in and the tower was no more than 3/16in off the vertical. Such precision was achieved by building six to eight

courses in Cornwall before sending them out to the Rock, the last course being held over to form the reference for the next. In all eighty-nine courses were laid, with the stones landed and set over a 118-day period.

One hundred years on, the stones remain bright, their joints true and the arrises of each stone as even as the day when Freeman's quarrymen in Penryn dressed them before shipment. The tower is a three-dimensional jigsaw. It is a monolith, made one by a system of dovetails and keys. No stone can be removed without removing all of those above, breaking the dovetail joint below and releasing the cement joint.

As much as it is easy to marvel at the feats of the day, it is easy to forget the human cost of such projects. Two men lost eyes building the tower. Foul weather brought frequent halts to the work, though another was caused when the quarry exhausted the best vein of granite. Some fifteen men lived in various huts during the tower's construction, being paid the princely sum of 2s. 6d. (12.5p) for a nine-hour day, plus an extra 1s. (5p) per day for working on the Rock, though they did have to provide their own food. In 1899 William Douglass retired owing to ill-health, never to see the finished work, while James Kavanagh died from apoplexy within weeks of its completion in 1904 and its first illumination on 21 June.

The gentleman Commissioners did, however, see the fruits of Douglass and Kavanagh's labours, for they made a tour of inspection aboard their steamer, *Alexandra*. Using a system of mirrors, they were able to measure the intensity of the new paraffin bioform light with that on Bull Rock. The Commissioners' scientific adviser, Sir Robert Ball concluded: 'It was a most beautiful optical phenomenon. Each great flash, as it swept past, lighted up the whole ship and rigging like a search light. The Fastnet is now, at length, provided with a monumental tower and a superb light well worthy of this lonely light, as being, from the navigator's point of view, the most important outpost in Europe.'

The light itself pioneered the technology of its day, with a ton of mercury to float the mechanism – which until its electrification had to be hand wound with a clockwork mechanism every forty minutes – a bioform lens made up of 726 pieces of glass. The bioform Chance lens marked real progress, for it produced a more powerful and a longer flash, 50 per cent efficiency if one half of the lens was ever damaged, and a cleaning platform between the two halves which did not obstruct the light. Together with speedier rotation made possible by the mercury bath, the Fastnet progressed the march towards better navigation.

For a long time now, the light has been electric, producing 2.5 million candela which gives a range of twenty-eight miles. When the light became operational in 1904, transatlantic traffic was such that the tower was both a Lloyd's signal and a Marconi wireless telegraphy station. As late as the 1960s, the keepers would have four liners a week as passing trade.

That has all changed now. Modern electronic fixing aids have made redundant the need for a visual fix before striding out across the ocean. The passing traffic is nil, and the Fastnet Race is responsible for bringing more sea-borne traffic than anything else.

Because of modern navigation aids and the employment cost of keepers, the light was de-manned in 1989, its operation conducted by remote control from the safety of the shore. No longer are there three keepers tending the light. When a helipad was built, it ended the chances of being stranded for weeks on end and of having to make the perilous trip by breeches buoy from the supply vessel to the derrick. The helipad also effectively ended the need for keepers, for maintenance crews can fly on to the Rock in all but the severest of weathers.

And now, every two years, a RORC crew also flies in to monitor the Fastnet Race.

*The Fastnet Rock and lighthouse (Yachting World)*

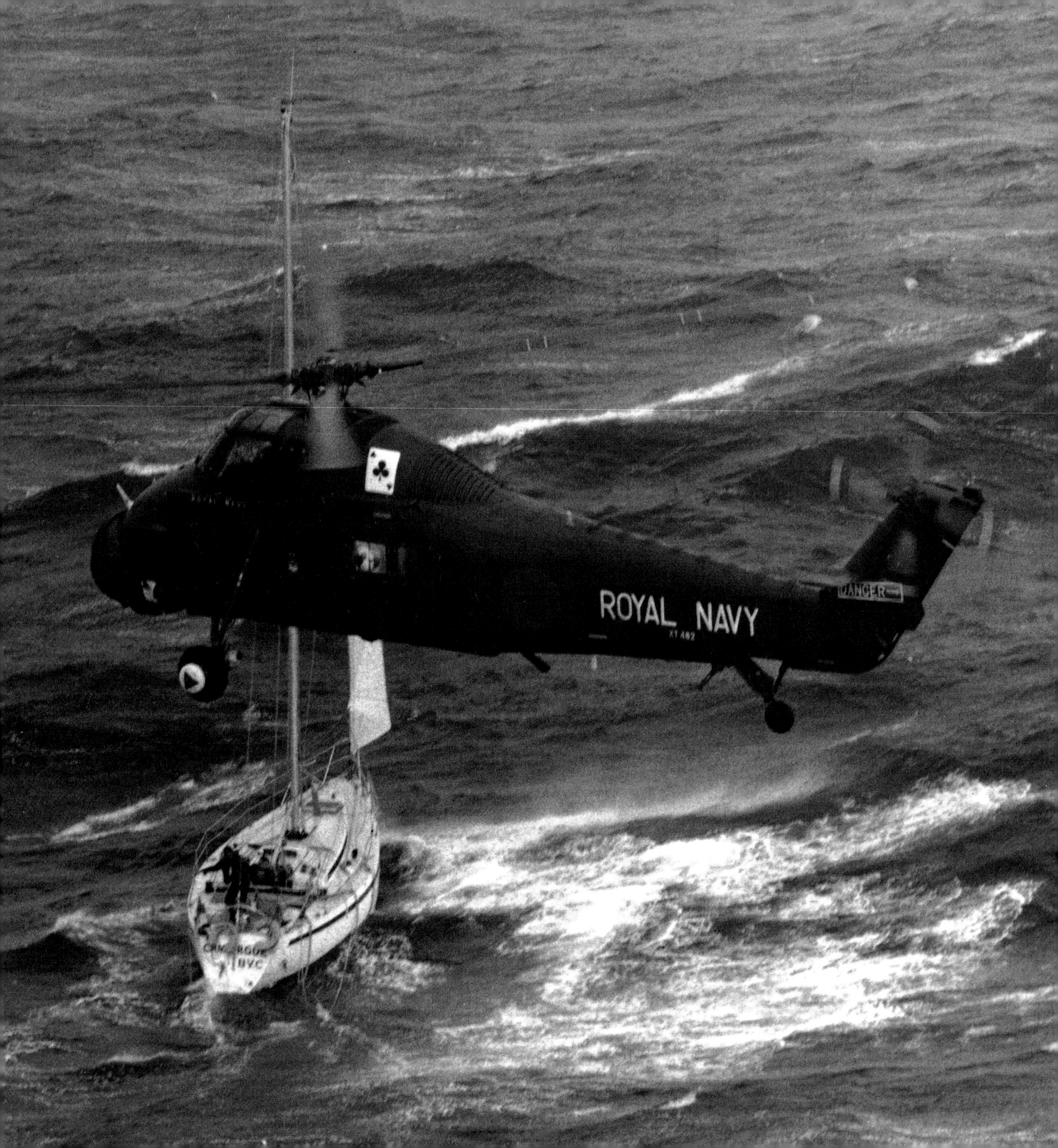
ROYAL NAVY
DANGER

# THE 1979 FASTNET RACE STORM

ALTHOUGH THE ADMIRAL'S CUP opened its account in 1957 with a heavy Fastnet Race, and there had been one previous fatality in 1931 when Colonel Hudson had been washed off the 51ft *Maitenes II*, it is the events between 14 and 15 August 1979 which caused the race that year to be remembered for the most infamous storm in yachting. From the Great Plains of the US mid-West, a storm galloped east, wrenching a roof off a toll booth on the New Jersey Turnpike and dropping trees in New York's Central Park. One bough fell on a woman, who became the storm's first casualty. With increasing ferocity, the storm raced across the Atlantic to strike the Fastnet fleet.

Tragically, fifteen lives were lost, plus a further four from a trimaran shadowing the 303-boat Fastnet fleet. Six were lost because their safety harnesses broke, while nine others were lost either to drowning or hypothermia in the water close to yachts and liferafts which had been capsized. Only 85 of the 303 starters completed the race, from 30-footers up to the 76ft maxi *Condor*, which broke the course record by more than eight hours. Twenty-four boats were abandoned, with five claimed by the raging sea in the Western Approaches. For a few brief days the sport of offshore racing, which must be the definitive participant sport as opposed to a spectator game, was suddenly thrust into the limelight. It made headlines around the world, led TV news bulletins and exposed sailing to the sort of scrutiny it had never before experienced.

Much of that fell on the Royal Ocean Racing Club. Normally they had only competitors to worry about; then the press arrived wanting immediate answers. Boats not reported in or not accounted for became casualties by default. Rumour became fact, as was illustrated when two American racers came ashore in Plymouth to find their obituaries had already been published at home.

The scale of the rescue operation was such that fixed-wing aircraft – principally RAF Nimrods, though with help from French and Irish planes – spent 135.5 hours aloft. Royal Navy helicopters were airborne for 195 hours, RAF and Irish Air Corps helicopters another 216 hours. Eight ships from the Services were involved, plus six fishing vessels, while even the official inquiry report on the disaster described the massive lifeboat operation from British and Irish stations as 'numerous'. It involved 169 hours at sea by lifeboats from thirteen different stations. In all, 136 sailors were recovered from liferafts, their yachts or the sea by the rescue services, fishermen, or fellow competitors, with a further seventy escorted back to safety by lifeboats.

The one inescapable truth about the 1979 race was that the storm developed very quickly, was exceptionally severe for August, hit the fleet in relatively shallow water after a major wind swing to generate an immensely difficult sea, and that all of these combined when there was a large concentration of small boats in its path.

The tall, steep-faced waves that swept the fleet in a cross pattern thumped down on the boats and their crews. More than a third of the fleet were laid flat, so that their masts were parallel to the raging sea. An even more terrifying statistic is that a quarter of the fleet – including the 46ft Admiral's Cupper *Jan Pott*, were inverted, many of them, rolling through a full 360 degrees. It scarcely needed the inquiry report to say: 'The sea showed that it can be a deadly enemy and those that go to sea for pleasure must do so in the full knowledge that they may encounter dangers of the highest order.'

*Low Y sped across the Atlantic and found more than 300 yachts in its path. A sharp shift in the breeze created a vicious crosswind which caused the damage (RNAS Culdrose)*

For something so awful, it started innocently enough. *The Daily Telegraph* on Monday 14 August headlined the race: *'Imp* among leaders, but pace slow.' Tony Fairchild's report ended: 'With a slow first twenty-four hours at sea, hopes of a brisker pace than for the last three Fastnet Races were beginning to recede.'

Known to few, Low Y had already begun its destructive course. Between midday Sunday and Monday, the depression had deepened slowly to 995mb, which suggested nothing menacing. The Paris National

*Ireland's Golden Apple of the Sun was the most newsworthy Admiral's Cup casualty, losing her rudder and having her crew airlifted off by helicopter. Here a Royal Navy crew from HMS Broadsword organise a tow rope on the afternoon of Tuesday 15 August, 20 hours after the storm's height (HMS Broadsword)*

twenty-four hour forecast issued at 0615 on Monday showed a small wave depression, yet by 1505 the BBC Shipping Forecast, which was the prime source for the fleet, issued the warning: 'Sole, Fastnet, Shannon. South-westerly gale Force 8 imminent.'

In forecasting terms, imminent means within six hours. The warnings were repeated in the 1750 Shipping Forecast on Monday, while forecasters at the Meteorological Office in Bracknell became increasingly aware that the isobars were tightening with rapidly

gathering pace. By 1905, the forecasters had upgraded their warnings to severe gale and by 2300 warnings of severe Force 9 gales were being forecast along with 'veering north-westerly and increasing Storm Force 10. Imminent.'

So, from the lunch-time shipping forecast, the fleet realised that the light-air race was going to be visited by a gale and, from the night-time forecast, that this had worsened to a storm. It's impossible to say whether by monitoring the BBC at other times, or by listening to forecasts from coast radio stations, the fleet could have been more forewarned, given the sudden deepening of Low Y. Or, if they were, whether it would have prompted crews to do anything thing more than check their vessels, their safety gear and prepare themselves for a big blow.

With the bigger yachts further down the course, it was they who signalled that events were starting to unfold disastrously and that the effect of the cross seas was beginning to be felt. The Irish Admiral's Cupper *Regardless* lost her rudder before midnight on Monday. The yachts *Wild Goose*, *Accanito* (a French AC yacht) and *Magic* had sent out maydays and by 0300 one British and three Irish lifeboats were at sea. The rescue operation got into full swing at 0345, when HM Coast-guard, the primary lifesaving service in British home waters and one which initiates and coordinates the civil SAR services, sent a message from their Land's End centre, whose patch is the Western Approaches, to the Southern Rescue Coordination Centre (SRCC) at Plymouth. They'd already overheard a radio telephone conversation between the maxi *Condor of Bermuda* and the smaller, rudderless, *Magic*, and had received reports of a red flare and three instances of distress.

The SRCC knew that the race was in progress so realised there were a lot of small boats in the wrong place at the wrong time. At first light, helicopters from the Royal Naval Air Station at Culdrose were dispatched, as was a Nimrod SAR aircraft from Kinloss in Scotland, the first moves in a massive operation.

The severity of the conditions was registered by the rescue services and some merchant ships. SAR aircraft reported 60-65 knot winds and 50-60ft seas, while windspeeds of 50 and 52 were noted by two ships.

The fifteen lives lost in the race, and the five yachts, were all from among the Fastnet Race fleet, but the Admiral's Cup boats did not escape unscathed. Hugh Coveney's crew aboard the Irish *Golden Apple of the Sun*, including designer Ron Holland, Harold Cudmore and triple Olympic medallist Rodney Pattisson, were the only AC team to be lifted off by SAR helicopter, when one came overhead the disabled yacht, which had lost her rudder and had the Scilly Isles forty miles to leeward.

German Frers was skippering the 51ft *Acadia*, which finished second in Class I. Twice she rolled far enough to put the mast's spreaders in the water. Malin Burnham, a noted San Diego sailor and banker, sliced off a toe nail on the deckhead of the 46ft *Williwaw* as he climbed the companionway ladder. In her 360-degree roll, the German *Jan Pott* was dismasted. Hong Kong's *Vanguard* was almost rolled right over when running under bare poles, and was later half-flooded when a wave broke over the boat as the No. 4 jib was being handed through the open companionway.

The British Class II winner, the 39ft *Eclipse*, was knocked down twice near the Rock. Skipper Jeremy Rogers considered retiring, mindful that the seas could be very dangerous between Cape Clear and the Rock, but *Eclipse* rounded at 0255 on Tuesday morning and set off back towards England under just the storm jib. 'Our speed was about seven knots, such a speed giving us useful control in the wild seas,' wrote navigator Peter Bruce. 'It seemed that a wave with a breaking crest would mount from one direction, then moments later, another wave would follow from a different direction.'

A crew packed with skilled helmsmen allowed *Eclipse* to press on, with a special effort made to keep the boat dry below and the crew fuelled up with hot soup, despite the stove having snapped its wire strop and jumped its anchorages. 'At daybreak the waves were spectacular,' added Bruce. 'They had become very large, very steep and breaking awkwardly.' As one of the lightest-built Admiral's Cup boats in the race, much was made of *Eclipse* coming through unscathed. But her internal ballast had already begun to move, and

Bruce speculates whether, because of their position in the race, they had been able to round the Rock during a lull at the depression centre, and then take the majority of the seas off the stern quarter.

*Morning Cloud*, Edward Heath's yacht, whose crew had already been chastened by the loss of their rudder in the Channel Race nine days before, was rolled down to 130 degrees some two hours after rounding the Rock. Helmsman Larry Marks was flung against the steering wheel and a stanchion. Two others were swept

*Anxious friends and relatives read the bulletin board at the RORC office in Plymouth's Millbay Dock (Rex Features)*

over the side, but, fortunately, their safety harnesses held. The yacht lay a-hull for while to take a breather. 'When daylight came, we thought, blimey, this is pretty bad,' recalled Marks. 'We were still pretty much dazed, and we all thought the best thing to do was sail home and sit by a fireside.'

The Dubois-designed 42ft downwind flyer, *Police Car*, was another to be knocked down but recovered, and her crew sped the boat up, even though she was under the storm jib (there was no storm trysail aboard), and found that this made control better as they started to run before the seas on the leg back from the Rock. The hugely experienced New Zealander, Chris Bouzaid, wrote in the American magazine *Yachting*: 'Every sea was different. Some of them we would just square away and run down the front of. Others were just too steep to do this. One imagines a sea to be a long sausagelike piece of water moving across the ocean. However, this was not the case at all as these seas had too many breaks in them and were not uniform. We found that in many cases we could pick our way through the seas, finding a little valley between seas and ducking through now that we had more boat speed. We found that we were managing to avoid all the breaking seas, either by cutting through the sea and going beyond the breaks, or bearing away on a sea prior to the break and avoid having it hit the boat.'

Thirteen of the fifty-seven Admiral's Cuppers failed to complete the race, a further three not having started.

The disaster threw up questions over press conduct.

After the tragic race, the Admiral's Cup management committee chewed over what had been reported. Dave Allen, an American, went so far as to say that harm had been created by incorrect reporting, so the press office should have been closed. But Alan Green, who had conducted himself and guided his staff with admirable control, understanding and tact during a stressful time, differed. To have closed it, he reasoned, would have worsened matters, as material would have been fabricated. Inquiries by the president of the United States Yacht Racing Union into some of the more bizarre reporting which cropped up in American papers had shown that there was considerable misunderstanding even among the yachting administrators in his own organisation, let alone amongst those outside it.

He had reason enough to be sensitive. Reports had circulated in the USA that *Imp* and *Williwaw* had sunk, with the *New York Times* running it as a front-page story, citing a USYRU source. It was into this atmosphere that Ted Turner, the flamboyant Atlanta media

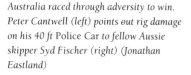

*Australia raced through adversity to win. Peter Cantwell (left) points out rig damage on his 40 ft* Police Car *to fellow Aussie skipper Syd Fischer (right) (Jonathan Eastland)*

magnate, commented on the arrival of *Tenacious* at the finish, that his greatest fear had been smashing into the smaller boats on the way back. 'That is the only thing that had me scared – that, and the fear than something on board *Tenacious* might break, causing us to lose the race.'

When *Williwaw* did finish, Dennis Conner adopted the same tough racer stance. 'It's no worse than the Indianapolis 500. We'll take our chances, The danger is part of it.'

As a former Prime Minister, Edward Heath and his *Morning Cloud* attracted acute interest. He found Plymouth ablaze with headlines such as 'The Suicide Armada', 'Cauldron of Death' and so forth. He showed the sensitivity expected of a senior statesman, who in 1974 had lived through the loss of his second *Morning Cloud* – and, with her, two crew, including a godson. The press clamoured for his views. He said simply, honestly: 'It was the worst experience I have ever had. We were fighting massive seas. It was very frightening – the sort of thing you would never want to experience again.'

For Alan Green, this was an unwelcome experience in his second year as RORC Secretary. He had shifted the race office from Cowes to Plymouth, anticipating no more than the painstaking process of receiving the position reports from the fleet and the radio relay vessels, calculating the results and arranging the prizegiving. He had been out on the Plymouth breakwater, checking the finish line, when the news of a disaster came through, and now he bore the full brunt of the media pressure as it was decided that the RORC would be the main source of information. This was on top of the unwelcome task of managing a considerable crisis.

Two press conferences a day were scheduled, with the Admiral's Cup press officer Roger Ware giving factual information but Alan Green being the sole voice of RORC actions and opinion. What he describes as 'the less well-bred members of the journalistic profession' used increasingly 'persuasive and invasive means' to get their stories. But Alan Green spoke only at the agreed times and gave only information which had been cross-checked and authenticated. He had to face with equanimity a press that was publishing 'Armada of Death' stories and turning every yacht unaccounted for into a total loss, while at the same time grilling him with variations on the same question: 'Why didn't you stop the race when the storm warnings became known?'

In his usual manner, Alan Green paused before answering such demands, the meaning of his words and their impact measured before utterance. 'The way the sport is organised,' he said during one particularly tense press conference at the height of the disaster, '...it is the skippers' responsibility whether to race or not.'

That, of course, was a reiteration of one of the RORC's principal conditions of entry to its races. 'Why should yachtsmen risk their lives and then put those who rescue them at risk too?' he was asked. 'Public opinion will have to make up its mind,' he replied. 'And sailors must make up their own minds whether to face the risks of the sea or not.'

Looking back on what must, for two days, have been the most unenviable job in the world, Alan Green said fourteen years later: 'It was hard work and difficult, requiring considerable amounts of fast decision-making on one's feet. I enjoy problem solving but the worst feature now, as it was at the time, was the consideration of the people who had lost relatives. I always felt then, and I do now, that they had a far harder time than any of us.'

Suprisingly, the Club came in for criticism from among its own number. Dick Nye, whose various *Carinas* had graced the Admiral's Cup in the 1960s, wrote of the race committee in the American journal

*Yachting*: 'You have an attractive nuisance. The Fastnet Committee (sic) is promoting a race which they are encouraging people to enter. To say there should be no special coverage for these yachts that have been encouraged to come by promoting the glamour of the Fastnet Race... is wrong. The race committee is totally abrogating (sic) its responsibility.'

Chris Bouzaid said much the same, though more colourfully: 'It's like running the Indianapolis 500 and having no fire-fighting equipment... it is the race committee's responsibility to prepare itself... handle something going wrong.'

But Mary Pera, no longer RORC secretary by 1979 and laid up during the storm in hospital with a viral infection, said: 'I've never felt the Club should feel the slightest bit guilty. We had done our best in specifying the most stringent safety regulations that we knew about at the time, we did our best to see that they were enforced. What more could we do?'

Communication proved exceptionally difficult. This was the era before faxes, and the phone lines and telex links between Land's End Coastguard and Plymouth soon became choked. Accounting for 300-plus yachts was one of the biggest operations the SAR agencies have had to cope with in UK waters, although the fleet was at least organised in the sense that yachts could be identified by the RORC through name, hull colour and sail number. But it was not until Wednesday that the precise number of starters was known. Just getting the printouts between the tip of Cornwall and Plymouth could take between three and six hours. Private aircraft and police vehicles were used to speed it up.

Alan Green was assisted by John Clothier, then a RORC rear-commodore and a senior partner in Clarks shoes, who set up a crisis desk, part of it a special unit manned by Sir David Mackworth and Keith Ludlow. With rapidly increasing efficiency, the various sources of information were screened until proper means validated a casualty as a death, when it fell to Sir David and Keith Ludlow to pass the information on to relatives. 'Everyone did a marvellous job, but it was those two who handled a particularly difficult task with great sensitivity,' Alan Green remembers.

The letters winging their way from St James's Place after the race was over said much about the people who rallied round to manage the crisis. Janet Grosvenor sent special thanks to her opposite number, Sue Fielden, at the Cowes Combined Clubs. The Commodore thanked press officer Roger Ware ('most competent, level-headed and reliable'), Sir David and Lady Mackworth (for planning the new IBM computer results service at Cowes, sorting out its utter failure in practice, and manning, without break, the next-of-kin phone in Plymouth), Rodney Hill (radio relay work and arranging another marquee at Cowes when the original was burnt down), Colonel James Myatt (who came down to Plymouth specially to man the office during a critical thirty-six hours). There were many others.

Alan Green said a month later: 'It is certainly a year we will never forget. I thought the frustrations of the two weeks in Cowes were bad enough, but the Fastnet tragedy made Cowes look like child's play.'

After it was all over, the RORC and the Royal Western YC offered a joint Christmas present to the Land's End Coastguard, just one of many gestures to recognise the assistance that had been given so willingly by so many people.

Through the myriad sensationalised press reporting, *The Daily Telegraph* ran a well-considered editorial: 'If we still value the qualities of daring, comradeship and endurance in our national life we should cherish the sports which foster them with the risks they carry. The lessons of the Fastnet should be studied carefully and applied sensibly but in the knowledge that they can never expel the danger from yachting and the conviction that it will be a sad and bad day when the seafaring people declines the challenge of the ocean.'

*Undertakers wait to carry out their grim duty as the Dutch race guardship, Overijssel, comes alongside in Devonport (Jonathan Eastland)*

# SPONSORSHIP – CASH AND THE CUP

PONSORSHIP FIRST CAME in the shape of the team backers. Inevitably, those for whom the cost of competing was the highest were the first to entertain commercial backing. In 1965 the Australian team were supported by Qantas Airlines and Rothmans of Pall Mall, the latter through their Rothmans Sports Foundation. A pointer to the future was that when Rob McAuley filmed the series that year, his budget was met by the team sponsors. Arguably, it was the first initiative of its type in ocean racing in Europe and involved fast launches and a helicopter. The team's press officer, Frank McNulty, was racing on Syd Fischer's *Ragamuffin* and while he was afloat, Richie Benaud, sometime Australian cricket captain, helped out with the PR.

Dunhill, the British team's first supporter, became involved in 1969 with both the Admiral's Cup and Cowes Week. With Dunhill's Pall Mall offices just a stone's throw away from the RORC clubhouse in St James's Place, the links with the Club were not just geographical but personal. Buster de Guingand's brother, Sir Francis de Guingand, was a director of Dunhill, as was Edmund de Rothschild, a considerable yachtsman himself. Already the support was being put to good use. Dunhill provided the appropriately named motor yacht, *Virginia Queen*, with meteorologist Alan Watts recruited to give the British sailors a met briefing.

Dunhill also provided inflatable runabouts, made the *Virginia Queen* available to the press, made a film of the series in conjunction with Rothmans' Australian endeavours, and furnished crews with team ties and badges. Branding had arrived. Dunhill's marketing manager, Derek Lee, sought to assure the previous RORC secretary, Alan Paul, that filming team meetings would pose no threat to security of tactics: 'Any film shot won't be processed for at least a month.'

In 1975, the then RORC secretary Mary Pera rang out the alarm that Dunhill had decided to withdraw from yachting. Not surprisingly, representations were made to Dunhill to reconsider and they agreed to sponsor Cowes Week in 1975 and support the press office, which would be used for both events. But it was a slimmed-down operation.

Dunhill's support of the RORC bar in Groves & Guttridge marina fell by the wayside and the Cowes Combined Clubs brought in outside caterers to provide a bar cafeteria. The showers and toilets at Plymouth, which Dunhill had sponsored in 1971 and 1973, were installed again, though the Plymouth council was asked to take care of this for future events.

Just as Dunhill were preparing an orderly withdrawal, so the visiting nations began to absorb some of the benefits of sponsorship. American Jeff Hammond became convinced that sponsorship was beneficial. 'Dunhill organised a press office, press boats, results distribution, portable heads, telephones, trophies, promotion posters and publicity which all contributed to the success of the event,' he wrote in *Sail* magazine after the 1975 series. 'In return, Dunhill is associated in the mind of the public with an exciting sport. Many yachting events in the USA could be improved by commercial sponsorship and possibly in the future an American will step forward to help promote the sport,' he added presciently.

Dunhill's Peter Huntley and his aide Terry Lees made a big contribution, but it was Anthony Churchill, later to navigate Edward Heath's *Morning Clouds*, who was one of the first to recognise the promotional opportunities of the sport through sponsorship.

So the first steps towards Champagne Mumm were made. Churchill persuaded an emissary of the Mumm champagne house, Gérard de Ayala, to come to Cowes.

*Graham Walker's 50 foot* Indulgence *rounding the leeward mark in the 1993 series.*

Mumm was part of the giant Canadian drinks conglomerate Seagram, who were looking to extend their sporting sponsorships and liked what they saw in the Admiral's Cup. Moreover, the Mumm chairman, Baron Alain de Gunzburg, was a former racing sailor himself,

*HRH Princess Anne with Baron Alain de Gunzburg of Champagne Mumm at the 1991 Royal Yacht Squadron Lawn Reception. The then RORC Commodore John Dare and Assistant Racing Director Janet Grosvenor look on*

maintaining a large cruise ketch in the Greek Islands, and he was particularly keen for Mumm to be involved in sailing.

'The marketing strategy was to find an event which was international – since Champagne Mumm ships abroad something like 70-80 per cent of its production – was upscale, well established and prestigious,' recalls Gérard de Ayala, who then worked in Mumm's marketing and export department, with the UK included in his territory. 'The countries involved, then including France, make up 98-99 per cent of the champagne market and yacht owners are right at the heart of that market.' De Ayala, who still plays a large roll in Mumm's involvement with the Cup, says it was felt that the UK was the right place to find such an event, a factor helped by Britain long being the biggest importer of champagne.

The Club asked Seagram to underwrite a party at the Royal Yacht Squadron and contribute to the series expenses, but David Edwards, chairman of the Cup's management committee, urged caution about the linked advertising which would inevitably follow and stressed the need to maintain discretion. Undaunted, Alan Green arranged to see the Mumm chairman, Baron Alain de Gunzburg. Green travelled to France at the end of the 1975 season with Terry Lees, who brought first-hand knowledge of Dunhill's experience, as well as their important pictorial record of their support. De Gunzburg gave his agreement, and so began what was to become one of the longest sports sponsorships ever.

The American computing giant, IBM, also entered the scene, offering to compute the results of the races in the Solent and Channel as well as interim positions while the races were in progress. The RORC tried to tease another terminal out of IBM so that the Fastnet results could be calculated in Plymouth too. For all of IBM's prowess, the results service was far from slick.

Mumm came formally onboard for the 1977 series. Pleased as the Club was, it had not entirely shed its blushing bride persona at the prospect of being in bed with a commercial sponsor. While the Cup's management committee went back to Mumm to see if they would be interested in additional support, a Champagne Mumm Trophy, for the newly instituted Third Inshore race, it was still necessary to ask the views of the Club's main committee about how this might affect the Club's other races.

Other offers were forthcoming. Delta Metals had concluded a three-year agreement with the Cowes Combined Clubs to support Cowes Week from 1977 onwards and had shown interest in the Admiral's Cup too. Their bid of £10,000 was considered too low, however, as the Club felt £29-30,000 was necessary. IBM wanted to continue its help with the results service, while Volvo and Hennessy had also made approaches.

But the strongest offer came from American Express. The proposal, comprehensive and carefully written, had been presented with considerable care and trouble. They offered £30,000 towards running the series, plus another £30,000 to Anthony Churchill and his associate Guy Pearse – promoters who had been part of the British ocean racing scheme for some time – to publicise the regatta. By offering to spend a further £30,000 on additional promotional activity, such as providing banking and credit card facilities to visiting yachtsman, the Amex bid topped £90,000.

For the RORC, as a private club, it marked a bold step forward. Its committee pondered the pros and cons. Sponsorship would bring publicity, which in turn could help crews secure time off work from their employers. It would also require the closest of controls, because 'there was always the slightest possibility that the promotion could move the face of the sport in a direction which would not be desired by those who took part in it'.

Amex were strong contenders to claim the 1977 series, though in retrospect the style of a corporation such as Amex was probably too assertive for the Club. Fortunately, Mumm were still interested and the Club pondered whether they would be interested as a subsidiary sponsor. Mumm were pleased with the results of their involvement in 1975. The sales of cases of Mumm champagne in the UK told their own story: in 1975 it had been 320 cases, a year later it was 620 and by 1977 it had risen to 1850.

When the Cup management committee plumped for the Amex proposal after an agonising debate, they found the offer could not be confirmed. Some expressed relief and the committee clearly felt happiest with its relationship with Mumm, who were supportive but not assertive and whose product sat so comfortably alongside high-level yachting. Even if its cash value was far less than the Amex deal, the association with Mumm has proved a fortuitious one.

Two years on, the Club was delighted to negotiate the contract with Mumm for £30,000, in a deal confirmed in March 1979. Besides £30,000 for the next series, Mumm agreed to support the series until 1985, based on the same figure, but adjusted according to the British government's Retail Price Index. For Mumm it was, and remains, their biggest sponsorship, their other main marketing thrust being in the field of gas-

tronomy. By sponsoring some famous chefs, the culture of *haute cuisine* and champagne is enhanced.

After the 1979 series, Gérard de Ayala broached the idea of buying the naming rights to the series. 'I told the RORC they were wasting quite a lot of energy and losing half of the coverage,' said de Ayala, 'When I suggested we call it the Champagne Mumm Admiral's Cup, there was some reluctance, as you can imagine. That's why we offered a ten-year contract. It was good for the Club because they were assured of a long-term sponsor, and it was good for Mumm because we were able to build a real marketing strategy.'

By 1983, a real partnership had been formed, consummated by a new ten-year arrangement, with Mumm purchasing the right to add their name to that of the

*The Champagne Mumm Admiral's Cup awaiting presentation at the close of the Fastnet Race outside the Royal Western YC in Plymouth (KOS)*

series. 'When the naming rights were made over to Champagne Mumm, it was major decision,' recalls Alan Green of the committee's deliberation. 'They found it a considerable step to take.' There were some reluctant voices on the committee, but they came round.

Signed on St Valentine's Day, 14 February 1983, the ten-year agreement required a contract drawn up by solicitors for both parties, whereas a simple exchange of letters had sufficed before. It was symptomatic of

term deal would enable them to buy property in Cowes as a permanent club premises on the Island. However, events overtook this idea, for the estate of Sir Max Aitken generously made 82 High Street available to the Club. This was The Prospect, the former Ratsey & Lapthorn sail loft which Sir Max had made into a museum, home and office.

By 1989, the game was certainly more costly. The budget for the 1989 series was set at £228,000, ranging

*Ryouji Oda celebrates Will's 1991 win in the Champagne Mumm Trophy Race with his own weight in champagne, Japan's first ever Admiral's Cup race victory*

the more complex and more businesslike arrangements. Tony Greener, the Club's honorary treasurer, joined the RORC's negotiating team. He was a sailor who had run Dunhill's smokers' accessory business, a brand which Greener turned into a luxury goods concern before joining the drinks giant, Guinness, as managing director.

One thing the RORC had in mind was that a long-

from large items such as marina berthing at £21,000 to a helpers' party at £500. The list of things to be budgeted for was staggeringly long. By 1991 it ran to seven pages, covering such items as artwork for the skippers' briefing, marshal boats to control the spectators and give the TV boats a clear shot, the Squadron reception, buoys and ground tackle, crew gear transport from Cowes to Plymouth, jury travel, accommodation and food, measurement and special regulations checks, timekeepers at Gillkicker, Plymouth and on the Fastnet Rock, scoreboards, photocopying, messenger runners, results service, office costs and portable radios. Press releases alone – sent world-wide to 1250 journals, newspapers, TV and radio stations – cost over £1,000 each mailshot. Even if entry fees generated close to £100,000, owing largely to the loading applied to sponsored boats, the costs to be met were, and remain, considerable.

Champagne Mumm were sensitive to the issue of registering their trademark, and put their foot down about the term Admiral's Cup being used on its own for a range of clothing produced by a prominent British manufacturer. Mumm had already gone to considerable lengths in regaining their Cup trademark from another company in the Far East.

The change in Mumm's disposition was plain to see, and not unreasonable. The 'value' of the event was discussed, especially as it had been purchased as a separate and substantial investment by Mumm. As Gerard de Ayala noted: 'Outside of the specialist yachting press, few people in the media are interested in covering the event. We have to sell it to them, which invariably costs money. This is becoming an industry trend as sponsors generally seek to enhance returns.'

In the last two agreements, other sparkling wines or champagne have been expressly excluded, with a 'no-bubbles' clause. That champagne and yachting get along together in terms of image is obvious. So, too, is the international status and prestige of the event. Throughout their involvment, a key figure for Mumm, however, is that 98 per cent of their production is shipped to countries involved in the series.

In 1987, when a study was made, Mumm put the TV coverage achieved around the world at £2.5 million and press coverage at £1 million. In some countries an audience level of 104 million had been achieved, according to an analysis of the TV coverage, with 2hr 42mins of news shown, plus 23hr 5mins of documentary coverage. They have also sold 7600 cases of their special Admiral's Cup cuvée in Britain and France alone, and between 1983 and 1993, when a new ten-year agreement was signed until 2003, Mumm moved from twelfth in the UK champagne market to be the third brand behind Moet et Chandon and Lanson. Gerard de Ayala admits this was due to a mix of marketing initiatives, but a survey carried out in the UK in the early 1990s showed that a majority of the sample interviewees associated Mumm with sailing.

A key to the longevity of the sponsorship is the association of Baron de Gunzberg and Gerard de Ayala, who have brought stability to a business which normally has a high turnover of personnel. 'Yachting is Champagne Mumm and Champagne Mumm is yachting,' admits Gerard de Ayala. 'We realise that continuity is good for the image, good for the product and good for the event. We are really happy with it, and now it seems we are considered the champagne of yachting.'

The contract is based on two budgets. A fixed management fee is given to the club to run each event and is negotiated for each series, though to assist with cash flow it is paid on a rolling annual basis. There is also a direct-cost budget which covers the actual expenditure required to run the event, from committee boat charter fees to mailshots, from rented accommodation to photocopier hire.

Augmenting this, each Seagram subsidiary or affiliate around the world tops up the budget by running their own promotion. When Mumm linked the Admiral's Cup with other events around the world to form the Champagne Mumm World Cup, these local budgets became especially important as key buyers and distributors were entertained at events such as Key West Race Week in Florida. Incentive schemes saw a party of forty-six from the USA come to Cowes for the 1993 Champagne Mumm Admiral's Cup.

After Mumm, it is the Swiss watchmaking company Corum who have made the biggest commitment to the event, largely through the enthusiasm of chairman Jean-René Bannwart. Corum came aboard in the 1983 series because they had developed a watch with flags on its face in place of numerals. Jean-René Bannwart's father had used the Admiral's Cup name back in the 1960s, when the series meant little outside the offshore racing community, and it was thought a good idea to

*The Corum Trophy presented to the winning team of the second inshore race. It is based on the ship's clock designed in the 18th century by the famous French royal naval watchmaker Ferdinand Berthoud, a fellow of the Royal Society*

revive the name to go with the new watch. The RORC and Mumm agreed.

Two years later, Corum presented their trophy for the Second Inshore race, often holding their prizegiving on the evening of the race on a large chartered vessel, such as the J-Class yacht *Velsheda*, moored in Cowes Roads.

'We have spent a lot of money and worked hard at making the name Admiral's Cup well-known throughout the world. Ten years ago, no one outside sailing knew what the event was. Now I think a lot more people do, thanks to our efforts,' said M. Bannwart in 1991.

That year was a landmark for Corum, for the French team won the Champagne Mumm Admiral's Cup in three boats either owned or chartered by Corum, each of which was named Corum, and with all three yachts and crews branded in colour coordinated livery. Only once had that been tried before, in 1987, when Alan Bond backed the Australian team and had two of the three yachts re-painted black and named *Swan Premium I, II* and *III* after his lager brand. An attempt in 1989 to brand the British team Swan Light in return for £150,000 from Allied Breweries came to nought.

Corum stepped beyond simple event support by becoming involved in boat ownership in 1987, at the instigation of La Rochelle-based designer Philippe Briand. He arranged a collaboration between volume boatbuilder Beneteau and Corum whereby the costs were shared. For Beneteau, the custom race boat did for them what rallying does for the likes of Toyota, Lancia or Peugeot, while for Corum it made their interest more focused.

'I think the boat made our involvement much more personal,' explained Jean-Rene Bannwart. 'Everybody who works for Corum in our workshops and retailing outlets could get behind the campaign. Also the event happens every two years, whereas the boat exists all the time; it can be followed. Our customers can also relate to a boat more easily; it is something more visible, both on the water and in magazine photographs, than sponsorship of an event.'

In 1989 a second 45ft Two-Tonner was built, which like her predecessor proved to be a good but not outstanding boat. Briand spent two years tinkering with her to – in the jargon of the sport – adjust her performance profile, but for the 1991 series he decided to play the boat's strength and revert back to her near-original trim when, in her conditions, she was really fast.

It was around the Two-Tonner, now called *Corum Rubis*, that the team was built, in collaboration with the Fédération François à Voile. For their One-Tonner, *Mean Machine* was chartered from the Netherlands to become *Corum Diamant*, while the 50-footer was secured through Briand, who had designed *Capricorno* for Rinaldo del Bono of Italy. The whole effort almost came crashing to the floor when *Capricorno* was involved in a three-boat collision in her first 50ft regatta at Key West, Florida, in January.

But the boat was given a new bow by her builder, Eric Goetz, and just got back to Europe in time for the Oracle Admiral's Cup warm-up regatta. Because of that mishap, the small boat's moderate showing in the One Ton Cup and the Two-Tonner's reputation as a heavy boat, the French team entered the 1991 Champagne Mumm Admiral's Cup as clear outsiders. That ignored the work done by Luc Gellusseau in securing crews, creating impressive back-up, putting in hours of planning and having the squad sailing according to a weather plan, rather than getting involved in the muck and bullets of boat-to-boat racing. Because of it, the French scored a win memorable both for its surprise and the smallness of its margin – just 0.62 points.

Corum, Beneteau and the FFV were delighted. They had, after all, spent £1 million on the sailing aspects of the campaign, quite apart from PR and advertising costs. 'It wasn't a fluke,' maintains Jean-René Bannwart. 'Some people will think it may well have been, but some of our opposition know damn well that while we had some luck, it was no fluke. Luc Gellusseau organised this whole thing, and did so incredibly precisely, even by Swiss standards. He was brilliant and must take much of the credit for this success.'

Ironically, a world-wide recession which upset Corum's sales figures made it impossible to determine the value of the 1991 victory.

Mumm and Corum work very closely to support each other's efforts. For instance, in preparing brochures or videos, they are careful to use clips or pictures of their respective products. And they are co-sponsors of the Champagne Mumm World Cup (run also by the RORC), with whom both work closely with the Japanese electrical giant Kenwood. 'We know how the other works,' said Gerard de Ayala, 'and we try and fulfil as much as we can on all sides. I don't know where you'd find sponsors with different products who would work together so closely.'

*From entering their own boat in 1987, Corum progressed to fielding the entire French team in 1991 and 1993. Here the 45ft* Corum Rubis *(left) leads the 40ft* Corum Diamant *and the 50ft* Corum Saphir *past the Royal Yacht Squadron*

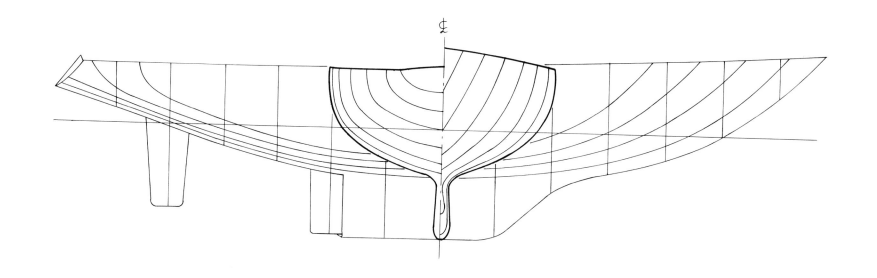

RABBIT

---

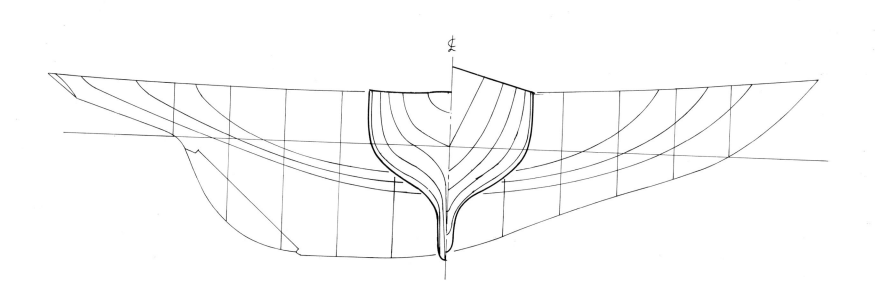

OLIVER VAN NOORT

---

# DESIGN DEVELOPMENTS

*U*NTIL 1993 the history of rating rules was a lot simpler than their technical workings, for the Admiral's Cup had to deal with only two: the Royal Ocean Racing Club Rule and the International Offshore Rule. The 1995 Champagne Mumm Admiral's Cup will be the first to use the IOR's successor, the International Measurement System.

The RORC rule can be traced back to the early tonnage rules of the eighteenth and nineteenth centuries, the word 'ton' deriving from a measure of tuns of wine a vessel could carry, calculated for revenue purposes. The object of such rules was to enable different yachts to race together, because if a boat's performance potential could be measured and rated, then time allowances could be generated too.

Several rules were attempted in nineteenth-century Britain as the fledgling sport of yacht racing grew, and it was to bring some order that the Yacht Racing Association was formed in 1875, although its early rule was not a huge success. It brought length, beam and displacement together in a formula which encouraged narrow and deep gutted hulls – the so-called plank-on-edge type. By contrast, the Americans were favouring the beamy, shallow-hulled approach.

The plethora of rules settled down at the turn of the century. In the USA Nathanael Herreshoff, 'the Wizard of Bristol' turned his attention from his fabulous America's Cup yachts towards creating the Universal Rule, divided into classes according to the alphabet. The J class was used in the America's Cup until 1937. In Britain, Brooke Heckstall-Smith of the Yacht Racing Association organised a sixteen-nation conference in London in 1906, a meeting which was the precursor of the sport's governing body, International Yacht Racing Union. A technical committee framed the International Rule, which continues today in the shape of, for example, the 6-metre class and which, unlike its American rival, demanded that yachts be sensibly and soundly built in accordance with the Lloyd's Register of Shipping scantling rule.

Neither was really suitable for passage racing yachts, so when the Bermuda race was run by some members of the recently created Cruising Club of America in 1923, a new rule was drafted. Then, when the Fastnet was sailed in 1925 and the RORC's predecessor, the Ocean Racing Club, was formed, it too wrote a new rule, both countries content to plough their own furrows. A gesture was made towards a harmonised pan-Atlantic rule when the 1928-32 Bermuda races and the 1926 Fastnet used an adapted Universal Rule.

Appropriately, it was Brooke Heckstall-Smith's brother, Malden, who was charged with finding a way for Britain's fledgling ocean racing fleet to race together. He based what became the RORC Rule on some of the premises of the 1912 Boat Racing Association Rule – yet another formula which had been created by yet another body.

In many ways, it was a relief that there were 'only' two rules for the offshore branch of the sport – and they were closer in spirit than many acknowledge, although the detail differences were many, with perhaps the measurement of length the fundamental thing that divided the two regulations. The Americans saw this as a 2-D problem and simply measured length as 4 per cent of the waterline length. The British considered it a 3-D problem, and established length by drawing two girths at the bow and stern, their location dictated by the fullness of the hull.

After the Admiral's Cup was established in 1957, American boats coming over to the UK became used to their CCA-inspired shapes accruing a higher rating when put through the RORC Rule parameters. Taking sail area off the boat became an accustomed rating reducing ploy for US boats.

Dick Carter was an American designer whose boats did rather well in Europe. Following *Rabbit's* 1965 Fastnet victory, he gave a talk at the New York Yacht Club, picking the theme of a single world rating system. 'Although the rules are very different, the boats are a lot closer than many people realise,' Carter told his audience.

Afterwards he was approached by Olin Stephens, then at the height of his considerable and enduring prowess. 'He came up in his inimitable style,' remembers Carter, 'of head lowered nervously and feet shuffling, to say he shared the same thoughts.' Stephens introduced Carter to the Offshore Racing Coordinating Committee, which was exploring the one-rule concept. 'Frankly, I was appalled at the things they were talking about,' recalls Carter. 'The New York YC's objective was not to manage the sport at all.'

But Carter and Stephens plugged on. 'I felt Olin and I made a terrific combination. He knew the people and I was able to ask the questions he felt too circumspect to pose.' The turning point came in 1967 when CCA Commodore Fred Adams wrote to the RORC Secretary, Alan Paul, suggesting that each club surrender the sovereignty over their rules. This cause was championed by a mailshot from Stephens and Carter, which set the scene for a meeting of the ORCC in the Fastnet Room at the RORC. 'That room was packed and loaded with tension,' says Carter. 'Buster de Guingand was chairing the two sides and heard RORC Commodore Mike Vernon reiterate that the RORC rule *was* international. Then the Norwegian delegate said, "Let's just agree to agree!" and the whole meeting took off.'

In November 1968, the combined rule was announced, called the International Offshore Rule and administered by the new Offshore Racing Council, which was a tenant of the RORC in 19 St James's Place. From 1971 the RORC used the IOR for all its races, including all the Admiral's Cups from then until 1993.

In the 1980s, the International Offshore Rule was slowly drowning under a sea of criticism. If there was any one fault to be used in evidence against the IOR,

then perhaps it was a failure to weigh boats in order to determine displacement. Instead, rather like the tonnage rules, point measurements were taken at predetermined locations on the hull to gauge its shape and hence how much of it was in the water. In time, displacement was scooped away between the measurement stations by designers as they sought to reduce wetted surface, and advances in glassfibre – and then composite – construction meant that the hull shells themselves weighed less and less. In order to have the sort of displacement the IOR rule needed for an effective rating, more and more internal ballast was needed to replace what had been removed. By the mid-1980s, it was becoming difficult to get sufficient lead in the floor of the boats, with great tombstones of lead often an integral part of the hull floor.

Part of this process saw the boats stripped out further until they became inhospitable shells which had to be sailed like dinghies. When all pretence of racing boats being dual purpose evaporated in the mid-1970s, so came the realisation that the IOR boats were not especially fast for their length to make up for the privations in sailing them offshore.

Yet the achievements of the IOR were profound. By the mid-1970s, there were more than 10,000 certificates around the world; for the first time an owner could have his boat built and rated in New Zealand and be able to race in Florida or the Solent with a valid rating. An IOR certificate was international currency. The Rule was also able to embrace boats from, say, 22ft overall length up to 84ft, and be used for gentle club day racing or round the world maxi marathons. Above all, it permitted excellent racing between disparate designs.

The style of offshore racing through four decades of the Admiral's Cup altered because of what happened to the design of yachts. The then and now picture can be painted with the help of Mary Pera. She started sailing with her father, an Army officer who became a barrister, in the 1930s out of West Mersea when offshore racing 'was considered totally out of the realm'. She raced extensively in the British and Italian waters throughout the 1940s, 1950s and 1960s. 'In those days, one did everything: foredeck, helm, navigate.' Being a woman navigator was considered quite extraordinary, although far more women raced then than in modern times.

'It was much less stressful then. You had a nice sail, took someone with you to cook, ate properly, drank nice wine and went to bed at night and slept,' remembers Mary Pera. 'It was a great deal more civilised till it came under pressure from the dinghy boys. It was the Admiral's Cup and Ton Cups of the 1960s which really did it in.'

The contrast by the early 1970s could not have been more profound. The boats were stripped out. Crews sat on the rail. Watch systems disappeared in favour of a buddy system, or even just letting the two most tired down below. Sleeping on the rail became common. Decent onboard meals, taken around the saloon table, gave way to prepared food, snacks, caffeine tablets and other stimulants. There was less and less pleasure involved in being at sea, other than for the competition.

The course of the Admiral's Cup has accurately reflected the progress of yacht design, based on a few landmark yachts, though, paradoxically, one of the most significant yachts of all, Captain John Illingworth and Peter Green's *Myth of Malham*, was ten years old when she competed in the first Cup in 1957. Even then she was still the most advanced yacht taking part. Though dubbed a dreadful-looking monstrosity, she pioneered the view that function can have a beauty of its own and that, just as in the inshore classes, offshore yachts could be designed to manipulate a rating rule.

As with *Myth*, Ricas van de Stadt from the Netherlands attempted wholly different ideas, though in truth his boats looked like model yachts designed years earlier. However, he did pioneer light displacement and split underbodies, which reduced wetted surface by separating the rudder from the trailing edge of the keel. His *Zeevalk* met with success when the wind piped up.

It was the evolutionary approach of Olin Stephens which was the dominant influence for the first two and half decades of the Admiral's Cup. Sparkman & Stephens' Madison Avenue office in New York was the engine-room of yacht design from the day *Dorade* won the Fastnet in 1931. An S & S boat was a safe bet for any owner, just as a Farr boat had become by the late 1980s. Dennis Miller and Derek Boyer beat a path to Olin Stephens for *Clarion* in 1963, and the two sister ships – *Firebrand* for Dennis Miller and *Prospect of Whitby* for Arthur Slater in 1965 – demonstrated, by Olin Stephens' own admission, that the racing Admiral's Cupper had arrived.

It was in the Ton Cup fleets, though, that real innovation was showing its head, particularly among the One-Tonners, where Dick Carter's *Tina* and *Rabbit* made the fin and skeg hull form work in a way van de Stadt had not managed. Stephens had already taken the rudder away from the keel, but Carter isolated the keel from the hull to such an extent that it was a true lifting surface, rather than a means of carrying ballast.

After such a big step, design stagnated, with boats getting heavier for their ratings until Carter struck again in 1973 with the One-Tonner, *Ydra*. She was relatively light, had a compact rig, an easily driven hull and a symmetrical waterplane.

It was those ideas that a young Californian, Doug Peterson, took to a far more effective conclusion in *Ganbare*, as did a young New Zealander, Ron Holland, with the Quarter-Tonner *Eygthene*, which transformed the sport. The jeans-and-dishevelled-hair brigade were on the brink of displacing their bow-tied elders.

The Holland/Peterson style – of a deep forefoot, negligible rocker and pinched pintail stern epitomised by Peterson's 1977 *Moonshine* – was a cul-de-sac. This style of boat exhibited great upwind form, but they were not great reaching boats and were positive bitches to get downwind in a blow. Their aptly named death roll was the result of big masthead rigs and beamy hulls with fine ends. It took a good helmsman to keep such a boat under the spinnaker.

Having come straight out of small boats, New Zealander Bruce Farr looked at offshore boats with a sharp mind, and he seemed to marry the two seemingly incompatible characteristics of light displacement with agreeable upwind form. His first offshore design was *Titus Canbe*, arguably more radical than *Myth* had been when she was launched.

Farr's first Admiral's Cup boat was *Gerontius* in 1975, and in the battle with the Peterson, Holland and German Frers type of medium-heavy masthead rigged boats over the next eight to nine years, it was the Farr-style boats which emerged superior, with their fuller sterns and fractional rigs.

While Peterson and Holland tipped their design balance more towards offwind speed, with Ron Holland's *Imp* from 1977 proving the point whilst pioneering the move away from alloy to glassfibre, it was Ed Dubois' *Police Car* from 1979 which helped paint the message that towards downwind orientated boats was the way to go. She highlighted a theme developed by Laurie Davidson's Half-Tonner *Waverider* and helped establish the smaller-ton cup sizes as the forcing ground for design. This led to a new crop of designers blossoming forth, best represented by France's Joubert/Nivelt, with their 1981 top boat *Diva*, and the German/Dutch partnership of Judel/Vrolijk with *Dusselboot*.

The offshore dinghy movement was well and truly underway, with Bruce Farr becoming by the end of the 1980s as dominant in terms of market share, results and reputation as Olin Stephens had been before him.

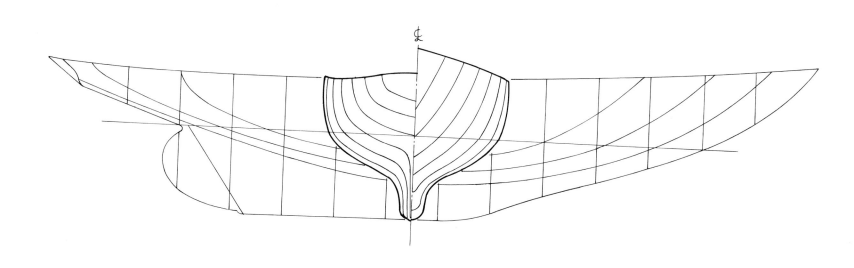

# CARINA (1957)

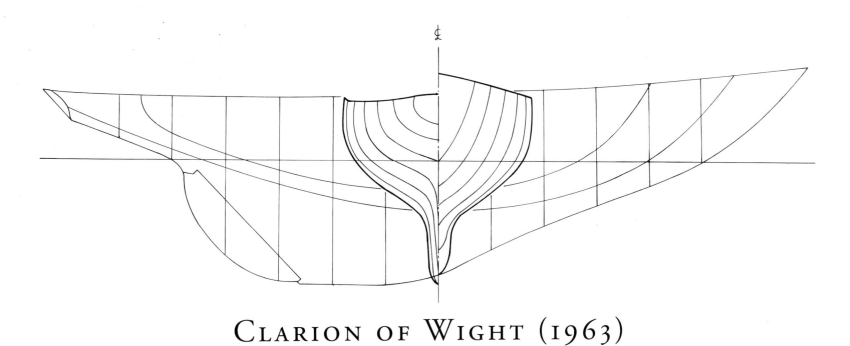

# CLARION OF WIGHT (1963)

*Clarion of Wight*'s drawings were done in the early summer of 1962. She was beautifully built by Clare Lallow of Cowes for Derek Boyer and Dennis Miller and delivered at the beginning of the 1963 sailing season. I was in Germany and drove to Rotterdam for the finish of the early race to the Hook of Holland and was able to join a happy crew, as *Clarion* had come in as the winner. This was the start of a good season as *Clarion* went on to become high point boat in the 1963 Admiral's Cup and that year's Fastnet winner.

There is nothing unusual about *Clarion*'s design. She came out at a time when I saw no loopholes in the RORC Rule. I had not yet found the opening offered by the scantling allowance. Her hull was relatively light and her ballast ratio high, about 50%. The ends were well-balanced and fine, especially aft. She was deeper in both her sections and her draught than an American CCA type yacht of the same period. I then had the impression, no longer so strongly held, that British racing meant heavy weather, so *Clarion*'s rig was decidedly snug and rather low, with a masthead foretriangle. This spelled a low rating for her size and, I think, for that summer at least, the strong wind gamble paid off. She could carry a No.1 genoa in a good breeze and her deep hull could keep going when well heeled over.

*Clarion*'s displacement/length ratio of about 360 seems very high today and probably was higher than many of her competitors. This made possible the high ballast ratio. Her windward ability was exceptional and more than made up for anything she lost down wind as even the lightest of her competitors did not have anything like the downwind performance that has become routine today. Beam was only what it had to be considering displacement and the shape of her sections. Her wetted area was moderate to low for a boat of her dimensions.

A detail that one would not see today is the sharp leading edge of the keel carried right down to the heel of the rudder. I am still not sure that this was a mistake along the keel, though I believe the sharp forefoot (as it was under the mast step) must have been wrong.

I think *Clarion of Wight* could be described as a tough boat for her size that liked rough water and plenty of wind. When it went light, because she was well handled, she could always be kept moving so a leftover chop did not stop her. The 1963 combination of crew, sails, weather and boat was a good one.

**OLIN STEPHENS**

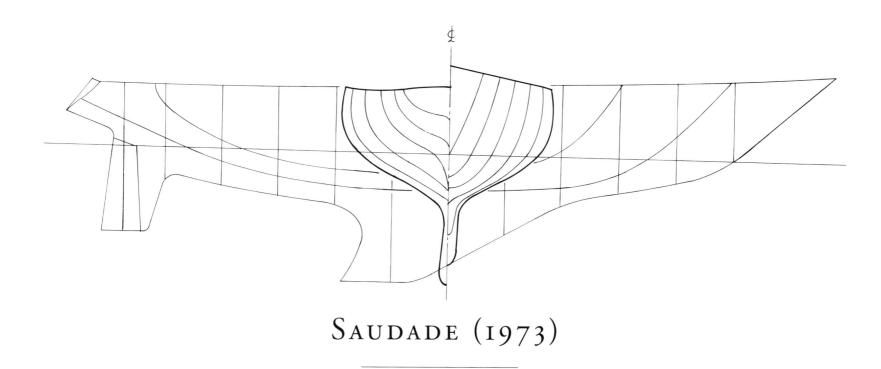

# SAUDADE (1973)

*Saudade* of 1973 was the high point scorer in that year's Admiral's Cup, as *Clarion of Wight* had been ten years earlier. And, just as *Clarion* came before the discovery of the weak points of the RORC Rule, so *Saudade* was built while the IOR was still seen to encourage a seagoing type. Later she led in the Florida Southern Circuit.

*Saudade*'s displacement/length ratio, though not light by today's standards, was about 72% that of her earlier sister, while her ratio, square root of sail over cube root of displacement, was about 5% greater. Her tall rig gave her even greater power.

Ten years, and the IOR, had brought two major changes: the separated keel and rudder and aluminum alloy hull construction, well executed by Wolter Huisman. The former reduced wetted area, emphasizing the effect of the more powerful rig, while the latter provided an even higher ratio of ballast to displacement, and thus greater stability. This was before the rating advantage of a low CGF was recognized. If half her ballast had been placed inside she might have been just as fast under most conditions and lower in rating. *Saudade*'s power made her fast to windward, even more so than *Clarion*, so that she was a winner in the days when races were won on the wind. I think that day has returned with IMS.

*Saudade*'s lines, in my view, are well balanced and relatively fine at both ends, but more noticeably aft. Her beam is relatively generous, though more so above the waterline than below. Her interior is conveniently arranged, with galley and navigating area aft near the companionway. Despite the high ballast ratio, designed as 58.5%, she was not stripped out below, nor was her interior sacrificed to the deck plan, though that was well studied for ease of handling.

Characteristically, for S&S boats of that time, *Saudade*'s separate rudder was hung on a large skeg. I felt that this was structurally desirable with the added benefit of 'putting feathers on the arrow'. This is no longer accepted on racing boats. As her designer, I should prefer to be on board *Saudade* in a tough offshore race than on many of her successors. This is for reasons of hull shape and proportions, layout on deck and below, and ruggedness of both hull and rig. But I am not as young as I used to be.

**OLIN STEPHENS**

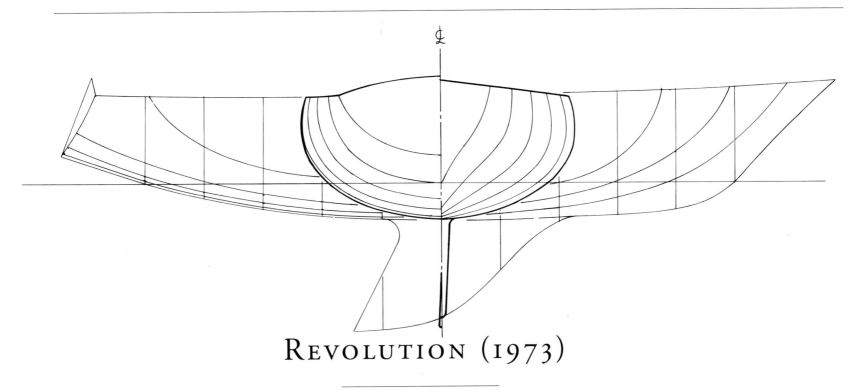

# REVOLUTION (1973)

*Revolution* was the first boat, in this size, which was designed taking account of principles we had perfected in smaller sized boats. She was a compromise trade-off between minimal wake caused by wave action, minimum fraction caused by hull drag and maximum stability.

We increased stability a lot, deliberately, to permit the carrying of the large sail plan. Therefore we designed a wide, flat hull form with a large sail area with the after section proportional to the mid-part in order to maintain good balance when the boat heeled.

This fullness in the ends of the hull was a good solution for offshore races, though for inshore races, with light winds and flat water, it was not so satisfactory.

We designed *Revolution* using CAD (computer aided design), still quite a novel idea at the time. Our concept for the hull was to create a form without any rating considerations: no distortion, no bumps. All the fittings, deck plan and rigging were designed with the same consideration of simplicity and efficiency.

Wolter Huisman in the Netherlands made a splendid job of building her aluminium hull for her owner Jean Louis Fabry.

The total of all these factors made *Revolution* a great racing yacht which won races repeatedly. She showed her supremacy in the RORC races and is still sailing.

**GROUPE FINOT**

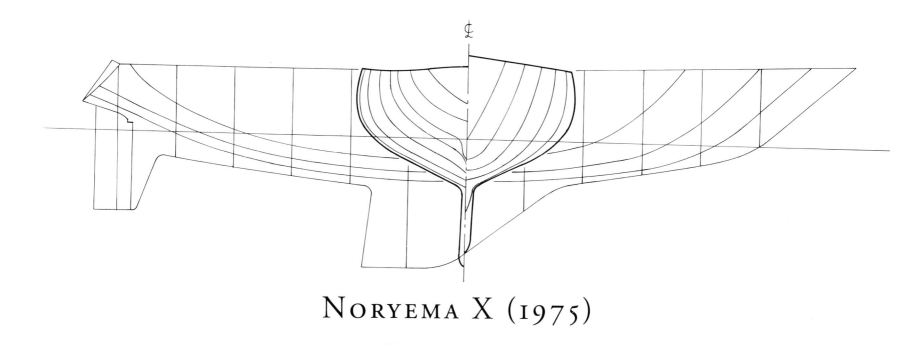

# NORYEMA X (1975)

*Noryema X* was Design No 622 and represented my last attempt to create a yacht entirely by intuition. The result sailed successfully to her rating under the IOR despite not taking advantage any of the obvious loopholes in the rule which were easy to obtain by designing a hull around a few measurement points.

My belief in 1974 in planning *Noryema X* for Ron Amey, was that the penalty I was having to pay for additional displacement without a proper corresponding rating credit was more than offset by the lesser total resistance of a fair hull. Designing around the Rule of introducing bumps and hollows was tempting at the time but, without the proper tools to measure the difference in total drag and the confidence of continuous success of earlier designs, made me delay my move towards the more stereotyped IOR shape until later.

This design not only proved highly successful in the Admiral's Cup, where she was the 1975 top scorer and her sister, *Red Rock IV* won one of the inshore races, but continued to be so as the Palmer Johnson 46 built in the USA. They had a string of wins lasting well into the 1980s, starting with *Rattler's* 1st place in Class 1 at the 1976 SORC.

Despite her racing intentions, I gave *Noryema* an interior layout with proper cruising comfort and I believe she was the last boat to do well in the Admiral's Cup with such comfortable accommodation.

The sail plan is typical of the mid-nineteen seventies, featuring a minimum mainsail carried behind a large, straight mast which did little to help the speed of the boat, and a very large foretriangle designed around the technology and sail material available at time.

She was built like a battleship in aluminium by Joyce Brothers in Southampton and finished off by Moody's at Swanwick.

**GERMAN FRERS JR**

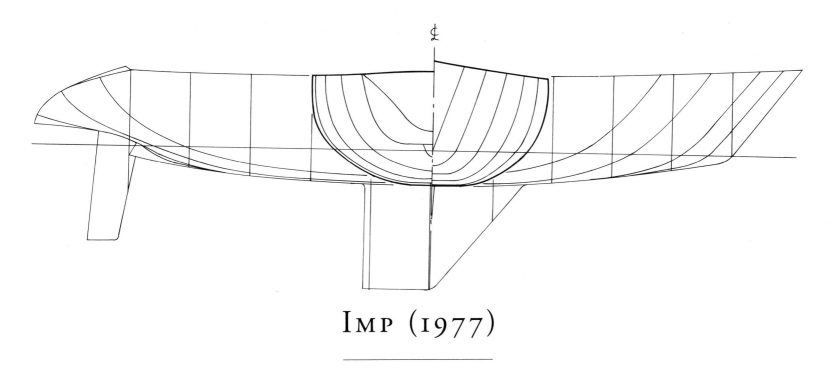

# IMP (1977)

Reflecting on the design of *Imp* and the success she gained at the highest levels of ocean racing, I have two immediate thoughts. The first is the good fortune to have gained Dave Allen's confidence that allowed me to receive this design commission. The second is to recall how I consciously departed from my earlier symmetrical water plane design concepts to enhance off the wind speed. This was encouraged by Dave Allen after his experience with the 'downwind sled' *Improbable*.

The hull lines and keel were certainly optimised to improve reaching and running speed and it was no surprise to me to see *Imp* lead her class out of Tampa Bay at the start of the 1977 SORC. What did surprise me was to see her still leading the fleet at the end of the race after a 50-mile beat against a fresh northerly wind. The apparent compromises made to windward speed were not noticeable and *Imp* went on to win selection in the 1977 and 1979 US Admiral's Cup teams.

Besides the hull and keel shape, developments related to the IOR Rule at that time, a significant factor with *Imp*'s performance must be related to her unique construction system that allowed her comparatively light weight to rigidly hold its shape in any conditions. Gary Carlin's Kiwi Boats, builder of *Imp*, took advantage of a suggestion by Lars Bergstrom to incorporate an aluminium tube internal 'space frame' structure. This structure, detailed by project manager, Ragar Harkensen, took rigging and keel loads away from the balsa core sandwich hull, allowing the overall weight of the yacht to be reduced with improved stiffness.

The combination of a courageous change in design philosophy, innovative construction and expert crewing under Californian Skip Allen allowed *Imp* to gain a string of successes over a six year period and established Ron Holland Design at the very top of the world racing events.

Happily, *Imp* is now owned by an Irish enthusiast and is located in my local harbour of Kinsale. She was an important design for me.

**RON HOLLAND**

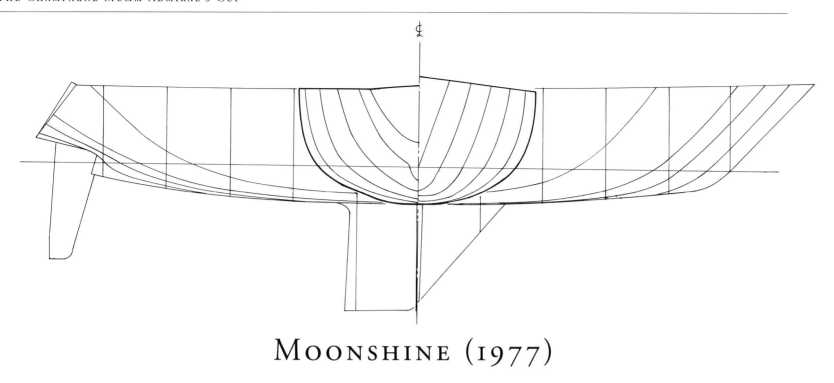

# MOONSHINE (1977)

The boats which followed my One-Tonner *Ganbare* were true upwind/downwind yachts, designed to go around fixed courses. *Ganbare* set the style which was to last for more than a decade. The sail area: wetted surface ratio was higher than the norm and with the U-sectioned bow and balanced ends, it was a shape which pointed very high. *Moonshine* was one of the final developments of that thinking, a very fast boat upwind and taken to new levels of construction sophistication by Jeremy Rogers and Bill Green.

Bill Green was a good friend of mine who had sailed on *Ganbare* and when he moved to England he worked for Jeremy Rogers. Before that he'd been my representative on *Yeoman XX* and though she wasn't top boat in the 1973 and 1975 Admiral's Cups, she'd been hammering the opposition all the time. Like *Yeoman*, when *Moonshine* changed hands and went to Italy as *Rrose Selavy*, she carried on winning races for years.

In time, the style was christened 'pin-tail'. I think it was East Coast sailors, probably Tom Whidden or the guys on the various *Love Machines*, who dreamed it up. The boats were so high-winded they just obliterated the opposition. Even the light-air orientated designs, such as *Yeoman* and *Moonshine*, went well in a breeze because they could point well and short tack well. That was important for Solent racing. Besides the balanced hull shape, the rigs of the pin-tails made a big impact. Tim Steam was quite a visionary, and his development of three spreader rig and its complex controls were the perfect complement to a hull which loved to point high.

*Moonshine* was probably the ultimate incarnation of this

pinched-ends shape before I started filling out the stems and gaining a little better reaching performance. That's because the problem with the pin-tails was that if you bore away and let the sheets out you didn't tend to go much faster. But the same thinking was still there in 1983, with the likes of *Scarlett O'Hara* and the Serendipity 43 types. It wasn't a new design then, but it was a rocket and extremely competitive, and *Scarlett* was the top inshore boat of the series, proving that the philosophy continued to work on beat-run types of courses.

The shape had a reputation for being a handful downwind. That was true when they were built heavy, such as in production boats, but the light custom boats really were very good straight downwind. They were fast for their rating. The reason for the style switching towards the lighter displacement type was the desire for higher speeds downwind in stronger breezes and, when fractional rigs finally became small and flexible, this became really effective on the lighter boats. That was a development which the IOR Rule encouraged, because it favoured the fractional rig by giving more sail area for rating and it pretty much changed the entire style of boats from the 1970s to the 1980s as a consequence.

There is no doubting the impact of boats like *Yeoman XX* and *Moonshine*. They made the rest of the fleet obsolete. Everything else was history. In fact, if you built a pin-tail style hull today and built it with current technology, filling the hull with inside ballast, I'm sure you would still get to the weather mark in good order.

**DOUG PETERSON**

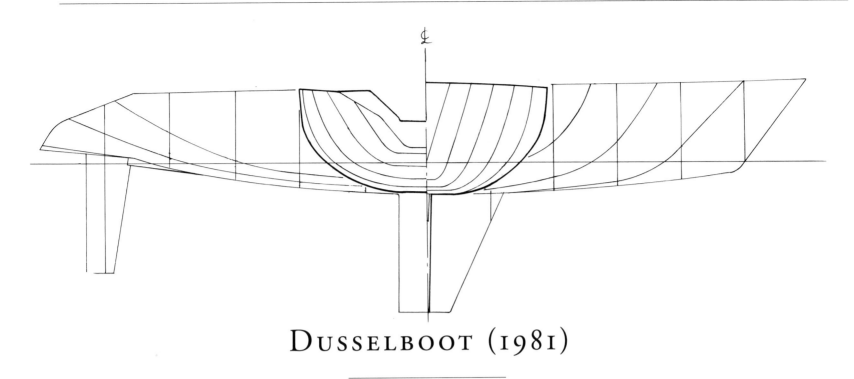

# DUSSELBOOT (1981)

*Dusselboot* was a development from our smaller Mini Tonner, Quarter Tonner and Half Tonner designs. She was one of the first big racing yachts where ideas and input from dinghy sailors determined nearly all aspects of the design without any compromises being made to non-racing abilities.

At the request of Michael Schmidt, who was the co-owner with Dieter Haensel, *Dusselboot* was built by his boatyard for the sole purpose of winning races. No other role for the boat was envisaged, certainly not a dual-purpose cruiser-racer role. Looking at today's yachts you can see that not so much has changed since 1981, and even the dimensions and relationships between length, displacement and sail area of the top One Tonners 10 years later were relatively close to those of *Dusselboot*. It is not without good reason that we claim that *Dusselboot* was one the forerunners of an entire style of boat.

The biggest question we faced in designing *Dusselboot* was whether the flexible fractional rig, which had proved so effective on smaller boats, could be controllable and safe on a 40ft yacht.

In consultation with Michael Schmidt, sparmaker Rudi Magg and North Sails Germany we finally decided to use the fractional rig and although *Dusselboot*'s failed during the 1981 Admiral's Cup, perhaps costing the German team first place, everyone took note of the speed of the boat.

Today, no one would consider a racing boat with a masthead rig to be competitive. The success of the same boat in 1983, when she raced at *Outsider* in the winning German team, proved once and for all that the concept was the right way to go.

The boat was a low-budget project. The hull and deck were a sandwich of PVC foam and simple R-glass. Carbon fibre, Kevlar, honeycomb cores and titanium fittings, then just making their appearance in racing boats, were miles outside the campaign budget. Even so, *Dusselboot*'s construction was relatively light, though put up against today's technology she seemed closer to a warship than a race boat. She is still racing in the USA.

**JUDEL/VROLIJK**

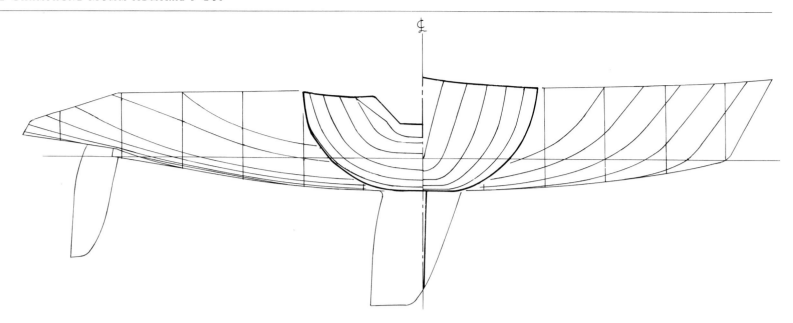

# PROPAGANDA (1987)

Design 182 was commissioned for a pair of One-Ton yachts, *Propaganda* and *Fairshare*, built in New Zealand with the hope of competing as members of the 1987 New Zealand Admiral's Cup team. This design featured a long and powerful hull shape to deliver exceptional upwind and reaching performance, which *Propaganda* clearly displayed as the top scoring yacht at the 1987 Admiral's Cup.

*Fairshare* missed selection for the Admiral's Cup team, but she

showed this design's strength at the 1987 Southern Cross Cup, placing third overall.

The following year, *Propaganda* again showed her transom to the 1988 One Ton Cup fleet in San Francisco, winning this series in close company with the seven other Farr designs which finished in the top ten places.

**BRUCE FARR**

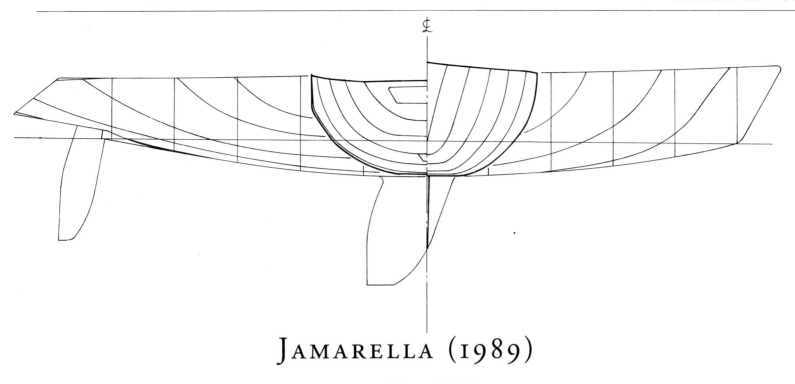

# JAMARELLA (1989)

Alan Gray commissioned Design 213 to compete as the big boat on the 1989 UK Admiral's Cup team. *Jamarella*'s design evolved from the first of the new breed of Farr 50-footers that had made their debut earlier that year in the 50-Footer fleet. These new 50's, *Carat VII* and *Windquest*, had a clear advantage over the existing fleet, showing superior light-air, and reaching performance. For the Admiral's Cup, rig and keel modifications were made to orient the design more for ocean racing courses and suit the slightly lower maximum rating limit established for the Admiral's Cup.

*Jamarella* was carefully constructed by a group of boat builders assembled in southern England, and her full potential was quickly realised through an intensive sailing/tuning schedule. *Jamarella* never finished out of the top four places throughout the 1989 Admiral's Cup, easily placing first overall and leading the UK Admiral's Cup team to victory.

**BRUCE FARR**

THE ADMIRAL'S CUP was originally set up on a two-year cyclical management system. In offering the Cup to the RORC, the five original donors prepared a five-page Deed of Gift which appointed two trustees to monitor compliance with its use. The trustees, themselves nominated by the RORC, nominated the Cup's management committee in conjunction with the RORC. The management committee begins its work immediately after each series finishes and has worked well in the past, increasing its non-British membership.

There are two vital clauses in the Deed of Gift: that the Fastnet race shall always be part of the Admiral's Cup series (the only race specified by name) and that if the event is not run for seven years or four consecutive Fastnets, the Cup shall revert to the Club.

During the 1989 and 1991 series, it became evident that the IOR rule was waning. After consideration, the committee of management decided that for 1993 they would stick with teams of three boats, one each from the 30.5, 34.5 and 40.0ft rating sizes. It was increasingly apparent that this was not going to attract sufficient teams: just five or six seemed likely, and the unthinkable – that Britain would fail to raise a team – looked like a real possibility. The days seemed over when the RORC could sit back and watch the challenges roll in.

The move towards more specialist and more expensive boats reduced the numbers who could take part, a situation which, combined with a worldwide recession and the collapse of interest in the IOR, seemed to threaten the 1993 series. The management committee responded by announcing that two-boat teams would be eligible.

It was already apparent that a longer-term strategy was needed than merely planning from one series to the next. Designers, owners and sailors wanted to know where the Champagne Mumm Admiral's Cup was

heading, and there was an initiative in early 1993 to begin a much longer term strategy than the management committee could create. 'I have particularly promoted the view that we should put together a steering group,' explained Alan Green. 'That will set a target which, if its work is well done, will give everyone else something to aim at.'

The idea was hatched over a breakfast between Alan Green, who had been involved with four decades of the Admiral's Cup, and the Club's admiral, Don Parr, and the then Commodore, John Dare, who set up and chaired the steering commitee. The trustees – David Edwards, who had succeeded John Bush, and Sir Peter Green, one of the original donors – were entirely pragmatic and willing to accommodate the change and formally asked the Club to do likewise.

The composition of the steering group reflected the huge change that had taken place in the sport. Player power was evident by the inclusion of Luc Gellusseau, head of the Corum Sailing Team sponsored by the Swiss watch company, and of Geoff Stagg, a New Zealand pro-sailor whose job as president of Farr International was to market Bruce Farr-designed race boats.

The steering group was deliberately made small to prevent it becoming too unwieldy and slow, and because of its modest size it was required to canvass views vigorously. 'If they were to discuss only their own ideas, the steering group would have failed in its purpose. It was plain that it had to go out in the by-ways of the sport,' said Alan Green who was a member, along with RORC rear-commodore Stuart Quarrie, and John Bourke, then chairman of the Offshore Racing Council and subsequently John Dare's successor as Club Commodore. The enormity of letting active sailors set the terms for the series was conceded by Alan Green: 'We are not replicating what has gone in

*1993 was the last Admiral's Cup to use the International Offshore Rule. In a bold move to regenerate ocean racing, the RORC promoted a new class of worldwide one-design, the Farr-designed Mumm 36 (Guy Gurney)*

the past. I am entirely convinced about it. We have got the right people. We have got the right tilt.'

Identifying the classes was the prime objective of the steering group. It did not need terms of reference laid out, for the task was plain enough: decide on the classes to be sailed and all the small matters such as dates, number of races, format of races and so forth would follow.

An event of the stature of the Champagne Mumm Admiral's Cup is such that it always requires a measure of conservatism if it is not to be veered around by every gust of wind, by every opinion voiced by a sailor, owner or sponsor who might compete in one series

and be gone the next. The 1990s, though, were so full of change that new directions were called for. Among the options considered was switching to the new International Measurement System and International Level Racing Rule in place of the IOR. In an attempt to keep costs down, make it easier for countries to send teams and create an 'entry level' boat, the steering committee decided to recommend the small boat in 1995 and 1997 be a one-design, a most radical decision.

A selection committee was established, chaired by John Dare, whose members were John Bourke, Chairman of the ORC and Vice Commodore of USA, Stuart Quarrie, Rear Commodore of the RORC, Don Gen-

*The Italian Mumm 36, Paolo Gaia's* Mumm a Mia! *racing at the 1994 SORC (Guy Gurney)*

itempo from the USA, David Kellett from Australia and Serge Paillard from France and Alan Green from the RORC. The RORC prepared an Invitation to Tender document which they sent to all the leading designers and builders around the world. Six proposals were returned – two from the US, three from Europe and one from Australia. Mumm were invited to support this effort and brand new boat, which they were pleased to do. On 26 July 1993 the selection committee met all day in the library of the Royal Yacht Squadron to consider the proposals. RORC people had visited all the proposers' yards and their reports were heard. Just before midnight the final decision was taken and Mumm 36 was born.

In the event, the Mumm 36 got the go-ahead. Designed by Bruce Farr, and built by Carroll Marine of the US, Beneteau in France, Astilleros de Estuario in Argentina and Cookson's in New Zealand, its brief was nothing less than the regeneration of the sport. The Mumm 36 falls between the price of a production boat and a custom boat: in effect a series-built one-off. Rather like Mercedes Benz and its 190 model or BMW's 3 series, the Mumm 36 is charged with bringing in a new generation of owners to offshore racing to replace the Fischers and Illbrucks when they finally hang up their sea boots. The boat should lend itself to ownership by clubs and small syndicates, as well as just being in the range of a salaried owner.

By far the most radical proposal considered by the steering group was to drop the Fastnet Race in favour of a 500-mile offshore finale, not only starting in Cowes but finishing there too, which would avoid the logistical nightmare of moving the entire show to Plymouth to finish the series. But that was no more than kite flying. Sir Peter Green said: 'I cannot ever anticipate a time, with the present trustees, when the Fastnet Race would be removed from the Deed. The idea was tried out, but like a lead balloon, it dropped beneath the waters of the Channel.' To no-one's real surprise, the Fastnet has stayed in. Without it, the series would be Wimbledon without the grass.

Although many bemoaned the demise of the IOR at the close of the 1993 Champagne Mumm Admiral's

Cup, the truth is that five years previously many of them would have built a new boat for each AC. At the very moment of the IOR's decline and fall, the most critical owners had found themselves enjoying up to five years' excellent racing out of the last boats to be built, because the rule had reached such high stability.

One reason why the IOR's adherents wanted to hold on for so long was distrust about its successor. Not only had the Offshore Racing Council taken a long time to state clearly their vision of the future, but the most likely successor, the IMS, was experiencing all sorts of teething problems. How long would carbon fibre stay banned under IMS was what sailors, designers and owners wanted to know. When would the Velocity Prediction Program, which is at the very core of the IMS's working, be stabilised? And when would the Offshore Racing Council turn around the disastrous public perceptions of the IMS, which variously portrayed the rule as an American conspiracy foisted on an unwilling world, and one of generating results full of mumbo-jumbo.

The praetorian guard who remain the bedrock of offshore racing have faced bigger challenges to their continuing interest than the switch to IMS, not the least being an inability to steer their own boats and the hiring of costly professionals.

At its annual meeting in London in November 1993, the Offshore Racing Council set out its store, with IMS clearly designated the grand prix rule of the future. Pent-up demand for new custom boats had already seen IMS race boats being built in gathering numbers in the USA. Now the rest of the world has to follow. The selection of the Mumm 36 proved a huge success, with more than a hundred being sold in the first nine months.

Not surprisingly, Alan Green looked back on the uncertain times of 1993 and reflected: 'There are times when leadership is easier than it is at other times and right now we are having to work harder to maintain that role.' However, prospects for a re-invigorated sport and the 1995 Champagne Mumm Admiral's Cup look promising. Like the world economy, the sport is on the upswing, having come out of recession changed but stronger.

| 1957 RACE RESULTS | | | RACE 1 CHANNEL RACE | | RACE 2 BRITANNIA CUP | | RACE 3 RORC SPECIAL RACE | | RACE 4 FASTNET RACE | | TOTAL (OVERALL POINTS) | OVERALL TOTAL (BY COUNTRY) |
|---|---|---|---|---|---|---|---|---|---|---|---|---|
| Country | Boat Name | Owner | Corrected time | Points | Corrected time | Points | Corrected time | Points | Corrected time | Points | | |
| Britain | **Myth of Malham** | **Capt J Illingworth/P Green** | **24.27.29** | **12** | **04.29.51** | **5** | **04.47.19** | **3** | **88.04.35** | **15** | **35** | |
| | Uomie | S B Slater | 24.36.57 | 10 | 04.27.40 | 6 | 04.43.32 | 5 | DNF | 0 | 21 | |
| | Jocasta | G P Pattinson | 26.09.44 | ANTC | 04.54.33 | 1 | 05.07.11 | 1 | 89.09.26 | 12 | 14 | 70 |
| USA | Carina | R S Nye | 24.38.44 | 8 | 04.39.33 | 3 | 04.56.45 | 2 | 82.55.50 | 18 | 31 | |
| | White Mist | G W Blunt White | 25.30 12 | 6 | 04 47 39 | 2 | 04 45 31 | 4 | 90 08 12 | 9 | 21 | |
| | Figaro | W T Snaith | dns | 0 | 04 34 12 | 4 | 04 41 46 | 6 | 90 09 50 | 6 | 16 | 68 |

| 1959 RACE RESULTS | | | RACE 1 CHANNEL RACE | | RACE 2 BRITANNIA CUP | | RACE 3 NEW YORK YC TROPHY | | RACE 4 FASTNET RACE | | TOTAL (OVERALL POINTS) | OVERALL TOTAL (BY COUNTRY) |
|---|---|---|---|---|---|---|---|---|---|---|---|---|
| Country | Boat Name | Owner | Corrected time | Points | Corrected time | Points | Corrected time | Points | Corrected time | Points | | |
| Netherlands | Zwerver | W N H van der Vorm | 30 10 08 | 10 | 07 56 26 | 9 | 05 47 23 | 6 | 102 50 11 | 18 | 43 | |
| | Olivier van Noort | A W Goudriaan | 29 46 32 | 14 | 08 23 20 | 8 | 05 54 50 | 5 | 101 36 46 | 24 | 51 | |
| | Zeevalk | C Bruynzeel | 32 40 35 | 4 | 09 50 31 | 6 | 05 47 23 | 7 | 116 14 54 | 12 | 29 | 123 |
| France | Eloise II | F Hervé | 30 48 16 | 8 | 08 53 31 | 7 | 06 30 41 | 2 | DNF | 0 | 17 | |
| | Marie Christine III | J-C Menu | 31 26 12 | 6 | 15 57 19 | 3 | DSQ | 0 | DNF | 0 | 9 | |
| | St François | G Craipeau | 35 15 16 | 2 | DNS | 0 | 05 29 46 | 9 | DNF | 0 | 11 | 37 |
| Britain | Ramrod | S Slater/R McLoughlin | 29 00 50 | 18 | 15 27 57 | 5 | 06 04 42 | 3 | 101 38 26 | 21 | 47 | |
| | **Griffin II** | **RORC** | **29 29 45** | **16** | **15 50 47** | **4** | **05 31 05** | **8** | **97 46 01** | **27** | **55** | |
| | Myth of Malham | Capt J Illingworth/P Green | 29 58 14 | 12 | 16 10 31 | 2 | 05 58 33 | 4 | 107 18 37 | 15 | 33 | 135 |

KEY  DNS  –  Did Not Start    DNF  –  Did Not Finish    DSQ  –  Disqualified    RTD  –  Retired    (P)  –  Includes Penalty    DNC – Did Not Compete    ANTC  –  Agreed not to count

| 1961 RACE RESULTS | | | RACE 1 CHANNEL RACE | | RACE 2 BRITANNIA CUP | | RACE 3 NEW YORK YC TROPHY | | RACE 4 FASTNET RACE | | TOTAL (OVERALL POINTS) | OVERALL TOTAL (BY COUNTRY) |
|---|---|---|---|---|---|---|---|---|---|---|---|---|
| Country | Boat Name | Owner | Corrected time | Points | Corrected time | Points | Corrected time | Points | Corrected time | Points | | |
| USA | Cyane | H B du Pont | 33 30 02 | 22 | 15 40 43 | 5 | 15 15 27 | 12 | 90 33 56 | 21 | 60 | |
| | Figaro | W Snaith | 33 26 22 | 24 | 15 27 48 | 12 | 15 23 41 | 8 | 86 29 05 | 33 | 77 | |
| | Windrose | J Isbrandtsen | 32 02 07 | 30 | 15 23 09 | 14 | RTD | 0 | 86 07 34 | 39 | 83 | 220 |
| Britain | Griffin II | rorc (Mjr G Potter) | 33 37 41 | 20 | 15 30 20 | 10 | 15 25 32 | 7 | 90 29 19 | 24 | 61 | |
| | Myth of Malham | Capt J Illingworth/P Green | 35 32 23 | 12 | 15 29 02 | 11 | 15 19 22 | 10 | 87 24 31 | 30 | 63 | |
| | Quiver III | S H R Clarke | 35 01 27 | 14 | 15 22 08 | 15 | 14 54 08 | 15 | 84 32 01 | 42 | 86 | 210 |
| Netherlands | **Zwerver** | **W N H van der Vorm** | **34 24 38** | **18** | **15 26 40** | **13** | **14 56 20** | **14** | **81 32 03** | **45** | **90** | |
| | Olivier van Noort | A W Goudriaan | 35 32 24 | 10 | 15 30 39 | 9 | 15 19 54 | 9 | 92 47 54 | 18 | 46 | |
| | Corabia | Dr J Kars | 36 18 39 | 6 | 15 41 26 | 4 | 15 14 19 | 13 | 95 48 20 | 6 | 29 | 165 |
| Sweden | Dione | O Wettergren | 34 51 06 | 16 | 15 34 12 | 7 | 15 25 38 | 6 | 92 47 56 | 15 | 44 | |
| | Anitra | S Hansen | 00 00 00 | 0 | 00 00 00 | 0 | 15 16 24 | 11 | 86 15 40 | 36 | 47 | |
| | Staika III | S H Roden | 32 53 39 | 26 | 15 35 10 | 6 | RTD | 0 | 88 05 18 | 27 | 59 | 150 |
| France | Striana | Dr Auclair/M Chassagny | 35 53 44 | 8 | 15 47 41 | 3 | DSQ | 0 | 112 18 05 | 3 | 14 | |
| | Marie Christine III | J-C Menu | 36 23 18 | 4 | 16 06 34 | 2 | 15 49 08 | 5 | 93 18 02 | 12 | 23 | |
| | Eloise II | F L Hervé | 32 45 45 | 28 | 15 34 08 | 8 | RTD | 0 | 93 22 08 | 9 | 45 | 82 |

KEY:   DNS  –  Did Not Start       DNF  –  Did Not Finish       DSQ  –  Disqualified       RTD  –  Retired       (P)  –  Includes Penalty       DNC – Did Not Compete

| 1963 RACE RESULTS | | | RACE 1 CHANNEL RACE | | RACE 2 BRITANNIA CUP | | RACE 3 NEW YORK YC CUP | | RACE 4 FASTNET RACE | | TOTAL (OVERALL POINTS) | OVERALL TOTAL (BY COUNTRY) |
|---|---|---|---|---|---|---|---|---|---|---|---|---|
| Country | Boat Name | Owner | Corrected time | Points | Corrected time | Points | Corrected time | Points | Corrected time | Points | | |
| Britain | Outlaw | Hon M Aitken/R Lowein | 36 02 09 | 16 | 05 33 55 | 4 | 03 28 27 | 17 | 91 02 30 | 36 | 73 | |
| | Noryema III | R W Amey | 37 03 09 | 2 | 05 15 40 | 14 | 03 28 39 | 16 | 91 16 32 | 30 | 62 | |
| | **Clarion of Wight** | **D Boyer/D Miller** | **34 53 13** | **28** | **05 08 09** | **15** | **03 26 58** | **18** | **86 34 13** | **54** | **115** | 250 |
| USA | Dyna | C Ewing | 36 52 25 | 4 | 05 22 25 | 11 | 03 41 40 | 12 | 90 40 16 | 42 | 69 | |
| | Figaro | W T Snaith | 35 44 57 | 22 | 05 21 46 | 13 | 03 42 46 | 10 | 88 24 54 | 48 | 93 | |
| | Windrose | J Isbrandtsen | 35 18 31 | 26 | 05 04 34 | 17 | 03 34 13 | 14 | 94 21 24 | 18 | 75 | 237 |
| Sweden | Vagabonde | G A Lindberg | 32 32 59 | 36 | 05 27 06 | 8 | DSQ | 0 | 91 04 07 | 33 | 77 | |
| | Dione | O Wettergren | 35 47 31 | 20 | 05 35 55 | 3 | 03 45 52 | 7 | 94 22 15 | 15 | 45 | |
| | Staika III | S Roden | 33 53 27 | 34 | 05 02 19 | 18 | 03 45 42 | 8 | 90 45 54 | 39 | 99 | 221 |
| Netherlands | Najade | Kon-Mar Y C | 36 45 02 | 6 | 05 04 34 | 7 | 03 40 11 | 13 | 92 44 14 | 21 | 47 | |
| | Corabia | Mrs J Kaars | 36 19 14 | 10 | 05 22 04 | 12 | 03 44 08 | 9 | RTD | 0 | 31 | |
| | Tulla | S de Wit | 34 39 14 | 30 | 05 04 48 | 16 | 03 34 11 | 15 | 88 08 51 | 51 | 112 | 190 |
| France | Glenan | Ctr Naut des Glénans | 36 10 05 | 14 | 05 30 22 | 5 | DSQ | 0 | 94 33 37 | 12 | 31 | |
| | Eloise II | F Hervé | 35 30 39 | 24 | 05 28 46 | 6 | 04 05 15 | 5 | 92 22 16 | 27 | 62 | |
| | Marie Christine III | J-C Menu | 36 01 43 | 18 | 05 25 11 | 9 | 03 55 45 | 6 | 92 36 22 | 24 | 57 | 150 |
| Germany | Diana II | H S Thomas | 36 25 14 | 8 | 05 38 39 | 2 | DSQ | 0 | 96 34 50 | 9 | 19 | |
| | Rubin | H-O Schumann | 34 08 22 | 32 | 05 23 19 | 10 | 03 42 09 | 11 | 89 46 43 | 45 | 98 | |
| | Inschallah | W Andreae | 36 10 16 | 12 | 05 43 19 | 1 | DSQ | 0 | 98 42 00 | 6 | 19 | 136 |

| KEY: | DNS – Did Not Start | DNF – Did Not Finish | DSQ – Disqualified | RTD – Retired | (P) – Includes Penalty | DNC – Did Not Compete |
|---|---|---|---|---|---|---|

| 1965 RACE RESULTS | | | RACE 1 CHANNEL RACE | | RACE 2 BRITANNIA CUP | | RACE 3 NEW YORK YC TROPHY | | RACE 4 FASTNET RACE | | TOTAL (OVERALL POINTS) | OVERALL TOTAL (BY COUNTRY) |
|---|---|---|---|---|---|---|---|---|---|---|---|---|
| Country | Boat Name | Owner | Corrected time | Points | Corrected time | Points | Corrected time | Points | Corrected time | Points | | |
| Britain | **Quiver IV** | **S H R Clarke** | **33 40 20** | **38** | **15 34 14** | **22** | **14 40 52** | **22** | **86 43 47** | **72** | **154** | |
| | Noryema IV | R W Amey | 33 01 04 | 44 | 15 31 40 | 23 | 14 48 48 | 19 | 88 25 48 | 66 | 152 | |
| | Firebrand | D P Miller | 32 53 13 | 46 | 15 43 23 | 20 | DSQ | 0 | 91 12 26 | 48 | 114 | 420 |
| Australia | Caprice of Huon | G W Ingate | 32 50 32 | 48 | 15 26 32 | 24 | 14 30 15 | 24 | 90 44 08 | 54 | 150 | |
| | Freya | T and M Halvorsen | 33 46 17 | 34 | 16 18 57 | 11 | 14 54 30 | 16 | 91 27 12 | 42 | 103 | |
| | Camille of Seaforth | R Swanson | 33 12 30 | 42 | 20 00 00 | 6 | 14 54 38 | 15 | 89 31 45 | 60 | 123 | 376 |
| Netherlands | Zwerver | O J van der Vorm | 35 13 18 | 22 | 16 04 12 | 17 | 14 56 33 | 14 | 91 45 41 | 39 | 92 | |
| | Tulla | S de Wit | 34 31 06 | 28 | 16 06 21 | 14 | 15 13 47 | 9 | 91 03 35 | 51 | 102 | |
| | Tonnerre de Breskens | P W Vroon | 33 43 07 | 36 | 16 05 55 | 15 | 15 15 09 | 8 | 88 44 18 | 63 | 122 | 316 |
| USA | Caper | H I Pratt | 35 16 26 | 20 | 16 04 24 | 19 | 14 36 41 | 23 | 90 20 01 | 57 | 119 | |
| | Figaro | W Snaith | 34 37 23 | 26 | 15 51 08 | 16 | 14 46 33 | 21 | 87 15 33 | 69 | 132 | |
| | Windrose | J Isbrandtsen | 34 11 56 | 32 | DSQ | 0 | RTD | 0 | 95 11 42 | 30 | 62 | 313 |
| France | Stiren | D Berthelin | 35 40 42 | 16 | 16 29 16 | 8 | 14 59 54 | 12 | 96 34 35 | 27 | 63 | |
| | Pen Duick II | E Tabarly | 35 08 36 | 24 | 16 01 42 | 18 | 14 57 17 | 13 | 93 28 26 | 33 | 88 | |
| | Varna II | F Fournier | 34 27 08 | 30 | 16 42 06 | 7 | 15 15 55 | 7 | 92 01 53 | 36 | 80 | 231 |
| Sweden | Vagabonde | G A Lindberg | 35 59 41 | 12 | DSQ | 0 | DSQ | 0 | RTD | 0 | 12 | |
| | Staika IV | S Rodén | 36 01 27 | 10 | 16 16 11 | 13 | 15 21 38 | 6 | 96 40 30 | 24 | 53 | |
| | Honey | H Myren | 33 12 56 | 40 | 15 40 03 | 21 | 15 02 03 | 11 | 91 14 16 | 45 | 117 | 182 |
| Ireland | Shelmalier of Anglesey | K A Wilby | 35 28 39 | 18 | 16 17 06 | 12 | 14 48 46 | 20 | 96 52 22 | 21 | 71 | |
| | Moonduster | D N Doyle | 37 03 19 | 8 | 16 19 59 | 10 | 14 54 25 | 17 | 96 55 25 | 18 | 53 | |
| | Myth of Malham | B and D Livingston | 35 41 49 | 14 | DSQ | 0 | 15 04 51 | 10 | 97 08 24 | 15 | 39 | 163 |
| Germany | Ortac | Hamburg Sailing Club | DNS | 0 | 16 27 11 | 9 | 14 49 23 | 18 | 98 23 03 | 12 | 39 | |
| | Lisoletta V | F Marggraff | DNS | 0 | DNS | 0 | DNS | 0 | DNS | 0 | 0 | |
| | Ariadne | H Vogeler | DNS | 0 | DSQ | 0 | 15 30 29 | 5 | 111 30 51 | 9 | 14 | 53 |

KEY:    DNS – Did Not Start      DNF – Did Not Finish      DSQ – Disqualified      RTD – Retired      (P) – Includes Penalty      DNC – Did Not Compete

| 1967 RACE RESULTS | | | RACE 1 CHANNEL RACE | | RACE 2 BRITANNIA CUP | | RACE 3 NEW YORK YC CUP | | RACE 4 FASTNET RACE | | TOTAL (OVERALL POINTS) | OVERALL TOTAL (BY COUNTRY) |
|---|---|---|---|---|---|---|---|---|---|---|---|---|
| Country | Boat Name | Owner | Corrected time | Points | Corrected time | Points | Corrected time | Points | Corrected time | Points | | |
| Australia | Balandra | R Crichton-Brown | 28 46 28 | 48 | 17 05 48 | 21 | 14 38 01 | 23 | 83 07 51 | 72 | 164 | |
| | **Mercedes III** | **E H Kaufman** | **28 37 19** | **50** | **16 34 17** | **27** | **14 34 03** | **25** | **82 04 23** | **75** | **177** | |
| | Caprice of Huon | G C Reynolds | 29 31 44 | 42 | 16 54 01 | 25 | 14 35 52 | 24 | 84 35 11 | 63 | 154 | 495 |
| Great Britain | Noryema V | R W Amey | 29 14 48 | 44 | 16 55 18 | 24 | 14 47 37 | 12 | 85 46 42 | 54 | 134 | |
| | Firebrand | D P Miller | 29 59 33 | 40 | 16 36 12 | 26 | 14 32 13 | 26 | 84 49 41 | 60 | 152 | |
| | Prospect of Whitby | A Slater | 30 31 22 | 30 | 16 59 09 | 22 | 14 43 26 | 17 | 101 41 29 | 33 | 102 | 388 |
| USA | Thunderbird | T V Learson | 30 16 10 | 36 | 17 08 05 | 18 | 14 49 49 | 10 | 85 05 43 | 57 | 121 | |
| | Figaro IV | W Snaith | 32 43 37 | 8 | 18 11 04 | 12 | 14 43 21 | 18 | 81 04 26 | 78 | 116 | |
| | Rabbit II | R E Carter | 29 13 56 | 46 | RTD | 0 | 14 30 43 | 27 | 95 17 16 | 48 | 121 | 358 |
| France | Pen-Duick III | E Tabarly | 27 57 17 | 54 | RTD | 0 | 14 57 50 | 6 | 78 39 19 | 81 | 141 | |
| | Oryx | F Bouygues | 30 27 07· | 34 | 17 08 03 | 19 | 14 44 02 | 15 | 83 46 01 | 66 | 134 | |
| | Gerfaut II | C/ P Renot | 32 17 09 | 16 | RTD | 0 | 14 40 22 | 21 | 100 29 34 | 39 | 76 | 351 |
| Germany | Rubin | H-O Schumann | 28 20 01 | 52 | 17 08 01 | 20 | 14 46 52 | 13 | 83 25 07 | 69 | 154 | |
| | Jan Pott III | N Lorck-Schierning | 30 15 43 | 38 | 17 58 39 | 14 | 14 42 17 | 20 | 106 39 27 | 18 | 90 | |
| | Hamburg VII | N R V | 31 21 57 | 22 | 17 33 16 | 16 | 15 23 15 | 4 | 113 48 15 | 9 | 51 | 295 |
| Finland | Lygaia | P Herlin | 30 29 15 | 32 | 16 58 31 | 23 | 14 43 33 | 16 | 99 30 16 | 42 | 113 | |
| | Can Can III | E Kindberg | 31 06 52 | 24 | 18 00 20 | 13 | 14 59 27 | 5 | 98 28 53 | 45 | 87 | |
| | Eva II | A Lindqvist | 31 59 38 | 20 | 17 24 18 | 17 | 14 38 15 | 22 | 104 37 46 | 27 | 86 | 286 |
| Netherlands | Pierrette III | W P J M Pierrot | 32 35 22 | 10 | RTD | 0 | 14 51 43 | 9 | 112 59 52 | 12 | 31 | |
| | Zeezot van Veere | P W Deerns | 30 57 14 | 28 | 17 33 28 | 15 | 14 49 46 | 11 | 103 32 12 | 30 | 84 | |
| | Tonnerre de Breskens | K Adlard Coles | 32 04 10 | 18 | RTD | 0 | 14 44 57 | 14 | 101 01 01 | 36 | 68 | 183 |
| Ireland | Moonduster | D N Doyle | 30 57 34 | 26 | 18 26 25 | 10 | DSQ | 0 | 93 10 52 | 51 | 87 | |
| | Jaynor | I I Selig | 33 00 57 | 6 | 18 13 48 | 11 | 14 55 15 | 7 | 104 51 09 | 21 | 45 | |
| | Fire Dancer | K A Wilby | 33 14 56 | 4 | DSQ | 0 | 14 53 41 | 8 | RTD | 0 | 12 | 144 |
| Spain | Artako | J M de Gamboa | 32 17 36 | 14 | RTD | 0 | 14 42 33 | 19 | 104 45 06 | 24 | 57 | |
| | Karmatan II | J Balleste | 32 22 17 | 12 | RTD | 0 | RTD | 0 | 109 51 32 | 15 | 27 | 84 |

KEY:  DNS – Did Not Start  DNF – Did Not Finish  DSQ – Disqualified  RTD – Retired  (P) – Includes Penalty  DNC – Did Not Compete

| 1969 RACE RESULTS | | | RACE 1 CHANNEL RACE | | RACE 2 BRITANNIA CUP | | RACE 3 NEW YORK Y C CUP | | RACE 4 FASTNET RACE | | TOTAL (OVERALL POINTS) | OVERALL TOTAL (BY COUNTRY) |
|---|---|---|---|---|---|---|---|---|---|---|---|---|
| Country | Boat Name | Owner | Corrected time | Points | Corrected time | Points | Corrected time | Points | Corrected time | Points | | |
| USA | Carina | R S Nye | 33 17 35 | 48 | 16 39 35 | 18 | 15 18 30 | 24 | 94 36 49 | 87 | 177 | |
| | Red Rooster | R E Carter | 32 39 50 | 60 | 16 01 55 | 29 | 15 07 59 | 31 | 91 38 37 | 93 | 213 | |
| | Palawan | T J Watson Jr | 35 52 53 | 12 | 16 50 10 | 14 | 15 32 59 | 8 | 97 56 25 | 72 | 106 | 496 |
| Australia | **Ragamuffin** | **S Fischer** | **32 38 49** | **62** | **16 21 11** | **25** | **15 09 14** | **29** | **92 54 26** | **90** | **206** | |
| | Koomooloo | D O'Neil | 32 57 08 | 50 | 16 18 11 | 26 | 15 11 44 | 28 | 116 50 47 | 36 | 140 | |
| | Mercedes III | H T Kaufman | 32 50 14 | 56 | 16 38 53 | 19 | 15 19 36 | 22 | 116 09 30 | 39 | 136 | 482 |
| Great Britain | Phantom | G P Pattinson | 32 52 52 | 54 | 16 31 49 | 22 | 15 16 23 | 26 | 95 19 40 | 84 | 186 | |
| | Prospect of Whitby | A Slater | 32 49 27 | 58 | 15 53 17 | 31 | 15 12 26 | 27 | 98 25 24 | 63 | 179 | |
| | Casse Tete III | D Johnson/M Hurrell | 36 53 21 | 8 | 16 22 33 | 24 | 15 18 59 | 23 | 109 17 28 | 51 | 106 | 471 |
| Italy | La Meloria | Mrs M Pera | 34 52 54 | 32 | 16 01 58 | 28 | 15 27 02 | 13 | 116 02 08 | 42 | 115 | |
| | Mabelle | S Zaffagni | 32 55 55 | 52 | 15 59 47 | 30 | 15 08 16 | 30 | 95 51 46 | 81 | 193 | |
| | Levantades | G Diano | 33 39 32 | 46 | DSQ | 0 | 15 23 07 | 19 | 96 16 25 | 78 | 143 | 451 |
| Germany | Rubin | H-O Schumann | 34 11 07 | 42 | RTD | 0 | 15 22 54 | 20 | 98 18 58 | 66 | 128 | |
| | Suca | W Kuhrt | 34 30 44 | 36 | 16 40 57 | 17 | 15 24 59 | 17 | 117 12 05 | 33 | 103 | |
| | Klaar Kimming | A H E von Zerssen | 35 14 36 | 28 | 16 35 58 | 21 | 15 17 41 | 25 | 117 36 30 | 30 | 104 | 335 |
| Finland | Lygaia | P Herlin | 34 45 59 | 34 | 16 25 51 | 23 | 15 28 51 | 12 | 121 49 54 | 12 | 81 | |
| | Runn | M Berner | 34 26 49 | 38 | 16 14 53 | 27 | 15 20 19 | 21 | 108 55 42 | 54 | 140 | |
| | Gabriella | Å Lindqvist | 35 16 54 | 24 | DSQ | 0 | 15 37 39 | 5 | 111 24 36 | 48 | 77 | 298 |
| France | Oryx | Société ORYX | 35 17 12 | 22 | RTD | 0 | 15 25 21 | 14 | 123 23 41 | 6 | 42 | |
| | Pacha | F Bouygues | 34 11 55 | 40 | 16 44 58 | 15 | 15 25 05 | 16 | 98 49 11 | 60 | 131 | |
| | Coriolan | C de Galéa | 35 15 45 | 16 | DSQ | 9 | 15 30 21 | 10 | 97 44 18 | 75 | 111 | 284 |
| Netherlands | Stormy | C Bruynzeel | 35 03 44 | 30 | 16 52 17 | 11 | 15 31 27 | 9 | 102 33 37 | 57 | 107 | |
| | Tonnerre de Breskens | P W Vroon | 35 32 32 | 18 | 16 50 24 | 13 | 15 34 10 | 7 | 120 41 17 | 21 | 59 | |
| | Pierrette III | W P J M Pierrot | 35 34 25 | 26 | 17 19 57 | 0 | 15 35 22 | 6 | 124 59 39 | 3 | 34 | 200 |
| Argentina | Fortuna | Capt A Heredia | 35 32 20 | 20 | RTD | 0 | 15 39 20 | 3 | 97 59 59 | 69 | 92 | |
| | Kuenda | A F Acevedo | 39 07 23 | 6 | 17 11 31 | 10 | 15 29 17 | 11 | 119 28 28 | 28 | 51 | |
| | Fjord V | G Frers | 35 37 59 | 14 | RTD | 0 | 15 38 04 | 4 | 121 27 29 | 18 | 36 | 179 |
| Bermuda | Quest of Paget | K F Trimingham Jr | 41 26 45 | 4 | RTD | 0 | RTD | 0 | 118 26 07 | 27 | 31 | |
| | Wizard of Paget | B de F Trimingham | 36 34 22 | 10 | 16 38 27 | 20 | 15 23 31 | 18 | 114 45 27 | 45 | 39 | 124 |
| Spain | Artako | J de Gamboa | 34 09 21 | 44 | 16 41 43 | 16 | 15 25 12 | 15 | 121 49 09 | 15 | 90 | |
| | El Monje | Capt J Balleste | 43 28 07 | 2 | 16 51 31 | 12 | 15 46 51 | 2 | 122 07 34 | 9 | 25 | 115 |

KEY:  DNS – Did Not Start  DNF – Did Not Finish  DSQ – Disqualified  RTD – Retired  (P) – Includes Penalty  DNC – Did Not Compete

| 1971 RACE RESULTS | | | RACE 1 CHANNEL RACE | | RACE 2 RORC TROPHY (FIRST INSHORE) | | RACE 3 RYS TROPHY (SECOND INSHORE) | | RACE 4 FASTNET RACE | | TOTAL (OVERALL POINTS) | OVERALL TOTAL (BY COUNTRY) |
|---|---|---|---|---|---|---|---|---|---|---|---|---|
| Country | Boat Name | Owner | Corrected time | Points | Corrected time | Points | Corrected time | Points | Corrected time | Points | | |
| Britain | Morning Cloud II | Rt Hon Edward Heath | 28 15 53 | 90 | 04 03 49 | 44 | 03 50 14 | 38 | 82 16 01 | 102 | 274 | |
| | Prospect of Whitby | A Slater | 27 53 19 | 94 | 04 00 36 | 46 | 03 47 00 | 43 | 82 06 43 | 108 | 291 | |
| | Cervantes IV | R C Watson | 28 28 07 | 86 | DSQ | 0 | 03 50 02 | 39 | 79 00 33 | 138 | 263 | 828 |
| USA | Bay Bea | P E Haggerty | 29 08 00 | 82 | 04 10 01 | 32 | 03 53 49 | 31 | 80 28 56 | 129 | 274 | |
| | Carina | R S Nye | 29 40 06 | 60 | 04 06 57 | 38 | 03 50 32 | 37 | 82 25 13 | 99 | 234 | |
| | Yankee Girl | D D Steere | 28 03 04 | 92 | 03 59 46 | 47 | DSQ | 0 | 79 37 25 | 135 | 274 | 782 |
| Australia | Koomooloo | N B Rydge | 29 50 39 | 58 | 04 06 19 | 39 | 03 46 46 | 44 | RTD | 0 | 141 | |
| | **Ragamuffin** | **S Fischer** | **29 27 41** | **70** | **04 05 45** | **41** | **03 46 43** | **45** | **76 08 38** | **141** | **297** | |
| | Salacia II | A W Byrne | 28 19 15 | 88 | 04 11 21 | 27 | 03 45 10 | 46 | 81 56 32 | 120 | 281 | 719 |
| Argentina | Matrero | E Kocourek | 29 24 51 | 74 | 04 04 35 | 43 | 03 49 59 | 41 | 83 35 05 | 87 | 245 | |
| | Recluta II | C A Corna | 29 38 45 | 64 | 04 10 06 | 30 | 03 58 55 | 20 | 83 07 09 | 90 | 204 | |
| | Shinda | A F Acevedo | 29 27 56 | 68 | 04 14 22 | 24 | 03 55 52 | 28 | 82 06 23 | 111 | 231 | 680 |
| Netherlands | Standfast | P Vroon & F Maas | 29 55 44 | 56 | 04 03 45 | 45 | 03 50 00 | 40 | 81 56 32 | 117 | 258 | |
| | Staron | Dr W M Oosterwyke | RTD | 0 | RTD | 0 | 03 56 34 | 26 | 83 45 37 | 84 | 110 | |
| | Belita VII | J S Bouman | 29 04 22 | 84 | 04 08 27 | 37 | 03 43 37 | 47 | 80 45 19 | 123 | 288 | 659 |
| South Africa | Jakaranda | T Bester | 29 27 30 | 72 | 04 08 40 | 36 | 03 53 40 | 32 | 80 41 54 | 126 | 266 | |
| | Mercury | G Neill | 30 58 17 | 34 | 04 10 01 | 32 | 03 54 31 | 29 | 87 35 05 | 48 | 143 | |
| | Omuramba | H Berker | 30 00 22 | 50 | 04 09 58 | 33 | 03 58 39 | 22 | 85 28 32 | 60 | 165 | 574 |
| Italy | Tarantella | A Raffaelli | 29 24 08 | 76 | 04 16 26 | 18 | 03 56 51 | 25 | 83 52 21 | 78 | 197 | |
| | Levantades | G Diano | 29 35 22 | 66 | 04 13 07 | 25 | RTD | 0 | 82 56 05 | 96 | 187 | |
| | Mabelle | Miss S Zaffagni | 30 04 12 | 46 | 04 05 59 | 40 | 03 57 21 | 24 | 84 46 24 | 69 | 179 | 563 |
| Bermuda | Cedrene | W Brown/G Jones | 31 33 00 | 26 | 04 13 22 | 24 | 04 01 16 | 15 | 91 22 29 | 33 | 98 | |
| | Firebrand II | D P Miller | 29 55 59 | 54 | 04 04 55 | 42 | 03 56 16 | 27 | 83 02 16 | 93 | 216 | |
| | Wizard of Paget | B de F Trimingham | 29 14 24 | 80 | DSQ | 0 | 03 51 37 | 36 | 82 04 38 | 114 | 230 | 544 |
| Germany | Rubin | H-O Schumann | 29 56 09 | 52 | 04 15 43 | 20 | 03 59 59 | 17 | 83 49 04 | 81 | 170 | |
| | Ree | H/K Redlefsen | 30 27 28 | 40 | 04 10 42 | 28 | 03 59 36 | 18 | 89 53 07 | 42 | 128 | |
| | Klaar Kimming | J H Anthon | 31 10 40 | 28 | DSQ | 0 | 03 53 00 | 34 | 89 35 02 | 45 | 107 | 405 |
| Brazil | Pluft | I Klabin | 29 22 42 | 78 | 04 12 39 | 26 | 04 04 32 | 13 | 84 35 03 | 72 | 189 | |
| | Villegagnon | Lt Cdr O M M Forte | 32 20 12 | 24 | 04 25 51 | 0 | 03 58 43 | 21 | 94 23 00 | 21 | 66 | |
| | Wa-Wa-Too | F L N de Abreu | 30 39 49 | 38 | 04 14 52 | 22 | 03 53 10 | 33 | 85 53 58 | 54 | 147 | 402 |
| Ireland | Moonduster | D N Doyle | 30 41 09 | 36 | DSQ | 0 | 04 06 45 | 12 | 89 09 43 | 39 | 87 | |
| | Tritsch Tratsch | Dr O Glaser | 30 22 41 | 42 | 04 10 18 | 29 | 03 54 09 | 30 | 82 11 10 | 105 | 206 | |
| | Clarion of Wight | Dr R O'Hanlon | 31 01 54 | 32 | 04 14 56 | 21 | 03 59 35 | 19 | 90 34 55 | 36 | 108 | 401 |
| Belgium | Phantom | A Moorkens | 29 39 45 | 62 | 04 16 20 | 0 | 04 00 49 | 16 | 85 00 09 | 63 | 141 | |
| | Callirhoé | A F Pauwels | 30 15 50 | 44 | 04 19 56 | 17 | 04 02 23 | 14 | 92 25 30 | 24 | 99 | |
| | Scarlett O'Hara | H Wolfs | 35 54 59 | 18 | 04 20 35 | 16 | 03 51 45 | 35 | 91 44 46 | 30 | 99 | 339 |

KEY:  DNS – Did Not Start    DNF – Did Not Finish    DSQ – Disqualified    RTD – Retired    (P) – Includes Penalty    DNC – Did Not Compete

| 1971 RACE RESULTS | Boat Name | Owner | RACE 1 CHANNEL RACE | | RACE 2 RORC TROPHY (FIRST INSHORE) | | RACE 3 RYS TROPHY (SECOND INSHORE) | | RACE 4 FASTNET RACE | | TOTAL (OVERALL POINTS) | OVERALL TOTAL (BY COUNTRY) |
|---|---|---|---|---|---|---|---|---|---|---|---|---|
| Country | | | Corrected time | Points | Corrected time | Points | Corrected time | Points | Corrected time | Points | | |
| Sweden | Sawadi | H Formgren | 31 05 07 | 30 | 04 15 46 | 19 | 03 58 32 | 23 | 84 53 07 | 66 | 138 | |
| | Madame II | B Högbom | 38 08 51 | 16 | 04 46 29 | 12 | 04 22 41 | 9 | 95 37 12 | 18 | 55 | |
| | Carina III | B Nylen | 32 25 26 | 22 | 04 06 57 | 14 | 03 50 32 | 11 | 92 21 42 | 27 | 74 | 267 |
| New Zealand | Improbable | D W Allen | 30 03 39 | 48 | 04 09 27 | 34 | 03 48 59 | 42 | 79 52 30 | 132 | 256 | 256 |
| France | Gitana V | Baron E de Rothschild | RTD | 0 | 04 08 44 | 35 | RTD | 0 | 83 56 10 | 75 | 110 | |
| | Pen Duick III | E Tabarly | DNS | 0 | 04 33 08 | 13 | DSQ | 0 | DNS | 0 | 13 | |
| | Izenah | M Holley | 33 03 08 | 20 | 04 21 37 | 15 | 04 12 04 | 10 | 85 43 19 | 57 | 102 | 225 |
| Austria | Iorana | W W Denzel | DNS | 0 | DNS | 0 | 00 00 00 | 0 | 86 00 26 | 51 | 51 | 51 |

KEY:   DNS  –  Did Not Start       DNF  –  Did Not Finish       DSQ  –  Disqualified       RTD  –  Retired       (P)  –  Includes Penalty       DNC – Did Not Compete

| 1973 RACE RESULTS | | | RACE 1 CHANNEL RACE | | RACE 2 RORC TROPHY (FIRST INSHORE) | | RACE 3 RYS TROPHY (SECOND INSHORE) | | RACE 4 FASTNET RACE | | TOTAL (OVERALL POINTS) | OVERALL TOTAL (BY COUNTRY) |
|---|---|---|---|---|---|---|---|---|---|---|---|---|
| Country | Boat Name | Owner | Corrected time | Points | Corrected time | Points | Corrected time | Points | Corrected time | Points | | |
| Germany | **Saudade** | **A Bull** | **30 44 17** | **90** | **05 50 50** | **48** | **05 15 47** | **48** | **115 27 57** | **126** | **312** | |
| | Rubin | H-O Schumann | 31 13 39 | 72 | 06 04 22 | 39 | 05 23 57 | 43 | 120 44 45 | 114 | 268 | |
| | Carina III | D Monheim | 31 16 34 | 70 | 06 06 53 | 36 | 05 30 51 | 27 | 119 59 17 | 117 | 250 | 830 |
| Australia | Ginkgo | G Bogard | 30 54 03 | 88 | 06 01 01 | 42 | 05 24 49 | 41 | 121 14 27 | 111 | 282 | |
| | Apollo II | A Bond | 32 24 58 | 74 | 05 57 15 | 45 | 05 23 28 | 44 | 115 46 13 | 102 | 265 | |
| | Ragamuffin | S Fischer | 31 34 02 | 50 | 05 57 54 | 44 | 05 25 10 | 39 | 122 43 29 | 99 | 232 | 779 |
| Britain | Frigate | A J Boyden & R Aisher | 30 38 58 | 94 | 06 11 18 | 35 | 05 21 12 | 45 | 117 28 37 | 123 | 297 | |
| | Quailo III | T D Parr | 32 08 47 | 16 | 05 56 57 | 46 | 05 25 34 | 38 | 112 23 32 | 129 | 229 | |
| | Morning Cloud III | Rt Hon Edward Heath | 30 59 50 | 82 | 06 02 56 | 40 | 05 18 49 | 47 | 128 56 07 | 54 | 223 | 749 |
| USA | Lightnin' | R E Turner | 30 40 19 | 92 | 06 16 33 | 32 | 05 25 06 | 40 | 122 48 15 | 96 | 260 | |
| | Charisma | J Philips | 31 54 28 | 30 | 05 58 35 | 43 | 05 28 57 | 34 | 106 49 03 | 138 | 245 | |
| | Salty Goose | W Frank/R Derecktor | 31 57 00 | 22 | 06 11 46 | 34 | 05 24 45 | 42 | 108 08 43 | 135 | 233 | 738 |
| Netherlands | Nymphaea | Th E Vinke/R Morelisse | 30 56 34 | 86 | 06 19 52 | 30 | 05 30 28 | 30 | 126 43 22 | 75 | 221 | |
| | Standfast II | F Maas/P Vroon | 31 30 09 | 58 | 06 25 07 | 23 | 05 29 00 | 33 | 127 53 06 | 69 | 183 | |
| | Polka Mara | W Kesteloo | 30 59 57 | 80 | 06 38 35 | 13 | 05 32 02 | 22 | 129 23 03 | 45 | 160 | 564 |
| Argentina | Recluta III | C A Corna | 31 04 50 | 76 | 06 01 55 | 41 | 05 19 18 | 46 | 105 38 24 | 141 | 304 | |
| | Atrevido | A Grandi | 31 42 15 | 40 | 06 30 51 | 21 | RTD | 0 | 128 32 50 | 66 | 127 | |
| | Matrero | E Kocourek | 31 49 40 | 34 | 06 04 34 | 38 | 05 30 57 | 25 | 132 05 24 | 24 | 121 | 552 |
| France | Revolution | J L Fabry/M Hennebert | 30 31 51 | 96 | 06 22 19 | 28 | 05 29 17 | 32 | 128 54 04 | 57 | 213 | |
| | Milene II | A Mirlesse | 31 35 58 | 46 | 06 23 03 | 26 | 05 36 29 | 15 | 122 24 59 | 105 | 192 | |
| | L'Orgueil V | G des Moutis | 31 33 58 | 52 | 06 47 44 | 7 | 05 30 24 | 21 | 129 39 44 | 42 | 122 | 527 |
| Bermuda | War Baby | W Brown/A Brown | 31 33 42 | 54 | 06 20 43 | 29 | 05 31 39 | 23 | 125 14 06 | 87 | 193 | |
| | Wizard of Paget | B H de F Trimingham | 31 00 41 | 78 | 06 36 44 | 14 | 05 35 06 | 17 | 128 58 30 | 51 | 160 | |
| | Firebrand III | D Miller | 32 17 11 | 12 | 06 24 22 | 24 | 05 42 18 | 11 | 124 30 08 | 90 | 137 | 490 |
| Italy | Sagittarius | G Carriero | 30 59 07 | 84 | 06 18 18 | 31 | 05 29 58 | 31 | 125 33 52 | 84 | 230 | |
| | Mabelle | Signorina S Zaffagni | 31 16 53 | 68 | 06 46 53 | 8 | 05 33 42 | 18 | 130 09 23 | 36 | 130 | |
| | Naif | R Gardini | 31 17 32 | 66 | 06 24 18 | 25 | 05 30 42 | 28 | 135 10 16 | (P) 6 | 125 | 485 |
| Brazil | Saga | E Lorentzen | 31 56 32 | 24 | 05 56 23 | 47 | 05 43 53 | 9 | 105 11 00 | 144 | 224 | |
| | Wa-Wa-Too III | F Nabuco de Abreu | 31 49 50 | 32 | 06 13 58 | 33 | RTD | 0 | 119 03 44 | 120 | 185 | |
| | Cangaceiro | D Barreto | 32 03 16 | 20 | RTD | 0 | 06 20 05 | 6 | 133 40 19 | 15 | 41 | 450 |
| Finland | Safari | P W Adams | 32 21 18 | 10 | 06 06 32 | 37 | DSQ | 0 | 108 46 52 | 132 | 179 | |
| | Carolina | T Koristo | 31 37 12 | 44 | 06 44 37 | 9 | 05 31 11 | 24 | 123 13 56 | 93 | 170 | |
| | Can-Can IV | E Kindberg | 34 13 25 | (P) 4 | 07 06 20 | 4 | 05 40 51 | 12 | 127 46 32 | 72 | 92 | 441 |
| South Africa | Jakaranda | ORI (B Bongers) | 31 47 45 | 38 | 06 26 01 | (P) 22 | 05 28 21 | 36 | 122 00 28 | 108 | 204 | |
| | Omuramba | H J Berker | 31 26 04 | 62 | RTD | 0 | 05 30 56 | 26 | 130 47 08 | 33 | 121 | |
| | Outburst | W C O'Reilly | 31 21 41 | 64 | 06 52 51 | 6 | 05 42 22 | 10 | 132 17 21 | 21 | 101 | 426 |

KEY:  DNS – Did Not Start   DNF – Did Not Finish   DSQ – Disqualified   RTD – Retired   (P) – Includes Penalty   DNC – Did Not Compete

| 1973 RACE RESULTS | Boat Name | Owner | RACE 1 CHANNEL RACE | | RACE 2 RORC TROPHY (FIRST INSHORE) | | RACE 3 RYS TROPHY (SECOND INSHORE) | | RACE 4 FASTNET RACE | | TOTAL (OVERALL POINTS) | OVERALL TOTAL (BY COUNTRY) |
|---|---|---|---|---|---|---|---|---|---|---|---|---|
| Country | | | Corrected time | Points | Corrected time | Points | Corrected time | Points | Corrected time | Points | | |
| Denmark | Tai Fat | J H Andersen | 31 40 45 | 42 | 06 38 56 | 12 | 05 28 05 | 37 | 126 35 43 | 78 | 169 | |
| | Kiss III | P Teichert | 31 56 23 | 26 | 06 33 48 | 19 | 05 44 57 | 7 | 125 40 44 | (P) 81 | 133 | |
| | Jet | J E Thomsen | 32 16 07 | 14 | 06 34 59 | 16 | 05 44 20 | 8 | 134 13 52 | 12 | 50 | 352 |
| Belgium | Colombe III | P d'Andrimont | 31 29 37 | 60 | 06 32 22 | 20 | 05 32 30 | 20 | 130 01 06 | 39 | 139 | |
| | Phantom II | A Moorkens | 31 48 55 | 36 | 06 34 14 | 17 | 05 28 54 | 35 | 131 21 06 | 27 | 115 | |
| | Dagon | P J Orban | 31 55 30 | 28 | 06 35 30 | 15 | 05 32 36 | 19 | 132 54 40 | 15 | 77 | 331 |
| Portugal | Rajada | V Polisaitis | 31 33 27 | 56 | 06 42 38 | 10 | 06 28 20 | 5 | 128 40 10 | 60 | 131 | |
| | Procelaria | F P Duarte | 32 05 31 | 18 | 06 40 21 | 11 | RTD | 0 | 128 33 55 | 63 | 92 | |
| | Foxhound | X Nogueira | 33 22 10 | 6 | 06 22 43 | 27 | 05 38 34 | 14 | 141 48 17 | (P) 3 | 50 | 273 |
| Ireland | Tritsch-Tratsch II | Dr O Glaser | 31 35 42 | 48 | RTD | 0 | 05 30 29 | 29 | 130 54 54 | 30 | 107 | |
| | Tam O'Shanter | J M Park | 32 26 39 | 8 | 07 00 50 | 5 | 05 38 58 | 13 | 129 16 55 | 48 | 74 | |
| | Moonduster | D N Doyle | RTD | 0 | 06 34 00 | 18 | 05 35 30 | 16 | 135 08 05 | 9 | 43 | 224 |

KEY:   DNS  –  Did Not Start      DNF  –  Did Not Finish      DSQ  –  Disqualified      RTD  –  Retired      (P)  –  Includes Penalty      DNC – Did Not Compete

| 1975 RACE RESULTS Country | Boat Name | Owner | RACE 1 CHANNEL RACE Corrected time | Points | RACE 2 RORC TROPHY (FIRST INSHORE) Corrected time | Points | RACE 3 RYS TROPHY (SECOND INSHORE) Corrected time | Points | RACE 4 FASTNET RACE Corrected time | Points | TOTAL (OVERALL POINTS) | OVERALL TOTAL (BY COUNTRY) |
|---|---|---|---|---|---|---|---|---|---|---|---|---|
| Britain | Battlecry | J O Prentice | 42 11 58 | 40 | 06 25 09 | 51 | 12 37 04 | 27 | 115 54 27 | 138 | 256 | |
| | **Noryema X** | **R W Amey** | **40 22 07** | **114** | **06 24 45** | **52** | **11 01 56** | **55** | **114 53 25** | **159** | **380** | |
| | Yeoman XX | R A Aisher/A Aisher | 40 59 05 | 90 | 06 21 57 | 56 | 10 33 29 | 57 | 115 44 56 | 141 | 344 | 980 |
| Germany | Pinta | W Illbruck | 40 41 10 | 106 | 06 23 21 | 54 | 12 27 30 | 40 | 115 22 50 | 144 | 344 | |
| | Rubin | H-O Schumann | 40 53 50 | 100 | 06 24 07 | 53 | 12 57 12 | 0 | 115 21 35 | 147 | 300 | |
| | Duva | P Lubinus | 41 07 30 | 80 | 06 33 31 | 41 | 12 54 22 | 17 | 117 54 26 | 93 | 231 | 875 |
| USA | Charisma | J Philips | 40 36 54 | 108 | 06 34 53 | 40 | 13 05 48 | 11 | 118 10 46 | 87 | 246 | |
| | Tenacious | R E Turner | 41 12 54 | 74 | 06 31 45 | 44 | 12 45 18 | 21 | 116 05 20 | 135 | 274 | |
| | Robin | T Hood | 40 36 22 | 110 | 06 22 18 | 55 | 12 33 47 | 32 | 116 16 58 | 129 | 326 | 846 |
| Netherlands | Easy Rider | J Martens | 40 28 39 | 11 | RTD | 1 | 12 42 32 | 23 | 118 21 51 | 81 | 171 | |
| | Standfast | P W Vroon/F L Mass | 40 46 48 | 104 | 06 30 33 | 45 | 12 41 43 | 24 | 126 27 22 | 165 | 338 | |
| | Goodwin | J van Drongelan | 42 16 22 | 34 | 06 44 24 | 19 | 12 33 23 | 33 | 109 82 08 | 171 | 257 | 766 |
| New Zealand | Gerontius | G Eder | 41 02 41 | 86 | 06 32 52 | 42 | 12 53 49 | 18 | 116 08 24 | 132 | 278 | |
| | Inca | E Julian | 41 06 23 | 82 | 06 36 58 | 31 | 12 08 06 | 48 | DSQ | 0 | 161 | |
| | Barnacle Bill | R Jarden | 41 16 22 | 72 | 06 35 23 | 34 | 12 34 18 | 31 | 117 20 04 | 108 | 245 | 684 |
| Spain | Sanumac | J Camunas | 41 53 45 | 54 | 06 26 48 | 49 | 13 33 20 | 7 | 120 14 55 | 69 | 179 | |
| | Flamenco | G Cryns | 41 07 39 | 78 | 06 53 33 | 13 | 12 28 35 | 38 | 110 08 05 | 168 | 297 | |
| | Mabelle | Fed Espanola de Vela | 45 22 55 | 4 | 06 50 11 | 15 | 12 25 55 | 41 | 116 04 24 | 123 | 183 | 659 |
| Ireland | Moonduster | D N Doyle | 42 01 04 | 52 | 06 40 53 | 24 | 12 35 10 | 30 | 121 41 16 | 45 | 151 | |
| | Assiduous | C Loves | 42 09 10 | 44 | 06 35 33 | 32 | 12 35 55 | 29 | 119 41 12 | 78 | 183 | |
| | Irish Mist | A O'Leary | 40 33 58 | 112 | 06 27 28 | 48 | 12 46 49 | 51 | 117 06 50 | 111 | 322 | 656 |
| Hong Kong | Ceil V | B Turnbull | 42 03 05 | 50 | DSQ | 0 | 12 46 49 | 20 | 122 07 03 | 39 | 109 | |
| | Trailblazer | W F Jeffrey | 41 47 06 | 60 | 06 35 21 | 35 | 12 27 56 | 39 | 114 38 51 | 162 | 296 | |
| | Casse Tête | H H Ross | 42 08 20 | 42 | 06 38 02 | 28 | 11 57 06 | 50 | 115 33 18 | 117 | 237 | 642 |
| Australia | Bumblebee 3 | J D Kahlbetzer | 40 55 45 | 96 | 06 28 37 | 46 | RTD | 1 | 121 23 29 | 54 | 197 | |
| | Love and War | P Kurts | 40 55 27 | 98 | 06 32 19 | 43 | 13 05 37 | 12 | 121 29 35 | 51 | 204 | |
| | Mercedes IV | H T Kaufman | 41 00 23 | 88 | DSQ | 0 | 12 49 05 | 19 | 117 46 34 | 96 | 203 | 604 |
| Switzerland | Altair | A Sutsch | 42 29 02 | 28 | 06 35 22 | 34 | 13 16 12 | 10 | 123 43 28 | 21 | 93 | |
| | More Opposition | B Guttinger | 40 56 13 | 94 | 06 26 26 | 50 | 12 31 06 | 35 | 121 35 50 | 48 | 227 | |
| | On Dit | H Ringeisen | 41 19 03 | 70 | 06 35 02 | 38 | 12 18 10 | 44 | 117 34 22 | 105 | 257 | 577 |
| France | Coriolan II | C de Gallea | 42 05 04 | 48 | 06 37 20 | 30 | DSQ | 0 | 127 27 59 | 9 | 87 | |
| | Katsou | A Viant/D Paul-Cavallier | 40 57 01 | 92 | 06 34 57 | 39 | 12 38 41 | 25 | 117 02 41 | 114 | 270 | |
| | Revolution | J L Fabry | 44 40 09 | 8 | RTD | 1 | 11 50 05 | 52 | 113 32 52 | 156 | 217 | 574 |
| Argentina | Matrero | E Kocourek | 41 50 14 | 36 | 06 39 20 | 27 | 13 37 45 | 6 | 124 11 22 | 18 | 87 | |
| | Red Rock III | B Mandelbaum | 41 05 02 | 84 | 06 21 06 | 57 | 11 17 03 | 54 | 117 38 33 | 99 | 294 | |
| | Don Alberto | G Frers | 41 12 22 | 76 | DSQ | 0 | 12 59 04 | 14 | 117 35 05 | 102 | 192 | 573 |

KEY: DNS – Did Not Start    DNF – Did Not Finish    DSQ – Disqualified    RTD – Retired    (P) – Includes Penalty    DNC – Did Not Compete

| 1975 RACE RESULTS | Boat Name | Owner | RACE 1 CHANNEL RACE | | RACE 2 RORC TROPHY (FIRST INSHORE) | | RACE 3 RYS TROPHY (SECOND INSHORE) | | RACE 4 FASTNET RACE | | TOTAL (OVERALL POINTS) | OVERALL TOTAL (BY COUNTRY) |
|---|---|---|---|---|---|---|---|---|---|---|---|---|
| Country | | | Corrected time | Points | Corrected time | Points | Corrected time | Points | Corrected time | Points | | |
| South Africa | Omuramba | H Berker | 43 08 03 | 12 | 06 39 23 | 26 | 12 36 07 | 28 | 116 55 58 | 90 | 156 | |
| | Golden Fleece | G J Neill | 43 10 16 | 16 | 06 45 28 | 18 | 12 58 56 | 15 | 118 42 51 | 84 | 133 | |
| | Frigate | CASA | 42 49 06 | 22 | 06 35 19 | 36 | 11 43 51 | 53 | 115 09 35 | 150 | 261 | 550 |
| Sweden | Humbug XIX | P Pettersson | 40 48 52 | 102 | 06 37 31 | 29 | 12 19 08 | 43 | 120 38 20 | 63 | 237 | |
| | Sawadi Song | H Formgren | 43 31 18 | 14 | 06 41 50 | 22 | 12 06 43 | 49 | 122 17 37 | 36 | 121 | |
| | Attaque | C Rydqvist | 44 54 27 | 6 | 06 47 16 | 17 | 12 16 56 | 45 | 116 44 26 | 120 | 188 | 546 |
| Brazil | Wa Wa Too II | F L Nabuco de Abreu | 42 33 06 | 24 | 06 35 18 | 37 | 13 16 14 | 9 | 121 13 15 | 60 | 130 | |
| | Nymphea | M Simoes | 41 43 53 | 46 | 07 54 46 | 10 | 12 58 35 | 16 | 113 55 52 | 153 | 225 | |
| | Procelaria | F J Pimentel Duarte | 43 50 48 | 10 | 06 53 42 | 12 | 12 30 10 | 37 | 119 47 08 | 72 | 131 | 486 |
| Norway | Ariel | G Wilhelmsen | 41 51 47 | 56 | 06 53 27 | 14 | 12 32 34 | 4 | 119 41 14 | 75 | 179 | |
| | Liz | J Godager | 42 18 41 | 32 | 06 28 10 | 47 | 12 37 07 | 26 | 120 35 06 | 66 | 171 | |
| | Sagamore | F Grape | 42 52 16 | 20 | 06 41 48 | 23 | 12 09 28 | 47 | 123 04 01 | 30 | 120 | 470 |
| Italy | Vihuela | F Violati | 42 28 04 | 30 | 06 43 00 | 21 | 13 04 13 | 13 | RTD | 3 | 67 | |
| | Mandrake | G Carriero | 41 47 33 | 58 | DSQ | 0 | 12 42 37 | 22 | 116 17 15 | 126 | 206 | |
| | Guia III | G Falck | 41 09 23 | 62 | DNF | 1 | 10 59 56 | 56 | 122 08 46 | 24 | 143 | 416 |
| Canada | Diva | B A Sully | 42 29 11 | 26 | 06 47 43 | 16 | 13 22 41 | 8 | 122 51 31 | 33 | 83 | |
| | Dynamo | G W Moog | 41 20 29 | 68 | RTD | 1 | 12 21 23 | 42 | 122 05 08 | 42 | 153 | |
| | Kanata | V Plavsic | 45 38 16 | 2 | 06 43 57 | 20 | 12 09 53 | 46 | 125 51 38 | 15 | 83 | 319 |
| Belgium | Dagon | P Orban | 42 28 53 | 18 | 06 58 27 | 11 | RTD | 1 | 125 03 37 | 12 | 42 | |
| | Phantom | A Moorkens | 41 47 16 | 38 | 06 39 33 | 25 | 13 41 22 | 5 | 121 58 39 | 27 | 95 | |
| | Colombe | P d'Andrimont | 41 06 01 | 64 | RTD | 1 | 12 30 50 | 36 | 116 43 44 | 57 | 158 | 295 |

KEY: DNS – Did Not Start    DNF – Did Not Finish    DSQ – Disqualified    RTD – Retired    (P) – Includes Penalty    DNC – Did Not Compete

| 1977 RACE RESULTS | | | RACE 1 RORC TROPHY (FIRST INSHORE) | | RACE 2 CHANNEL RACE | | RACE 3 * RYS TROPHY (SECOND INSHORE) | | RACE 4 (THIRD INSHORE) | | RACE 5 FASTNET RACE | | TOTAL (OVERALL POINTS) | OVERALL TOTAL (BY COUNTRY) |
|---|---|---|---|---|---|---|---|---|---|---|---|---|---|---|
| Country | Boat Name | Owner | Corrected time | Points | Corrected time | Points | Corrected time | Points | Corrected time | Points | Corrected time | Points | | |
| Britain | Moonshine | J C Rogers/W L Green | 05 28 31 | 57 | 37 33 27 | 78 | 05 43 59 | 55 | 04 25 22 | 47 | 141 32 31 | 168 | 405 | |
| | Yeoman XX | R A/A Aisher | 05 34 01 | 51 | 37 40 29 | 76 | 06 06 34 | 29 | 04 25 53 | 45 | 141 36 25 | 165 | 366 | |
| | Marionette | C A F Dunning | 05 37 19 | 48 | 38 09 03 | 58 | 05 43 32 | 56 | 04 24 21 | 50 | 146 42 12 | 147 | 359 | 1,130 |
| USA | **Imp** | **D Allen** | **05 31 52** | **54** | **36 38 48** | **110** | **05 52 47** | **47** | **04 13 54** | **57** | **141 26 53** | **171** | **439** | |
| | Scaramouche | C Kirsch | 05 54 08 | 22 | 36 35 45 | 114 | 05 50 02 | 53 | 04 28 26 | 41 | 151 16 43 | 123 | 353 | |
| | Bay Bea | P E Haggerty | 05 28 53 | 56 | 39 32 00 | 28 | 05 51 55 | 49 | DSQ | 0 | 145 06 49 | 159 | 292 | 1,084 |
| Hong Kong | Vanguard | D Lieu | 05 29 26 | 55 | 36 47 09 | 106 | 06 00 17 | 36 | 04 17 15 | 56 | 162 10 24 | 84 | 337 | |
| | White Rabbit | J Ma | 05 45 24 | 34 | 37 11 55 | 92 | 05 58 21 | 38 | 05 20 42 | 54 | 158 18 22 | 99 | 317 | |
| | La Pantera | E de Lasala/C Ostenfeld | 05 33 53 | 52 | DSQ | 0 | 05 57 44 | 40 | 04 30 47 | 34 | 147 45 09 | 141 | 267 | 921 |
| Germany | Champagne | P Westphal-Langloh | 05 36 15 | 45 | 37 00 25 | 96 | 05 50 40 | 51 | 04 19 08 | 55 | 149 10 30 | 135 | 382 | |
| | Pinta | W Illbruck | 05 32 04 | 53 | 36 59 34 | 98 | DSQ | 0 | 04 28 36 | 40 | 143 28 24 | 162 | 353 | |
| | Duva | Dr P Lubinus | 05 59 37 | 15 | 39 31 19 | 30 | 05 50 15 | 52 | 04 37 16 | 20 | 170 08 38 | 24 | 141 | 876 |
| Italy | Moby Dick | L F Bortolotti | 05 38 15 | 46 | 36 38 26 | 112 | DSQ | 0 | 04 26 27 | 44 | 157 51 36 | 102 | 304 | |
| | Vanina | V Mandelli | 05 45 45 | 32 | 38 45 00 | 46 | 05 53 13 | 46 | 04 22 42 | 52 | 153 39 31 | 111 | 287 | |
| | Mandrake | G Carriero | 05 45 14 | 35 | 37 26 02 | 82 | DSQ | 0 | 04 31 58 | 32 | 149 30 23 | 132 | 281 | 872 |
| France | Revolution | J L Fabry | 05 35 50 | 50 | 36 49 24 | 102 | 06 04 15 | 33 | 04 35 13 | 25 | 159 13 29 | 96 | 306 | |
| | Emeraude | J Dewailly | 05 56 11 | 20 | 39 11 44 | 38 | 05 55 29 | 42 | 04 37 57 | 19 | 148 29 46 | 138 | 257 | |
| | Alexandre | M Marchais/J Carpentier | 05 53 24 | 26 | 37 41 13 | 74 | 05 57 51 | 39 | 04 32 46 | 30 | 164 00 48 | 63 | 232 | 795 |
| Australia | Ragamuffin | S Fischer | 05 43 56 | 36 | 37 59 26 | 66 | 05 52 15 | 48 | 04 29 36 | 37 | 150 43 00 | 126 | 313 | |
| | Runaway | J Hardy | RTD | 0 | 36 53 52 | 100 | 06 05 20 | 28 | 04 33 10 | 28 | 162 31 27 | 81 | 237 | |
| | Superstar | K Farfor | 05 42 24 | 38 | 37 59 49 | 64 | 05 46 13 | 54 | 04 24 45 | 48 | 170 04 44 | 27 | 232 | 782 |
| Ireland | Big Apple | Coveney/Fielding/Love | 05 41 52 | 40 | 36 48 54 | 104 | 05 40 57 | 57 | 04 25 06 | 48 | 155 40 24 | 108 | 357 | |
| | Irish Mist II | A O'Leary | 05 40 13 | 44 | 38 01 47 | 60 | 06 12 17 | 22 | 04 32 40 | 31 | 164 11 04 | 54 | 212 | |
| | Golden Leigh | N Cordiner | 05 42 10 | 39 | 37 47 17 | 72 | DSQ | 0 | 04 31 15 | 33 | 163 46 00 | 66 | 210 | 779 |
| Spain | Yachtman | Sindicato AC77 | 05 38 15 | 47 | 37 13 14 | 90 | RTD | 0 | 04 29 25 | 38 | 145 27 57 | 156 | 332 | |
| | Azahara | Duke of Arion | 05 49 24 | 29 | 38 12 57 | 56 | 06 04 17 | 32 | 04 34 15 | 27 | 156 06 54 | 105 | 249 | |
| | Odiseus IV | L Garcia Meca | 05 53 52 | 23 | 39 14 06 | 36 | 05 54 50 | 43 | 04 35 14 | 24 | 163 36 09 | 72 | 198 | 779 |
| Argentina | Recluta IV | C A Corna | 05 48 03 | 30 | 37 48 23 | 70 | 05 54 41 | 44 | 04 35 26 | 23 | 153 13 00 | 114 | 281 | |
| | Fortuna II | Armada Argentina | 06 08 13 | 9 | 37 59 56 | 62 | 05 54 27 | 45 | 04 53 02 | 3 | 151 20 29 | 120 | 239 | |
| | Victoria | E Kocourek | 05 53 35 | (P) 25 | 38 53 34 | 42 | 06 27 33 | 7 | 04 28 19 | 42 | 152 02 43 | 117 | 226 | 746 |
| Netherlands | Standfast | P W Vroon/F L Maas | 05 43 26 | 37 | 38 13 56 | 54 | 06 12 31 | 20 | 04 44 04 | 13 | 149 47 53 | 129 | 253 | |
| | Schuttevaer | Dr J C W van Dam | 05 45 35 | 33 | 37 22 37 | 84 | 06 25 27 | 9 | 04 34 29 | 26 | 159 44 53 | 93 | 245 | |
| | Nymphæa | A Goudriaan/Th E Vinke | 05 50 38 | 27 | 39 26 24 | 32 | 06 19 59 | 14 | 04 43 51 | 14 | 164 08 49 | 60 | 147 | 645 |
| Brazil | Orion III | E Barth | 05 40 17 | 43 | 37 10 18 | 94 | 06 21 53 | 13 | 04 44 16 | 1 | 163 28 07 | 75 | 226 | |
| | Tigre | F P Duarte | 05 41 18 | 41 | RTD | 0 | 06 13 01 | 19 | 04 23 55 | 48 | 159 50 34 | 90 | 200 | |
| | Kamaiura | E Falkenberg | 06 09 37 | 7 | 37 57 01 | 68 | 06 16 11 | 16 | 04 43 13 | 15 | 164 10 46 | 57 | 163 | 589 |

* 1st attempt abandoned; eventually raced Thursday after Third Inshore

| KEY: | DNS – Did Not Start | DNF – Did Not Finish | DSQ – Disqualified | RTD – Retired | (P) – Includes Penalty | DNC – Did Not Compete |

| 1977 RACE RESULTS | Boat Name | Owner | RACE 1 RORC TROPHY (FIRST INSHORE) | | RACE 2 CHANNEL RACE | | RACE 3 * RYS TROPHY (SECOND INSHORE) | | RACE 4 (THIRD INSHORE) | | RACE 5 FASTNET RACE | | TOTAL (OVERALL POINTS) | OVERALL TOTAL (BY COUNTRY) |
|---|---|---|---|---|---|---|---|---|---|---|---|---|---|---|
| Country | | | Corrected time | Points | Corrected time | Points | Corrected time | Points | Corrected time | Points | Corrected time | Points | | |
| Norway | Liz of Hankø | J B Godager | 05 53 38 | 24 | 37 19 45 | 86 | 06 08 44 | 25 | 04 25 32 | 46 | 145 36 41 | 153 | 334 | |
| | Synergy | E Koefoed | 05 58 33 | 17 | 38 17 00 | 52 | 06 04 22 | 32 | 04 44 26 | 9 | 169 03 10 | 30 | 139 | |
| | Jan Pott | L Hubert | 05 56 59 | 19 | 38 31 56 | 50 | 06 16 09 | 17 | 04 47 44 | 5 | 171 50 04 | 12 | 103 | 576 |
| Austria | Iorana III | W W Denzel | 05 40 34 | 42 | 36 46 42 | 108 | 05 55 52 | 41 | 04 21 38 | 53 | 146 15 39 | 150 | 394 | |
| | Brother Cup | Osterreichischer S V | RTD | 0 | 38 47 24 | 44 | 06 14 44 | 18 | 04 37 08 | 21 | RTD | 3 | 87 | |
| | Rubin | Osterreichischer S V | 06 05 12 | 12 | 41 17 46 | 12 | 06 11 55 | 23 | 04 48 44 | 7 | 170 41 16 | 21 | 75 | 556 |
| Switzerland | Assiduous | N Berger | 05 50 20 | 28 | 37 30 21 | 80 | 06 09 06 | 24 | 04 32 53 | 29 | 147 12 00 | 144 | 305 | |
| | Atair | A Sutsch | 06 04 15 | 13 | 38 33 49 | 48 | 06 05 31 | 24 | 04 30 12 | 32 | 170 56 42 | 15 | 132 | |
| | Milene III | A Mirlesse | 05 58 49 | 16 | 40 49 05 | 18 | 06 05 32 | 23 | 04 28 45 | 39 | 170 52 41 | 18 | 114 | 551 |
| Sweden | Good Will | H Formgren | 05 47 20 | 31 | 39 52 33 | 24 | 06 19 04 | 15 | 04 29 43 | 36 | 164 49 11 | 48 | 154 | |
| | Victoria | G Lundberg | 05 54 39 | 10 | 39 44 10 | 26 | DSQ | 0 | 04 39 58 | 17 | 163 41 22 | 69 | 129 | |
| | Susette | C W Edstrom | 05 57 40 | 18 | 44 06 07 | 6 | 06 25 49 | 8 | 04 45 09 | 11 | 166 17 06 | 36 | 79 | 362 |
| Belgium | Raveling | L van den Bossche | 06 05 21 | 11 | 38 57 37 | 40 | 06 29 35 | 5 | 04 51 26 | 4 | 161 14 08 | 87 | 147 | |
| | Soizic | J Dobbelaere | 06 06 07 | 10 | 40 04 02 | 22 | 06 24 38 | 10 | 04 36 36 | 22 | 164 46 21 | 51 | 115 | |
| | Phantom II | A Moorkens | 06 17 00 | 6 | 40 52 45 | 14 | 06 22 27 | 12 | 04 49 01 | 6 | 166 57 34 | 33 | 71 | 333 |
| Japan | Sunbird V | T Yamasaki | 06 03 05 | 14 | 40 49 55 | 16 | 06 12 17 | 22 | 04 39 04 | 18 | 163 26 52 | 78 | 148 | |
| | B B III | Y Sawano | 06 19 13 | 4 | 39 18 21 | 34 | 06 27 53 | 6 | 04 42 10 | 13 | 165 30 23 | 42 | 99 | |
| | Miyakadori III | H Okasaki | 06 18 40 | 5 | 43 25 23 | 8 | 06 22 50 | 11 | 05 00 51 | 2 | RTD | 3 | 29 | 276 |
| Poland | Bumerang | Jacht Klub Stal | 06 08 58 | 8 | 40 04 03 | 20 | RTD | 0 | 04 46 15 | 10 | 165 41 49 | 39 | 78 | |
| | Bolinski Hajduk | E Hoffmann | RTD | 0 | 41 45 26 | 10 | 06 38 40 | 4 | 04 47 01 | 9 | 165 02 56 | 45 | 66 | |
| | Spaniel | Jacht Klub Pasat | RTD | 0 | RTD | 0 | 06 52 40 | 3 | 04 50 57 | 5 | RTD | 3 | 14 | 158 |

KEY:   DNS – Did Not Start   DNF – Did Not Finish   DSQ – Disqualified   RTD – Retired   (P) – Includes Penalty   DNC – Did Not Compete

| 1979 RACE RESULTS | | | RACE 1 RORC TROPHY (FIRST INSHORE) | | RACE 2 RYS TROPHY (SECOND INSHORE) | | RACE 3 CHANNEL RACE | | RACE 4 CHAMPAGNE MUMM TROPHY (THIRD INSHORE) | | RACE 5 FASTNET RACE | | TOTAL (OVERALL POINTS) | OVERALL TOTAL (BY COUNTRY) |
|---|---|---|---|---|---|---|---|---|---|---|---|---|---|---|
| Country | Boat Name | Owner | Corrected time | Points | Corrected time | Points | Corrected time | Points | Corrected time | Points | Corrected time | Points | | |
| Australia | Police Car | P R Cantwell | 05 05 59 | 51 | 05 19 52 | 55 | 33 03 41 | 100 | 04 47 07 | (P) 41 | 97 56 26 | 162 | 409 | |
| | Impetuous | G Lambert /J Crisp | 05 15 12 | 28 | 05 20 01 | 54 | 33 22 24 | 78 | 04 52 17 | 35 | 97 53 33 | 165 | 360 | |
| | Ragamuffin | S Fischer | 05 07 43 | 45 | 05 24 07 | 49 | 33 45 05 | 54 | 04 51 33 | 36 | 100 17 47 | 135 | 319 | 1088 |
| USA | Imp | D W Allen | 05 07 35 | 46 | 05 27 04 | 44 | 32 47 43 | 108 | 04 51 03 | 40 | 97 57 09 | 159 | 397 | |
| | Williwaw | S Sinett | 05 04 17 | 56 | 05 21 43 | 52 | 33 47 59 | 46 | 04 40 24 | 57 | 101 38 23 | 129 | 340 | |
| | Aries | M Swerdlow | 05 06 50 | 48 | 05 26 31 | 46 | 33 58 12 | 26 | 04 41 48 | 56 | 104 39 10 | 90 | 276 | 1013 |
| Hong Kong | La Pantera III | C Ostenfeld /E de Losala | 05 04 17 | 55 | 05 24 33 | 48 | 33 38 19 | 60 | 04 47 14 | 51 | 99 43 36 | 147 | 361 | |
| | Vanguard | D T V Lieu | 05 05 31 | 53 | 05 27 48 | 39 | 33 30 57 | 64 | 04 56 04 | 23 | 102 47 27 | 120 | 299 | |
| | Uin-na-Mara IV | H Ross | 05 05 29 | 54 | 05 21 29 | 53 | 37 08 15 | 26 | 04 48 02 | 49 | 103 34 55 | 102 | 284 | 944 |
| Italy | Vanina | V Mandelli | 05 09 52 | 42 | 05 34 35 | 29 | 33 27 01 | 72 | 04 47 46 | 50 | 100 12 52 | 144 | 337 | |
| | Yena | S Doni | 05 07 27 | 47 | 05 30 07 | 35 | 33 43 18 | 56 | 04 48 46 | 47 | 100 15 38 | 138 | 323 | |
| | Rrose Selavy | R Bonadeo | 05 09 55 | 41 | 05 29 25 | 36 | 33 47 44 | 50 | 04 52 34 | 34 | 102 21 28 | 123 | 284 | 944 |
| Argentina | Red Rock IV | E Mandelbaum | 05 16 09 | 27 | 05 30 41 | 33 | 33 51 44 | 40 | 04 50 57 | 41 | 98 35 05 | 156 | 297 | |
| | Acadia | B Beenan | 05 12 48 | 35 | 05 27 27 | 42 | 34 43 25 | 12 | 04 44 07 | 54 | 98 42 30 | 153 | 293 | |
| | Sur II | D P Ramos | 05 16 33 | 26 | 05 31 59 | 31 | 33 14 49 | 94 | 04 59 29 | 15 | 103 28 47 | 105 | 271 | 861 |
| Britain | **Eclipse** | **J C Rogers** | **05 06 07** | **50** | **05 21 45** | **51** | **32 44 05** | **110** | **04 49 49** | **44** | **97 05 27** | **171** | **426** | |
| | Blizzard | E G Juer | 04 58 56 | 57 | 05 43 07 | 16 | 34 52 57 | 10 | 04 46 50 | 53 | 105 25 49 | 81 | 217 | |
| | Morning Cloud V | Rt Hon Edward heath | 05 07 46 | 44 | 05 28 40 | 37 | RTD | 4 | 04 51 15 | 39 | 104 39 56 | 87 | 211 | 854 |
| France | Revolution | J L Fabry | 05 19 30 | 22 | 05 40 09 | 23 | 32 42 41 | 112 | 04 52 37 | 32 | 98 42 30 | 153 | 342 | |
| | Jubilé VI | H Hamon | 05 22 21 | (P) 3 | 05 38 00 | 25 | 33 16 48 | 90 | 04 59 56 | 13 | 97 40 15 | 168 | 299 | |
| | Accanito | S Poli | 05 13 57 | 32 | 05 41 04 | 19 | 33 01 24 | 102 | 04 50 12 | 43 | RTD | 3 | 199 | 840 |
| Ireland | Regardless | K Rohan | 05 09 22 | 43 | 05 18 21 | 57 | 32 36 29 | 114 | 04 49 41 | 45 | RTD | 3 | 262 | |
| | Golden Apple | H Coveney | 05 05 35 | 52 | 05 18 54 | 56 | 33 21 33 | 82 | 04 49 16 | 46 | RTD | 3 | | |
| | Inishanier | B Bramwell/B Buchanan | 05 17 30 | 24 | 05 56 58 | 4 | 33 05 45 | 98 | 04 53 28 | 28 | 106 32 49 | 72 | 226 | 727 |
| Switzerland | Assiduous | N Berger | 05 13 40 | 33 | 05 27 03 | 45 | 32 59 22 | 104 | 04 52 47 | 31 | 101 22 08 | 132 | 345 | |
| | Silver Apple | B Guttinger & G Nolan | 05 11 12 | 37 | 05 23 33 | (P) 22 | 33 20 16 | 88 | 04 50 41 | 42 | RTD | 3 | 192 | |
| | Milene IV | A Mirlesse | 05 31 10 | 4 | 05 56 02 | 5 | 34 17 49 | 22 | 05 09 13 | 4 | 117 50 29 | 57 | 92 | 629 |
| Spain | Campsa | J Cusi | 05 14 22 | 31 | 05 27 04 | 44 | 33 21 07 | 84 | 04 55 25 | 26 | 102 08 04 | 126 | 311 | |
| | Tornado | W Singleton | 05 22 44 | 13 | 05 42 38 | 17 | 33 06 03 | 96 | 04 51 32 | 21 | 123 38 41 | 51 | 198 | |
| | Yachtman II | R Montagut | 05 24 12 | 9 | 05 46 18 | 10 | 33 25 36 | 74 | 04 54 23 | (P) 1 | RTD | 3 | 97 | 606 |
| Germany | Rubin | H O Schumann | 05 13 16 | 34 | 05 31 39 | 32 | 33 15 20 | 92 | 04 53 16 | 29 | 103 49 07 | 93 | 280 | |
| | Tina | T Friese | 05 06 36 | 49 | 05 25 43 | 47 | 33 54 58 | 38 | 04 42 43 | 55 | RTD | 3 | 192 | |
| | Jan Pott | N Lorck-Schierning | 05 14 39 | 30 | 05 28 07 | 38 | 34 03 39 | 28 | 04 59 16 | 16 | RTD | 3 | 115 | 587 |
| Japan | Ko Teru Teru II | T Yamaguchi | 05 17 32 | 23 | 05 37 38 | 26 | 33 41 01 | 58 | 04 56 11 | 22 | 103 19 31 | 108 | 237 | |
| | Togo VI | Dr T Yamada | 05 22 47 | 12 | 05 42 33 | 3 | 33 46 15 | 52 | 05 56 00 | 24 | 102 53 07 | 117 | 208 | |
| | Gekko VI | S Namiki | 05 20 14 | 18 | 05 43 33 | 15 | 33 20 25 | 86 | 04 54 26 | (P) 16 | RTD | 3 | 138 | 583 |

KEY:   DNS  –  Did Not Start      DNF  –  Did Not Finish      DSQ  –  Disqualified      RTD  –  Retired      (P)  –  Includes Penalty      DNC – Did Not Compete

| 1979 RACE RESULTS | Boat Name | Owner | RACE 1 RORC TROPHY (FIRST INSHORE) | | RACE 2 RYS TROPHY (SECOND INSHORE) | | RACE 3 CHANNEL RACE | | RACE 4 CHAMPAGNE MUMM TROPHY (THIRD INSHORE) | | RACE 5 FASTNET RACE | | TOTAL (OVERALL POINTS) | OVERALL TOTAL (BY COUNTRY) |
|---|---|---|---|---|---|---|---|---|---|---|---|---|---|---|
| Country | | | Corrected time | Points | Corrected time | Points | Corrected time | Points | Corrected time | Points | Corrected time | Points | | |
| Netherlands | Formidable | P W Vroon | 05 10 24 | 40 | 05 27 44 | 40 | 33 51 20 | 42 | 04 53 11 | 30 | 100 13 07 | 141 | 293 | |
| | Dagger | J L Dolk/Th E W Vinke | 05 39 45 | 3 | 05 49 53 | 7 | 33 29 42 | 66 | 05 05 47 | 6 | 106 36 05 | 69 | 151 | |
| | Schuttevaer | Dr J C W Van Dam | 05 14 46 | 29 | 05 46 30 | 9 | 33 37 32 | 62 | 04 55 34 | 25 | RTD | 3 | 124 | 568 |
| Belgium | Darling Dee | A Nelis | 05 12 20 | 36 | RTD | 0 | 33 22 52 | 76 | 04 52 34 | 34 | 103 42 37 | 99 | 246 | |
| | Pinta | P C d'Andrimont | RTD | 0 | 05 40 25 | 22 | 33 21 33 | 80 | 04 59 39 | (P) 1 | 118 26 59 | 54 | 158 | |
| | Incisif | A Loisse | 05 28 29 | (P) 1 | 05 40 31 | (P) 20 | 34 18 26 | 20 | 04 57 42 | 2 | 106 29 04 | 75 | 136 | 540 |
| Sweden | Midnight Sun | J Pehrsson | 05 20 11 | 19 | 05 32 44 | 30 | 35 01 10 | 8 | 04 51 30 | 37 | 109 23 12 | 66 | 160 | |
| | Carat | V Forss | 05 21 50 | 17 | 05 36 59 | 28 | 34 03 27 | 32 | 05 02 11 | 11 | 112 03 31 | 63 | 150 | |
| | Big Shadow | S Bjerser | 05 16 36 | 25 | 05 37 03 | 27 | 33 27 28 | 70 | 04 58 26 | 17 | RTD | 3 | 142 | 452 |
| Singapore | Apollo IV | J Barry/A Bond | 05 10 46 | 38 | 05 27 42 | (P) 13 | 34 25 16 | 18 | 04 48 24 | 48 | 103 49 05 | 96 | 213 | |
| | Wild Goose | j e g ayres | 05 19 49 | 20 | 05 38 28 | 24 | 32 55 10 | 106 | 04 51 18 | 38 | RTD | 3 | 191 | |
| | Bugis | D Riley | 05 26 45 | (P) 1 | 05 47 01 | 8 | 34 26 53 | 16 | 05 05 28 | 7 | DNS | | 335 | 439 |
| Poland | Hadar | Yacht Club Stal | 05 25 05 | 8 | 05 42 21 | 18 | 34 03 38 | 30 | 04 58 19q | 18 | 105 24 44 | 84 | 158 | |
| | Cetus | Yacht Club Stal-Stocznia | 05 23 32 | 11 | 05 40 27 | 21 | 34 52 53 | 14 | 05 02 55 | 9 | 106 20 00 | 78 | 133 | |
| | Nauticus | Yacht Club Kotwica | 05 29 09 | 5 | 05 44 38 | 13 | 34 13 15 | 24 | 05 04 08 | 8 | 112 31 07 | 60 | 110 | 401 |
| Canada | Magistri | C Bentley | 05 20 38 | 17 | 05 50 01 | 6 | 33 47 51 | 48 | 04 58 08 | 19 | 102 59 50 | 114 | 204 | |
| | Pachena | J Newton | 05 24 06 | 10 | 05 45 55 | 11 | 33 29 23 | 68 | 05 02 20 | 10 | RTD | 3 | 102 | |
| | Evergreen | D Green | 05 19 35 | 21 | 05 45 39 | 12 | 33 48 52 | 44 | 05 08 54 | 5 | RTD | 3 | 85 | 391 |
| Brazil | Indigo | S Eotelho | 05 10 32 | 39 | 05 30 15 | 34 | 34 01 18 | 34 | RTD | 3 | 103 15 46 | 111 | 221 | |
| | Noryema | S Haymes | 05 22 01 | 15 | 05 44 31 | 14 | 35 12 50 | 6 | dns | 1 | DNS | 3 | 39 | |
| | Winsome Gold/ | | RTD | 0 | DNS | 2 | DNS | 1 | DNS | 3 | | | 7 | |
| | Madrugada | P Paolo | DNS | 0 | | | | | | | | | 1 | 268 |

KEY:  DNS – Did Not Start    DNF – Did Not Finish    DSQ – Disqualified    RTD – Retired    (P) – Includes Penalty    DNC – Did Not Compete

| 1981 RACE RESULTS | | | RACE 1 RORC TROPHY (FIRST INSHORE) | | RACE 2 RYS TROPHY (SECOND INSHORE) | | RACE 3 CHANNEL RACE | | RACE 4 CHAMPAGNE MUMM TROPHY (THIRD INSHORE) | | RACE 5 FASTNET RACE | | TOTAL (OVERALL POINTS) (BY COUNTRY) | OVERALL TOTAL |
|---|---|---|---|---|---|---|---|---|---|---|---|---|---|---|
| Country | Boat Name | Owner | Corrected time | Points | Corrected time | Points | Corrected time | Points | Corrected time | Points | Corrected time | Points | | |
| Britain | Victory of Burnham | P de Savary | 05 24 26 | 33 | 04 06 55 | 48 | 05 24 26 | 84 | 04 11 41 | 47 | 110 29 25 | 102 | 314 | |
| | Dragon | Mr & Mrs B S Cooper | 05 34 06 | 19 | 04 40 23 | 7 | 05 34 06 | 70 | 04 41 16 | 15 | 110 01 51 | 114 | 225 | |
| | Yeoman XXIII | R A Aisher | 05 32 24 | 23 | 04 09 34 | 47 | 05 32 24 | 90 | 04 19 16 | 43 | 112 06 12 | 72 | 275 | 814 |
| USA | Stars & Stripes | W Martin | 05 19 42 | 40 | 04 29 07 | 22 | 05 19 42 | 74 | 04 43 51 | 13 | 108 55 54 | 129 | 278 | |
| | Intuition | P E Malloy | 05 30 49 | 25 | 04 16 44 | 42 | 05 30 49 | 34 | 04 48 45 | 9 | 109 57 52 | 120 | 230 | |
| | Scaramouche | C Kirsch | 05 22 32 | 36 | 04 15 17 | 44 | 05 22 32 | 14 | 04 28 55 | 39 | 112 02 11 | 75 | 208 | 716 |
| Germany | Dusselboot | M Schmidt/H Hensel | 05 21 03 | 38 | 04 30 22 | 21 | 05 21 03 | 2 | 04 31 57 | 32 | 108 48 38 | 132 | 225 | |
| | Pinta | W Illbruck | 05 12 56 | 46 | 04 23 30 | 32 | 05 12 56 | 22 | 04 39 58 | 17 | 110 17 15 | 108 | 225 | |
| | Container | U Schutz | 05 30 24 | 26 | 04 18 44 | 41 | 05 30 24 | 66 | 04 34 09 | 27 | 110 34 29 | 96 | 256 | 706 |
| Ireland | Moonduster | D N Doyle | 06 02 42 | 6 | 04 22 00 | 37 | 06 02 42 | 94 | 04 36 08 | 25 | 120 51 30 | 15 | 177 | |
| | Regardless | K Rohan | 05 25 17 | 32 | 04 22 42 | 34 | 05 25 17 | 40 | 04 14 16 | 46 | 107 25 23 | 144 | 296 | |
| | Woolly Jumper | Walsh/O'Donovan/Ryan | 05 17 00 | 43 | 04 27 09 | 2 | 05 17 00 | 72 | 04 48 44 | 10 | 111 19 01 | 81 | 208 | 681 |
| New Zealand | **Swuzzlebubble** | **I Gibbs** | **05 22 38** | **35** | **04 27 40** | **25** | **05 22 38** | **92** | **04 34 00** | **28** | **108 38 41** | **135** | **315** | |
| | Inca | E Julian/D Winstone | 05 44 37 | 14 | 04 26 31 | 27 | 05 44 37 | 18 | 04 41 09 | 16 | 115 38 20 | 39 | 114 | |
| | Wee Willie Winkie | S Brentnall | 05 25 19 | 31 | 04 31 24 | 12 | 05 25 19 | 36 | 04 36 53 | 23 | 110 23 25 | 105 | 207 | 636 |
| Canada | Runaway | B Kirby/J Spain | 05 20 30 | 39 | 04 31 13 | 16 | 05 20 30 | 78 | 04 48 53 | 8 | 110 49 37 | 93 | 243 | |
| | Amazing Grace | J R Plaxton | 05 26 41 | 30 | 04 28 12 | 24 | 05 26 41 | 68 | 04 31 59 | 31 | 116 16 38 | 27 | 180 | |
| | Pachena | J Newton | 05 19 03 | 42 | 04 32 31 | 14 | 05 19 03 | 16 | 04 34 50 | 26 | 109 59 43 | 117 | 215 | 629 |
| Italy | Almagores | G Borremeo | 05 11 10 | 47 | 04 24 57 | 30 | 05 11 10 | 26 | 04 10 01 | 48 | 111 05 59 | (P) 54 | 205 | |
| | Brava | P Landolfi | RTD | 1 | 04 23 05 | 33 | RTD | 60 | 04 22 15 | 17 | 121 00 24 | 12 | 123 | |
| | Mandrake | G Carriero | 05 19 29 | 41 | 04 22 11 | 36 | 05 19 29 | 64 | 04 17 21 | 45 | 110 50 42 | 90 | 276 | 604 |
| Australia | Hitchhiker | P Briggs | DSQ | 0 | 04 30 42 | 6 | 05 34 03 | 56 | 04 29 30 | 37 | 112 40 52 | 63 | 162 | |
| | Apollo V | A Bond | 05 21 20 | 37 | 04 20 17 | 39 | 05 21 20 | 50 | 04 19 12 | 44 | 116 00 51 | 33 | 203 | |
| | Ragamuffin | S Fischer | 05 27 16 | 28 | 04 22 28 | 35 | 05 27 16 | 86 | 04 32 18 | 30 | 112 43 23 | 60 | 239 | 604 |
| Sweden | Ra Carat | W Forss | 05 33 04 | 21 | 04 11 47 | 46 | 05 33 04 | 88 | 04 29 28 | 38 | 115 51 07 | 36 | 229 | |
| | Attaque | K A Rydqvist | 05 13 39 | 44 | 04 31 00 | 17 | 05 16 39 | 26 | 04 37 30 | 0 | 109 40 04 | 126 | 213 | |
| | Hurrycane | K Bruneflod | 05 50 38 | 9 | 04 35 30 | 10 | 05 50 38 | 20 | 04 47 57 | 11 | 110 14 48 | 111 | 161 | 603 |
| Netherlands | Formidable | P W Vroon | 05 32 31 | 22 | 04 25 01 | 29 | 05 32 31 | 32 | 04 27 39 | 40 | 114 28 27 | 54 | 177 | |
| | Pro-motion | J L Dolk | 05 38 03 | 18 | 04 16 26 | 43 | 05 38 03 | 82 | 04 30 55 | 36 | 110 14 48 | 57 | 236 | |
| | Schuttevaer | Dr J C W van Dam | 00 00 00 | 1 | 04 32 10 | 15 | RTD | 30 | 04 36 13 | 24 | 112 36 26 | 66 | 136 | 549 |
| France | Tahiti | M Blanck | 05 47 13 | 11 | 04 24 38 | 31 | 05 47 13 | 24 | 04 51 59 | 6 | 115 25 54 | 45 | 117 | |
| | Lady Be Good | B Moureau/P Faure | 05 38 24 | 16 | 04 37 06 | 9 | 05 38 24 | 58 | 04 32 21 | 29 | 110 29 31 | 99 | 211 | |
| | Midnight Sun | J Pehrson/J L Fabry | 00 00 00 | 1 | 04 12 56 | 45 | RTD | 96 | 04 20 21 | 42 | 117 41 23 | 21 | 205 | 533 |
| Spain | Bribon | J Cusi | 05 36 26 | 18 | 04 30 32 | 19 | 05 36 26 | 2 | 00 00 00 | 1 | 109 45 52 | 123 | 163 | |
| | Potitos | J Vich | 05 53 54 | 7 | 04 42 44 | 4 | 05 53 54 | 44 | 04 56 47 | 4 | 119 02 07 | 18 | 77 | |
| | L'Emporda | J Pla/V Sagi | 05 45 10 | 13 | 04 35 17 | 11 | 05 45 10 | 76 | 04 31 13 | 35 | 107 52 24 | 141 | 276 | 516 |

KEY:  DNS – Did Not Start    DNF – Did Not Finish    DSQ – Disqualified    RTD – Retired    (P) – Includes Penalty    DNC – Did Not Compete

| 1981 RACE RESULTS | Boat Name | Owner | RACE 1 RORC TROPHY (FIRST INSHORE) | | RACE 2 RYS TROPHY (SECOND INSHORE) | | RACE 3 CHANNEL RACE | | RACE 4 CHAMPAGNE MUMM TROPHY (THIRD INSHORE) | | RACE 5 FASTNET RACE POINTS) | | TOTAL (OVERALL (BY COUNTRY) | OVERALL TOTAL |
|---|---|---|---|---|---|---|---|---|---|---|---|---|---|---|
| Country | | | Corrected time | Points | Corrected time | Points | Corrected time | Points | Corrected time | Points | Corrected time | Points | | |
| Switzerland | Nadia | J Christen | 05 23 49 | 34 | 04 33 11 | 13 | 05 23 49 | 62 | 04 38 31 | 19 | 116 15 13 | 30 | 158 | |
| | Chouette | N W Berger | 05 39 05 | 15 | 04 41 48 | 5 | 05 39 05 | 54 | 04 43 22 | 14 | 111 04 43 | 87 | 175 | |
| | Accanito | S Poli | 05 27 06 | 29 | 04 45 06 | 1 | 05 27 06 | 52 | 04 37 35 | 21 | 111 26 31 | 78 | 181 | 514 |
| Hong Kong | La Pantera | C Ostenfeld/P Laidlaw | 00 00 00 | 1 | 04 18 51 | 40 | RTD | 48 | 04 38 56 | 18 | 114 58 54 | 51 | 158 | |
| | Vanguard | D T V Lieu | 05 13 18 | 45 | 04 28 21 | 23 | 05 13 18 | 80 | 04 31 44 | 33 | 115 33 43 | 42 | 223 | |
| | Uin-na-Mara | H H Ross | 00 00 00 | 1 | 04 30 25 | 20 | RTD | 12 | 04 37 45 | 20 | 123 15 00 | 9 | 62 | 443 |
| Belgium | Incisif | A Lousse | 05 27 23 | 27 | 04 39 18 | 8 | 05 27 23 | 42 | 04 46 59 | 12 | 108 08 34 | 138 | 227 | |
| | Red Rock III | P Bruninx | 05 45 28 | 12 | 04 25 12 | 28 | 05 45 28 | 8 | 05 03 29 | 2 | 114 37 10 | 48 | 98 | |
| | Tyfoon | G Versluys | 05 50 01 | 10 | 04 54 15 | 1 | 05 50 01 | 10 | 04 59 65 | 3 | 116 31 15 | 24 | 48 | 373 |
| Bermuda | Flirt of Paget | B de F Trimingham | 05 31 03 | 24 | 04 47 48 | 2 | 05 31 03 | 2 | 04 50 39 | 7 | 112 21 01 | 69 | 104 | |
| | Caiman II | J C Hooper | 05 07 26 | 48 | 04 21 35 | 38 | 05 07 26 | 28 | 04 31 20 | 34 | 120 30 23 | 0 | 148 | |
| | Panda | D W McCowan | 05 51 22 | 8 | 04 40 39 | 0 | 05 51 22 | 38 | 04 53 53 | 5 | 111 45 38 | 0 | 51 | 303 |

KEY: DNS – Did Not Start    DNF – Did Not Finish    DSQ – Disqualified    RTD – Retired    (P) – Includes Penalty    DNC – Did Not Compete

| 1983 RACE RESULTS | | | RACE 1 RORC TROPHY (FIRST INSHORE) | | RACE 2 RYS TROPHY (SECOND INSHORE) | | RACE 3 CHANNEL RACE | | RACE 4 CHAMPAGNE MUMM TROPHY (THIRD INSHORE) | | RACE 5 FASTNET RACE | | TOTAL (OVERALL POINTS) | OVERALL TOTAL (BY COUNTRY) |
|---|---|---|---|---|---|---|---|---|---|---|---|---|---|---|
| Country | Boat Name | Owner | Corrected time | Points | Corrected time | Points | Corrected time | Points | Corrected time | Points | Corrected time | Points | | |
| Germany | Pinta | W Illbruck | 05 51 00 | 35 | 04 22 37 | 38 | 49 52 48 | 52 | 05 30 20 | 38 | 100 21 11 | 120 | 283 | |
| | **Sabina** | **H Noack** | **06 10 15** | **21** | **04 28 15** | **24** | **48 50 07** | **88** | **05 45 38** | **27** | **99 40 24** | **126** | **286** | |
| | Outsider | T Hansen | 06 10 21 | 20 | 04 23 22 | 36 | 48 55 09 | 84 | 05 40 38 | 33 | 101 31 52 | 105 | 278 | 847 |
| Italy | Almagores | G Borremeo/Boniello | 05 46 20 | 43 | 04 23 58 | 33 | 49 59 14 | 50 | 05 31 58 | 37 | 100 12 42 | 123 | 286 | |
| | **Brava** | **P Landolfi** | **05 47 20** | **42** | **04 22 26** | **39** | **50 32 21** | **28** | **05 25 18** | **42** | **99 33 19** | **132** | **283** | |
| | Primadonna | G Bassi | 06 16 26 | 14 | 04 32 30 | (P) 0 | 49 38 36 | 64 | 05 52 40 | (P) 0 | 105 24 07 | 33 | 111 | 680 |
| USA | Scarlett O'Hara | M Wingate | 05 49 13 | 40 | 04 18 42 | 45 | 50 02 29 | 46 | 05 30 02 | 39 | 103 01 03 | 60 | 230 | |
| | Locura | G de Guardiola | 05 51 14 | 33 | 04 19 26 | 44 | 50 47 03 | 20 | 05 47 57 | 26 | 102 23 51 | 72 | 195 | |
| | Shenandoah | W L Palmer Jr | 06 10 43 | 18 | 04 24 34 | (P) 16 | 49 04 23 | 80 | 05 42 50 | 32 | 102 04 06 | 84 | 230 | 655 |
| Australia | Hitchhiker | P Briggs | 05 43 04 | 45 | 04 29 17 | 23 | 49 46 07 | 62 | 05 45 24 | 28 | 103 40 11 | 51 | 209 | |
| | Bondi Tram | D O'Neil | 05 50 03 | 38 | 04 31 14 | 14 | 49 48 06 | 58 | 05 50 09 | 14 | 101 37 00 | 102 | 226 | |
| | Once More Dear Friends | P Kurts | 06 42 11 | 5 | 04 25 24 | 28 | 49 10 59 | 70 | 05 46 13 | 23 | 102 31 15 | 69 | 195 | 630 |
| Canada | Amazing Grace | R A Herron | 05 51 13 | 34 | 04 24 05 | 32 | 50 42 29 | 22 | 05 34 02 | 36 | 102 49 20 | 63 | 187 | |
| | Magistri | P Farlinger | 06 10 11 | 22 | RTD | 1 | 48 45 18 | 90 | 05 49 14 | 17 | 100 51 32 | 114 | 244 | |
| | Charisma V | R Kennedy | 05 55 34 | (P) 5 | 04 27 25 | (P) 3 | 49 49 38 | 54 | 05 36 30 | 35 | 101 47 02 | 96 | 193 | 624 |
| New Zealand | Lady B | P Blake | 05 54 56 | 29 | 04 20 45 | 42 | 51 13 11 | 8 | 05 44 36 | 29 | 101 49 31 | 90 | 198 | |
| | Swuzzlebubble IV | I O Gibbs | 06 13 14 | 16 | 04 29 55 | 17 | 49 10 27 | 72 | 05 49 10 | 18 | 101 09 01 | 111 | 234 | |
| | Shockwave | N A Crichton | 06 00 14 | (P) 2 | 04 19 44 | 43 | 50 33 15 | 26 | 05 22 26 | 44 | 103 09 47 | 57 | 172 | 604 |
| Netherlands | Bierkaai | H Klunder | 05 50 50 | 36 | 04 23 56 | (P) 25 | 50 23 13 | 32 | 05 47 46 | 22 | 102 32 00 | 66 | 181 | |
| | Pro-motion | J L Dolk | 05 52 56 | 32 | 04 22 40 | (P) 14 | 50 09 05 | 42 | 05 43 01 | 31 | 100 39 21 | 117 | 236 | |
| | Caiman | G Jellof | 05 53 32 | 30 | 04 31 01 | 15 | 50 38 32 | (P) 6 | 05 37 08 | 34 | 102 05 27 | 78 | 163 | 580 |
| Britain | Indulgence | G Walker/J Wooderson | 05 58 48 | 26 | 04 23 33 | 35 | 49 46 48 | 60 | 05 46 11 | 24 | 108 06 39 | 15 | 160 | |
| | Dragon | Mr & Mrs B S Cooper | 06 11 58 | 17 | 04 24 37 | 29 | 49 11 15 | 68 | 05 48 44 | (P) 11 | 102 19 08 | 75 | 200 | |
| | Black Topic | D Atkinson | 06 16 26 | 14 | 04 33 59 | 7 | 49 09 52 | 74 | 05 49 43 | 15 | 101 13 12 | 108 | 219 | 579 |
| Austria | Container | U Schutz | 05 50 25 | 37 | 04 21 49 | 40 | 50 24 26 | 30 | 05 24 46 | 43 | 105 25 34 | 30 | 180 | |
| | Container 79 | E Moritz | 06 19 09 | 13 | 04 26 03 | 27 | 50 02 43 | 44 | 05 51 01 | 13 | 104 34 14 | 42 | 139 | |
| | Espada | W Passegger | 06 28 29 | 11 | 04 30 59 | 16 | 49 00 24 | 82 | 05 51 40 | 12 | 101 58 28 | 87 | 208 | 527 |
| Papua New Guinea | Di Hard | B Tardrew | 05 49 29 | 39 | 04 29 20 | (P) 0 | 49 49 31 | 56 | 05 51 51 | 20 | 101 45 34 | 99 | 214 | |
| | Sure Foot | PNGYA | 06 38 33 | 9 | 04 32 18 | 11 | 50 54 37 | 14 | 05 49 36 | 16 | 102 05 01 | 81 | 131 | |
| | Too Impetuous | G Lambert | 05 52 56 | (P) 9 | 04 29 28 | 21 | 50 01 20 | 48 | 06 00 43 | 3 | 101 48 26 | 93 | 174 | 519 |
| Ireland | Moonduster | D N Doyle | 05 48 42 | 41 | 04 31 51 | 12 | 53 19 36 | 4 | 05 26 28 | 41 | RTD | 6 | 104 | |
| | Justine IV | F X Woods | 06 10 38 | 19 | 04 29 28 | 21 | 48 53 45 | 86 | 05 44 07 | 30 | 99 33 51 | 129 | 285 | |
| | Stormbird | C P Foley | 06 43 42 | 4 | 04 31 46 | 13 | 51 10 25 | 10 | 05 48 15 | 21 | 103 45 28 | 48 | 96 | 485 |
| France | Diva | B Moureau/P Faure | 05 46 09 | 44 | 04 21 08 | 41 | 49 06 55 | 76 | 05 46 00 | (P) 16 | 99 16 08 | (P) 129 | 306 | |
| | Ossian | P Ratzel | 06 20 44 | 12 | 04 29 48 | 18 | 50 10 50 | 40 | 05 52 09 | 10 | 107 50 15 | 21 | 101 | |
| | Passion | J L Fobry | 06 29 49 | 10 | 04 32 19 | 10 | 50 15 08 | 36 | 05 52 54 | 7 | DNS | 3 | 66 | 473 |

KEY:   DNS – Did Not Start   DNF – Did Not Finish   DSQ – Disqualified   RTD – Retired   (P) – Includes Penalty   DNC – Did Not Compete

| 1983 RACE RESULTS | | | RACE 1 RORC TROPHY (FIRST INSHORE) | | RACE 2 RYS TROPHY (SECOND INSHORE) | | RACE 3 CHANNEL RACE | | RACE 4 CHAMPAGNE MUMM TROPHY (THIRD INSHORE) | | RACE 5 FASTNET RACE | | TOTAL (OVERALL POINTS) | OVERALL TOTAL (BY COUNTRY) |
|---|---|---|---|---|---|---|---|---|---|---|---|---|---|---|
| Country | Boat Name | Owner | Corrected time | Points | Corrected time | Points | Corrected time | Points | Corrected time | Points | Corrected time | Points | | |
| Belgium | Mariner | F Van Nufel | 05 56 44 | 27 | 04 36 14 | 4 | 50 22 07 | 34 | 05 52 16 | 9 | 103 35 03 | 54 | 128 | |
| | Incisif III | A Lousse | 06 39 27 | 8 | 04 35 34 | 5 | 50 51 22 | 16 | RTD | 1 | 105 38 10 | 27 | 57 | |
| | Black Lion | F C M v Leeuwen | 06 45 09 | 3 | 04 39 33 | 3 | 49 06 27 | 78 | 05 54 06 | 5 | 104 18 27 | 45 | 134 | 319 |
| Sweden | Carat | W Forss | 06 04 56 | 23 | 04 27 40 | 25 | 53 31 39 | 2 | 05 21 19 | 45 | 105 19 18 | 36 | 131 | |
| | Bla Carat | R Gustafsson | 06 48 38 | 2 | 04 29 35 | 19 | 52 56 32 | 6 | 05 26 40 | 40 | 105 09 49 | 39 | 106 | |
| | Paper Tiger | S E Sahlin | 07 12 50 | 1 | 04 46 48 | (P) 0 | 50 13 25 | (P) 20 | 06 04 18 | 2 | RTD | 6 | 29 | 266 |
| Japan | Formidable | P Vroon | 06 00 32 | 24 | 04 24 28 | 31 | 50 49 30 | 18 | 05 53 58 | 6 | 108 00 48 | 18 | 97 | |
| | Togo VII | T Yamada | 06 40 46 | 7 | 04 34 22 | 6 | 49 14 07 | 66 | 05 54 11 | 4 | 107 46 45 | 24 | 107 | |
| | Flirt of Paget | NORC | 06 40 48 | 6 | 04 33 57 | (P) 0 | 51 00 58 | 12 | 05 48 52 | 19 | 111 42 23 | 12 | 49 | 253 |

KEY:  DNS – Did Not Start  DNF – Did Not Finish  DSQ – Disqualified  RTD – Retired  (P) – Includes Penalty  DNC – Did Not Compete

| 1985 RACE RESULTS Country | Boat Name | Owner | RACE 1 RYS TROPHY (FIRST INSHORE) Corrected time | Points | RACE 2 CORUM TROPHY (SECOND INSHORE) Corrected time | Points | RACE 3 CHANNEL RACE Corrected time | Points | RACE 4 CHAMPAGNE MUMM TROPHY (THIRD INSHORE) Corrected time | Points | RACE 5 FASTNET RACE Corrected time | Points | TOTAL (OVERALL POINTS) | OVERALL TOTAL (BY COUNTRY) |
|---|---|---|---|---|---|---|---|---|---|---|---|---|---|---|
| Germany | Outsider | T Hansen | 03 58 50 | 104 | 05 01 37 | 98 | 28 08 32 | 156 | 04 58 07 | 80 | 82 59 45 | 265 | 703 | |
| | Rubin G VIII | H O Schumann | 04 02 37 | 78 | 05 04 17 | 88 | 28 19 08 | 147 | 04 54 00 | 96 | 83 27 59 | 250 | 659 | |
| | Diva | F Diekell/P Westphal-Langloh | 04 03 03 | 72 | 05 05 54 | 80 | 29 08 49 | 84 | 05 06 32 | 78 | 84 27 18 | 230 | 544 | 1,906 |
| Britain | **Phoenix** | **L Bankson/G Walker** | **03 58 57** | **102** | **05 00 44** | **100** | **28 23 45** | **141** | **04 51 07** | **108** | **83 22 21** | **255** | **706** | |
| | Jade | L Wooddell | 03 58 59 | 100 | 05 08 33 | 40 | 28 05 28 | 162 | 05 03 52 | (P) 22 | RTD | 15 | 339 | |
| | Panda | P T Whipp | 04 02 05 | 87 | 05 07 57 | (P) 0 | 28 07 54 | 159 | 04 58 22 | 64 | 82 45 18 | 270 | 581 | 1,626 |
| New Zealand | Exador | M Clark | 03 57 06 | 108 | 05 05 16 | 84 | 28 25 40 | 135 | 05 01 15 | 60 | 83 07 24 | 260 | 647 | |
| | Epic | T Geldard | 04 02 47 | 76 | 05 06 13 | 76 | 28 27 54 | 129 | 04 56 23 | 88 | RTD | 15 | 384 | |
| | Canterbury | C Collins | 04 03 01 | 74 | 05 03 27 | (P) 62 | 28 42 17 | 111 | 05 07 13 | 24 | 85 56 25 | 185 | 456 | 1,487 |
| Australia | Challenge III | L J Abrams | 04 03 13 | 66 | 05 16 04 | 14 | RTD | 3 | 04 59 45 | 72 | 85 11 01 | 205 | 360 | |
| | Drake's Prayer | P Kurts | 04 00 20 | 96 | 05 06 43 | 72 | 29 13 34 | 75 | 04 59 01 | 76 | 85 52 18 | 190 | 509 | |
| | Intrigue | D C Calvert | 04 02 05 | 88 | 05 07 56 | 54 | 28 24 35 | 138 | 04 59 54 | 70 | 85 03 04 | 210 | 560 | 1,429 |
| Denmark | Maitresse | P Kruuse | 04 01 57 | 90 | 05 01 54 | 96 | RTD | 3 | 05 05 19 | 42 | 96 36 23 | 135 | 366 | |
| | Euro | I B Andersen | 03 57 07 | 106 | 04 59 29 | 106 | 28 15 17 | 153 | 04 53 43 | 100 | 84 31 52 | 225 | 692 | |
| | Krone | P Jespersen | 04 05 24 | (P) 0 | 05 06 25 | 74 | 28 40 37 | 114 | 05 05 25 | (P) 34 | RTD | 15 | 237 | 1,295 |
| Singapore | Highland Fling | I A S Laidlaw | 04 01 02 | 94 | 05 00 29 | 102 | 28 26 16 | 132 | 04 56 29 | 86 | 84 34 47 | 220 | 634 | |
| | Pocket Battleship | C Griffiths | 04 04 00 | 62 | 05 10 07 | 30 | 29 21 19 | 57 | 04 55 36 | 92 | 86 38 38 | 170 | 411 | |
| | Marionette | S Loh | 04 04 58 | 54 | 05 18 37 | 4 | 28 57 02 | 90 | 05 03 57 | 52 | RTD | 15 | 215 | 1,265 |
| France | Espace du Desir | B Moureau | 04 02 17 | 84 | 05 07 04 | 66 | 29 32 27 | 45 | 05 06 00 | (P) 0 | DNS | 2 | 197 | |
| | Coyote | B Trouble | 04 02 34 | 80 | 05 08 22 | 46 | 28 17 01 | 150 | 04 57 29 | 82 | 84 55 59 | 215 | 573 | |
| | Fiére Lady | E Duchemin | 04 05 18 | (P) 0 | RTD | 2 | 28 34 47 | 126 | 05 05 38 | 38 | 84 15 35 | 240 | 406 | 1,176 |
| Austria | Container | U Schutz | 04 00 04 | 98 | 04 59 53 | 104 | 28 38 33 | 117 | 04 54 47 | 94 | RTD | 15 | 428 | |
| | I-Punkt | T Friese | 04 05 54 | 38 | 05 12 59 | 16 | 28 46 24 | 102 | 05 00 50 | (P) 8 | RTD | 15 | 179 | |
| | Pinta | W Illbruck | 04 03 04 | 70 | 05 11 50 | (P) 22 | 28 43 11 | 108 | 04 55 37 | 90 | 84 15 20 | 245 | 535 | 1,142 |
| USA | Sleeper | L North | 04 12 35 | (P) 0 | 05 08 59 | 38 | 28 58 48 | 87 | 04 53 43 | 102 | RTD | 15 | 242 | |
| | Sidewinder | C F Short | 04 02 23 | (P) 28 | 05 07 06 | 64 | 29 14 41 | 69 | 04 53 44 | 98 | RTD | 15 | 274 | |
| | High Roler | W F Power | 04 04 54 | 58 | 04 57 46 | 108 | 28 50 02 | 99 | 04 52 52 | 104 | 84 25 17 | 235 | 604 | 1,120 |
| Ireland | Justine V | F X Woods | 04 05 14 | 52 | 05 08 16 | 48 | 29 11 36 | 81 | 05 07 57 | 16 | 87 17 24 | 160 | 357 | |
| | Hero | D Andrew | 04 05 18 | 50 | 05 12 48 | 18 | RTD | 3 | 05 09 14 | 14 | 95 11 15 | 140 | 225 | |
| | Yeoman of St Helier | S Mansfield | 04 05 23 | 44 | 05 08 32 | 42 | 28 19 16 | 144 | 05 01 44 | 58 | 86 12 27 | 180 | 468 | 1,048 |
| Netherlands | Caiman II | G Jeelof | 04 03 08 | 68 | 05 03 52 | 92 | 28 53 29 | 93 | 04 52 40 | 106 | 86 37 54 | 175 | 534 | |
| | The Way of Living | P B de Ridder | 04 03 13 | 66 | 05 07 43 | 60 | RTD | 3 | 05 10 24 | 10 | RTD | 15 | 154 | |
| | Mustang | W Noordzij | 04 09 46 | (P) 0 | 05 08 22 | 46 | 28 36 45 | 120 | 05 00 01 | 68 | DNS | 2 | 265 | 924 |
| Italy | Brava | P Landolfi | 04 08 27 | (P) 0 | 05 08 01 | 50 | 28 35 34 | 123 | 05 06 22 | 30 | 85 44 27 | 195 | 398 | |
| | Templars' C | M del Lago | 04 13 35 | 2 | 05 04 49 | 86 | 29 28 53 | 51 | 05 10 24 | 10 | RTD | 15 | 164 | |
| | Almagores | C Nappi | 04 06 10 | 36 | 05 04 08 | 90 | 29 21 06 | 60 | 05 01 57 | 56 | RTD | 15 | 257 | 819 |

KEY:  DNS – Did Not Start    DNF – Did Not Finish    DSQ – Disqualified    RTD – Retired    (P) – Includes Penalty    DNC – Did Not Compete

| 1985 RACE RESULTS | | | RACE 1 RYS TROPHY (FIRST OFFSHORE) | | RACE 2 CORUM TROPHY (SECOND OFFSHORE) | | RACE 3 CHANNEL RACE | | RACE 4 CHAMPAGNE MUMM TROPHY (THIRD OFFSHORE) | | RACE 5 FASTNET RACE | | TOTAL (OVERALL POINTS) | OVERALL TOTAL (BY COUNTRY) |
|---|---|---|---|---|---|---|---|---|---|---|---|---|---|---|
| Country | Boat Name | Owner | Corrected time | Points | Corrected time | Points | Corrected time | Points | Corrected time | Points | Corrected time | Points | | |
| Sweden | Diva | P Elmer | 04 01 56 | 92 | 05 06 56 | 70 | 28 44 45 | 105 | 05 06 32 | 28 | RTD | 15 | 310 | |
| | Carat | W Forss | 04 06 39 | 30 | 05 10 29 | 28 | RTD | 3 | 05 04 02 | 50 | 85 35 38 | 200 | 311 | |
| | Indispensable Too | P Wallenberg | 04 07 15 (P) | 0 | 05 06 57 | 68 | 29 13 02 | 78 | 05 07 53 | 18 | RTD | 15 | 179 | 800 |
| Brazil | Carro Chefe | A Laurits v Lachmann | 04 07 32 | 24 | 05 06 04 | 78 | RTD | 3 | 04 57 25 (P) | 78 | 87 18 29 | 155 | 338 | |
| | Saga IV | E Lorentzen | 04 10 08 | 10 | 05 05 52 | 82 | RTD | 3 | 05 06 17 | 32 | 0 | (P) 0 | 127 | |
| | Indigo | I Botelho | 04 06 16 | 32 | 05 17 33 | 12 | 29 20 09 | 66 | 04 59 05 | 74 | 87 25 06 | 150 | 334 | 799 |
| Papua New Guinea | Sudpak | L Green | 04 07 08 | 28 | 05 07 52 | 56 | 29 13 57 | 72 | 05 07 51 | 20 | RTD | 15 | 191 | |
| | Cifraline 3 | P Jenkins | 04 08 20 | 20 | 05 09 33 | 34 | 28 52 52 | 96 | 05 09 50 | (P) 0 | 89 46 57 | 145 | 262 | |
| | Hitchhiker | P Briggs | 04 09 47 | 14 | 05 07 48 | 58 | 29 21 40 | 54 | 05 06 02 | (P) 12 | RTD | 15 | 153 | 606 |
| Canada | Amazing Grace | B Herron | 04 04 56 (P) | 34 | 05 18 26 | 6 | 29 32 12 | 48 | 05 04 11 | (P) 16 | 86 42 26 | 165 | 269 | |
| | Impetus | R Koehler | 04 04 41 | 60 | 05 11 32 | 24 | 30 16 11 | 42 | 05 05 07 | (P) 38 | RTD | 15 | 179 | |
| | Pachena III | J Newton | 04 11 23 | 8 | 05 12 23 | 20 | 30 21 30 | 39 | 05 12 27 | 4 | RTD | 15 | 86 | 534 |
| Portugal | Bigamist | P Mendonca | 04 06 10 (P) | 0 | 05 09 49 | 32 | RTD | 3 | 05 06 36 | (P) 0 | RTD | 15 | 50 | |
| | Snake Oil | J Pinheiro | 04 05 48 | 40 | 05 11 16 | 26 | RTD | 3 | 05 00 27 | 66 | RTD | 15 | 150 | |
| | Al Gharb | B Pinheiro | 04 05 18 | 48 | 05 07 18 | 62 | RTD | 3 | 05 07 47 | (P) 16 | RTD | 15 | 146 | 346 |
| Belgium | Mariner | F Van Nuffel | 04 13 27 | 4 | 05 18 04 | 8 | RTD | 3 | 05 20 38 | 2 | DNS | 2 | 19 | |
| | Formidable | J Rogge/P W Vroon | 04 08 15 | 22 | 05 17 56 | 10 | 29 20 48 | 63 | 05 10 50 | (P) 0 | RTD | 15 | 110 | |
| | Poinciana | A Lousse/T Vinke | 04 10 01 (P) | 0 | 05 09 01 | 36 | RTD | 3 | 05 04 56 | 46 | RTD | 15 | 100 | 229 |

KEY:  DNS – Did Not Start   DNF – Did Not Finish   DSQ – Disqualified   RTD – Retired   (P) – Includes Penalty   DNC – Did Not Compete

| 1987 RACE RESULTS | | | RACE 1 RORC TROPHY (FIRST INSHORE) | | RACE 2 CHANNEL RACE | | RACE 3 CORUM TROPHY (SECOND INSHORE) | | RACE 4 CHAMPAGNE MUMM TROPHY (THIRD INSHORE) | | RACE 5 FASTNET RACE | | TOTAL (OVERALL POINTS) | OVERALL TOTAL (BY COUNTRY) |
|---|---|---|---|---|---|---|---|---|---|---|---|---|---|---|
| Country | Boat Name | Owner | Corrected time | Points | Corrected time | Points | Corrected time | Points | Corrected time | Points | Corrected time | Points | | |
| New Zealand | Goldcorp | M Canning | 04 59 42 | 18 | 31 07 30 | 111 | 05 01 22 | 66 | 04 52 46 | 70 | 87 06 42 | 160 | 425 | |
| | **Propaganda** | **A Burr** | **04 52 30** | **48** | **30 55 34** | **126** | **04 52 56** | **84** | **04 52 06** | **74** | **86 37 29** | **195** | **527** | |
| | Kiwi | P Walker | 04 40 43 | 70 | 31 23 55 | 72 | 04 57 57 | 80 | 04 51 12 | 76 | 87 50 04 | 115 | 413 | 1,365 |
| Britain | Jamarella | A Gray | 04 48 03 | 58 | 30 55 50 | 123 | 04 58 54 | 78 | 05 01 11 | 38 | 86 35 32 | 200 | 497 | |
| | Juno | M Peacock | 04 58 22 | 24 | 31 08 57 | 108 | 05 02 57 | 54 | 05 05 39 | (P) 0 | 86 35 27 | 205 | 391 | |
| | Indulgence | G Walker | 04 49 51 | 54 | 31 11 38 | 105 | 05 00 21 | 72 | 04 52 13 | 72 | 88 15 03 | 90 | 393 | 1,281 |
| Australia | Swan Premium I | L Abrahams | 04 57 57 | 30 | 31 15 20 | 96 | 05 04 15 | (P) 24 | 05 03 33 | 14 | 86 44 10 | 185 | 349 | |
| | Swan Premium III | P Kurts | 04 35 03 | 78 | 31 57 32 | 21 | 05 01 05 | 68 | 04 50 25 | 78 | 87 48 10 | 120 | 365 | |
| | Swan Premium II | G Appleby | 04 51 16 (P) 36 | | 31 12 28 | 102 | 05 00 50 | 70 | 04 59 45 | 48 | 87 25 40 | 135 | 391 | 1,105 |
| Ireland | Jameson Whiskey | B Butkus | 05 01 04 | 10 | 31 15 12 | 99 | 05 07 16 | 16 | 05 06 42 | (P) 0 | 87 13 54 | 150 | 275 | |
| | Turkish Delight | H Bezman | 04 47 42 | 62 | 31 31 01 | 42 | 05 03 03 | 52 | 04 48 58 | 80 | 88 04 33 | 100 | 336 | |
| | Irish Independent Pelt | S Fein | 04 47 47 | 60 | 31 21 46 | 84 | 05 03 06 | 49 | 05 04 39 | 24 | 86 33 43 | 210 | 427 | 1,038 |
| Germany | Container | U Schutz | 05 02 03 | 8 | 31 06 20 | 117 | 05 03 06 | 49 | 05 00 43 | 44 | 86 48 19 | (P) 170 | 388 | |
| | Saudade | A Bull | 04 53 27 | 44 | 31 21 20 | 87 | 05 04 21 | 38 | 05 03 10 | (P) 0 | 86 47 40 | 175 | 344 | |
| | Diva | P Westphal-Langloh | 05 07 06 (P) 0 | | 31 20 34 | 90 | 05 02 03 | 62 | 04 58 15 | (P) 38 | 88 48 51 | 80 | 270 | 1,002 |
| USA | Sidewinder | R Short | 04 34 52 | 80 | 31 23 57 | 69 | 04 59 11 | 76 | 04 48 49 | 82 | 87 14 36 | 145 | 452 | |
| | Blue Yankee | R Towse | 05 05 35 | 6 | 33 06 12 | 3 | 05 02 50 | 57 | 04 59 23 | 50 | 88 01 58 | 105 | 221 | |
| | Insatiable | B Krehbiel/D Tank | 04 40 38 | 74 | 31 32 11 | 39 | 05 03 53 | 42 | 04 47 04 | 84 | 89 48 14 | 60 | 299 | 972 |
| Denmark | Original Beckmann Pletfjerner | P Jespersen | 04 32 53 | 84 | 31 20 32 | 93 | 05 02 50 | 57 | 04 52 47 | 68 | 87 07 04 | 155 | 457 | |
| | Andelsbanken | V Greulich | 04 52 51 | 46 | 31 24 33 | 66 | 05 04 34 | 36 | 05 03 34 | 28 | 88 42 04 | 85 | 261 | |
| | Stockbroker Lief | J Host | 04 56 09 | 40 | 31 24 56 | 60 | 05 04 40 | 34 | 05 05 34 | (P) 0 | 88 10 47 | 95 | 229 | 947 |
| France | Xeryus | B Trouble | 05 00 28 | 12 | 31 36 49 | 33 | 05 05 28 | 24 | 04 03 29 | 32 | 86 46 33 | 180 | 281 | |
| | Centurion-Musclor | J P Dick | 04 54 30 | 42 | 31 22 16 | 81 | 05 04 53 | (P) 16 | 05 04 57 | 18 | 86 39 00 | 190 | 347 | |
| | Corum | Beneteau | 04 40 39 | 72 | 31 29 16 | 45 | 05 01 56 | 64 | 04 56 17 | 62 | 89 15 59 | (P) 55 | 298 | 926 |
| Austria | Pinta | W Illbruck | 04 43 43 | 68 | 31 24 53 | 63 | 05 02 26 | 60 | 04 58 00 | 56 | 87 19 13 | 140 | 387 | |
| | Ritec | T Vinke | 04 58 08 | 26 | 31 46 18 | 24 | 05 10 22 | 6 | 05 08 26 | 4 | --- | 20 | 80 | |
| | I-Punkt | T Friese | 04 58 01 | 28 | 31 02 47 | 120 | 04 55 15 | 82 | 05 06 15 | 12 | 91 00 38 | 50 | 292 | 759 |
| Spain | Anquin's Too | A Quinteiro | 04 57 17 (P) 0 | | 32 10 28 | 15 | 05 05 22 | 26 | 05 00 08 | 46 | 89 07 42 | 70 | 157 | |
| | Mayurca | G Cryns | 04 51 44 (P) 8 | | 31 06 22 | I14 | 05 06 12 | 20 | 04 56 46 | (P) 36 | 87 05 40 | (P) 115 | 293 | |
| | Vento | M Fernandez | 04 57 29 | 32 | 31 22 39 | 78 | 05 05 33 | 22 | 05 04 54 | 20 | 87 29 02 | 130 | 282 | 732 |
| Netherlands | Mean Machine | P de Ridder | 05 00 13 | 14 | 31 25 51 | 54 | 05 03 18 | 46 | 05 02 30 | (P) 0 | 87 29 39 | 125 | 239 | |
| | Caiman | G Jeelof | 04 45 58 | 66 | 32 05 44 | 18 | 05 03 27 | 44 | 05 00 56 | 40 | 90 06 25 | (P) 45 | 216 | |
| | Pro-Motion V | B Dolk | 04 34 03 | 82 | 32 48 13 | 0 | 05 10 08 | 8 | 04 57 29 | 58 | 91 44 21 | 40 | 188 | 640 |
| Italy | Merope | Marina Militare | 04 56 10 | 38 | 31 38 10 | 3 | 05 09 15 | 10 | 05 04 19 | 26 | --- | 25 | 102 | |
| | Marisa – Konica | U Lucarelli | 04 36 32 | 76 | 31 37 34 | 30 | 04 59 48 | 74 | 04 57 11 | 60 | RTD | 15 | 255 | |
| | Mandrake – Krizia | G Carriero | 04 48 47 | 56 | 31 27 08 | 51 | 05 05 16 | 28 | 04 55 42 | 64 | 89 02 47 | 75 | 274 | 631 |

KEY:  DNS – Did Not Start    DNF – Did Not Finish    DSQ – Disqualified    RTD – Retired    (P) – Includes Penalty    DNC – Did Not Compete

| 1987 RACE RESULTS | | | RACE 1 RORC TROPHY (FIRST INSHORE) | | RACE 2 CHANNEL RACE | | RACE 3 CORUM TROPHY (SECOND INSHORE) | | RACE 4 CHAMPAGNE MUMM TROPHY (THIRD INSHORE) | | RACE 5 FASTNET RACE | | TOTAL (OVERALL POINTS) | OVERALL TOTAL (BY COUNTRY) |
|---|---|---|---|---|---|---|---|---|---|---|---|---|---|---|
| Country | Boat Name | Owner | Corrected time | Points | Corrected time | Points | Corrected time | Points | Corrected time | Points | Corrected time | Points | | |
| Sweden | Royal Blue | R Gustafson | 04 46 18 | 64 | 32 24 07 | 9 | 05 06 40 | 18 | 04 54 43 | 66 | 91 16 38 | 45 | 202 | |
|  | Civic | J Norrman | 05 00 04 | 16 | 31 22 40 | 75 | 05 05 15 | (P) 4 | 05 00 50 | 42 | --- | 035 | 172 | |
|  | Eurocard | S Ball | 04 57 12 | 36 | 31 35 02 | 36 | 05 08 01 | 12 | 05 02 11 | 6 | --- | 030 | 120 | 494 |
| Belgium | CGI | TFV/B Decré | 04 57 15 | 34 | 31 25 24 | 57 | 05 07 54 | 14 | 05 04 53 | 22 | 87 53 55 | 110 | 237 | |
|  | REF Val Maubuée | J Dumon | 05 07 39 | 2 | 32 19 25 | 12 | 05 13 18 | 4 | 05 07 21 | 8 | DNS | 2 | 28 | |
|  | Port du Crouesty | Port du Crouesty | 04 58 25 | 22 | 31 28 18 | 48 | DNF | 2 | DNF | 2 | DNS | 2 | 76 | 341 |

KEY: DNS – Did Not Start    DNF – Did Not Finish    DSQ – Disqualified    RTD – Retired    (P) – Includes Penalty    DNC – Did Not Compete

| 1989 RACE RESULTS | Boat Name | Owner | RACE 1 RORC TROPHY (FIRST INSHORE) | | RACE 2 CHANNEL RACE | | RACE 3 CORUM TROPHY (SECOND INSHORE) | | RACE 4 CHAMPAGNE MUMM TROPHY (THIRD INSHORE) | | RACE 5 LONG INSHORE | | RACE 6 FASTNET RACE | | TOTAL (OVERALL POINTS) | OVERALL TOTAL (BY COUNTRY) |
|---|---|---|---|---|---|---|---|---|---|---|---|---|---|---|---|---|
| Country | | | Corrected time | Points | Corrected time | Points | Corrected time | Points | Corrected time | Points | Corrected time | Points | Corrected time | Points | | |
| Britain | Jamarella | A Gray | 04 55 13 | 42 | 30 17 27 | 60 | 04 11 52 | 41 | 04 24 54 | 40 | 05 59 53 | 41 | 90 22 36 | 97 | 321 | |
| | Juno IV | M Peacock | 05 05 52 | 17 | 36 34 17 | 28 | 04 17 20 | 32 | 04 30 12 | 22 | 06 07 04 | 32 | 92 30 21 | 77 | 209 | |
| | Indulgence VII | G Walker | 04 57 49 | 40 | 36 07 00 | 52 | 04 18 35 | 26 | 04 31 03 | 16 | 06 09 54 | 25 | 93 18 29 | 57 | 217 | 748 |
| Denmark | 4K | F Thomsen | 05 06 33 | 16 | 36 28 09 | 39 | 04 23 14 | 13 | 04 30 53 | 19 | 06 13 21 | 16 | 92 22 47 | 82 | 185 | |
| | Andelsbanken IV | V Greulich | 05 03 36 | 26 | 30 03 51 | 61 | 04 12 08 | 40 | 04 27 07 | 35 | DNF | 1 | 89 49 31 | 100 | 263 | |
| | Stockbroker's Container | J Host | 05 09 52 | 11 | 34 19 25 | 58 | 04 10 38 | 42 | 04 26 12 | 38 | 05 59 02 | 42 | 91 09 49 | 90 | 281 | 730 |
| New Zealand | Librah | D Richwhite/M Fay | 04 56 52 | 41 | 36 25 09 | 48 | 04 14 22 | 36 | 04 28 11 | 31 | 06 03 13 | 37 | 90 51 05 | 92 | 285 | |
| | Fair Share | J Benton | 05 02 06 | 34 | 36 25 10 | 39 | 04 19 37 | 23 | 04 28 04 | 32 | 06 13 57 | 15 | 93 04 57 | 60 | 203 | |
| | Propaganda | T Bailey | 05 05 47 | 18 | 36 37 29 | 24 | 04 14 30 | 35 | 04 29 32 | 26 | 06 10 14 | 23 | 93 26 47 | 52 | 179 | 667 |
| France | CGI | TF/B-Decre | 05 05 07 | 20 | 36 00 12 | 54 | 04 19 47 | (P) 1 | 04 31 02 | 17 | 06 12 50 | 18 | 92 26 01 | 80 | 190 | |
| | Xeryus de Givenchy | B Trouble | 05 02 29 | 31 | 36 31 46 | 36 | 04 24 17 | 7 | 04 36 36 | (P) 0 | 06 11 07 | 21 | 92 41 46 | 70 | 165 | |
| | Corum 89 | P Briand | 05 02 28 | 32 | 36 25 56 | 43 | 04 14 11 | 37 | 04 24 00 | 42 | 06 00 01 | 40 | 92 34 44 | 72 | 267 | 622 |
| Australia | Madeline's Daughter | P Kurts | 05 02 44 | 30 | 36 38 20 | 21 | 04 17 40 | 30 | 04 26 00 | 39 | 06 06 45 | 34 | 93 44 37 | 47 | 201 | |
| | True Blue | L Klopper | 04 58 53 | 39 | 36 32 58 | 34 | 04 19 51 | 21 | 04 32 41 | 12 | 06 14 30 | 14 | 93 22 11 | 55 | 175 | |
| | Joint Venture III | R Elliott | 05 02 16 | 33 | 35 53 15 | 24 | 04 15 42 | 33 | 04 27 23 | 34 | 06 07 13 | 31 | 92 02 22 | 85 | 240 | 617 |
| USA | Great News | Calvert-Jones | 05 04 52 | 23 | 36 46 36 | 9 | 04 13 44 | 38 | 04 32 16 | 13 | 06 01 36 | 38 | 89 09 10 | 105 | 226 | |
| | Sagacious V | D Allen/G Appleby | 05 04 53 | 22 | 36 25 50 | 45 | 04 23 05 | 14 | 04 30 05 | 24 | 06 16 37 | 10 | 91 37 02 | 87 | 202 | |
| | Bravura | I Loube | 05 04 40 | 24 | 36 23 49 | 49 | 04 17 44 | 29 | 04 26 58 | 36 | 06 08 59 | 28 | DNF | 5 | 171 | 600 |
| Japan | Will | R Oda | 05 01 29 | 35 | 29 59 34 | 63 | 04 12 47 | 39 | 04 26 49 | 37 | 06 00 52 | 39 | 90 34 05 | 95 | 308 | |
| | Arecan Bay | Nippon Challenge | 05 03 34 | 27 | 36 37 38 | 22 | 04 20 39 | 18 | 04 30 29 | 21 | 06 19 45 | 5 | 93 30 26 | 50 | 143 | |
| | Turkish Delight | Nippon Challenge | 05 14 41 | 2 | 36 40 38 | 13 | 04 20 25 | 20 | 04 36 01 | 7 | 06 09 45 | 26 | 95 04 17 | 32 | 101 | 552 |
| Germany | Rubin XI | H Schumann | 05 14 44 | 1 | 36 36 21 | 25 | 04 17 35 | 31 | 04 30 32 | 20 | 06 05 37 | 35 | 92 44 31 | 65 | 177 | |
| | Pinta | W Illbruck | 05 09 31 | 13 | 36 42 12 | 12 | 04 24 00 | 10 | 04 33 34 | 10 | 06 10 06 | 24 | 92 34 39 | 75 | 144 | |
| | Beck's Diva | P Westphal-Langloh | 05 12 37 | 5 | 36 34 32 | 27 | 04 21 29 | 17 | 04 28 37 | 28 | 06 03 27 | 36 | 89 28 36 | 102 | 215 | 537 |
| Italy | Mandrake Krizia | G Carriero | 05 11 32 | 8 | 36 27 04 | 40 | 04 15 15 | 34 | 04 24 48 | 41 | 06 06 59 | 33 | 92 54 51 | 62 | 219 | |
| | Bellatrix | Marina Militare | 05 00 23 | 38 | 36 26 03 | 42 | 04 24 41 | (P) 0 | 04 38 34 | 2 | 06 17 05 | 9 | 94 50 09 | 35 | 126 | |
| | Aria | C Bixio | 05 07 01 | 0 | 36 13 36 | 51 | 04 18 44 | 25 | 04 28 19 | 30 | 06 12 21 | 20 | 95 11 27 | 27 | 153 | 498 |
| Netherlands | Mean Machine | P de Ridder | 05 03 21 | 28 | 35 53 01 | 57 | 04 18 50 | 24 | 04 28 29 | 29 | 06 09 34 | 27 | 92 44 14 | 67 | 232 | |
| | Amsterdamed | J Visser | 05 07 44 | 14 | 36 45 56 | 3 | 04 24 30 | (P) 0 | 04 31 51 | 14 | 06 17 21 | 8 | 96 55 40 | 17 | 56 | |
| | Pro-motion VI | J Dolk | 05 09 43 | 12 | 36 33 34 | 31 | 04 22 41 | 15 | 04 37 04 | 3 | 06 12 23 | 19 | 95 09 37 | 30 | 110 | 399 |
| Norway | Elkem Yeoman XXVII | T Knutsen | 05 12 12 | 6 | 37 24 19 | 3 | 04 23 19 | 12 | 04 31 12 | 15 | 06 07 45 | 30 | 99 23 58 | 15 | 81 | |
| | Hydro | P Lunde | 05 01 25 | 36 | 36 34 14 | 30 | 04 28 01 | 3 | 04 28 38 | (P) 6 | 06 14 39 | 13 | 94 06 35 | 40 | 128 | |
| | Fram XI | HH Crown Prince Harald | 05 00 35 | 37 | 36 29 42 | 37 | 04 23 46 | 11 | 04 27 24 | 33 | 06 13 20 | 17 | 94 00 43 | 42 | 178 | 387 |
| Sweden | Kiwi | A Lonnqvist | 05 12 55 | 4 | 36 38 23 | 19 | 04 20 26 | 19 | 04 30 12 | 22 | 06 10 55 | 22 | 93 51 30 | 45 | 132 | |
| | Greve Duckula | J Norman | 05 04 13 | 25 | 36 33 24 | 33 | 04 34 07 | 1 | 04 33 37 | 9 | DNF | 1 | DNF | 2 | 71 | |
| | Full Pelt | B Bernholm | 05 03 14 | 29 | 36 55 29 | 6 | 04 24 13 | 8 | 04 30 55 | 18 | 06 17 55 | 6 | 104 54 13 | 10 | 77 | 280 |
| Ireland | Platon Finans II | J Neilsen | 05 11 41 | 7 | 36 40 13 | 15 | 04 18 00 | 28 | DNF | 1 | 06 08 02 | 29 | 95 40 48 | 22 | 102 | |
| | Citroen | W Borel | 05 05 47 | 18 | 37 26 19 | 1 | 04 28 08 | 2 | 04 36 45 | 5 | 06 20 15 | 4 | 95 56 13 | 20 | 51 | |
| | Hitchhiker III | P Briggs | 05 04 55 | 21 | 36 40 02 | 16 | 04 24 01 | 9 | 04 33 59 | 8 | 06 16 03 | 11 | 94 15 21 | 37 | 103 | 256 |
| Argentina | Daphne | G Frers | 05 11 26 | 9 | 36 58 22 | 4 | 04 27 16 | 4 | 04 36 58 | 4 | 06 23 38 | 3 | DNF | 5 | 29 | |
| | Jockey Club | A Urani | 05 10 01 | 10 | 36 49 08 | 7 | 04 22 32 | 16 | 04 29 45 | 25 | 06 17 37 | 7 | 101 10 54 | 12 | 78 | |
| | Tango Too | Schmiegelow/Haymes | 05 13 36 | 3 | 36 39 21 | 18 | 04 18 25 | 27 | 04 33 32 | 11 | 06 15 50 | 12 | 95 25 47 | 25 | 96 | 203 |

KEY:  DNS – Did Not Start    DNF – Did Not Finish    DSQ – Disqualified    RTD – Retired    (P) – Includes Penalty    DNC – Did Not Compete

| 1991 RACE RESULTS | | | RACE 1 RORC TROPHY (FIRST INSHORE) | | RACE 2 CHANNEL RACE | | RACE 3 CORUM TROPHY (SECOND INSHORE) | | RACE 4 CHAMPAGNE MUMM TROPHY (THIRD INSHORE) | | RACE 5 LONG INSHORE | | RACE 6 FASTNET RACE | | TOTAL (OVERALL POINTS) | OVERALL TOTAL (BY COUNTRY) |
|---|---|---|---|---|---|---|---|---|---|---|---|---|---|---|---|---|
| Country | Boat Name | Owner | Corrected time | Points | Corrected time | Points | Corrected time | Points | Corrected time | Points | Corrected time | Points | Corrected time | Points | | |
| France | **Corum Saphir** | **R D Bono** | **03 54 38** | **5 00** | **31 10 36** | **9 00** | **04 00 37** | **7 00** | **03 53 17** | **7 00** | **05 19 22** | **8 25** | **98 59 27** | **20 63** | **56 88** | |
| | Corum Rubis | Corum Sailing Ltd | 04 09 07 | 3 00 | 31 51 30 | 10 50 | 04 20 38 | 2 00 | 04 12 04 | 2 00 | 05 26 51 | 8 25 | 101 22 53 | 17 50 | 43 25 | |
| | Corum Diamant | L Dewulf | 04 18 42 | 1 00 | 32 55 16 | 6 00 | 04 32 01 | 3 00 | 04 25 17 | 3 00 | 05 39 40 | 5 00 | 101 02 16 | 20 63 | 38 63 | 138 75 |
| Italy | Mandrake Krizia | G Carriero | 03 51 06 | 8 25 | 31 03 38 | 12 38 | 04 03 24 | 2 00 | 03 54 38 | 4 00 | 05 22 56 | 6 00 | 100 27 44 | 10 00 | 42 63 | |
| | Larouge | G D Gennaro | 04 04 55 | 5 00 | 31 53 12 | 9 00 | 04 14 16 | 7 00 | 04 04 51 | 7 00 | 05 32 49 | 6 00 | 101 57 11 | 10 00 | 44 00 | |
| | **Brava** | **P Landolfi** | **04 11 36** | **8 25** | **32 43 36** | **7 50** | **04 31 32** | **4 00** | **04 23 10** | **6 00** | **05 35 52** | **8 25** | **102 23 15** | **17 50** | **51 50** | 138 13 |
| USA | Champosa VII | M Morita | 03 55 08 | 4 00 | 31 15 52 | 7 50 | 04 01 31 | 5 00 | 03 53 42 | 6 00 | 05 24 53 | 4 00 | 100 17 02 | 12 50 | 39 00 | |
| | **Bravura** | **I Loube** | **04 05 08** | **4 00** | **31 47 27** | **12 38** | **04 21 13** | **3 00** | **04 08 15** | **5 00** | **05 34 39** | **3 00** | **101 21 35** | **20 63** | **48 00** | |
| | Vibes | D Clarke | 04 12 27 | 6 00 | 32 36 15 | 10 50 | 04 27 54 | 8 25 | 04 20 02 | 8 25 | 05 40 24 | 4 00 | 102 34 01 | 10 00 | 47 00 | 134 00 |
| Britain | Juno V | M Peacock | 03 52 24 | 7 00 | 31 19 26 | 4 50 | 04 01 15 | 6 00 | 03 53 59 | 5 00 | 05 20 56 | 7 00 | 101 42 57 | 5 00 | 34 50 | |
| | Wings of Oracle | Oracle | 04 04 24 | 7 00 | 31 57 18 | 7 50 | 04 18 47 | 5 00 | 04 09 32 | 2 00 | 05 29 58 | 5 00 | 102 32 49 | 5 00 | 31 50 | |
| | Port Pendennis | E Dubois | 04 14 24 | 4 00 | 32 34 38 | 12 38 | 04 28 38 | 7 00 | 04 23 21 | 5 00 | 05 37 17 | 7 00 | 102 29 30 | 12 50 | 47 88 | 113 88 |
| Germany | Container | U Schuetz | 03 56 38 | 2 00 | 31 16 26 | 6 00 | 03 58 19 | 8 25 | 03 55 45 | 2 00 | 05 29 22 | 1 00 | 99 32 18 | 15 00 | 34 25 | |
| | Rubin XII | H O Schuemann | 0401 43 | 8 25 | 31 58 45 | 6 00 | 04 17 42 | 6 00 | 04 06 17 | 6 00 | 05 34 27 | 2 00 | 101 50 10 | 12 50 | 40 75 | |
| | ABAP/4 | H Plattner | 04 14 06 | 5 00 | 33 50 31 | 4 50 | 04 30 36 | 3 00 | 04 20 59 | 7 00 | 05 41 40 | 2 50 | 105 54 245 00 27 00 | | 102 00 | |
| Denmark | Tuborg | I U Andersen | 03 56 04 | 3 00 | 31 20 05 | 3 00 | 04 03 15 | 3 00 | 03 56 47 | 1 00 | 05 27 11 | 2 00 | 100 55 55 | 7 50 | 19 50 | |
| | Unibank | V Greulich | 04 04 50 | 6 00 | 32 02 35 | 1 50 | 04 12 56 | 8 25 | 04 03 54 | 8 25 | 05 34 13 | 5 00 | 102 27 19 | 7 50 | 36 50 | |
| | Z Forsikring | J E Hoest | 04 17 11 | 3 00 | 32 39 29 | 9 00 | 04 29 06 | 6 00 | 04 24 30 | 4 00 | 05 38 30 | 6 00 | 102 24 24 | 15 00 | 43 00 | 99 00 |
| Japan | Will | R Oda | 03 54 20 | 6 00 | 31 05 55 | 10 50 | 04 01 38 | 4 00 | 03 50 35 | 8 25 | 05 24 35 | 5 00 | 99 19 20 | 17 50 | 51 25 | |
| | Carino | T Yamada | 04 11 25 | 0 00 | 33 16 07 | 0 00 | DNF | 1 00 | DNC | 1 00 | DNC | 1 00 | DNC | 2 50 | 5 50 | |
| | Spica | M Muroi | 04 17 39 | 2 00 | 35 04 00 | 1 50 | 04 38 29 | 2 00 | 04 30 10 | 1 00 | DNF | 1 00 | 122 57 39 | 2 50 | 10 00 | 66 75 |
| Australia | Cyclone | M Ryan | 03 57 24 | 1 00 | 31 44 48 | 1 50 | 04 06 59 | 1 00 | 03 55 20 | 3 00 | 05 26 05 | 3 00 | 102 14 57 | 2 50 | 12 00 | |
| | Bimblegumbie | K Jacobs | 04 10 07 | 2 00 | 32 40 31 | 3 00 | 04 22 08 | 2 00 | 04 11 33 | 3 00 | 05 38 07 | 2 00 | 101 33 40 | 15 00 | 27 00 | |
| | Shardana II | C Jacobsen | 04 12 16 | 7 00 | 34 46 26 | 3 00 | DNF | 1 00 | 04 26 03 | 2 00 | 05 41 40 | 2 50 | 104 42 29 | 7 50 | 23 00 | 62 00 |

KEY:  DNS – Did Not Start    DNF – Did Not Finish    DSQ – Disqualified    RTD – Retired    (P) – Includes Penalty    DNC – Did Not Compete

| 1993 RACE RESULTS | | | RACE 1 RORC TROPHY (FIRST INSHORE) | | RACE 2 CHANNEL RACE | | RACE 3 CORUM TROPHY (SECOND INSHORE) | | RACE 4 CHAMPAGNE MUMM TROPHY (THIRD INSHORE) | | RACE 5 KENWOOD RACE | | RACE 6 KENWOOD RACE | | RACE 7 FASTNET RACE | | TOTAL (OVERALL POINTS) | OVERALL TOTAL (BY COUNTRY) |
|---|---|---|---|---|---|---|---|---|---|---|---|---|---|---|---|---|---|---|
| Country | Boat Name | Owner | Corrected time | Points | Corrected time | Points | Corrected time | Points | Corrected time | Points | Corrected time | Points | Corrected time | Points | Corrected time | Points | | |
| Germany | **Pinta** | **W Illbruck** | **04 14 42** | **05 00** | **25 32 53** | **21 00** | **04 13 05** | **05 00** | **04 12 03** | **21 00** | **02 03 30** | **30 00** | **02 00 01** | **05 50** | **90 58 45** | **42 50** | **63 50** | |
| | Rubin XII | H A Schuemann | 04 12 08 | 07 00 | 25 19 52 | 31 50 | 04 07 36 | 17 00 | 04 13 42 | 12 00 | 02 02 02 | 08 00 | 01 57 21 | 11 63 | 91 04 47 | 35 00 | 75 13 | |
| | Container | U Schuetz | 04 08 57 | 16 00 | 25 28 35 | 25 50 | 04 06 52 | 19 50 | 04 13 41 | 13 00 | 02 00 09 | 08 00 | 01 58 44 | 08 50 | 87 59 49 | 50 00 | 140 50 | 279 13 |
| Australia | Ninja | P Kurts | 04 15 25 | 04 00 | 25 41 21 | 6 00 | 04 10 12 | 8 00 | 04 13 51 | 11 00 | 02 02 52 | 06 00 | 02 00 43 | 04 00 | 91 22 56 | 25 00 | 31 00 | |
| | Great News II | J Calvert-Jones | 04 06 08 | 20 00 | 25 19 02 | 33 00 | 04 07 33 | 18 00 | 04 11 38 | 22 00 | 02 02 55 | 05 50 | 01 59 18 | 06 50 | DNF | 07 50 | 99 50 | |
| | **Ragamuffin** | **S Fischer** | **04 04 30** | **23 25** | **25 37 37** | **12 00** | **04 05 48** | **21 00** | **04 13 00** | **17 00** | **01 59 17** | **11 63** | **01 57 30** | **11 00** | **87 47 12** | **52 50** | **148 38** | 278 88 |
| France | Corum Diamant | Corum Sailing Team | 04 11 18 | 10 00 | 25 35 20 | 15 00 | 04 09 49 | 10 00 | 04 13 04 | 16 00 | 02 02 25 | 06 50 | 02 00 30 | 04 50 | 91 33 27 | 22 50 | 27 00 | |
| | Corum Rubis | Corum Sailing Team | 04 09 34 | 13 00 | 25 24 17 | 30 00 | 04 08 08 | 14 00 | 04 14 30 | 08 00 | 02 01 16 | 09 00 | 01 59 11 | 04 50 | 90 52 43 | 45 00 | 123 50 | |
| | Corum Saphir | Corum Sailing Team | 04 10 26 | 12 00 | 25 33 18 | 18 00 | 04 09 11 | 12 00 | 04 15 39 | 06 00 | 02 03 01 | 04 50 | 02 01 32 | 02 50 | 87 40 48 | 55 00 | 97 00 | 247 50 |
| Italy | Brava Q8 | P Landolfi | 04 11 43 | 9 00 | 25 30 28 | 22 50 | DNF | 02 00 | 04 12 23 | 18 00 | 02 03 15 | 03 50 | 01 58 25 | 09 50 | 91 05 47 | 32 50 | 68 00 | |
| | Larouge | G D Gennaro | 04 08 58 | 15 00 | 25 16 30 | 34 88 | 04 07 42 | 11 00 | 04 12 14 | 19 00 | 02 00 41 | 09 50 | 01 58 09 | 10 50 | DNF | 07 50 | 107 38 | |
| | Mandrake | G Carriero | 04 04 57 | 21 00 | 25 35 12 | 16 50 | 04 05 04 | 23 25 | 04 10 39 | 23 25 | DNF | 02 00 | DNC | 02 00 | DNC | 05 00 | 67 50 | 242 88 |
| Japan | Nippon | T Yamasaki | 04 10 40 | 11 00 | 25 43 28 | 4 50 | DNF | 02 00 | 04 12 05 | 20 00 | DNC | 01 50 | DNC | 02 00 | DNF | 07 50 | 31 00 | |
| | Swing | S Suzuki | 04 12 23 | 06 00 | 25 27 25 | 27 00 | 04 05 08 | 22 00 | 04 13 19 | 14 00 | 02 02 21 | 07 00 | 01 58 56 | 07 50 | 91 19 49 | 30 00 | 107 50 | |
| | Champosa | M Morita | 04 06 40 | 19 00 | 25 38 33 | 09 00 | 04 09 13 | 11 00 | 04 16 53 | 03 00 | 01 59 53 | 11 00 | 01 59 33 | 06 00 | 88 07 15 | 47 50 | 103 50 | 242 00 |
| Britain | GBE International | P Morton | 04 12 07 | 08 00 | 25 37 45 | 10 50 | 04 11 43 | 07 00 | 04 15 31 | 07 00 | 02 02 16 | 07 50 | 02 00 25 | 05 00 | 91 20 56 | 27 50 | 40 00 | |
| | Provezza Source | D Woods | DSQ | 00 00 | 25 30 22 | 24 00 | 04 06 52 | 19 50 | 04 14 29 | 09 00 | 02 00 09 | 10 25 | 01 58 49 | 08 00 | 91 03 47 | 37 50 | 108 25 | |
| | Indulgence | G Walker | 04 04 56 | 22 00 | 25 39 35 | 07 50 | 04 12 16 | 06 00 | 04 15 49 | 04 00 | 02 03 00 | 05 00 | 01 58 22 | 10 00 | 87 40 22 | 58 13 | 90 13 | 238 38 |
| Ireland | Jameson 1 | J Storey | DNF | 01 00 | DNC | 01 50 | DNC | 01 00 | DNC | 01 00 | DNC | 01 50 | DNC | 02 00 | DNC | 05 00 | 02 00 | |
| | **Jameson 2** | **J Storey** | **04 08 43** | **17 00** | **25 26 34** | **28 50** | **04 07 45** | **15 00** | **04 14 08** | **10 00** | **02 02 00** | **08 50** | **01 58 38** | **09 00** | **91 03 39** | **40 00** | **128 00** | |
| | Jameson 3 | J Storey | 04 09 21 | 14 00 | 25 35 58 | 13 50 | 04 09 53 | 09 00 | 04 13 12 | 15 00 | 02 03 09 | 04 00 | DSQ | 00 00 | DNF | 07 50 | 63 00 | 193 00 |
| Netherlands | Ace | M D Lange | DNS | 01 00 | 26 12 19 | 03 00 | 04 21 43 | 04 00 | 04 24 08 | 02 00 | DNC | 01 50 | DNC | 02 00 | 97 06 01 | 20 00 | 33 50 | |
| | Promotion VII | B Dolk | 04 08 01 | 18 00 | 25 32 54 | 19 50 | 04 08 20 | 13 00 | 04 15 44 | 05 00 | YMP | 06 13 | YMP | 06 13 | YMP | 30 63 | 98 38 | 131 88 |

KEY  DNS – Did Not Start    DNF – Did Not Finish    DSQ – Disqualified    RTD – Retired    (P) – Includes Penalty    DNC – Did Not Compete    YMP – Yacht Materially Prejudiced

## BIBLIOGRAPHY

*The Daily Telegraph*
*Yachting World*
*Yachting Monthly*
*Seahorse*
*Boat International*
*Yachting (USA)*
*Sail (USA)*

*British Ocean Racing*, Douglas Phillips-Birt (Adlard Coles)
*Fastnet Force 10*, John Rousmaniere (Nautical)
*Fastnet: The Story of a Great Ocean Race*, Ian Dear (Batsford)
*Fastnet: One Man's Voyage*, Roger Vaughan (Seaview)
*Further Offshore*, John Illingworth (Adlard Coles)
*Ocean Racing Around the World*, Antrobus/Ross/Hammand (Angus & Robertson)
*Sacred Cowes*, Anthony Heckstall-Smith (Anthony Blond)
*Sailing: A Course of My Life*, Edward Heath (Sidgwick & Jackson)
*Sailing Year*, Ed. Timothy Jeffery (Hazelton)
*The Admiral's Cup*, Bob Fisher (Pelham)
*The Champagne Mumm Book of Ocean Racing*, Ian Dear (Severn House)
*The Guinness Book of Yachting Facts & Feats*, Peter Johnson (Nautical)
*The Leading Edge*, Sandy Weld (Barre)
*The World of Yachting*, Ed. Gerard Asaria (Editions de Messine)
*To Win the Admiral's Cup*, Dick Kenny (Nautical)
*Who's Who in Yachting*, Erroll Bruce (Nautical)
*Yachting World Annual*, various years